*Fixing Stories*

T0382162

News "fixers" are translators and guides who assist foreign journalists. Sometimes key contributors to bold, original reporting and other times key facilitators of homogeneity and groupthink in the news media, they play the difficult but powerful role of broker between worlds, shaping the creation of knowledge from behind the scenes. In *Fixing Stories*, Noah Amir Arjomand reflects on the nature of news production and cross-cultural mediation. Based on human stories drawn from three years of field research in Turkey, this book unfolds as a series of narratives of fixers' career trajectories during a period when the international media spotlight shone on Turkey and Syria. From the Syrian Civil War, Gezi Park protest movement, rise of authoritarianism in Turkey and of ISIS in Syria, to the rekindling of conflict in both countries' Kurdish regions and Turkey's 2016 coup attempt, Arjomand brings to light vivid personal accounts and insider perspectives on world-shaking events alongside analysis of the role fixers have played in bringing news of Turkey and Syria to international audiences.

NOAH AMIR ARJOMAND is the Mark Helmke Postdoctoral Scholar in Global Media, Development, and Democracy at Indiana University in Bloomington and the Center for International Media Assistance. A sociologist, filmmaker, and documentary photographer, Arjomand has published writings and photography in *Public Culture*, *Dissent*, and *Profil*. His first feature-length film, *Eat Your Catfish*, premiered at the International Documentary Film Festival Amsterdam in 2021.

The Global Middle East

*General Editors*

Arshin Adib-Moghaddam, *SOAS, University of London*
Ali Mirsepassi, *New York University*

*Editorial Advisory Board*

Faisal Devji, *University of Oxford*
John Hobson, *University of Sheffield*
Firoozeh Kashani-Sabet, *University of Pennsylvania*
Madawi Al-Rasheed, *London School of Economics and Political Science*
David Ryan, *University College Cork, Ireland*

The Global Middle East series seeks to broaden and deconstruct the geographical boundaries of the "Middle East" as a concept to include North Africa, Central and South Asia, and diaspora communities in Western Europe and North America. The series features fresh scholarship that employs theoretically rigorous and innovative methodological frameworks resonating across relevant disciplines in the humanities and the social sciences. In particular, the general editors welcome approaches that focus on mobility, the erosion of nation-state structures, travelling ideas and theories, transcendental techno-politics, the decentralization of grand narratives, and the dislocation of ideologies inspired by popular movements. The series will also consider translations of works by authors in these regions whose ideas are salient to global scholarly trends but have yet to be introduced to the Anglophone academy.

## Other books in the series:

1. *Transnationalism in Iranian Political Thought: The Life and Times of Ahmad Fardid*, Ali Mirsepassi
2. *Psycho-nationalism: Global Thought, Iranian Imaginations*, Arshin Adib-Moghaddam
3. *Iranian Cosmopolitanism: A Cinematic History*, Golbarg Rekabtalaei
4. *Money, Markets and Monarchies: The Gulf Cooperation Council and the Political Economy of the Contemporary Middle East*, Adam Hanieh

# Fixing Stories

Local Newsmaking and International Media
in Turkey and Syria

NOAH AMIR ARJOMAND
*Indiana University*

# CAMBRIDGE
## UNIVERSITY PRESS

Shaftesbury Road, Cambridge CB2 8EA, United Kingdom

One Liberty Plaza, 20th Floor, New York, NY 10006, USA

477 Williamstown Road, Port Melbourne, VIC 3207, Australia

314–321, 3rd Floor, Plot 3, Splendor Forum, Jasola District Centre, New Delhi – 110025, India

103 Penang Road, #05–06/07, Visioncrest Commercial, Singapore 238467

Cambridge University Press is part of Cambridge University Press & Assessment, a department of the University of Cambridge.

We share the University's mission to contribute to society through the pursuit of education, learning and research at the highest international levels of excellence.

www.cambridge.org
Information on this title: www.cambridge.org/9781009048750

DOI: 10.1017/9781009049337

First published 2022
First paperback edition 2023

*A catalogue record for this publication is available from the British Library*

*Library of Congress Cataloging-in-Publication data*
Names: Arjomand, Noah Amir, author.
Title: Fixing stories : local newsmaking and international media in Turkey and Syria / Noah Amir Arjomand, Indiana University.
Description: Cambridge, UK ; New York : Cambridge University Press, 2022. | Series: The global Middle East | Includes bibliographical references and index.
Identifiers: LCCN 2021039465 (print) | LCCN 2021039466 (ebook) | ISBN 9781316518007 (hardback) | ISBN 9781009048750 (paperback) | ISBN 9781009049337 (epub)
Subjects: LCSH: Foreign news. | Foreign news–Turkey–21st century. | Foreign news–Syria–21st century. | Reporters and reporting–Turkey. | Reporters and reporting–Syria. | BISAC: POLITICAL SCIENCE / World / General
Classification: LCC PN4784.F6 A75 2021 (print) | LCC PN4784.F6 (ebook) | DDC 079/.561–dc23/eng/20210930
LC record available at https://lccn.loc.gov/2021039465
LC ebook record available at https://lccn.loc.gov/2021039466

ISBN    978-1-316-51800-7    Hardback
ISBN    978-1-009-04875-0    Paperback

*For Brett*

# Contents

# Figures & Tables

# Acknowledgments

This study was made possible first and foremost by the fixers, reporters, producers, and editors who generously offered their time as I interviewed, observed, and otherwise bothered them with little to offer in return. I am deeply grateful for their help and, in many cases, their friendship.

Barbara Demick, Paul Salopek, and Anna Badkhen inspired my initial interest in the world of international journalism, and all three encouraged and advised my writing during my undergraduate years. The Eliot Kalmbach '09 Award for Turkic Studies, generously funded by Whitney Kalmbach Moore, enabled my first foray into studying journalists in Turkey as a Committee to Protect Journalists intern in 2010.

Many thanks to Diane Vaughan, Michael Schudson, Gil Eyal, Peter Bearman, and Karen Barkey for the formative influence they had on my graduate training and doctoral dissertation. Joshua Whitford, Shamus Khan, Herbert Gans, and Ann Cooper also provided valuable guidance about this project and otherwise supported my work. My fellow graduate students at Columbia University offered good advice and good company throughout my time at the program; in particular, I thank Nathanael Shelley, Ryan Hagen, Adrianna Bagnall Munson, Olivia Nicol, Philipp Brandt, Pierre-Christian Fink, Anand Gopal, Owen Miller, and the late great Devon Tyrone Wade.

Outside of Columbia, Zeynep Devrim Gürsel, Sinem Aydınlı, Iddo Tavory, Burce Çelik, Ebru Diriker, Bilge Yeşil, Erika Gilson, and Aslı Tunç each made helpful suggestions about various aspects of the research during my graduate studies. I also thank the student participants and organizers of the NYLON working group, especially Anna Skarpelis and Liz Koslov, from whom I learned a great deal as I shared my work in progress.

As the Mark Helmke Postdoctoral Scholar in Global Media, Development, and Democracy at Indiana University – Bloomington and the Center for International Media Assistance, I benefited from feedback on this project and moral support from Thomas Gieryn, Koji Chavez, Nick Benequista, Art Alderson, Keera Allendorf, Byunkyu Lee, Purnima Bose, and the organizers and participants of the Media School Colloquium; Political, Economic and Cultural Sociology Workshop; Center for the Study of the Middle East; and Zürich University events at which I presented elements of this book.

I owe a debt of gratitude to my editors at Cambridge University Press, Maria Marsh and Atifa Jiwa, who provided essential guidance through the publishing process, and to copy-editor Beth Morel. A huge thanks also to Joe Sacco for allowing me to use a panel from his comic *The Fixer* for the book cover and to Tora Aghabayova for the artwork at the start of Parts I–V.

I am lucky to have a family full of intellectuals willing to read my drafts. My father, Saïd; sister, Minou; and brother-in-law, Harel Shapira, all blazed a trail for me and helped me think through my research, presentations, and chapters. Most of all I thank my wife, Brett, who was at my side for all the highs and lows of this project, gave it a name, and penned the sharpest edits of anyone. My mother, Kathryn, sadly did not live to see me complete this project, but her faith in me was a powerful motivator and her strength in the face of devastating illness and disability an inspiration.

The National Science Foundation and Institute of Turkish Studies provided financial support for my research and have my sincere thanks. To formally acknowledge the former: this material is based on work supported by the National Science Foundation Graduate Research Fellowship under Grant No. 201214092. Any opinions, findings, and conclusions or recommendations expressed in this material are those of the author and do not necessarily reflect the views of the National Science Foundation.

Figure 0.1  Map of Turkey and Syria

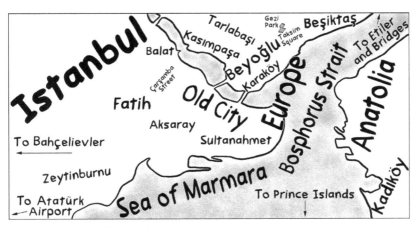

Figure 0.2  Map of Istanbul

# Introduction: A Tale of Two Fixers

"I call myself a rat," Solmaz confessed to me over posh coffee at a café on Istanbul's European side. It was 2016, and Turkey was the center of the world. Istanbul was a boom town for correspondents reporting on the European refugee crisis, the Syrian civil war, the Kurdish conflict, jihadist terrorism, and Turkey's own controversial president. It was also a boom town for the fixers who assisted those foreign correspondents.

Solmaz was new to the fixing game. She had recently left a career as a journalist in Turkey's national press. When her newspaper changed ownership and started printing government propaganda, a colleague advised she parlay her combination of English language and reporting abilities into a fixer's day rate that would keep her afloat. But as we sipped our coffees, she was soul-searching after a particularly grating experience with a foreign correspondent I will call Fred. Fred covered the whole of the Middle East for his newspaper and had recently arrived for a brief trip. A parachutist, in journo lingo. He hired Solmaz to help him get around town, connect him with sources, translate, provide background information.

Fred came to Istanbul to do a feature on the country's beleaguered LGBT community, but then had the mixed luck of also being in town on the occasion of a suicide terrorism attack. Fred and Solmaz rushed to the scene of the crime. Solmaz translated for Fred and convinced witnesses to do interviews. Fred wanted to get close to the blast site for photos, but police made him stay back from an area that they had cordoned off. He angrily protested that the cops had a "typical third-world mentality," and his anger extended to Solmaz for not fighting or sweet-talking strongly enough to get him better access – part of her job as his fixer, as he saw it.

Once the attacker was identified as an operative of the self-proclaimed Islamic State (ISIS), Fred next wanted to go to Çarşamba, Istanbul's most religiously conservative neighborhood, infamous as a recruiting ground for ISIS and other extremist groups. Solmaz refused, saying that it was too dangerous.

By this time, she had decided that Fred was too bullheaded and conspicuous for her to trust him to be sensitive to cultural difference or to keep a low profile. He did not seem to be listening to her coaching: open with small talk, answer sources' questions about yourself before asking questions of them – especially sources steeped in a tradition of paranoia about foreign agents.

Fred meanwhile mistook Solmaz's unwillingness to broker man-on-the-street interviews with ultraconservatives – coupled with her ease talking with LGBT activists for their previous story – for antipathy toward religion. He categorized Solmaz as a secular elitist and grew dismissive of her advice and explanations. He did not trust her to be objective.

"I understand Islam!" Fred huffed in response to Solmaz's attempt to correct one of his misperceptions. Fred had to rely on Solmaz nonetheless, and the pair ended up settling on a routine story for the foreign press that year: the decline of tourism to beautiful, historic, tragic Istanbul in the wake of the latest violence. It was an easy compromise for a reporter and a fixer who were at odds and under deadline. At the Grand Bazaar, they talked to shopkeepers and tourists who said predictable shopkeeper and tourist things, and Solmaz secured Fred an interview with a tourism official – nobody she had labored to cultivate as a source, no bridge she worried Fred would burn. Despite her assistance, Fred decided, without consulting her, against giving Solmaz a "contributed to this report" credit on the articles they produced together. She griped to me of this snub to her sense of professionalism, even as she claimed not to want her name on his cliché stories anyway. Fred flew out a few days later, on to another country and another fixer.

Solmaz called herself a rat because she felt at that moment that her job, fundamentally, was to betray sources, to open doors and feed information to foreign reporters who did not respect those sources or consider their views beyond categorizing them according to lazy stereotypes. Fred, at least in Solmaz's telling, seemed to consider her a rat of another kind: betraying journalism for a secret allegiance to a local political faction (secular elitists, in his misunderstanding).

Fixers are caught between reporters and sources, between worlds with different cultural and political norms. Fixers' in-betweenness is both what makes them useful in the first place and the principal source of their stress and self-doubt. Fixers face reporters' expectations from one side and sources' expectations from the other. When those expectations clash, fixers are thrust into states of moral ambivalence. Fred demands that Solmaz press dubious sources with uncomfortable questions, while those sources simultaneously demand Solmaz side with them against the suspicious foreigner. Solmaz feels like a rat because it can feel immoral to act as a proxy for a reporter – especially one like Fred – in extracting what they want from resistant local sources.

To avoid being caught in the middle of conflict, fixers get creative. They matchmake between compatible reporter–source pairs, like a writer who thinks their editor will be happy with a piece on the plight of Istanbul tourism and bazaar merchants glad to have an audience for their grumbles. They avoid matching short-term clients whom they do not trust with long-term sources with whom they have built up trust. They act as a buffer or reconcile differences between potentially clashing reporters and sources, as when Solmaz tried to coach Fred on culturally appropriate ways to approach sources and broach sensitive topics.

These strategies are not always possible and do not always work; sometimes, as with Solmaz, fixers' very attempts to manage the contradictions of in-betweenness discredit them to reporters or sources. But in success or failure, they shape what becomes news. An article appeared one day, in June 2016 in a major newspaper, about the deep discounts that tourists could find in Istanbul shops, in lieu of an article about ISIS recruitment in the same city, because Solmaz was more comfortable bringing Fred to the Grand Bazaar than to Çarşamba. Despite her part in determining what would become international knowledge about Turkey, Solmaz remained invisible to readers.

A Canadian reporter whom I will call Sally and a Syrian fixer whom I will call Karim chased that same terror attack story. Also based in Istanbul, Sally and Karim had a network of sources within Syria to tap, once authorities identified the suicide bomber as a Syrian national who had recently crossed into Turkey from the south. Unlike Fred and Solmaz, Sally and Karim had worked together for some time, long enough to trust each other, to know each other's blind spots, to become friends. Lovers too, but we will get to that later.

Karim reached out by phone to ISIS defectors and to sources with relatives in the Islamic State, asking if they knew the bomber. One heard a rumor he was from a town where Karim had a friend. Karim called the friend, who put Karim in touch with people who had known the bomber growing up. Karim also posted on Facebook that he was on the hunt for information; another friend responded that one of his own Facebook contacts had just posted about knowing the bomber from years back and being shocked. Both friends were willing to vouch for Karim as trustworthy and so help persuade sources to consent to interviews via Facebook or WhatsApp or Skype.

Sally was able to write a long profile on the bomber within days of the attack thanks to Karim's efforts and social network. Crucially, Karim was not only just a few degrees of social separation from the bomber, but also willing to call in favors and stake his own reputation that Sally would report the story in a way that maintained Karim's bridges to his contacts and kept sources living under militant rule in Syria out of danger.

Differences in the fixer–reporter relationship explain some differences between Solmaz's and Karim's respective performances on the Istanbul bombing story. Fred parachuted in and hired Solmaz for a few days' work. That was not enough time for much trust to develop or for them to understand each other beyond the level of stereotype. It was no wonder that Solmaz was unwilling to risk long-term relationships with sources for a client who would soon move on to the next country. By contrast, Karim and Sally had devoted years to their mutual apprenticeship, Karim learning about journalism and Sally about Syria. Sally expected to continue working with Karim and so had greater reason than Fred to care about her fixer's morale and rapport with sources.

Differences in Karim's and Solmaz's respective places in the history that was unfolding around them also help explain the direction each took in reporting the event. Their individual stories were embedded in the larger stories of the era's Turkish politics and Syrian civil war, and the larger-still history of the region's interactions with the rest of the world.

Each fixer was on their own trajectory within these larger histories: Solmaz from a local reporter for an opposition press being crushed by an authoritarian president to a behind-the-scenes broker learning to view her country through foreign eyes; Karim from penniless refugee to central player at the intersection of Syria-focused journalism, humanitarianism, militancy, and espionage. These trajectories influenced whom they interacted with, on what terms, and with what aspirations. As our protagonists' stories unfold, you will see how fixers' strategies for brokering information and managing relationships with reporters and sources evolve hand in hand with their own positions in journalism and in local societies.

Broad trends of cultural politics are also among the cards that fixers are dealt. Fred's confidence in applying half-baked stereotypes and his sense of entitlement and distrust for Solmaz were not merely personal idiosyncrasies. Whether he realized it or not, Fred's understanding of the world and his place within it was informed by a well-worn master narrative, which literary critic Edward Said (1978) called **Orientalism**, that presents an exotic, backward Middle East as a foil for the rational, modern West and justifies Western domination over Muslims especially.

The point is, if we want to understand why the international media covers stories the way it does, we need to burrow all the way down into fixers' ever-changing moral worlds without losing sight of their connections to larger political contexts.

\* \* \*

Before proceeding, though, I must mention that Solmaz, Karim, Fred, and Sally are all composite characters created out of multiple real people. I conducted ethnographic research in Istanbul and in the eastern city of Diyarbakır from 2014 through 2016. I interviewed and observed reporters, fixers, producers, and editors at work and contributed – sometimes as a fixer, sometimes as a reporter – to news stories myself.[1] The stories you will read in this book are grounded in

---

[1] I met the participants of my study using a "snowball" method of recruitment: I asked people I knew in the field of journalism to introduce me to their colleagues, then asked those colleagues for contacts, and so on. When I began my research, I already knew a few foreign reporters based in Turkey from my previous time there and in Afghanistan and Iran and through Columbia University contacts. The foreign reporters with whom I initially connected were kind enough to put me in touch with fixers with whom they had worked and with other reporters and producers who did likewise. However, reliance on a snowball sample rolled from the nucleus of my initial contacts limited my own knowledge of the world I was studying and my ideas about the range of perspectives in that world. Stories in this book are of newsmaking for North American, European, Gulf Arab, and a few Japanese news organizations, but other foreign media do operate in Turkey. There are Russian and Chinese news outlets with offices in

real data that I collected in these encounters but remixed into composite narratives. The foreign news and aid organizations that appear in the text are likewise renamed and, in many cases, remixed composites.

Creating composites gave surer anonymity to the participants in my research. Reporters and fixers produce publicly available work, maintain large social networks, and rely heavily on their reputations with both colleagues and sources. Together, these factors mean that if I were only to change names, individuals and news organizations could easily be unmasked. In some cases, they could then face professional or even legal or physical harm.

As you will read, some of my interlocutors or their collaborators behaved in ways that violated standards of journalistic ethics; some were highly critical of armed groups or Turkish or Syrian governments. Journalists have been jailed at alarming rates in Turkey and killed at appalling rates in Syria in recent years.[2] My writing could put them in further danger.

A thread running through this book is that fixers come up with creative ways to maintain relative anonymity or to shift focus, credit, or blame onto others when safest for them to appear neutral or as mere technicians carrying out mechanical tasks. Although I will show how fixers, in general, actually have a good measure of influence and autonomy, I have no wish to spoil the *I'm-just-an-innocent-translator* cover story of any particular fixer in the real world.

The nice thing about composites is that a reader cannot recognize a character in the text as a real person and then deductively attribute everything else the character does and says to that

Istanbul, but they did not respond to my inquiries. I sought out fixers with experience working for those news outlets, but none of the 62 people who participated in my study had worked or knew anyone who worked for Russian, Chinese, or other countries' media. That in itself is an interesting finding, pointing to separate labor networks for different national media, but not as interesting as it would have been to actually talk to people in those other networks.

[2] As of 2020, the Committee to Protect Journalists (CPJ n.d.-a) confirmed 26 journalists – both national and foreign – murdered for their work in the two countries since the outbreak of Syrian civil war in 2011, not to mention many more killed in crossfire or under unclear circumstances (all those murdered in Turkey were reporting on Syria). Rates of other violence and threats against journalists in or reporting on Syria are far higher. According to CPJ (n.d.-b), Turkey has vied with, and most years exceeded, China as the world's most active jailer of journalists since 2012, with less than one seventeenth of China's total population.

individual. The challenge was to create composites responsibly. After all, by combining multiple people's experiences into a single character, I compounded the risk – if not temptation – that all social scientists and journalists face: I could spin too-tidy tales, cherry-picking convenient data from here and there to "prove" my initial assumptions. I explain in the appendix how I did my best to create composite character narratives that were accountable to empirical data and followed a systematic logic, which served as tools to sharpen rather than dull my thinking.

I may have tried to keep myself accountable to the data I collected, but a composite narrative makes it impossible for readers to fact-check my work. Most frustratingly of all, the character Noah who appears in the following chapters is himself a composite character that I created to prevent the unmasking of certain research subjects to clients and bosses who knew they were participating in my research. Some of my own experiences are attributed to other characters, and some of other people's actions are attributed to my character, so you cannot even know what I actually did or witnessed firsthand and what is based on secondhand accounts.

Since composite narratives cannot be fact-checked in a conventional way, my recommendation is that you instead evaluate this book through comparison. Does my argument about fixers' moral ambivalence hold up when compared to brokers of other kinds? Does my point about labeling and social status claims help to explain your own peers' gossip about one another? Have you reacted similarly to the book's protagonists when pressured to squeeze your knowledge into an ill-fitting framework by a superordinate who knows far less about the topic than you do? Theories, after all, should be useful for explaining more than just the case at hand. They should also provide you with new ways to think about other cases. The sociological fiction of composite characters serves as a tool for identifying and illustrating patterns and building theories that you can test against your own experience of the world.

I hope to get you thinking not just about news fixers, but about how knowledge of all kinds is mediated through chains of brokerage. Perhaps the most important difference between sociology and journalism is that I am more concerned with providing theories that people can use to interpret facts, while the journalists I study are more concerned with pinning down facts that people can use to substantiate claims, build their own theories, and make decisions.

This book will explain how fixers, reporters, and others create international news and why the news turns out the way it does. I will argue that the newsmaking process is contentious from start to finish, a series of unequal negotiations and sly translations that link together news contributors who are closest to events on the ground with the far-off expectations and narratives of media organizations headquartered on the other side of the world. Caught in the middle of local and global interests and values, fixers mediate between clients and sources in ways that reconcile political and cultural conflicts and transmit information across their divides. The role of the intermediary is precarious, offering fixers opportunity for status and power if they play their cards right, but disrepute and dissolution if they play them wrong.

The book is organized into five parts, subdivided into short chapters that recount the careers of fixers like Solmaz and Karim. I do not follow the usual template for academic monographs, which dictates that every section begin with an introduction that tells the reader exactly what is coming and a literature review that tells how the coming arguments fit into debates within the author's field. That style helps professors and graduate students efficiently extract theories for seminars and citations, but also makes academic books boring to read, like jokes that begin with the punch line or mysteries that begin with the solution (Hunter 2018). Instead, I foreshadow coming themes in introductory sections (as in the previous paragraph and the chapter summaries below) but then allow my full argument to accrue organically as I shift back and forth between character narratives and reflections on what they tell us about fixers' place in newsmaking. I hope this style makes for a more enjoyably surprising, if less tidy, read.[3]

There is nonetheless an order to the book's progression, consisting of a gradual zoom into the worlds of fixers. At each focal length, I will overlay outlines offered by different schools of social theory to help

---

[3]  If you prefer a more conventional social scientific reading experience, I recommend you read the last chapter of each part before continuing to the narrative sections titled with character names.

show patterns in our protagonists' stories, and together, the various theoretical lines will converge into a unified picture. Along the way, I will also tell the story of Turkey's and Syria's transformations over the past two decades through the eyes of newsmakers. These histories are important in their own right, but also essential for us to make sense of characters' careers and the conflicts they mediated between their local and foreign interlocutors.

Part I is about the social origins of people who became fixers in 2010s Turkey and Syria. I explain why reporters need fixers and why fixing appeals to some people using classic oppositions of relational sociology: insider and outsider, order and disorder (Douglas [1966] 2001; Merton 1972; Emirbayer 1997).

Part II looks at the position of fixers within the field of journalism. Actor-Network Theory (Latour 2005b) and Gatekeeping Theory (Shoemaker and Vos 2009) will help us see how media production involves collaboration along a chain of participants with diverse but interconnected interests and perspectives. Labeling Theory (Becker [1963] 1997; Goffman 1963, 1968) and Field Theory (Bourdieu 1984, 1993) will help explain how participants in journalism evaluate one another and strive to raise their own status.

Part III deals with the individual level of fixers as moral actors caught between competing expectations. Interactionist theories (Goffman 1959, 1969, 1974) about strategic self-presentation will guide my discussion of how fixers try, with mixed success, to manage their relationships with clients and sources and save face as the latter two come into conflict.

Part IV zooms in all the way to news stories and fixers' transformations of the information that passes from source to reporter. I will deploy concepts from Information Theory and Cybernetics (Shannon [1949] 1964; Weaver [1949] 1964; Wiener 1954; Bateson 1972) to answer a question that might arise in your mind: Why should I care about fixers and their problems, aside from motivations of curiosity or empathy? My response is that fixers' backgrounds, status struggles, and conflict-management strategies all come together at moments of interaction with reporters and sources in ways that shape what becomes news and informs your perception of the world.

By way of conclusion, Part V widens the frame back out to the global level, fitting fixers' careers into the international news economy and flow of knowledge. I draw on the hybrid theoretical approach developed in previous chapters to explain why there can be no journalism without insider-outsider brokers (whether or not they are called fixers, whether or not they are even human) and yet why journalism's constitutive brokerage relationships are necessarily in constant flux.

Finally, a methodological appendix explains how I created composite characters for those of you still skeptical and/or interested in the relationship among social science, fiction, and truth.

# PART I

# Beginnings

# Noah

I first heard of fixers when I participated in the Foundry Photojournalism Workshop in Istanbul in summer 2010, fresh out of college. Each student had to pursue their own photo stories over the course of a week, and workshop organizers provided us with a list of local fixers. Though I had taken undergraduate courses on international journalism, I had only the vaguest of ideas about what I was supposed to ask of the people on the list.

I had already learned decent Turkish, both at Princeton University and during a year I had taken off in the middle of college to wander around Turkey, Iran, and Iraqi Kurdistan in search of adventure and connection to my roots (my father is from Iran). I had not much considered it at the time, but for each of the photographic and reporting stories I pursued during that trip, whether about underground rap music in Tehran or the last vestiges of nomadic pastoralism in Bingöl or land-mine eradication in Sulemani, there had been an informal, ad hoc fixer, an insider who opened doors for me and made my (in most cases nonetheless botched) projects possible.

At the Istanbul photojournalism workshop two years later, I learned that there was a semiformal label for such people and considered for the first time that they were providing a form of labor that merited remuneration. I also learned, when I hired a political science student at one of Istanbul's English-language universities from the list, that different fixers are helpful in different ways.

I wanted to do a photo essay about an urban renewal project that was slated to evict residents from a historic and decrepit neighborhood called Tarlabaşı. My new fixer and I met and chatted about gentrification before going together to the neighborhood. I had already been there on my own several times but thought that having a real, live, authentic Turk beside me would change everything, give that true local access for which I yearned. I had photographed people in Tarlabaşı's streets and colorful laundry hanging between apartment windows on my solo visits, but I wanted more. I had an exoticist desire to get into the tidy hovels of the virtuous working poor, the brothels of transgender sex workers, the squats of thieves and junkies.

It turns out that fixers are not magical. They also find it awkward to invite themselves into the homes of strangers, and possessing the same national identity card as those strangers does not guarantee entrée or mutual understanding. Yet somehow, because of the way the workshop teachers had described and I had imagined the fixer as a local *in*, it had not occurred to me that a middle-class Turkish woman would be something of an outsider to impoverished Kurds and Romani.

Despite my bratty frustration over my fixer not opening the doors that I expected, I learned a huge amount from the conversations that the two of us had as we walked Tarlabaşı. We discussed urban planning, city politics, the neighborhood's Ottoman history, the place of sex work in Turkish society. She turned out to be a great fixer, not by securing exclusive access or even by following my directions, but by changing the way I made sense of Istanbul. At least she was a great fixer for a kid who was ultimately more interested in exploration than producing a sellable piece of news. If I had an editor and a deadline, it might have been different.

*** *** ***

I went to graduate school a year later to study sociology (as did that first fixer, actually, at another American university). I thought I would focus on political sociology, studying international military interventions and state-building. But when I went to Afghanistan to research American wartime development projects, I found that the foreign diplomats, humanitarians, journalists, and businesspeople, ostensibly running their respective organizations, tended to have very limited knowledge of what was actually going on outside of their Kabul bubble, or even outside of the walls of the guarded compounds that they rarely left. The most knowledgeable and interesting people that I met were the bicultural Afghans who functioned as intermediaries between the international organizations and local society. I discovered that news fixers have their analogs in many fields. Yet even among these various and fascinating behind-the-scenes players, fixers stuck out to me as potentially offering the purest case study for how local realities get mediated and transformed into foreign knowledge.

Knowledge – international news – is precisely the product of their work.

To be honest, I was also attracted to news fixers as an object of study because there was something about conducting my international development research in Afghanistan behind blast walls, in heavily air-conditioned trailers that defied power outages, through conversations with other Americans, that offended my own quest for uninsulated adventure. For ethnographers, as for journalists, there is a rugged ideal of working in the field, of exposing oneself to the chaos of a foreign world, that can be belied by the normality of researcher life. Following a long and unsavory tradition of Orientalists using the East as a land of fulfillment for their exotic fantasies, I wanted to pick a dissertation topic that would throw me into a vaguely imagined *real world* (Said 1978).

I remembered my experience in Tarlabaşı, remembered the other workshop student projects my first fixer had described to me, which led her to drag queen parties, to ultranationalist tattoo parlors, to days of shadowing garbage collectors. Fixers, I thought, are constantly doing interesting things with interesting people, and by attaching myself to them as an observer, some of that adventure would rub off onto me.

In the end, well aware of the cases of Ajmal Naqshbandi and Sultan Munadi, Afghan fixers who in the preceding years had been abducted with foreign clients and subsequently killed (Packer 2009), I decided that journalism in war-torn Afghanistan was too dangerous for my taste. Turkey seemed to promise tamer adventure as a research site. When I booked my flight from Kabul to Istanbul in summer 2014, I did not anticipate the violence that would soon be spilling over into Turkey too.

# Between Worlds

Kids do not tell their parents that they want to be fixers when they grow up, nor do their parents pressure them into the occupation. Students do not study in school to be fixers or attend career fairs with fixer kiosks. Many accounts of becoming a fixer involve serendipitous encounters or friendships unexpectedly evolving into careers.[1] Though I became accustomed to hearing that people got into fixing by accident, fixers' backgrounds and social and geographical positions led them to be in the right place at the right time to assist a foreign reporter and then to want to continue doing so.

There are important differences among fixers' origin stories. Some start off as local **insiders** with strong social ties to sources, links that help reporters gain access and trust. Others are relative **outsiders** from the beginning, closer in perspective to client reporters, which better positions them to help clients make sense of local realities and transform them into international news (Merton 1972; Bossone 2014; Palmer 2019: 8–10; Plaut and Klein 2019b).[2] Depending on where they come from and where they want to go, some fixers seek out adventure through reporting while others hope that the foreign press will be their anchor of stability.

If fixers' positions in their own societies and in relation to the world of foreign correspondents are important, then it follows that the larger context in which they become fixers matters. In order to understand how and why our characters became fixers, we will need to consider events that reshaped Turkey and Syria in the early twenty-first century: the government takeover of Turkey's national media, the Kurdish conflict, the Syrian civil war, and the Gezi Park protest movement.

---

[1] Swidler and Watkins (2017: 22–35, 108–112) cite a similar pattern of the seemingly miraculous encounters that kindle "romances" between local brokers and international AIDS activists in Malawi.

[2] See also Clifford's (1997: 18–24) analogous distinction between "natives" and "travelers" among the informants to ethnographic research.

# Orhan

I often met Orhan at a bustling coffee shop in Beşiktaş, a secularist-leftist enclave on Istanbul's European side. He called the café his office. Our conversations were continually interrupted by his acquaintances stopping in for a coffee or passing on the street, but he seemed to thrive in the chaos. Orhan was in his late 30s when I got to know him, a decade and a half older than me and much cooler, dressed most days in a rock concert tee-shirt and ripped jeans.

Orhan was a reporter who turned to fulltime fixing when he decided it had become too difficult to earn a living and avoid trouble in the Turkish media. To explain how and why he became a fixer, it is necessary to backtrack to the era following Turkey's 1980 coup d'état.

The September 12, 1980 military coup was the third in the short history of the Republic of Turkey. The armed forces seized control after years of instability in the country's parliamentary system and escalating violence between right- and left-wing militants. Several years of hardline military rule gave way to elections and the liberalization of the media. Private newspapers and then TV stations proliferated. Business tycoons with commercial interests ranging from port management to mining to banking owned the largest news outlets (Yeşil 2016: loc. 791–1084).

Those tycoons used their media power to smear rival companies and to curry favor with government officials and the still-dominant military (Finkel 2000; Yeşil 2016: loc. 741–875). The mainstream media backed secularist generals in 1997 when they pressured a coalition government led by the Islamist Welfare (*Refah*) Party into collapse and the prime minister into resignation (Över 2017: 76–77).

Orhan grew up during this period of chaotic semi-democracy. In his teens in the early 1990s, Orhan got into Istanbul's growing heavy metal music scene. He fancied himself an outsider and a skeptic, and so growing his hair out and becoming a *metalci* was a logical step for Orhan. Metalheads were on the bleeding edge of cultural rebellion in western Turkey, the subject of moral panic in the media and accusations of sadism and Satanism (Hecker 2016).

Orhan led something of a double life, rocking out at night but doing well in public school and later studying economics at a respectable state university by day. He did, however, credit music and not school for his English language skills, which were still a bit rough two decades later.

The ouster of the Welfare Party was succeeded by weak coalition and caretaker governments that failed to pass economic reforms and oversaw a string of corruption scandals and the collapse of the country's banking sector. The overtly religious Welfare Party was succeeded by the AK (*Adalet ve Kalkınma* – Justice and Development) Party, which adopted a more moderate and liberal platform. The AKP won big in the 2002 parliamentary elections, drawing voters disgusted by the previous years of corrupt politics and economic crisis, and formed a single-party government under Recep Tayyip Erdoğan.[1]

In the early 2000s, Orhan began working as a business reporter for *Sabah*, a large, tycoon-owned newspaper with a liberal-centrist editorial line. He buttoned down, pulling his grungy hair back into a neat ponytail for work and wearing a tie to interviews with Turkish executives and foreign investors. Orhan learned that he had to be careful about whom he covered critically:

"There was always that kind of pressure on the business journalist in Turkey, from the … big corporations, from the state ministries, state banks, blah blah. … In those days it [was] always hard to write negative" about the companies associated with the country's Kemalist political-economic establishment. (**Kemalism** refers to the secular nationalist ideology of the Republic of Turkey's founding president Mustafa Kemal Atatürk.)[2]

The owner of *Sabah*, a powerful player in that secularist establishment, had helped bring down the country's banking sector in 2000 by borrowing extravagantly from foreign lenders and engaging in a variety of fraudulent backroom deals. The new AKP government, pledging reform, killed two birds with one stone by going after its

---

[1] Erdoğan faced a 5-year ban from political office for reading an Islamist poem in 1998 while mayor of Istanbul, which meant he could not join parliament to become prime minister until 2003.
[2] See Gürpinar (2013) on the varieties and evolution of Kemalism.

political opponents' media holdings as punishment for their financial misdeeds.

On April Fools' Day 2007, black-suited police showed up at *Sabah*'s headquarters unannounced and, after a brief brawl with security guards, announced to Orhan and his startled colleagues that *Sabah* was now under state ownership. The government's banking regulator then auctioned the newspaper and the tycoon's other seized media assets off to an AKP-aligned businessman, who received generous financing from a state bank for the purchase. Prime Minister Erdoğan's son-in-law's brother became chief executive officer (Yeşil 2016). For all the AKP's talk of reformism and success convincing the world that it offered a new vision of Muslim democracy, this was an early sign that the party was playing a familiar, corrupt game.

Orhan had always faced pressure to report favorably on, in his words, "the good boys" (allies of the newspaper's owner) and enjoyed a free hand to dig into the business problems and misconduct of the "bad boys" (the owner's rivals). But under the new ownership, the script for whom Orhan was to cast in each role flipped. Now, businesses affiliated with the AKP and the religious movement of Fethullah Gülen were to be the good boys.

Fethullah Gülen is a cleric with a large following in Turkey who has lived in self-imposed exile in Pennsylvania since 1999. At the time of the newspaper takeover, Gülen was a close ally of Erdoğan and was enjoying a good deal of success in internationally branding his movement as a moderate and liberal face of Islam. Within Turkey, though, secularists like Orhan were deeply suspicious of Gülen followers, upon whom the AKP relied for technocratic expertise and global image management. Critics accused them of infiltrating state, financial, and media institutions with the secret goal of turning Gülen into the country's master puppeteer, if not of transforming the republic altogether into a theocracy (Hendrick 2013).

As AK Party and Gülen Movement loyalists gradually replaced *Sabah* upper management and editorial staff, Orhan's business desk was increasingly pressured to attack businesses controlled by AKP opponents and favor businesses close to the party and the Gülen Movement. "Even the simple stories start to become a problem," Orhan recalled, "I mean like 8 p.m. the demands start to come to change the news, to change the headlines, even to change the sentences."

The Gülen Movement and AKP cadres who came to control *Sabah* were not the first to use the paper as a tool to serve political and financial goals. But as a center-left secularist, Orhan found himself marginalized and uncomfortable with the new editorial orthodoxy.

The immediate cause of Orhan's departure, though, was that his new straitlaced and pious editor demanded that he cut his ponytail. Orhan's long hair was his thing; he would still let it down on the weekends to headbang to the heavy metal he loved. That was the last straw and he quit.

Orhan found work at another secular-leaning newspaper, only to watch as the tycoon who owned it was hit with a multi-billion-dollar tax penalty. The newspaper had enraged Erdoğan by covering a court case that implicated AKP supporters in a charity embezzlement scheme (Corke et al. 2014: 7). As part of the tax settlement, in a pattern becoming familiar, Orhan's newspaper was sold off to a businessman close to Erdoğan. And once again, Orhan's place in the newsroom gradually became marginal:

My last days at the paper, it was like hell, like seriously, *yani* [I mean] because you write stuff, you write stuff, and they are not get published, and then you feel like freaking out. *Yani* if you're a journalist, of course you want to see your articles published in the paper, right?

* * *

Years earlier, Orhan had befriended Geert, a freelance Belgian reporter based in Istanbul. Domestic and foreign journalism worlds overlap. Domestic journalists like Orhan, particularly in hubs like Istanbul, meet foreign reporters as they frequent the same press briefings and cover the same events. Foreign and domestic journalists are also in virtual contact: They read each other's stories and have overlapping networks on social media. Foreign journalists mine local reporting for story ideas, and local journalists are curious what the international press is saying about their country.

When a foreign reporter and a local reporter get to know each other, the line between friendship and fixing can blur. Geert never bothered to learn Turkish and would sometimes ask for Orhan's help translating, as well as contacting interviewees and navigating bureaucracy. Geert also relied heavily on Orhan's explanations – usually over beers and loud music – of the backgrounds to issues Geert was reporting. Orhan would travel with Geert on days off from his business news job and enjoyed exploring the country beyond his own beat. One day they would interview a soccer team, the next be invited to dance with Kurdish shepherds. It was also nice not to worry about the heavy hand of an editor caught up in Turkish factional politics. Geert would pay for all their travel expenses, but beyond that Orhan refused payment. He was helping out as a friend.

Working with the international media also held an exotic appeal for Orhan. Name-dropping the world-renowned outlets for which he and Geert reported signaled to Orhan's local colleagues and to himself a prestigious worldliness and social audacity.

Geert liked working with Orhan throughout the country because, as a career journalist himself, Orhan was more of an outsider to local sources than other potential fixers. When a foreign reporter goes to an unknown place, they can usually find someone local who speaks serviceable English to recruit as an ad hoc fixer. If they wander around a town babbling in English – at least in Turkey where both a norm of hospitality and people who have studied the language exist – locals will eventually direct them to someone who can translate and is generous or bored enough to help out for free. Yet reporters like Geert will instead make the more expensive choice of traveling with their own fixer, even to places that fixer does not know well.

Orhan's English was decent, and he had access to some valuable contacts, but as important, Orhan entered into fixing already equipped with a journalistic perspective. Having covered Turkish business news for years, Orhan had learned how to look at a happening in the world and imagine whether and how it might be turned into a news story. Orhan's extracurricular experiences also contributed to his fixing abilities. You cannot dive as deep into an international cultural scene as Orhan did into heavy metal music without developing an understanding of foreign perspectives and blind spots.

Geert was even more of an outsider, but so far outside the communities they were covering that he could not even make sense of much of what he heard and saw. He needed Orhan as a partial outsider and cultural interpreter to explain backgrounds and cultures and politics, to extend Geert's sensemaking abilities.[3]

---

[3] I use the term "sensemaking" and not "understanding," because it does not presume correct interpretation. Sensemaking can, to the contrary, employ "working misunderstandings" that allow reporter and source to align without actually understanding one another (Swidler and Watkins 2017).

The terms **outsider** and **insider** are relational – one must be outside or inside *of something* – and meaningless without reference to what news stories a journalist is covering (Emirbayer 1997). Orhan was an outsider for stories about soccer teams and Kurdish shepherds. But he would be an insider for a story on heavy metal, and was an insider years later when I hired him to help me with a story about the crackdown on the Turkish national press.

As Orhan prepared to quit his job after his second newspaper's resale to a government minion and planned his next move, he recalled that Geert, in their many arguments about Orhan accepting money for his services, had told him that fixers were usually paid about $150 a day, more for TV work. Orhan decided that he could live decently off that wage if he could find a steady flow of reporter clients. Besides, he felt hopeless about his prospects in the Turkish domestic media. Orhan asked Geert to start sending colleagues who needed fixers his way. Geert also added Orhan's contact information and summary of qualifications to a "fixer and translator list" circulating online among foreign journalists in Turkey.

Orhan was an early addition to the trickle of Turkish reporters flowing into fixing jobs due to the capture of national media by Prime Minister Erdoğan's allies.[4] At the same time that government-allied conglomerates bought up opposition outlets one after another, Turkey became the world's most prolific jailer of journalists who persisted in reporting critically. It became safer to work in relative anonymity for the foreign press (Finkel 2015; Beiser 2016).

---

[4] Gülen Movement–affiliated non-governmental organizations (NGOs) were competitors to news fixers in that they offered to help foreign journalists learn about Turkey and meet locals. Suzy Hansen (2017: 61), an American reporter who moved to Turkey the same year that Orhan's newspaper was seized, remembered,

Every month, Gülen representatives held seminars for foreign journalists in Istanbul, where they offered lectures related to the news of the day: the history of the AK Party, the compatibility of Islam with democracy. They introduced us to religious scholars and intellectuals, to young women pursuing PhDs who could confidently articulate their own reasons for wearing a head scarf. The Gülenists were aggressively helpful to foreigners.

Fixing allowed Orhan to live in a way he had come to value as he assimilated to both *metalci* culture and professional journalism. He could ditch the business-correspondent suit and tie for an Iron Maiden tee most days, and he could contribute to stories without having to please government-aligned managing editors. He would soon recognize, though, that foreign reporters and editors shackled him with a whole new set of expectations.

# *Nur*

Orhan and other secularist Turks considered the 2010s to mark a low point of political oppression.[1] But for minority ethnic Kurds living in eastern Turkey, the 1990s were crushing.

The Kurdistan Workers' Party (*Partîya Karkerên Kurdistanê* or PKK) staged its first attack on the Turkish military in 1984. The PKK's ultimate goal was to carve out an independent nation-state of Kurdistan under the Marxist-Leninist leadership of Abdullah Öcalan (Marcus 2007: 33–81). The Turkish state, which had long suppressed Kurdish cultural and political identity, responded with violence. The brutality of insurgency and counterinsurgency reached a climax in the '90s, just as Nur was growing up.

Nur was born and raised in a medieval maze of backstreets in the Old City of Diyarbakır, the unofficial capital of Northern Kurdistan in Turkey's southeast.[2] At home she spoke Kurdish, a language closer to Persian than to Turkish. But at school it was Turkish only, and her instruction was heavily laced with Turkish nationalist propaganda from ethnic Turkish teachers dispatched to the southeast on a state-led assimilationist mission (İnce 2018: 113–135).

The pitched fighting between the PKK and the Turkish state took place in the countryside, but assassinations were common in Diyarbakır. Journalism was a particularly dangerous profession: dozens of PKK-sympathetic journalists and even newspaper vendors were murdered in never-solved cases. Militants of Kurdish Hizbullah

---

[1] See Över (2017: 161–164) on unfavorable comparisons of the 2010s with the post-1980 coup era among mainstream journalists.

[2] The world's non-diasporic Kurdish population is split among Turkey, Iraq, Syria, and Iran. Kurdish nationalists who want to reference those borders without explicitly acknowledging the nation-states speak in the coded language of North (Turkish), South (Iraqi), East (Syrian), and West (Iranian) Kurdistan.

(unrelated to the Lebanese organization), supposedly Islamic revolutionaries but informally allied to Turkish security forces, were suspected in many of those murders (Kurt 2017: 18–38).

In Nur's older brother's high school, ordinary students passed through metal detectors, but Hizbullah-affiliated students flashed knives and handguns. Her brother strongly suspected them of killing his favorite teacher, who had veered from the curriculum to lecture about the importance of peace and tolerance. Nur's family coached her to keep her head down, and though she retained a rebellious streak, she did learn the lesson that it can be safest to remain behind the scenes.

In 1998–1999, Turkey struck two decisive blows against the PKK. The insurgents had long enjoyed bases of operation in Syria, where they agreed not to stir up trouble among Syria's own oppressed Kurds in exchange for safe harbor. But after Turkey massed troops on its southern border and threatened to invade Syria, Hafez al-Assad – father and predecessor of current Syrian President Bashar al-Assad – evicted the PKK. Months later, after an international game of cat-and-mouse, Turkish intelligence captured PKK leader Abdullah Öcalan (Marcus 2007: 269–276).

The PKK did not disappear with the imprisonment of Öcalan. Fighting resumed in 2004 and continued off and on. But at the same time, as Nur entered her teenage years, the Kurdish Movement transformed, redoubling emphasis on civil society activism and democratic politics. Öcalan himself underwent a political transformation while in Turkish prison. Though a Stalinist who maintained absolute control over his party and brooked no dissent during his years at the head of the insurgency (Marcus 2007), from prison Öcalan began to espouse an ideology of radically decentralized "democratic confederalism" that included environmentalist and feminist tenets. The Kurdish Movement followed his lead, focusing on local democratic politics inclusive of other minority groups and women.

Nur adopted the politics of autonomy and non-violent rebellion on a personal level – leather jacket, cigarettes, and all. She also stood out for her intelligence, earning a place at a prestigious English-language state university in Ankara, Turkey's capital, in the late 2000s. To the chagrin of her parents, Nur studied philosophy over a subject with better prospects for a stable income like health or education. She would return to her hometown during school breaks to volunteer and translate at Kurdish political parties'[3] and Kurdish Movement–aligned NGO events and conferences. These organizations were shorthanded when it came to English speakers who could get their messages out to a European and North American audience that might pressure Turkey into reform.

At one public meeting during the 2011 parliamentary election campaign, an American reporter pulled Nur aside during a cigarette break. She introduced herself as Alison and said that while she was in town for election coverage, she was also interested in doing a radio story about *dengbêjan*: traditional Kurdish singer-storytellers. The *dengbêjan* were old men who would gather daily to sit on rustic couches in the municipal Dengbêj House's stone courtyard, drink tea, and regale fellow bards and a small audience seated opposite them in plastic chairs.

Would Nur like to help report on them? Alison could pay her a modest day rate. Nur jumped at the opportunity. She considered assisting Alison an extension of her work for the Kurdish Movement, which was promoting *dengbêj* in an effort to reawaken Kurdish traditions and so foster a distinctive cultural identity after decades of Turkish assimilationism (Scalbert-Yücel 2009).

There was a smaller pool of potential fixers for Alison in Diyarbakır than in Istanbul. There are fewer local journalists in provincial cities who speak English well enough to be recruited as ad hoc fixers. Alison's budget may have allowed her to bring an outsider fixer like Orhan from Istanbul, but some reporters prefer to work with insiders.

Alison used Nur not only as a fixer for the *dengbêjan* story but also as a source: a youthful activist interested in the Kurdish cultural reawakening. Alison discovered Nur to be both eager to talk politics and a fount of human-interest story ideas. She knew of numerous other educational and cultural enterprises popping up around town in that season of "Kurdish Spring."

---

[3] Since the 1990s, the Kurdish Movement has been represented by a string of legal political parties that have regrouped under new names and color schemes each time the Constitutional Court shuttered them for separatism: The People's Labor Party, Democracy Party, People's Democracy Party, Democratic People's Party, Democratic Society Party, Peace and Democracy Party, and most recently a coordinated Peoples' Democratic Party for the national level and Democratic Regions Party for the local level. These name changes also reflected fusions and fissions within the movement.

Alison ended up extending her stay in Diyarbakır so that she could continue covering stories with Nur. Nur's English was not flawless, and Alison suspected that her translations were a bit spotty, but that was not the most important thing, particularly for radio journalism.

"[She] was really good at emotion," Alison later told me, so much so that Alison ended up including many clips of Nur's translations directly in her stories.

So [her] actual translations word-for-word weren't great, but [she] was really great – for the purpose of public radio – at relaying the emotion of the people I was interviewing, and I ended up crying in an interview because of it. . . . [Nur] was really good at mimicking the tone, probably because [she] was very empathetic. [She] was also active in the . . . [Kurdish] Movement, and so [Nur] was really good at relaying the emotion. . . . For the purposes of what I was doing, that trumped the word-for-word, because in the end the message, like what was being delivered got delivered. It was a personal experience that [she] was describing.

If Alison had worked with an outsider like Orhan on the same story, he may have been able to fly into Diyarbakır. He may even have been able to find the same Kurdish activists. But would they have been as open to talking with Alison if Orhan, an ethnic Turkish stranger, were mediating? And would Orhan's voice have quivered with emotion while translating in a way that Alison thought perfect for radio?

If outsiders are good for sensemaking, able to explain local ways and happenings in terms a foreigner can understand, then insiders are good for access. By access, I do not mean just getting sources into the same room as reporters. Fixers help reporters access sources' perspectives and emotional states. Nur could provide Alison access to the inner worlds of Kurdish Movement activists because of her personal affiliation with the group. She was able to elicit and communicate into English their feelings about issues they found important, even if Nur's word-for-word translations did not always make sense to Alison.

Yet because Alison thought of Nur as an activist rather than a fellow professional journalist, she also considered Nur biased, too close to the story to be trusted when it came to editorial input at a higher level than translation. Alison was interested in Nur's views, but felt she could not rely on Nur alone to make sense of Diyarbakır. When they first met, Alison told me, Nur was very ideological, always pushing her to talk with politicians from the Kurdish Left. Alison had to course-correct.

She did her best to find other sources to balance those whom Nur recommended and took Nur's claims and explanations with a grain of salt.

After that first introduction to fixing, Nur returned to college in Ankara. Upon graduating, she moved back to Diyarbakır and continued working as a translator and interpreter for NGOs and occasionally visiting diplomatic teams from Europe. Alison added her name to the foreign press fixer/translator directory, and new reporter clients began to contact her. Then they would refer their friends to her, and those friends would refer their friends, and she began charging more for her services.

The payment reporters offer fixers is high for some fields and low for others. Reporters poach fixers from low- or non-paying activist work, from grad school or English teaching, not from corporate public relations positions or comfortable public-sector employment.[4] Had Nur studied medicine instead of philosophy, had she become an interpreter out of college for a well-heeled company instead of for resource-strapped NGOs, fixing would have held less financial appeal.[5]

But for Nur, the realization that she could get by comfortably working as a fixer for a few clients each month was liberating. Fixing provided the right mix of income, schedule, and xenophilic fulfillment of interaction with foreigners. The job enabled Nur to afford her own apartment (difficult though it was to find a landlord willing to rent to a single woman) a safe distance from her parents and to adopt the bohemian lifestyle of the urban Kurdish freethinker.

---

[4] See Paterson et al. (2012) for a case study of Kosovar journalists learning that they could earn far more money fixing for the international press than at their jobs for the domestic media.

[5] In other economic contexts, you find different patterns of fixer backgrounds. When I first became interested in fixers during my fieldwork in Afghanistan, I learned that medical doctors were overrepresented in the cohort of news fixers recruited to cover the post-9/11 US war. They were among the few Afghans who spoke English, and foreign news organizations could pay them far more than they had earned practicing medicine. In Turkey too, the financial appeal of fixing has varied over time. When the Turkish economy floundered and the exchange value of the lira plummeted in the early 2000s and again in the late 2010s, being paid in US dollars or euros became a more attractive proposition.

# *Karim*

South of the border, Karim was unknowingly starting down his own path as a fixer. He was from the Syrian capital Damascus but grew up partly in the United Arab Emirates, where his father was a business-man and where English is more the lingua franca than Arabic. Karim returned to Syria in the early 2000s to study economics at university and then start a job at a luxury hotel. He would sometimes lead VIP guests around on tours, learning both to charm foreigners and to objectify and neatly package Syria for them.

Tall and handsome, Karim was a playboy and bon vivant, ignoring politics and concerning himself with work, family, romance, and fun in the relatively socially permissive but politically stagnant milieu of pre–civil war Damascus.

Bashar al-Assad had succeeded his long-ruling autocratic father, Hafez, as president of Syria after the latter's death in 2000. After initially presenting himself as a reformist – especially to international audiences – it did not take Bashar long to crack down on political dissent and continue in his father's footsteps, relying on a security state and tightly controlled national media to keep citizens in line (George 2003). Syria was meanwhile buffeted by shock waves of the sectarian civil war that engulfed Iraq after the American invasion, hosting more than a million Iraqi refugees (Campbell 2017).

Like many young Syrians, Karim was both astonished and inspired by anti-government protests that erupted in 2011 as "Arab Spring" uprisings shook the whole region. When security forces massacred protesters, Karim was propelled into activism for the first time.

He began volunteering with one of the coordination committees (*tansiqiyat*) that sprang up across the country to organize nonviolent resistance and document events (Yassin-Kassab and Al-Shami 2016: 57–60). Karim was tasked with running English-language social media accounts, posting hour-by-hour updates about military raids and demonstrations and shootings, captioning videos and photos, corresponding with foreign media who got in touch.

It was chaotic and amateurish. The state had previously repressed or co-opted civil society and independent media, so none of these newfound activists knew what they were doing (Yassin-Kassab and Al-Shami 2016: 18–21). Despite their lack of experience, the *tansiqiyat* members quickly realized that they would be taken most seriously, both inside and outside the country, if they adopted an objective news style emphasizing information over emotion. Karim began to learn how to present information in ways outsiders would find credible:

> I would just volunteer as much time as I could to translate the news. . . . And what I liked about it was, at least when I was there, they had a standard of like, you know, no emotion, no *Bismullahs* ["in the name of God"], no nothing. It's just like, "This happened on this street to this person." Next. Just really, it was very much like a breaking news, kind of like a wire.[1]

Damascus was still under state control, and after some months, intelligence services found and arrested Karim. He was held for several weeks, tortured, then released. He fled to a suburb of the city under rebel control and began working for a media office that gathered and disseminated information from a *tansiqiyat* network. He now worked more closely with foreign reporters, arranging their visits and for security provided by revolutionary fighters.

In those early revolutionary days, the conflict had not yet descended into a sectarian civil war, but there were already signs that religiously radical or simply venal rebel commanders were gaining in power.[2] A hodgepodge of Islamist and socialist militias controlled the suburb and faced the challenges of being the de facto government while under siege. The militias not only fought the regime but also competed with

---

[1] By "wire" he refers to international news agencies like Reuters, Associated Press, and Agence France-Presse.

[2] The Assad government encouraged the radicalization of resistance by selectively granting amnesty to imprisoned sectarian hardliners, many of whom had served Al Qaeda in Iraq after the 2003 US invasion and would go on to become founding members of Jabhat al-Nusra and ISIS (Yassin-Kassab and Al-Shami 2016: 120; Ackerman 2019: 31–32). As Ackerman (2019: 14) notes, "Assad emptied the prisons of jihadists in 2011. Assad had hoped the jihadists would fight against him; a regime under siege by radical Islamists is more likely to garner international support than a regime under siege by democratic activists. To Assad's credit, it worked."

one another, sometimes violently, for funding and to monopolize the delivery of aid and public services (Alsaafin 2015; Yassin-Kassab and Al-Shami 2016: 85–86, 121–125).

I cannot say with confidence exactly what Karim's connection was with local militias or what his role was in their power struggle. He told me he was never a fighter, though the first time we met, he did proudly pull back various articles of clothing to expose scars and invited me to feel shrapnel still lodged under his skin.

Karim continued to wield his pen, angering one powerful militia's leadership in 2013 by accusing the group of corruption on social media. He received threats, and friends advised him that he was in danger, so Karim fled to Turkey across what was still a porous border.

There, Karim reunited with relatives who had recently crossed into Turkey for their own reasons and settled in a new refugee camp in the south of the country. It was not the squalid tent city that the term "refugee camp" might conjure. The Turkish government had built row upon row of neat container homes equipped with hot water and satellite TV for their Syrian "guests." Streets, schools, and playgrounds were clean and safe (McClelland 2014).

Karim was nonetheless eager to get back to work and soon moved out of the camp to the nearby city of Antakya. There he took on various Arabic–English translation gigs for the aid agencies and political organizations growing in pace with the Syrian exile community in southern Turkey.

In early 2014, though, Karim drew the ire of an up-and-coming splinter group that had recently broken off from Al Qaeda's Syrian franchise, Jabhat al-Nusra ("The Victory Front"). The splinter group called itself the Islamic State of Iraq and Syria and was less concerned with fighting against the Assad regime than with carving out territory under its own control, where it enforced a radical vision of religious rule. It was again social media that got Karim in trouble. He criticized ISIS on Facebook, after which an ISIS-style cease-and-desist letter slid under his Antakya apartment door: *shut up or we will kill you.*

After hearing through the grapevine that they might kill him regardless, Karim fled again, away from Antakya and also from his family in the refugee camp to whom he did not want to bring his troubles, all the way northwest to Istanbul.

He was short on money and did not know anyone in the new city who could help him. Karim slept sitting upright in 24/7 internet

cafes – cheaper lodging than even the dingiest hostel. It was a far cry
from his days charming rich tourists at a Damascene luxury hotel.
When he gave up trying to sleep, he would log on to his social media
accounts looking for opportunities.

Luckily for Karim, he was Facebook friends with a Turkish fixer named
Orhan. Back when Karim worked at the revolutionary media center
outside Damascus, Orhan had contacted him on behalf of a Belgian
reporter doing a story on Syria. Karim had helped Orhan out then, and
now Orhan saw from Karim's English-language Facebook posts that he
had an opportunity to return the favor. The two met for beers, and Orhan
put Karim in touch with a German TV crew from channel DDT who had
recently arrived to report on the Syrian conflict's effects in Turkey.

Karim proved useful to DDT primarily for the access he could
provide. He still had his connections with rebels and others back in
Syria whom he could convince to sit down for Skype interviews. Karim
was enough of an insider to blur the boundary between fixer and
source. The Germans interviewed Karim about his own escape from
Syria, making him a character in one of their reports (without acknowledging to viewers that he was on payroll). Karim also had insider
access to the refugee camp where his relatives still lived in southern
Turkey. As a fixer–source hybrid, he traveled – as discretely as he could
beside a crew of Germans toting A/V equipment – back to the camp to
interview and be interviewed with his family.

He may have had the access of an insider, but Karim was also in the
process, started when he led hotel tours of Damascus and further
advanced during his time at the revolutionary media center, of learning
to see Syria and Syrians from an outsider's perspective, to gauge
newsworthiness and understand what client reporters did and did not
need to know.

* * *

If in normal times there is a trickle of potential fixers into the field,
once in a while, foreign journalists flood into a region to cover a big,
developing story, and suddenly the demand for fixers far outstrips
existing supply, and that trickle becomes a wave.

The Syrian conflict had become one of the world's biggest stories by
2014. News organizations desperately sought Syrians with English and
some combination of journalistic instincts and access to rebels or other
sought-after sources like smugglers. Events like the Syrian civil war

create new generations of fixers out of people who come into contact with foreign reporters, have reason to work with them, and have the rudiments of a fixer skill set, even if they have no idea what a fixer is before they become one.

Historical and political circumstances affected who became a fixer covering Syria from Turkey and who did not. I did not, for instance, meet or hear of any fixers working in Turkey from Syria's Armenian minority. There is a sizable and well-educated Syrian–Armenian middle class from whom competent fixers could no doubt be recruited (Payaslian 2007: 117–120), but its members have not sought refuge in Turkey in large proportion. They have fled in the tens of thousands, but to Armenia or Lebanon (Johnson 2015; Keshishian 2015).

Concurrent to the exodus of refugees from Syria, neighboring countries saw a smaller influx of young members of the Syrian diaspora concerned with events in the homeland. They offered their services as reporters, fixers, and/or humanitarians (e.g. Malas 2019). Relative outsiders to Syrian domestic politics, diasporic fixers tended to scorn sectarianism and to sympathize with the secular liberal revolutionaries of the early Arab Spring days.

Syrian fixers, whether refugees or diasporic, did not come from backgrounds as journalists for their national media, as in Turkey. Under the pre-2001 Assad autocracy, there was no opposition press inside Syria aside from informal social media channels (Yassin-Kassab and Al-Shami 2016: 39–40). The Syrian news workers who would be instrumental to the state's loss of control of the war's narrative both inside and outside Syria were overwhelmingly starting from scratch without formal training or experience. The background training that prepared them for the job of brokering international news was cultural, not professional: they were tour guides, English teachers, and third culture kids who leaned secular and cosmopolitan in outlook (Smith 2019: 137–138).[3]

These circumstances meant that there was a pattern to the political dispositions of Syrian fixers in Turkey, and in turn a pattern to the sources they could and would connect with client reporters. The Syrian voices most prominently featured in Turkey-based journalists' coverage of the early years of civil war were of secular-leaning opposition Sunnis.

---

[3] See also Andén-Papadopoulos and Pantti (2013) on the role that Syrian diaspora activists from similar backgrounds have played in brokering content from "citizen journalists" and others within Syria to news organizations.

# *Habib*

Syrians were not the only ones fleeing to or through Turkey in the 2010s. There were Iraqis, Iranians, Somalis, Congolese. The second largest national group, after Syrians, were Afghans (UNHCR 2018).[1]

The Afghan community in Istanbul goes back to the 1980s. The Soviet Union occupied Afghanistan for most of that decade to prop up the country's communist state, fighting against *mujahideen* insurgents backed by the United States and other Soviet rivals. Some Afghans escaping the conflict settled in Zeytinburnu, a working-class neighborhood of multistory concrete west of the Old City.

Zeytinburnu's Afghan population grew over the next decade, as civil war among rival *mujahideen* factions gave way to the harsh fundamentalist rule of the Taliban over most of Afghanistan. The community continued to grow in the 2000s as the US occupation of Afghanistan followed the Soviet precedent of devolving into a bloody quagmire. Young men hoping to support their relatives from abroad and whole families who saw no future for themselves in their homeland traveled overland through neighboring Iran to Turkey (Arjomand 2016a). Many thousands lived undocumented in Turkey; many

---

[1] Turkey has an unusual refugee policy. The country is a signatory to the 1951 Refugee Convention, but maintains a "geographic limitation" of granting asylum solely to refugees from Europe. Refugees from the east and south can come to Turkey, apply to be officially designated as refugees by the United Nations High Commissioner for Refugees (UNHCR), and then for resettlement in another country, but they will not find a permanent legal home in Turkey (with the recent and uncertain exception of Syrians [Ombudsman Institution 2018]). Asylum seekers in 2010s Turkey faced a massive, years-long backlog among the multiple bureaucracies processing their cases, and per international refugee law, people must remain in the country where they initially apply while they await official refugee status designation. For these reasons, it made sense for Afghans and others to remain undocumented in Turkey and cross over into the European Union, applying for asylum only after they reached Greece or Bulgaria, or better yet countries like Germany or Sweden that were actually accepting large numbers of refugees.

thousands registered with the UN refugee agency as asylum seekers; many thousands crossed illegally from Turkey into the European Union.[2]

Habib, though, came to Turkey on a student visa after he graduated from a Gülen Movement high school in Afghanistan. Orhan and other secularists within Turkey might have been deeply suspicious of Fethullah Gülen, but the cleric's movement had a very different image abroad. In the United States, Gülen Movement supporters were busy founding institutes, hosting interfaith forums, and organizing all-expenses-paid tours for influential Americans to movement-affiliated schools, hospitals, and newspapers in Turkey. In Afghanistan, the Gülen Movement ran boys' and girls' schools, some of the very best schools for education in secular subjects like math and science, despite the dangers of operating in a war-torn country where female education was still controversial and where much foreign educational aid was lost to waste and corruption (Hendrick 2013: 159–160, 206–216). Habib studied English and Turkish as foreign languages, and his teachers encouraged him to continue his education in Turkey when he graduated from high school. Habib was accepted with a scholarship into a private university in Istanbul affiliated with the Gülen Movement, where he joined his older brother Abdullah.

The latter had already come to Turkey to study, then stayed upon finding employment as an interpreter for an international NGO called Civic Aid[3] that worked with Persian- and Pashto-speaking asylum seekers. Habib moved in with Abdullah, who introduced him to the city's Afghan community and international aid worker scene. As Habib went on from his studies to follow in his brother's footsteps as an NGO interpreter, Abdullah and expat Civic Aid staff began sending reporter friends Habib's way when they asked for referrals to a fixer.

Habib was always hired to cover one aspect or another of the same story: Afghan migrants. Insider fixers are specialists, and Habib's specialization was particularly narrow.[4] There was not enough

---

[2] Colloquially, anyone fleeing war or other danger back home is called a "refugee." Officially, though, a refugee is someone who has been granted refugee status designation by the UNHCR. Until granted that status, a person is an "asylum seeker."

[3] Civil Aid, like news organizations that appear in this text, is a composite with a name I invented.

[4] See Palmer (2019: 92–94) for examples of generalist vs. specialist fixers.

demand for Afghan refugee stories – as opposed to Kurdish issue stories that provided Nur a steady income or Syrian crisis stories that gave Karim a career – for Habib to become a full-time fixer. Instead, he kept a day job at Civic Aid that, we will see, afforded him different fixing tools than available to our other protagonists.

# *Elif*

The same year that Habib graduated from university, and a year before Karim fled Syria for Turkey, an invigorated opposition movement shook up Turkish politics. Environmentalists occupied Istanbul's Gezi Park in late May 2013 to protest municipal plans to replace the park next to central Taksim Square with a shopping mall. The main construction contractor was a conglomerate that would soon acquire Orhan's former newspaper *Sabah* as it was passed around from one pro-government businessman to the next. Prime Minister Erdoğan was a witness at the owner's wedding (RSF and bianet 2016).

Police ousted the peaceful environmentalist protesters from the Beyoğlu-district park with batons, pepper spray, and water cannons. In response, tens of thousands flooded into the park, a disparate collective united by antipathy toward the AK Party government and organized using newly popular social media tools (Tüfekçi 2017: 45–53). They charged that Erdoğan was no reformist but a corrupt authoritarian amassing power and trampling anyone who got in the way.

The police eventually withdrew amid violent clashes, and the protesters erected barricades of graffitied dumpsters, junk, and crowd-control barriers. They dug in for a long-term occupation. The Gezi Movement's aims expanded well beyond environmentalism: within days they were calling for Erdoğan's resignation (Göle 2013).

The Gezi Movement was, like the Syrian civil war but on a quicker, smaller, and less violent scale, a transformative event that spawned a new generation of fixers, among them a young woman named Elif. She was not originally part of the Gezi Movement; she got into the business not as a source–fixer hybrid but by dating a foreign reporter. Fixing, in turn, gave her a chance to make new local connections.

Elif was in her mid-20s like Nur, but had grown up between the United States and Turkey and attended an elite English-language university in Istanbul. As in many countries in the age of globalization, a cosmopolitan stratum floats between Turkey's metropolises and the larger world, moored only tenuously to the culture and economy of the nation-state (Ong 1999).

In Turkey, the labels "White Turk" and its less often heard antonym "Black Turk" map roughly onto class, urban–rural, religious, and educational divisions seen between a west-coast elite and the common folk of the hinterland. The archetypal White Turk is the opera-going blonde who looks down on the rest of the country with a mix of patronizing distaste and civilizing zeal; the archetypal Black Turk is the superstitious hick targeted by that civilizing mission. Erdoğan embraced the Black Turk label to signal a populist, anti-elite identity (Demiralp 2012).[1] Elif, a blonde, would call herself a "White Turk" in a checking-my-privilege way when acknowledging to me – usually over cappuccinos at one of the hipster cafes she took pride in knowing before they got *too* popular – her elite position and limited understanding of the country outside her own cosmopolitan milieu.

In 2013, Elif held a boring but well-paid office job at her father's company. She hung out regularly with English-speaking journalists and other expats and in the labyrinth of Beyoğlu's side-street cafes and bars.

The Istanbul international journalist scene is small. For my research, I would offer to meet foreign reporter interviewees at places of their choosing, and I became accustomed to them selecting one from the familiar set of fashionable Beyoğlu coffee shops catering to the market between touristy and provincial, where we would often run into their colleagues.

Elif thus had far more opportunity to befriend foreign reporters than anyone outside Istanbul's central districts.[2] There is some circularity at

---

[1] "White" and "Black Turk" are socioeconomic and cultural, not racial, categories. However, Erdoğan and other politicians have sometimes used the explicitly racial term "*zenci*" to describe themselves and their supporters, which some have translated as "Negro." This use of a racial term for Blackness serves to underline politicians' claims to be fighting for an underclass against institutionalized discrimination and a decadent elite (Ferguson 2013; *BirGün* 2018).

[2] Compare this to Nur's situation in Diyarbakır, where there is no international journalist social scene. Apart from a single Dutch reporter in residence who would be deported in 2015, foreign journalists came to the city to do stories and then left. Diyarbakır-based fixers meet their first client not by rubbing elbows at cafes or bars, but as sources themselves or through institutions drawing international media attention like Kurdish political parties and NGOs. It is not a coincidence, then, that Nur entered the field of international journalism with a different background and trajectory than those of Elif.

play here: foreign journalists base themselves in Beyoğlu not just because of its geographic centrality, but because the neighborhood is known as the kind of cosmopolitan place where people like Elif are found.

Elif was dating Tim, a reporter for the American TV channel XYZ, when the Gezi Park Movement erupted and a new wave of foreign journalists descended on Turkey. Tim told her that the parachutists who had just arrived were looking for fixers and all the good ones were booked. Would she help a colleague of his for a day or two?

Her first day as a fixer, Elif discovered a new world in Gezi Park. She had previously walked through the encampment on her own out of curiosity, but had been shy to talk to anyone. It was very different visiting the park with Tim's friend, who with no discernible social anxiety demanded Elif initiate conversation on his behalf with anyone who caught his eye.

There was a mix of people and ideologies seldom found together in the same place and with whom Elif had never spoken, all spending their days peaceably debating politics and eager to explain themselves to the foreign press. There were LGBT activists, Kurdish nationalists, soccer hooligans, right-wing secularists. A group calling themselves Anti-Capitalist Muslims approached Elif to ask her to explain their religious objections to the AKP's neoliberal agenda to the reporter.

Elif related to these sources as an outsider, though of a different kind than career-journalist-turned-fixer Orhan. Elif was, like Orhan, strong on the sensemaking side of fixing, able to translate and explain ideas in terms she knew Tim's friend would understand. Whereas Orhan's sensemaking skills were grounded in his professional training, her abilities stemmed from her personal experience living in both Turkey and the United States and socializing with foreigners.

Where Elif exceeded Orhan (aside from the occasional metalhead reporter with whom Orhan could readily bond) was in building rapport. Elif and her first client chatted casually about their shared friends, backgrounds, and opinions about protests and politics as they worked. The lack of cultural barriers and the overlap in their social networks set him at ease, and he was soon treating Elif as confidante in a way that reporters did not treat Orhan, Nur, Karim, or Habib on Day One. Elif would later tell me that she credited her fluency in American pop culture and humor as much as any practical skills for her rapid rise through the ranks of journalism.

Elif thought helping Tim's friend with interviews was a one-off favor, but the next day she got a phone call from a freelance reporter she had never met named José, who asked if she was available that week to fix for him. José had gotten her number from Tim's friend. José offered her $50 a day to translate from Turkish to English, help him find activist leaders and experts who could comment on the protests, and fill him in on background information. He was new to the country.

Elif did not particularly need the money, but it sounded like fun. Fixing offered an adventure and a window into the unknown, allowing Elif to engage new people with a directness that would otherwise feel intrusive. If becoming a plumber gives a person special dispensation to engage in the ordinarily unacceptable behavior of walking into strangers' houses and poking around their bathrooms and kitchens, becoming a fixer provides special dispensation to walk into strangers' lives and poke around their histories and worldviews.[3]

From Cairo's Tahrir Square to New York's Zuccotti Park to Istanbul's Gezi Park, there seemed to be a wave of political awakenings bringing together citizens from all walks of life, and Elif had come to believe that living in a White Turk bubble was a problem. Fixing, she hoped, could help her burst out of that bubble. Elif and José continued to report together even after the police crushed the Gezi occupation a few days later.

---

[3] Others have noted that the role of media professional can liberate a person from normal constraints. Sontag ([1977] 1989) argued that Diane Arbus, a famed photographer of the grotesque who similarly to Elif grew up in privileged boredom, was drawn to photography because it licensed her to seek adventure and intrude into strangers' lives:

"Photography was a license to go wherever I wanted and to do what I wanted to do," Arbus wrote. The camera is a kind of passport that annihilates moral boundaries and social inhibitions. ... The photographer is supertourist, an extension of the anthropologist, visiting natives and bringing back news of their exotic doings and strange gear. The photographer is always trying to colonize new experiences or find new ways to look at familiar subjects – to fight against boredom. (41–42)

# Order and Chaos

The world is disorderly and dangerous, at least to an outsider. But cultures and professions impose order on their corners of the world, providing insiders with classification systems, explanations, and rituals to make sense of things (Abbott 1981; Zelizer 1993). Max Weber ([1918] 1946a), a founding father of sociology, used the term **disenchantment** for the domestication and rationalization of the previously mysterious and magical. A disenchanted world is orderly, predictable, safe, pure, and boring.

But outside of a culture's little world or a profession's jurisdiction lie other worlds, which look both chaotic and dangerous from the outside, even though those other worlds may feel safe and boring to their own insiders. Order and chaos are in the eye of the beholder (Gleick 2011: 272).

If I am a computer scientist, a well-established insider to cybersecurity, the patterns of computer hacking may be familiar, the problems and solutions of data protection routine, whereas politics seems disorderly and unpredictable. If my friend Temel (a purely theoretical being, not a composite fiction like our other characters) is a political scientist and confident that his science offers comprehensive explanations and predictions about the political process, the data on the politics he analyzes can be both boring and comprehensible, whereas the world of computer hacking may seem like dark magic to him. (Whether Temel's analyses are correct is irrelevant; the point is that politics make sense to him.) When a political hacking scandal erupts, though, Temel's and my little worlds may be thrown together and each of us exposed to the disruption of what, to each of us, looks like chaos.

There exists, then, not just one world but a multitude of small social worlds with fuzzy and overlapping boundaries, which some sociologists following Pierre Bourdieu (1993) call **fields**. The center of each field is at once the most orderly and the most boring spot for its insiders (whom field theorists have variously called "incumbent," "orthodox," or "core" players in contrast to "dissident," "heretical," or "peripheral" outsiders [Cattani et al. 2014]).

**Adventure,** on the contrary, is pursued in the trading zones between fields (Simmel [1911] 1971; Benson and Neveu 2005; Galison 2010). The adventurer is charismatic, taking on an attractive mystique from their exposure to and mastery of disorder (Weber [1922] 1946b; Douglas [1966] 2001; Abbott 1981). Chunks of the world we do not understand can seem dangerous and threaten to pollute the tidy order we know, but they also offer an exotic break from the ho-hum familiar (Simmel [1911] 1971: 187–188). When we do not understand how something works, we can see chaos, or we can see magic.

In dramatic portrayals of journalism – or any other job – the charismatic heroes are outsiders who live and work on the fringes of organizations, on the front lines between clashing cultural fields. Drama comes from their proximity to danger. Heroes' very exposure to the contamination of the world outside their established fields helps them to transcend received understandings and assumptions, to go off script, create change, broker peace. The by-the-books managing editors, police chiefs, and bureaucrats of dramas are conformist insiders, unheroic in their attachment to the comfort of order and xenophobic hostility to the impure hero who does not play by their rules or within familiar boundaries.

"Purity," writes anthropologist Mary Douglas, "is the enemy of change, of ambiguity and compromise" (Douglas [1966] 2001: 163). Impurity, on the other hand, carries the potential for new ideas, for excitement and reconciliation with the formerly strange. It is also essential for dealing with the messy reality of the wide world (Douglas [1966] 2001: 163–170).

Part of what attracted me to fixers as a topic of study was that they seemed the quintessential boundary-spanning heroes of journalism. For reporters, fixers' usefulness stems from their ability to cross into the unknown and bring back information that reporters then domesticate into news stories comprehensible to foreign audiences. Fixers who are insiders to sources can reach into the depths of fields unfamiliar to reporters, while outsider fixers can help purify the unfamiliar into an order that reporters recognize.

Foreign reporters (and ethnographers like me) are not the only ones attracted to the unknown. The promise of adventure can also be a strong motivation for people who become fixers. Before she started fixing, Elif's days followed a familiar, orderly routine. And in her social bubble, Elif felt herself an outsider to great inscrutable swathes of Turkish society. Of course, her own elite subculture had an established classification scheme for making sense of those masses, purifying them into Black Turk and other stereotypes that could be comfortably explained and dismissed. Yet Elif was inspired by pluralistic democracy experiments around the world, by talk of the 99 percent and reaching out across cultural divisions, as Gezi's mosaic of different groups had. Fixing gave her the opportunity to expose herself to the exotically unfamiliar of her own country and to try, through the nosiness that the job licensed, to make more empathetic sense of it.

What appears dully orderly and what appears excitingly disorderly depends on your position in intersecting fields, though. Nur was also chasing adventure, but for her, that adventure derived from contact with foreigners more than with locals. Speaking with fellow Diyarbakır residents about their everyday lives, their hopes and fears was not new to Nur. What was new and exciting was the opportunity to argue politics with an exotic outsider like Alison, to try to make sense of the unfamiliar foreign gaze onto the world she knew.

There is a grass-is-always-more-enchanting-on-the-other-side element to this argument. Americans' charismatic appeal had gone stale for Elif through her exposure to them, first living in the United States and then hanging out with them for years in Istanbul. Yet compatriot Others were full of fresh charismatic promise to Elif. The reverse was true for Nur.

Other fixers, caught up in upheaval within once-familiar worlds, are motivated more by hope for a restoration of order than by the promise of adventure. Orhan, remember, worked for years in the national press. Journalism, for him, already made sense when he began fixing. Working as a fixer offered a return of order to his life as the world of national journalism became dangerous and chaotic: colleagues were going to jail or losing their jobs; the government was orchestrating the capture of the mainstream media outlets where Orhan had once assumed he would enjoy a long career.

For Karim and Habib, each escaping their own civil war, working for international organizations offered a less dangerous, more orderly alternative. Some fields, those subject to violent and revolutionary change like Syrian society, are objectively – and not just in the eyes of outsiders – less stable and more disorderly than others. Karim was new to journalism, but fixing at least looked something like the comfortable routine of guiding tourists around Damascus. Had he continued to participate in the Syrian revolutionary struggle as an activist, dodging both the Assad regime and insurgents who did not brook criticism, he could have expected nothing but continued chaos.

# PART II

# Fitting In

# Are Fixers Journalists?

The role of the intermediary bridging disparate worlds is not new. Centuries before fixers mediated between journalists and sources, *dragoman* diplomats (from *tercüman*: translator) mediated between European states and Ottoman sultans (Lewis 2004). Oft-stigmatized "middleman minorities" and "edge people" have long found themselves in the role of bridges between worlds: Christians in the Middle East (most *dragomans* were ethnic Greeks), Chinese in Southeast Asia, Indians in East Africa, Jews in Europe, mixed-race people in colonial settings, upwardly mobile members of marginalized communities, immigrants and refugees everywhere (Bonacich 1973; Ong 1999; Lewis 2004; Pattillo 2007: 113–147; Yannakakis 2008; Judt 2010).

The label of "fixer," though, is new. Jackson and Hellyer's 1914 dictionary of criminal slang defines a fixer as "one who acts as go-between for thieves and bribe takers." In the early twentieth century, the term was used pejoratively to describe brokers doing shady deals in criminal and political contexts – for instance, lobbyists who bought off public officials (e.g. Irwin 1909).[1] In Hollywood, "fixers" were powerful behind-the-scenes studio operatives who brokered between the film industry and the press, though often by doing the opposite of our news fixers: killing scandal stories of stars' abortions, addictions, or homosexuality before they made headlines (Fleming 2004). Fans of the TV show *Scandal* will recognize elements of both definitions in Olivia Pope, a fictional "fixer" who manages Washington, DC, crises and scandals from the Beltway shadows (Rhimes 2012–2018).

*News* fixers have existed in all but name since the creation of the newspaper as we know it in the nineteenth century, yet the label has only recently come into journalistic parlance (Palmer 2019: 14–15).

---

[1] Recently, authors have similarly referred to lawyers Roy Cohn, Michael Cohen, and Rudy Giuliani as Donald Trump's "fixers," quietly handling illicit and unsavory transactions on their client's behalf (e.g. Palazzolo and Rothfeld 2020).

The *Oxford English Dictionary* traces the first use of "fixer" in the field of journalism to a 1971 article in *The Guardian* about Victor Louis leaking former Soviet leader Nikita Khrushchev's memoirs to *Life* magazine (Zorza 1971).

Louis, née Vitaly Yevgenyevich Lui, began his life as an international information broker working in low-level staff jobs at foreign embassies in 1940s Moscow, only to end up serving years in the Gulag on espionage charges. After making a deal with the KGB that secured him early release from the labor camp, he took the name Victor Louis and began hanging around the US embassy, chatting up foreign diplomats and journalists with impunity.

Louis's intelligence and Kremlin connections made Western journalists at once distrust and value him. He had incomparable access to both real and doctored breaking stories – for instance, of Khrushchev's imminent ouster in 1964 – that satisfied both foreign news editors and his KGB handlers. Over three decades, Louis worked for outlets including *CBS News*, *The London Evening News*, *Washington Post*, *New York Times*, *France-Soir*, and *Time* magazine (Vronskaya 1992; Whitney 1992; Schechter 2012). Ever since the fixer became a recognized role as broker between reporters and news sources, the term has carried a slightly unsavory connotation, carried over from etymological forebearers who mediated between dangerous underworlds and respectable society.

After that first description of Victor Louis, the term did not go mainstream for another two decades. Sydney Schanberg, whose 1980 article "The Death and Life of Dith Pran" became the basis for the film *The Killing Fields*, refers to Pran not as a fixer but as an "assistant" or "guide and interpreter" who goes on to become a "stringer" when he receives an official contract and retainer from the *New York Times* (Schanberg [1980] 2013).

In Peter Weir's 1982 film *The Year of Living Dangerously* about foreign correspondence in Sukarno-era Indonesia, the protagonist Guy Hamilton's fixer in Jakarta introduces himself simply and ambiguously as "Kumar, from Jakarta office." Hamilton refers to Kumar as "my assistant" at one point to get him through a military checkpoint. In keeping with the recurring trope of suspect or split loyalties among fixers, Kumar is secretly affiliated with communist revolutionaries and thwarts Hamilton's reporting as often as he facilitates it.

The label "fixer" only became commonplace among international journalists around the time of the 1991 Persian Gulf War (RSF 2017). In the twenty-first century, when journalists seek assistance reporting in a foreign country, they overwhelmingly use the word "fixer" when querying online forums or email lists; "translators" are sometimes sought, usually for the specific task of translating media the journalist has already accessed, and broadcast journalists occasionally ask for "field producer" contacts. "Local journalist," "local partner," or "freelance producer" are also up-and-coming politically correct codes for "fixer" used in such communications. "Fixer" is on rarer occasions also applied in domestic news contexts to intermediaries who open doors to hard-to-access communities (e.g. Terry 2011).

The term has its detractors. Some consider labeling a person as a fixer to be a demeaning, if not colonialist, way to brand them as an "epistemic other," less capable and trustworthy than Western journalists (Bishara 2013: 50–56; Seo 2016; Khan 2019).

The **fixer** label, in this view, minimizes the contributions of the labeled and establishes a boundary between them and a **journalist,** justifying attribution of greater status and credit to the latter (Palmer 2019: 2–19).[2] Critics say that such **boundary-work** (Gieryn 1983) is not backed up by actual differences between what those called journalists and those called fixers actually do. Rather, the **fixer** label is foremost a weapon that foreign reporters wield against potential local competitors, who might do the same job better than they could, to maintain a privileged position in the professional field (e.g. Borpujari 2019).[3]

Determining who counts as a journalist is not as straightforward as determining who counts, for example, as a doctor or nurse (Tuchman 1978; Nicey 2016). Journalism does not regulate its labels through professional licensing or academic credentials like medicine or other fields. Some but not all journalists hold some form of accreditation, and not everyone agrees who has the authority to issue a press card. Holding a master's degree from a journalism school might help you convince colleagues of your professional legitimacy, but it is not a

---

[2] See also Sanjek (1993) on a similar criticism of anthropology's erasure of the contributions of local fieldworkers.

[3] It is a well-established pattern that insiders to fields of cultural production protect themselves against the encroachment of outsiders by setting criteria for legitimacy and success that exclude those outsiders or put them at a competitive disadvantage (Cattani et al. 2014).

requirement to practice journalism.[4] The question of who is inside and who is outside of journalism is becoming trickier still in the Internet Era, when audiences get their news from a mix of influencers, bloggers, and comedians, and news organizations rely on user-generated content, aggregation, and unpaid "citizen" and "participatory" journalism models (Deuze 2005; Zelizer 2007: 421–424; Shirky 2008: 81–108; Hermida 2010; Nicey 2016).

The best way to assess criticism of journalism's boundary-work is to map out the professional field and the ways various people fit into it. What is the substantive difference between a fixer and a translator, a guide, a news assistant, a stringer, a producer? Does each one do different tasks? Does being labeled as one or the other change how a person is perceived and what is expected of them?

To think about differences in what people actually do to contribute to journalism, it is useful to start with verbs rather than nouns: fixing, writing, filming, rather than fixers, reporters, producers (Becker 2007: 15–16). We can define fixing as brokering between news sources and the credited authors of news stories, who are usually called "reporters."[5]

**Brokerage** – mediation between otherwise disconnected parties – is central to journalism as a whole and to fixing specifically. (I will use the terms "broker," "mediator," "intermediary," and "gatekeeper" interchangeably.) Journalism mediates a connection between audiences and far-off people and events. If we zoom in to the level of individual contributors to news production, we find a chain of microlevel brokers, fixers among them.[6] These brokers bridge gaps in social and

[4] Zelizer (1993: 220–223) argues that because journalism relies on informal socialization and hierarchization, it might be more illuminatingly framed as an "interpretive community" rather than as a profession like law or medicine. I nonetheless discuss the definition and boundaries of "professional journalism" because news contributors themselves use "professionalism" as a keyword to frame their status claims and evaluations of one another.

[5] Although news production is the focus of this book, many of my interlocutors did not fix exclusively for journalists. They also worked for documentary filmmakers and indeed for academics. There is a lot of overlap between fixing and research assistance (Palmer 2019: 19).

[6] Bishara (2013: 50–67, 159–161) describes the chain of brokerage through which news is produced as "accumulated authorship." Tumber and Palmer (2004) discuss war correspondents' practice of embedding with military units as creating another such brokerage relationship. Gürsel (2016) describes the brokerage of images by photo agencies and visual editors in newsrooms.

cultural connection and so allow the sharing of information across those gaps. In the process, they catalyze new relationships between the parties they mediate (Stovel and Shaw 2012: 141).

**Fixing** includes bringing sources and reporters into physical or virtual proximity, preparing them to interact, translating, and guiding each one's interpretations of information gleaned from the interaction (Packer 2009; Murrell 2015; Palmer 2019; Plaut and Klein 2019a, 2019b). Writing and filming – activities at the next link in the chain – are in turn ways of brokering between fixers and sources on the one hand and news headquarters on the other.

We might define the noun **fixer**, then, as someone whom reporters pay to fix for them.[7] The trouble is that people labeled fixers are not the only ones who fix, and fixing is not the only thing they do (Plaut and Klein 2019b).

Labels matter, nonetheless. Because they signal competencies to others, labels like **fixer** and **producer** similarly affect the way we treat each other. We make sense of the world and calibrate our expectations based on labels that arrange things and people into categories.[8] Successfully securing a particular label for yourself changes how others treat you, particularly new acquaintances who will use the label as a rough-and-ready compass for their preconceptions. A label functions as a temporary substitute for getting to know a person and a guide to doing so. Labels' meanings are in constant flux, though, and so you must not only secure the right label, but also police its usage and reinforce its distinction from other labels.

It is worth analyzing the field of journalism and fixers' place within it through the lens of labels, because labeling negotiations and strategies

---

[7] Incorporating the direction that money flows (from reporter to fixer) into the definition of fixer is important for distinguishing fixers from "parajournalists" like public relations representatives and volunteer activists (Schudson 2003: 3–6, 20–21) and from the public bureaucracies who play an important broker role in setting the news agenda and informing journalists (Fishman 1980).

[8] Labeling Theory in sociology has focused mostly on deviant labels (Becker [1963] 1997; Goffman 1963) that are used to control and limit people, but the theory's insights can be applied to favorable labels as well. Labels not only restrict but also license action. If my friend Temel is successful in labeling himself as a journalist, he can do things that would be otherwise socially unacceptable, like invite himself into the home of strangers grieving a family death or hang out in online jihadist chatrooms.

add up to determine who contributes which elements to news stories. World news as it appears on the page or screen is not only a description of reality but also an outcome of the struggles, compromises, and intrigues over status and control along the chain of media production that labeling makes semi-visible.

# Elif and José

Elif happily adopted the label of fixer, at least in the early days. The title did not entirely make sense (what was broken and how did she fix it?) but sounded cool and signaled that her project of becoming intimately familiar with the Other Turkey was succeeding, that she was not an insulated bourgeois but a gritty on-the-ground woman of action. After her initial, thrilling induction into the craft during the Gezi protests, though, her duties as a fixer quickly became less adventurous and more mundane.

Elif continued working with José, the American freelance writer, on the side of her day job at her father's company. Fixing became primarily desk and café based. José would email English-language news stories to her on subjects he wanted to cover or Turkish-language stories of which he had made rough sense using Google Translate. Elif would dig deeper with online research and translate what she found. José also paid her an hourly rate to sit with him and explain Turkish politics and history over tea.

"At first I didn't think it – I felt very weird to be paid [for] a conversation because I was enjoying it as well," Elif told me. "I mean we had a lot of conversations without [pay] as well. We became friends afterwards. But at first, [he] was literally like, 'Okay, we started at 12. We talked for 3 hours. I think I should pay you three hours.'"

As time went on, they increasingly talked about Turkish politics and history "as friends" without payment. They occasionally traveled together within Istanbul to interview people, but José was so cash poor that he could not spend many days each month reporting in the field with Elif.

José was in his mid-20s with a slight build and wisp of beard. He had come to Turkey in 2013 after studying journalism and deciding that he wanted to move straight into the international arena instead of a local news beat. He was raised and schooled in the American Midwest and found it oppressively boring. The Mideast promised an adventurous

escape. José chose Istanbul as his new home on a professor's advice
that it was where a lot of foreign correspondents based themselves. He
knew little about the country beyond the cliché that it is an exotic
bridge between West and East.

There had been no mention of fixers in any of José's journalism
classes. The professor who recommended Turkey did, however, introduce him to Alison, an American radio reporter who had been in the
country for a few years. She helped José plug into the Istanbul foreign
journalist scene, where he quickly learned that hiring fixers was a
routine part of reporting.

Cost was a problem, though. Established fixers like Orhan on the list
that Alison forwarded to José charged US$150 a day or more and did
not appreciate his attempts to haggle. José could expect a couple
hundred dollars from online publications, a bit more from newspapers,
for an article that might have taken him a full week to report. And
those were the articles that got published. Others he reported first and
then submitted as drafts on spec to editors – the only way he knew,
without personal connections, to establish a relationship with a new
publication. Many an article failed to sell and ended up as another
frustrated post on his blog.

Some reporters are forced or choose to operate without fixers' help,
but to gain access to and make sense of a foreign place without an
insider's guidance takes much more work or merely shifts dependency
to other forms of mediation. Working with only intermittent help from
novice and ad hoc fixers, José relied heavily on Google-translated
Turkish media and English-language newspapers like *Hürriyet Daily
News* and *Today's Zaman* for story ideas. These newspapers served, in
effect, as brokers. They were intermediaries between José and Turkish
society that shaped José's local knowledge, and he had to be wary of
their insider bias just as he did when he relied on human fixers.

José used his human and virtual brokers to keep one another in
check. Elif taught him to keep up to date on the latest takeovers of
opposition media outlets to better make sense of those newspapers'
changing editorial lines. *Hürriyet Daily News*, for instance, was highly
critical of the government in the early 2000s but started softening its
opposition after the paper's parent company was cowed by a tax
penalty (the turn of events that finally drove Orhan out of the domestic
press and into full-time fixing). *Today's Zaman* was affiliated with the
Gülen Movement and was pro-government until the end of 2013,

when the paper abruptly switched sides as a schism opened between Fethullah Gülen and Recep Tayyip Erdoğan.

Once he got accreditation from the prime minister's press director-ate, José was added to a government public relations email list that notified foreign correspondents of upcoming press conferences and official functions. He followed the Twitter accounts of all the Turkey experts, correspondents, and politicians he could. He sought guidance from established journalists about whom to follow and interview and how to contact them.

José's first story, before he met Elif, was on the Ecuadorian street vendors who were mysteriously ubiquitous in Istanbul's touristy spots. As a bilingual American whose parents had migrated from Mexico, José could speak Spanish with them, and they were easy to find. After weeks of shopping the story of an indigenous family that lived in squalor while saving money for remittances and airfare, bringing Ecuadorian trinkets to Turkey and then Turkish fabric back to Ecuador, he sold it for a pittance to an online start-up specializing in cultural stories of obscure interest.

After that, José did a story on Istanbul's tiny atheist community after reading about it in *Hürriyet Daily News*. Alison put him in touch with a pundit and commentator on religious issues often interviewed by foreign journalists to contribute the Moderate Turkish View for bal-ance. Alison helpfully coached José on what to expect and take with a grain of salt from the pundit, a reliably glass-half-full liberal who professed that Turkey offered a model for the reconciliation of reli-gious belief with pluralistic tolerance.

José also walked alone to the Istanbul office of an organization for Turkish atheists. He got lucky: there were a couple English speakers present who were willing to sit for interviews and to translate what the others hanging out in the office said.

Even once he began working with Elif and other fixers – mostly English-speaking students in need of beer and cigarette money – José tried to do as much as possible on his own to save costs without exploiting them. To cover events and get vox pop quotations, he made the most of the rudimentary Turkish he was learning from a grammar handbook found in a used bookshop. José would write out questions for potential interviewees with help from Elif or a barista at the hipster café that functioned as José's office. When he arrived at the event, José would profile people based on stereotypes that he was constantly refining (headscarves were a useful guide) and hope that they represented the range of views he needed. José would introduce himself and ask the questions he had rehearsed in Turkish, then record answers on his phone without understanding them. At the end of the day, he would send Elif the recordings to transcribe and translate on her own, thereby reducing fixer expenses from a half or full day to an hour or two. Follow-up questions were of course impossible with this method.

Professional fixers are not the only ones who mediate reporters' relationships with sources. Reporters also recruit ad hoc, unpaid brokers on the spot, like the friendly atheists who translated for José. I said José got lucky to find them, but it was no coincidence that the atheists were a well-educated and cosmopolitan bunch. Reporters, especially freelancers without expense budgets, learn to predict, on a story-by-story basis, when they will really need a paid fixer and when they will be able to make do with whomever they find on the scene. Will there be people around who speak English? Will it be easy to gain access? Do I have time and ability to do the necessary research on my own? If so, then why give half my paycheck to a fixer?

The relative value of time and cash to a reporter is a key determinant of their reliance on paid fixers. Reporters can find workarounds and do many of the specific tasks themselves, but with much more trouble. José had to devote many hours to learning Turkish to reduce his need to delegate linguistic translation to a fixer.[1]

More convenient workarounds to hiring a professional fixer tend to rely on technology. As substitutes for or complements to a human fixer, reporters delegate work to machines like Twitter or Google Translate (Latour 1988a). The former helped José find sources and the latter helped translate their words.

Communication technology changes with time, and with it the ease and consequences of replacing human fixers with machines. When José first started using Twitter as an information broker in 2013, it was a hassle to translate Turkish tweets by copying and pasting them into an external translator. It was easier to simply pay attention to those tweeting in English. The next year, though, Twitter added a built-in

---

[1] See Latour's (1988a: 299) definition of both "delegation" and "translation" as the "transformation of a major effort into a minor one."

translation tool to its iPhone app, allowing José easier access to what potential sources were saying in Turkish (Brown 2015).

Local English-language newspapers play a key role as budget fixers for the international press, lending those publications influence beyond their small circulations. *Hürriyet Daily News*, itself the product of a brokerage chain linking human journalists and machines like the computer and the printing press, fixed for José when the paper gave him both the idea to do a story on Turkish atheists and the name and location of their organization. *Hürriyet Daily News* bridged a gap between him and the people who would become his sources.

Locally experienced foreign reporters also often informally fix for neophyte and parachutist colleagues, as long as they are not direct competitors.[2] Take Alison: she brokered between author and source when she introduced José to the pundit and coached him on how to interpret the latter's words. The currency of exchange in such interactions is not money but social capital and prestige: those journalists build a network of people who owe them favors and respect them as plugged in to the local scene.

When reporters find their sources through other reporters, the press comes to rely on a small pool of vetted interviewees like the pundit José interviewed. By contrast, when José struck out on his own to explore obscure corners of Turkish society, he began developing a nuanced view of Istanbul and a roster of contacts off the beaten path for foreign journalists.

The problem was that his growing network of sources did not line up with American and European editors' narratives about Turkey, themselves derived from previous (and often Orientalist) coverage of the country. Editors (like everyone else) make sense of the world by metaphorical fitting unique phenomena into more general **frames** (some scholars prefer "frameworks"). **Framing** aggregates all phenomena of the same type, ranks the importance of various classes of

---

[2] On the division within the international press between long-timers and "parachutists" or "spiralists," see Hannerz (2012: 39–42, 83–88). "Parachutist," derogatorily meaning a journalist who is not based in a country but metaphorically parachutes in when something newsworthy happens, is a good example of a label wielded in the struggle over status between insiders and outsiders. Fixers and foreign correspondents long serving in the same country apply the term to highlight so-labeled parachutists' superficiality and distance from the societies on which they report, in contrast to the labelers' own insider expertise.

phenomena, and provides a script for how those subjects should be addressed.[3] Each editor does not invent their frames all on their own, but rather follows ever-shifting cultural conventions for classifying the world (Gans [1979] 2004). The unique phenomenon of a particular person in Istanbul on a spring day saying they do not believe in God only has the potential to be newsworthy if it fits within a larger frame that an editor has learned to recognize, like the Islamic World's Struggle between Faith and Reason, and only realizes its news potential if the reporter collects the right information to link that phenomenon to the larger issue.

José's pitches needed the right framing to attract editors' interest. The frames that mainstream editors wanted filled were Turkey's floundering democracy, relations with the European Union, fallout from the civil war heating up in Syria, political Islam versus secular Kemalism. José sold the atheism article by fitting it into the Besieged Secularism frame, though the story was still "a bit in the weeds," as the editor put it.

The Ecuadorian story is about as pure an example as I could find of a reporter coming up with a story idea not derived from antecedent news stories.[4] José saw his sources in the street and became curious. Not coincidentally, José struggled to sell that story. Turkish–Ecuadorian migration did not fit editors' frames.

---

[3] My conception of a frame collapses together the distinction that has emerged in journalism studies between the powers of **agenda setting** (what is discussed) and **framing** (how and in what context it is discussed). The division between the two was always shaky. Journalism studies drew (via Gans [1979] 2004) on Goffman's (1974) concept of framing, wherein a frame delineates the boundaries of both what should be done and how it ought to be done, but then needed to distinguish "framing" from "agenda-setting," a concept developed by political communication scholars interested in how mass media determined which issues occupied the public's attention (McCombs and Shaw 1972; Scheufule and Tewksbury 2007). I return to Goffman's earlier and broader conception of the frame.

[4] In Gatekeeping Theory terminology, José's Ecuadorian story was a rare case of information flowing through an "enterprise channel" – a reporter noticing a something in the world and taking the initiative to investigate it – rather than a "routine channel" of established contacts (Shoemaker and Vos 2009: 22–24).

# *Elif and Burcu*

Elif and José continued to work together occasionally. After a couple of years of painful lessons about what stories would and would not sell, José secured a "string" with a syndicated news website, an informal agreement that they would accept his work on an ongoing basis, even though he was still paid per article as a freelancer. This arrangement allowed him to focus on one article at a time with the confidence that he would be paid, if often belatedly and only after complaints to the editor. As a stringer, José could also sometimes expense Elif's fees instead of paying them out of pocket. She would type up a receipt for "translation services" for him to forward along to the editor.

For her part, Elif began to fix for other reporters, with mixed results. Sometimes facilitating newsmaking meant acting as a personal aide. In one case, Elif, recounted, "I felt more like his assistant than his fixer sometimes. ... I babysat his daughter a bunch of times; just like shit like that. They were rebuilding his house so I would just be with the workers sometimes." Such tasks infuriated Elif as an affront to her claim to be an emerging professional, not a teenager in need of a few extra bucks.[1]

---

[1] Following the globally well-worn pattern of expectations that women engage in "caring work" and "emotional labor" (Hochschild 1983; Ehrenreich and Hochschild 2003), clients are more likely to ask women fixers to do non-journalistic domestic work like nannying than their male counterparts. (That said, I ended up taking care of one reporter's kids on a couple of occasions so she could go chase stories.) The gendering of care extends to journalistic work as well: more than one reporter told me that they favor women fixers as more nurturing and emotionally supportive toward sources who need coaxing to address sensitive or painful topics (see also Palmer 2019: 102–104). Feminine subservience can also be an unspoken selling point for women fixers: the Belgian reporter Geert enjoyed working with women because they "don't tell me how to do my job" the way male fixers did.

Elif's big break, like her initial discovery of fixing in Gezi Park, came by surprise. Once again, she was in the right place at the right time to satisfy an unmet need sparked by an unforeseen event.

In May 2014, Elif was about to attend a yoga class when she got a phone call from Burcu, a producer at XYZ, her ex-boyfriend Tim's TV channel. Tim had recently moved on from Turkey (and Elif) to another news bureau, but by then Elif had already befriended Tim's circle of journalists.

Burcu told Elif that there had been a huge explosion at a coal mine in Soma, five hours' drive south of Istanbul, and asked if Elif could accompany the XYZ team. Elif rushed out of the yoga studio, called her dad to say that she would miss work for a while, bought cargo pants and an army-style field jacket on her way to the XYZ office, then packed into a car with a driver, a cameraperson, a correspondent, and a load of gear.

The story was a big one both because of the scale of death – 301 miners would become the final figure – and because weeks earlier the AK Party had voted down an opposition party motion in parliament for an investigation into safety at that very mining complex (HDN 2014). And miners were trapped and fires burning under Soma just three months before Prime Minister Erdoğan was expected to run for president.[2]

The first day, the XYZ team did mostly live shots: the correspondent standing in front of the disaster area explaining what had happened. After that, Elif later recounted to me,

> They told me, like, "We need like an emotional story; we need a family." And so I was talking to a waiter at the hotel we were staying in. And he told me, "Oh you should go talk to this *bakkal* [grocer]." I went; I was talking to this guy. ... He was like, "Ah I know a family lost their kid in this one village. Maybe you should talk to the *muhtar* [local administrator]." So he gave me his number; I called the *muhtar*.

Elif introduced herself as calling from channel XYZ and asked about the dead miner's family. "He was like 'No, you know, we really – they should be left alone.'" Elif consulted her colleagues, who were still

---

[2] In the Turkish political system at the time, the prime minister was the head of government, while the president was a supposedly non-partisan role with limited executive powers. The balance of power would shift drastically in favor of the presidency after Erdoğan's election to the position, however.

breakfasting at the hotel (unlike the mostly pious locals, nobody in her crew was fasting for Ramadan) and were interested in this lead. Elif called the *muhtar* back.

I was like, "Look, the world needs to see the story, you know, otherwise no one's gonna know. Can you help? Like, we're – we'll be sensitive, and we won't be in their hair too long." And he said, "Okay fine, meet us; come to the village." ... I was pretty nervous because I don't know how it's going to end up.

Elif, though still a rookie, intuitively adopted a couple strategies that took advantage of her ambiguous position as a go-between. When she did not have the right contacts herself, she acted as a meta-fixer, recruiting a chain of ad hoc sub-fixers to bridge the social gaps that remained between her and the sources XYZ wanted. She chatted with a waiter who directed her to a *bakkal* who connected her to a *muhtar* who introduced her to the miner's family. Elif even outsourced the task of persuading sources to participate to the *muhtar*.

She also recognized that it was strategically advantageous to present herself, in that moment, as an official representative of her news organization. Elif's introduction of herself to the gatekeeping *muhtar* in Soma as an employee of XYZ invested her with the authority to promise, "We'll be sensitive, and we won't be in their hair too long" on behalf of the channel – not that it was really Elif's call how long they would stay or what questions they would ask.

Elif's approach worked. The family was hospitable, and various relatives packed into the house to talk with the journalists. The crew was very pleased with the footage they got. The coal miner's wife even collapsed sobbing on camera. When family members broke down in tears as they recounted their last memories of the young man, Elif, seated cross-legged beside them on the living room floor, cried too.

When it came to editing the video, Burcu, the producer back in Istanbul, decided to keep a shot of Elif crying. In the segment that aired on American TV, the correspondent narrates and provides voice-over translation of everything said in Turkish, with Elif's field translations cut off except at one moment when her voice shakes with emotion. The correspondent signs off at the end and is named in the video's online description, but Elif is never identified despite her appearance in several shots.

Elif and I discussed that story a couple of times in my interviews with her the next year.

NOAH:  I remember with Soma ... you appeared on the camera.
ELIF:  Yeah.
NOAH:  Also you burst into crying, and they thought that was like a good moment.
ELIF:  Yeah, how cheesy. [laughs]
NOAH:  Does that ever happen now? Do they tend to use you –
ELIF:  [scoffs] Crying?
NOAH:  Or to use you as like – I thought that was like an interesting thing because you became part of –
ELIF:  – part of the story –
NOAH:  – the evidence, like you were a Turkish citizen for a second, not a fixer. Has that happened more recently also?
ELIF:  I think I was – I think I was not necessarily a Turkish citizen there. It was both, Turkish-citizen-slash-fixer.

Elif thought about it for a moment and told me that, no, she did not appear on camera anymore. "But I choose – I don't want to be in it either. I think – then I didn't have the experience. Like, then I just listened to them and . . . it was like we were sitting on the floor and everyone was on camera, basically. But now I know to stand behind my correspondent."

She may have looked back on her performance on the Soma story with mild embarrassment, but it was also the turning point after which she decided to quit her day job at the family business. She had already recognized that her hourly earnings were far higher than those of a struggling writer like José, and the US$250 day rate and compliments on a job well done that XYZ paid her for Soma were enough to convince her that she could be a full-time freelance fixer. Burcu promised to send more work her way.

Elif did not mind that XYZ staff credited her only privately and not in program credits. In fact, she was afraid that if her name did appear on news stories, it might attract government trouble, like an unexpected tax audit of her father's company.

\* \* \*

**Fixer** is an odd label because, despite its common usage, it does not appear in official vocational texts or in news organizations' employment records. Journalism students are not taught how to collaborate with fixers, news organizations' ethics guides do not specifically instruct fixers or their clients on best practices (e.g. *New York Times* 2004; *Toronto Star* 2011; NPR 2012; Reuters 2020), and almost nobody is officially a fixer (Bossone 2014; Palmer 2019: 17–19; Plaut and Klein 2019a).

When fixers are credited at all in an article, it is not with an "Elif, fixer," byline but with an ambiguous formulation in the footer like "Elif contributed to this article." The same "contributed" credit may be given to a staff correspondent at a different bureau who helps with a story involving multiple countries. If a high-status fixer makes what the reporter deems to be a significant contribution, they may be credited as a second author without distinction from the article's writer. In video journalism, fixers tend to be credited as "line produ-cer" or "researcher."[3] When someone receives a contract to officially join a news organization's staff, they are hired as a "news assistant" or "producer." When they fix as independent contractors, they invoice something like "interpretation and transportation services," not "fixing," on formal documentation.

Fixers do not get pensions or press cards until they become news assistants or producers. Official accreditation is a double-edged sword, though, opening some doors but also putting you on the government's radar. As far as Elif was concerned, the risk of attracting unwanted attention to her and to the family business outweighed the benefits of a press card.

The very ambiguity of fixers' place in newsmaking can be useful for both fixers and their clients. Fixers can be left invisibly behind the scenes in news reports or included in those reports as members of local society, as when Elif appeared on the screen as a tearful Turkish-citizen-slash-fixer. Fixers' association with news organizations can be downplayed when expedient, but also played up when strategically utile, as when Elif made promises to the *muhtar* on behalf of XYZ.

The **producer** label, on the other hand, denotes higher rank and is usually formal, written down on a contract that officializes a person's link to a news organization.[4] But that is not the only meaningful

---

[3] One exception to the trend of fixers' not receiving credit as such is that some long-form documentary and travel shows roll "fixer" credits.

[4] There is such a thing as a freelance producer; in fact, anyone can label themselves thusly. But for the self-labeling to be successful, for colleagues to also refer to them as such, they must build up a reputation as being on a higher level of professionalism than a freelance fixer, more closely tied to journalism in general if not to one specific employer.

distinction between producer and fixer, even though both **fix** in the sense of brokering between reporters and sources by arranging logistics, making introductions, translating interviews, and explaining each one's world to the other. Producers are higher in rank and status within journalism and engage with news stories at a higher level of abstraction than fixers.

When I asked Burcu, the XYZ producer, what the difference was between her job and Elif's, she recalled how Elif's then-boyfriend Tim had first recruited Elif to help a colleague from the channel who had flown in to assist with Gezi protest coverage back in 2013.

I was like, "[Tim], I'm desperate. I don't need a producer. I don't need a fixer. I need somebody who speaks English and Turkish. Can you recommend somebody?"

So Elif had started out not as a producer or even a fixer, though she had since developed into the latter. A fixer, Burcu explained, can do more than just translate. They have an idea of how to contact the right sources for a story, where and when to film. A producer like Burcu, though, is "in charge of a wider picture" that includes not only the local events they cover but also the news organization and the audience it serves.[5]

Producers know what duration and format the organization requires for segments, how to navigate the organization's bureaucratic and technological processes, and what story frames the organization expects filled. This knowledge of a wider picture invested Burcu, unlike XYZ's fixers, with the ability and authority to routinely pitch story ideas and to say No to correspondents and to XYZ headquarters when they made unreasonable suggestions, then propose alternatives that would work for XYZ and its audience. A producer knows how to convince her channel that a viewer in rural Arkansas will be interested in the story she is pitching. (Burcu often referenced this imaginary Arkie as her target viewer.) The capacity to act as producer was hard

---

[5] There is variation across different media subcultures in the meaning of the word **producer**, and the same goes for **reporter**. In the radio/podcasting world, for example, a producer might be anyone from a reporter in the field to the segment presenter to the editor managing postproduction to the researcher who actually reads the books about which the host interviews guests. In print journalism, **producer** is not a commonplace label. Whatever the semantic variations, analogous hierarchies of status and formality of positions exist across the news media. For the sake of clarity I will stick to just one set of definitions.

to find in Turkey, Burcu told me between sips of wine and compulsive glances at her phone at a swank bar near XYZ's Beyoğlu office:

The quality of the people we work with here generally is really not that good. Whether it be cameramen or producers – who are not really producers – something's always lacking: either an understanding of television, an understanding [of] how to put television together, or the – I don't know if it's an inability, but I'm going to call it an inability for now – the inability to understand what an audience outside of Turkey would be interested in hearing.

Note that the "quality" that is "lacking" in those "who are not real producers" is not intelligence, curiosity, bravery, or skill with a camera or keyboard. Their problem is that they lack affinity to the outside worlds of the profession and of the audience.[6]

Even among nominal producers there are different levels, Burcu said. She remembered how, although her official title at XYZ was "bureau producer" from the start, she began substantively as a fixer. Only later was there a shift among foreigners working at XYZ from "[Burcu] is our local staff" to "[Burcu] is our Turkey producer."[7]

This shift, she thought, came with their recognition that she could set aside her opinions for the job. The formal title on her contract was not enough: she had to demonstrate that she was a true producer by convincing the foreigners running XYZ of her objectivity. I use the term **objectivity** both in the sense journalists that use the word – lack of bias toward particular local sources or interests[8] – and in the sense of a capacity to **objectify** sources and events into products packaged to

---

[6] See also Blacksin (2021: 10–12) for examples of foreign reporters hierarchically distinguishing themselves from fixers because the latter "have trouble with the bigger picture that needs to be conveyed."

[7] See also Murrell (2015: 127) and Bishara (2013: 57) on the same hierarchy of fixer and producer labels among international media in Iraq and Palestine, respectively.

[8] Much scholarly ink has been spilled debunking the simplistic idea that journalists or other observers of society can ever truly lack bias. The actor recognized in any field of knowledge production as "objective" is rather the one whose subjectivity adheres most closely to that field's **doxa**: the unquestioned shared beliefs that appear self-evident to insiders (Bourdieu 1977: 164). In the field of international journalism, local subjectivities (i.e. those outside the field of journalism) are more readily recognized as biased than the doxic foreign subjectivities of the higher-status participants in the field.

meet news organizations' technical standards and foreign audiences' interests.[9]

If you want to be trusted to make big picture decisions about news stories, you have to convince colleagues that you are objective in both senses. Only then can you legitimately exercise **frame control**, not just contributing access and information but determining the overall theme and angle of news stories.[10]

It is easier to be objective in the free-of-peer-recognized-bias sense when you have the social and moral distance from sources of an outsider to local society (Merton 1972: 30–36; Pedelty 1995: 21–25). Objectivity in the second sense – the capacity to objectify and transform reality to fit an editorial template – comes from intimate familiarity with your news organization's routines and worldview, from being an insider to the field of journalism (Gans [1979] 2004; Fishman 1980).[11]

Social and moral distance are signaled by and easier to maintain with physical distance. Burcu sat in an office most of the day, far from events being reported but close to other journalists. As Elif rose in the ranks from translator to fixer and toward producer, she increasingly observed a physical distance from sources that mirrored her growing emotional distance: she went from sitting cross-legged beside them to standing behind her correspondent. By the time I interviewed Elif a year after the Soma disaster, she had professionalized enough to laugh at her former emotional involvement – crying alongside the dead miner's family – as "cheesy."

When Burcu criticized the "quality of the people we work with here" and highlighted her own objectivity, she was engaging in

---

[9] I will discuss a third way of conceptualizing objectivity – as a cultivated enlargement of the capacity to perceive the world beyond received stereotypes – in Part IV (Lippmann 1922; Galison 2015).

[10] See Giddens's (1991: 34) discussion of **trust** as "confidence in the reliability of a person or system, regarding a given set of outcomes or events, where that confidence expresses a faith in the probity or love of another, or in the correctness of abstract principles." Journalists convince colleagues to trust them with frame control through ritual performances of professional probity and allegiance to abstract principles of objectivity.

[11] See also Simmel ([1908] 1971: 146), Park (1928), Turner (1967: 134–147), and Rabinow (1977: 94–95, 152) for arguments that the insider-outsider figure of the "marginal man" or "stranger" is most capable of objectivity in both senses.

**boundary-work** (Gieryn 1983), policing who else got called a producer and preventing the unworthy from contaminating the label. In drawing lines between producers like her and fixers like Elif, Burcu did her part to ensure that the **producer** label remained a meaningful distinction, a signal of respectability and authority. Burcu was also justifying a hierarchy in which producers get press cards and pensions and frame control and boss fixers around.

Burcu, discerning though she was about shades of difference among news workers, could also appreciate how blurring the boundaries among producers, fixers, and interpreters served a strategic function in certain situations. She admitted to me that she liked to play "just the translator" when working on a controversial story. Burcu was usually the one at the XYZ office to answer phone calls from powerful people angry about unfair coverage, and her favorite way to deflect such anger was to join in trash-talking the Western media as if she only translated for XYZ to make ends meet and had no editorial power. When talking with other journalists (or with a foreign researcher like me), Burcu might fiercely assert her status as a true producer and defend the title's boundaries, but she was nonetheless capable of presenting herself as morally distant from foreign journalism when expedient.

Burcu told me that one nice thing about Elif, who had become a proper fixer if not yet a producer, was that she "doesn't need that much micromanaging." Burcu increasingly trusted her even to work independently of a foreign correspondent, to interview sources and work with a cameraperson on capturing supplemental B-roll footage. Burcu would work with Elif at the preproduction stage of choosing interviewees and deciding on the general direction and framing of stories, but then allow Elif relative autonomy when it came to actual reporting in the field.

With [Elif] it's, "Look, I need this very sensitive piece." We're dealing, for example, ... [with] the 100th anniversary of the Armenian genocide. And we had to be more careful than usual with the people that we chose to be our objective analyst-slash-expert, as they call them in the States. And it was a painstaking process. Like [Elif] was throwing out ... names and I'd Google them, and then there'd be one sort of anti-government tirade, or there'd be a staunch sort of Armenian stance in an article that they'd written like two years ago. ... This was a particularly sort of sensitive story. But ... I would say what I want, and then eventually [Elif would] come up with a name [of a source] that would fit perfectly to a T. We'd talk about what the story is, and then of course there's a cameraman as well. Then they'd go out and shoot it. So I usually give them sort of direction and then they'll sort of go out and prosper.

It was not a one-way street of progress in Elif's professionalization. Two months after the April 2015 Armenian Genocide anniversary coverage, Burcu did have to step in to micromanage Elif. She recalled dressing Elif down for including allegations of electoral fraud in XYZ's piece on the June 2015 parliamentary elections:

BURCU:   During elections, or election coverage, I called [Elif]. I'm like "Um why on earth would you pick this soundbite?" It was an incredibly provincial soundbite.

NOAH:   Do you remember what it was?

BURCU:   Yes. One of the [leftist-Kurdish] HDP[12] guys, it may even have been [party-co-chair Selahattin] Demirtaş. ... The opposition folks, who have pretty much everything at stake – before the polls closed, before anything, before votes were started to count they came out with these allegations of like voter fraud and like, "This whole entire – this election process has been riddled with fraud and blah blah blah blah blah." And they ended up in [Elif's] edit, but I'm like... "What the fuck? What is this doing here and why is it in the edit?" Because I heard on television what they had said, and there were plenty of other things that could have been put in the edit as opposed to this totally unfounded – like, how do you know? Voting hasn't even started. Like how do you know there's rampant fraud? ... So it was – it shouldn't be, but it was staggering to me that [an] otherwise smart [fixer] would choose that as *the* soundbite on Election Day from Turkey. Does this make sense?

NOAH:   Absolutely. And do [you] remember what [Elif] said? Do you [have a] sense of why [she] wanted to use [that soundbite]?

BURCU:   ... [T]ruth be told, my personal opinion on why that happened, and it continues to happen, and it will happen for a long long long long time: there is a fine line between activism and journalism in this country, particularly with the young folks, and it is almost impossible to separate the two in their minds. And those soundbites were a – because I know [Elif is] staunchly anti-government, and in [her] mind it's like, perhaps not consciously,

---

[12] Halkların Demokratik Partisi (Peoples' Democratic Party)

but perhaps subconsciously, it's like "Ah-ha, this is what I'm
thinking; this is what I want this guy to say."

NOAH:  So is a significant part of your job as a producer making sure that
your employees stay on the journalism side of that line?

BURCU:  Absolutely, it is *the* main part. It is the main part. Because you –
we're all human, right? We all have our opinions. I'm extremely
opinionated. Obviously I vote. I know who I like, who I don't
like – but it doesn't affect my job.

Whether or not we believe Burcu, the important thing to note is that
she claimed producer status and differentiated herself from fixers by
splitting herself into an opinionated voter self and an unbiased professional self. At the fixer level, a person is well on their way to understanding how to objectify, to transform local realities into objects
called news stories or packages. But when it comes to certain issues,
the fixer is too morally close, too "provincial." They cannot be fully
trusted. They threaten to pollute journalism with political activism.
A true producer, Burcu would have us believe, has transcended to a
greater level of objectivity, pure of local bias whatever the topic and no
matter how she votes in private. Burcu had risen in status by convincing her colleagues of her moral transcendence, and now pretty much
ran the XYZ bureau.

**Status** is relational, something that other insider participants in a
field recognize in a person. Status is not public fame; in fact, fame
among outsiders can detract from one's status within a field.[13] The
highest-status journalists are not the ones news audiences have most
likely heard of, or even the ones with the highest pay.[14] They are the
ones who are most trusted within the field to behave according to
its standards.

---

[13] Fields are for our purposes the same as "status groups" and "interpretative
communities" (Weber [1921] 2010: 142–148; Zelizer 1993; Schudson 2003:
41–45).

[14] Elif, for instance, earned more than José per hour, but was lower in professional
status. Those on the fringes of news organizations may earn good money on a
per-story basis, but benefits like insurance and pension that go through official
channels and imply long-term service and moral proximity to an organization
*are* connected to status. Following the money also is important insofar as the
direction that money flows is an easy first indicator of insider vs. outsider status.
Public relations agents are paid by sources and have good access but are biased
insiders; fixers are paid by journalists and are closer to the outsider pole of
the spectrum.

The highest-status journalists are those with the greatest distance from the contaminating influences of the outside world that threaten to spoil their objectivity (Abbott 1981: 820–827). Their allegiance is to the internal order of journalism and not to sources or provincial values or political factions.

The highest-status journalists consider news stories from the most abstract, bird's-eye view. Elif had to worry about concretes: which specific family to interview, how to translate particular words, where exactly to sit. Burcu was of higher status and involved at a level of greater abstraction: which events were newsworthy, what generic building blocks were needed to construct a disaster story, which political views fit within the bounds of mainstream acceptability.[15] Burcu's boss back at XYZ's US headquarters considered the channel's Turkey coverage from a yet more abstract viewpoint, as a disaster package X seconds in length, more or less interchangeable with all the other disaster packages from around the world that might air in the same time slot that evening.

The trade-off of high status is a loss of magic. The heroic allure of journalism comes precisely from exposure to local chaos and complexity. Elif was excited at the prospect of getting to know more of the country. José was attracted to journalism in the first place for its promise of an escape from the order of a safe suburban American life.

Purity, status, and order are the enemies of adventure. While the charismatic adventurer follows their own path (or at least appears to from the vantage point of one of the fields they bridge), the high-status functionary follows the rules and stays within the orderly walls of their office.

The opposing pulls of status and adventure create a paradox for journalists. Their public claim to legitimacy rests on their ability to access communities around the world, and their charismatic ideal is the rugged correspondent comfortably interacting with the foreign. Yet within the field of journalism, exposure to the outside world is simultaneously a status threat.[16] There is a tension between the status of

---

[15] On evaluations of newsworthiness and the boundaries of viewpoints acceptable within news media, see Lippmann (1922: 338–357), Gans ([1979] 2004), Herman and Chomsky (1988), and Shoemaker and Vos (2009).

[16] See also Pedelty (1995: 69–83, 201–213) on status hierarchy among reporters covering El Salvador's civil war for the foreign media. On the hierarchy from cosmopolitan to national to district to volunteer brokers in the world of international AIDS altruism, see Swidler and Watkins (2017: 78–105).

being a disinterested outsider to local messiness, objective and authoritative within the news organization, and the charisma of being an eyewitness insider with contacts everywhere and credible war stories to tell (Pedelty 1995: 29–39, 69–83; Zelizer 2007; Bishara 2013: 109–111).

Even Burcu felt this tension. Not long after the Soma disaster, she lamented to me that she was "still a bit jealous" for missing out when the police teargassed a team she had dispatched to the Syrian border. She had sacrificed the thrilling chaos of the field for the status and professional purity of the office.

# *Orhan*

Orhan, the *metalci* former national newspaper reporter, covered the Soma mine accident with an American news site. He was established in the fixing game by then and had developed routines for finding sources even when he lacked direct personal contacts. Instead of, like Elif, driving to the site first and hoping to meet the right victim once he arrived, Orhan monitored the Turkish media, skimming every story reported on location. He found an article mentioning an Alevi village that had lost more than a dozen men in the disaster, many of them related. Erdoğan and the governing AKP, with their increasingly sectarian Sunni Muslim identity politics, had a contentious relationship with the country's Alevi religious minority, and Orhan knew his clients would bite at a story framed by not just sadness but also oppression.[1] And with so many dead, they would find someone willing to talk.

Orhan got in touch with the author of the Turkish-language report on the Alevi village through an erstwhile colleague at the latter's news agency. Orhan called and explained that he was working for the American press on the story, which both impressed the author and made him willing to share contacts, as he did not view foreign English-language outlets as competitors.

In that case, because it was an unpredictable story in an unfamiliar place, Orhan recruited the local journalist to function as his informal and unpaid sub-fixer. Orhan may have found that journalist on the fly, but he did so by following a routine that had worked for him in the past.

Fixers are often asked to provide insider access to a huge geographic and social expanse, and fixers can no more pull that off than can reporters. Nobody can be local everywhere.[2] Anyone who hopes to quickly extend their social reach must rely on a chain of brokers.

---

[1] On Turkey's Alevi community and its relation with the Turkish state, see Shankland (2003).
[2] See also Palmer's (2019: 150–151) discussion of differing levels of insider-ness among fixers.

High-level fixers become experts at meta-fixing. They connect with and delegate tasks to a next level of brokers. Sub-fixers are to meta-fixers as fixers are to reporters and as reporters are to editors. **Meta-fixer** and **sub-fixer** are my words; Orhan just called everyone "friends" (a classic label for obfuscating relations of reciprocity and hierarchy).[3]

Sometimes a meta-fixer functions as a permanent **buffer** between foreign reporters and sub-fixers. Other times, a meta-fixer is a **catalyst**, introducing their clients to more local fixers with whom the reporters then work directly (Stovel and Shaw 2012). Had the Turkish journalist who alerted Orhan to the Alevi miners spoken English, and had Orhan been too busy to take a road trip to Soma, Orhan might have catalyzed a new fixer–client relationship between the Americans and the Turkish journalist and moved on. However, that sub-fixer did not speak English and Orhan needed the work, and so he acted as a buffer and filtered, translated, and passed information from the sub-fixer to his American clients.

Orhan's meta-fixing expertise was evident in the way he relied on a tried-and-true method for finding a sub-fixer even for the nonroutine Soma story: scouring Turkish news until he found a local journalist who had the right contacts. When it comes to predictable stories, the advantage of the experienced meta-fixer becomes even more pronounced. Orhan had a long, precious list of friends on his phones and Facebook account to whom he could turn.

One such friend was a Syrian woman named Leyla who had fled the civil war with her husband, Aziz, for the southern Turkish city of Gaziantep (abbreviated Antep). Leyla had been an English teacher and translator of literature back in Syria. Aziz was a political activist and spoke little English. The couple were in their late 30s and scraped by a living with work in Antep's growing Syrian affairs sector: Leyla as an interpreter for humanitarian organizations and anyone else trying to reach an international audience, Aziz for a Syrian opposition-aligned NGO.

Leyla spoke the English of a schoolteacher who had never traveled abroad: precisely enunciated, with a large vocabulary that often missed the idiomatic mark. The hardships and precarities of being Syrian in

---

[3] Like many of the terms I employ, **meta-** and **sub-fixer** are relational. You are a meta- or sub-fixer only in relation to another news contributor, and the same person can be both a meta-fixer to one colleague and a sub-fixer to another.

Turkey were "perplexing situations" that left her "unrelaxed." She spoke with more erudition, but also hesitantly with less colloquial ease, than Orhan, a difference emblematic of their respective orientations toward foreigner journalists. Orhan was closer to clients in culture and perspective.

Orhan and Geert, the Belgian reporter with whom he often worked, met Leyla and Aziz on a trip to Antep to report on the Syrian opposition in exile. They were interested in Aziz's NGO, and Aziz called in Leyla to translate. Between the two of them, Orhan and Geert realized, the couple had both the connections and the language skills to be useful as a fixing team. A chain of information brokers was established.

Leyla would keep Geert and Orhan updated via WhatsApp group chat about developments inside Syria and in the Turkey–Syria border region, based on what she heard from Aziz and other family and friends. If Geert was interested in doing a story on events she mentioned, Leyla would rely on Aziz's help to set Geert up with sources inside Syria. Leyla would translate three-way WhatsApp chats with Geert and the source, along with roundups of online news. She scanned social media, opposition coordination committees still operating in Syria, and the country's state press. Sometimes Geert would have her conduct the interviews herself via phone or Skype and send him any important quotations. Geert told me that exchanging ideas with Leyla and Aziz was, given their local vantage point, an important part of his process:

[They] will regularly say like, "Hey, I met this person. ... I was meeting up with a friend of mine, and they introduced me to their uncle or their cousin that came from [ISIS's capital] Raqqa, and they say that this is happening,"... and then we'll write a story about it. ... Or I'll say, "Look, this is what I'm hearing. Can we write a story about this? Who do you know?" And [they]'ll be like, "Oh, that's such a coincidence. I was speaking to somebody about that very thing in a café the other day. They said that they got a call from their mother in Urfa or Deir al-Zour."

Geert informally enjoyed a right of first refusal on these tips, but if he passed on a story, then Orhan might shop it around to other reporters. He would also sometimes reuse the same contacts and stories with other (none-the-wiser) clients after Geert was done with them, "double-dipping," as another foreign reporter disapprovingly called it.

In many cases, Aziz fed tips to Leyla, but on occasion Leyla was herself the insider with the useful connection. One WhatsApp text update that Geert did not find newsworthy was Leyla's cousin Hiba's marriage and divorce. The civil war had widowed Hiba, and after fleeing to Turkey with her young child, she had married a Turkish man twice her age in the hope of finding security and stability. The groom already had a wife, though. So they were married in an illegal ceremony that granted Hiba no legal rights or protections. (Turkey is a formally secular country that only recognizes monogamous marriage, but some imams will "marry" a man to up to four women in accordance with Islamic law.) A few days later, the husband unceremoniously "divorced" Hiba after his Turkish wife threatened to leave him over the matter.

Orhan thought that despite Geert's uninterest, a female reporter might see these events as newsworthy if he added his own sensemaking service on top of Leyla's access. He pitched it to an American radio reporter named Alison as one case of a larger phenomenon: Not just Hiba, but Syrian women across the country were marrying Turkish men, and Orhan could find them. Alison in turn recognized Orhan's idea as newsworthy because it fit into a still broader and more abstract frame of interest to American listeners: the vulnerability and exploitation of women displaced by war.

She hired him to accompany her on a trip to Antep and other cities along Turkey's southern border in search of Syrian second wives. Ahead of their visit, Orhan gave Leyla a list of requested sources that he and Alison had drafted: Syrian women happily and unhappily married to Turkish men, underaged brides, a women's rights expert. Asking around her community of displaced Syrians and using her NGO connections, Leyla was able to put together an Antep itinerary to satisfy Alison and Orhan. When the time came for interviews, Leyla interpreted for Alison while Orhan sat quietly in the background or stepped outside for a cigarette with the husband, catalyzation complete.

Orhan and Alison had less success in the city of Şanlıurfa (abbreviated Urfa), the next stop on their trip. There, Orhan's sub-fixer was a Syrian Kurd, nom de guerre Jimmy, whom we will meet more intimately at the siege of Kobani. Jimmy assured them that he had worked hard and found some Syrian wives who fit the bill, then brought them to a house where he said a group of sources had agreed to meet. Inside, a Syrian man, whom Jimmy translated as saying he was one of the women's relative, stood gloweringly present in the background.

Alison and Orhan felt that something was not quite right as the women told stories that matched one another's very closely.

After the interview, Orhan queried neighbors who confirmed their suspicions that the women were sex workers and the man their pimp. A twinkle in his eye, Jimmy said yes, maybe he had been fooled as well, and they were actually prostitutes. He then asked for money to pay the sources for their time, and when Alison refused, for US$150 for a driver to drive them the short way back to the airport. Alison did pay Jimmy his day rate, which had risen to $200 by then.

"He is very charming," Alison conceded of Jimmy. But she would not work with him again, and she was angry with Orhan for hiring Jimmy as their Urfa fixer. Orhan, she later complained to me, knew how to pitch a good story idea, but then had a habit of not following through. On the Syrian wives story, she said, "He was promising A-B-C and he delivered, you know, A."

When the system works, the sub-fixer provides the meta-fixer with sources and information that the meta-fixer can both vet for suitability and objectify without an insider's moral attachment. The sub-fixer handles access and the meta-fixer handles sensemaking, while also protecting the reporter from local bias and lies that threaten journalistic ethics. Orhan failed as a meta-fixer when he allowed his sub-fixer Jimmy to nearly corrupt Alison's story by hiring sex workers to play Syrian second wives (see Figure 2.1).

## Chain of Contributors to the Syrian Wives Story in Urfa

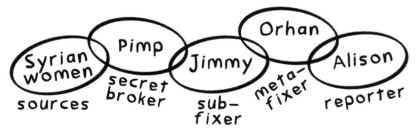

**Figure 2.1** Chain of contributors to the Syrian wives story

Orhan conceded to me that he should not have trusted Jimmy because Jimmy was not really a professional fixer. Meta-fixers, like every other player in the field, engage in boundary-work to police the way their subordinates are labeled. This boundary-work consists of highlighting the difference between true fixers and mere translators, activists, or middlemen like Jimmy or even the pimp. As Orhan complained to me over beers at a street-side Beyoğlu bar,

Sometimes [reporters] think that they hire fixer but they hire translators. The [nominal] fixer sometimes don't have the sources. Sometimes they are biased. They are the translators. ... Sometimes the person might say she's a fixer but she or he is only a translator. Because I think that a fixer might have – *should have* the capacity to improve your story, because you're in a country that you don't know.

Mirroring Burcu's distinction between fixers and producers, Orhan defined **translators** as news contributors who might superficially do the same job as a fixer but lacked a true fixer's journalistic savvy. As a buffer meta-fixer, Orhan had to differentiate himself from his translator "friends" and justify his continued mediation between reporters and those friends, stressing how the latter were incapable of seeing what was interesting to foreign reporters.[4] Friends could not be trusted to work directly with foreign reporters because they were too caught up in their own little worlds, both biased and incapable of gauging international newsworthiness.

ORHAN: So of course [near the Syrian border] local journalists, like human rights associations, NGOs and all these, *yani* [I mean] I'm kind of getting all kind of connection. Who[ever] is useful, you know? Like it might be a local journalist, but stupid guy, you know? He's worthless. I mean I don't – I keep friendship but I don't use him as a connection or all these things. In Kilis, there was a guy who's keep calling me all the time. There's some news but stupid, you know? Like he was like saying, "Oh, there was a municipality doing a pavement work." So what [the] fuck?[5] I mean –

---

[4] See also Palmer (2019: 125–132) for examples of fixers engaging in boundary-work to differentiate themselves from "basic translators" even in the act of translation itself. The fixers claim expertise in translating that facilitates sensemaking.
[5] Note that in both Orhan's and Burcu's boundary-work (see her complaints about Elif's bias, above), "What the fuck?" serves as a rhetorical coup de grâce

NOAH:     He would try to give you stories?
ORHAN:    He was giving me some information. It's like, "There was a
          wedding ceremony between Syrian and Turk."

Orhan would use this friend as a bottom-rung intermediary and source
of information when he needed someone in Kilis. But Orhan found him
useless as a fixer or producer with the vision to frame stories for a
foreign audience because the friend could not distinguish between
locally significant and internationally significant events.

The difference between "information" and "stories" in our conversation corresponds to the differences between lower- and higher-order
fixing and between access and sensemaking. Information depends on
local access, but to become a story, someone must make journalistic
sense of that information and fit it within a newsworthy frame.

Leyla likewise provided Orhan with information, which Orhan
sifted through for story material, as he found in Leyla's information
about her cousin's marriage and divorce. "A wedding ceremony
between Syrian and Turk" is not inherently interesting to foreign
clients in its raw informational form, but an expert meta-fixer can
cook it into a story idea palatable to outsider taste.[6]

Even as her list of clients grew from Orhan's sub-contracting, Leyla
did not call herself a fixer. She for one preferred the *translator* label.
"So when people contact me," Leyla told me, "They ask if I could fix
things. So I tell them that I am not a fixer. I can help them with the
translation and the interpretation."

Leyla might have done many of the same tasks as other fixers,
introducing reporters to sources and sometimes traveling with them,
but nonetheless she insisted to me, "Although I worked as fixer, I think
I'm translator." This was in part, she said, because she relied on her
husband's relationships for contacts, whereas a true professional fixer
would have their own network.

---

   hammering home the inferiority of the lesser fixer. *What the fuck?* is a rhetorical
   device signaling that the contrast between the speaker and whatever they are
   describing is so great that they cannot or need not explain it any further.
[6] It is not always the case, though, that reporters actually want to be shielded from
   local contamination. Sometimes they are attracted to adventure and chaos, but
   buffer-fixers block their access to it. Thus, we should not take Orhan at his word
   (which justifies his fee as a buffer) that foreign clients always and necessarily want
   him filtering and making sense of disorderly information from his sub-fixers,
   cleaning it up into neatly packaged stories for them.

Calling herself a translator also related her experience in journalism to her NGO work, and perhaps more importantly, to her lost life in Syria translating literature she loved instead of grant reports and atrocity news. I have focused on labels' meanings within the field of journalism, but it is not necessarily the only or even the primary field in which fixers live. For Leyla, **fixer** was a journalism label, and her identity did not lie in journalism. **Translator** was not to her a lesser version of **fixer**, but a respectable occupation in its own right that charted her temporary dabbling in journalism onto the larger map of her past as an English teacher and literary translator and on course to a future career that she hoped to find after passing through the purgatory of Turkey.

Securing a respectable and exclusive label for oneself is essential for a sense of self-worth and membership in a moral community. That is the emotional side of boundary-work.

# *Karim*

After fleeing Damascus, first for Antakya and then to Istanbul after ISIS threatened him, Karim cobbled together a living from fixing gigs. Orhan had connected him with his first reporters, and Karim continued to sub-fix for Orhan on occasion. He also began to recruit clients of his own. Karim knew from his luxury hotel days how to hang out with foreigners, how to play the coolly exotic Syrian and not the desperate or aggressive one, and proved entrepreneurial in using journalist parties to meet potential clients and reduce his dependence on Orhan.

Everything Karim worked on, his specialist beat, focused on the fallout from the Syrian civil war. But what he did and how presented himself changed dramatically from story to story and as time went on.

For one early story Karim did with the German TV channel DDT, his correspondent posed as a museum curator interested in buying stolen artifacts looted from Syria. Karim played the part of a go-between (a fixer in the early twentieth-century sense) with an antiquities smuggler and arranged a meeting. DDT equipped Karim with a hidden camera and pushed him to convince the smuggler to show off as much merchandise as possible and to state the provenance of his wares on video.

Karim's affiliation with journalism was something to hide from sources who wanted to avoid public awareness but something to highlight for those who sought such attention. When Karim talked with Syrian revolutionaries and activists eager to win international sympathy, he was sure to lead with the name of the outlet employing him and a sentence about its wide impact.

Activists spanning the spectrum from diaspora social media devotees to official NGO representatives to public relations firms also fix.[1]

---

[1] See Powers (2018) and Wright (2018) on the way NGOs increasingly shape journalistic coverage of their issues and even directly produce and distribute media that circumvents traditional news outlets.

Meta-fixers and reporters turn to them for access, though activists' editorial input can be a threat to objectivity. Activists are by definition biased advocates for particular causes. They try to win journalists over and to use the news to broadcast and add authority to their perspectives. The journalist–activist relationship is marked by both mutual distrust and mutual reliance (Breindl 2016).

One of a fixer's **sensemaking** duties is to help reporters vet activists. They explain to their clients how and to what degree an activist is biased toward this or that cause, providing the reporter a guide to interpret the activist's input and avoid naïve acceptance of their sloganeering. At the same time, one of a fixer's **access** duties is to help activists vet reporters. An activist must be convinced that a reporter is receptive to their message and works for an influential enough outlet to be worth the activist's time (Andén-Papadopoulos and Pantti 2013).

In mid-2014, Geert read an American news article about Syrian Civil Defense, a volunteer emergency response organization operating in rebel-held areas of Syria. Syrian Civil Defense had recently rebranded as the White Helmets and set up a fundraising site with the help of a newly founded UK-based publicity/activist organization called the Syria Campaign. Nobody in the Belgian press had yet covered the White Helmets and Geert's editor at the newspaper *Het Nieuws* was excited at the story idea.

Geert asked Orhan to connect him to a team of search-and-rescue workers. Orhan in turn reached out to Karim, who despite his own revolutionary activist background did not know anyone involved with the organization. Fortunately, emailing the Syria Campaign contact email listed at the bottom of the White Helmets website worked. After vetting Karim and Geert (Orhan had stepped aside after catalyzing the project by recruiting Karim), the Syria Campaign put them in touch with volunteer emergency workers in northern Syria.

"[Geert] just said, I want to do something about the White Helmets … I didn't have any contacts; I didn't have anything," Karim later remembered.

I just had a Syrian name and Arabic and like [*Het Nieuws*] behind me, and so I think – I mean not that Syrians know what [*Het Nieuws*] is, so I guess that didn't really help. But when they would type [*Het Nieuws* into a search engine], something would pop up, so I think that really helps when you're starting out, as opposed to being like a freelance journalist or fixer. … Like, it's hard to convince people to talk to you. 'Cause they feel so tired some-times. They're like, "What is this going to do for me?"

Not only fatigue but suspicion can affect sources' and activists' will-ingness to contribute to news stories. The White Helmets and Syrian Campaign would soon face a well-organized Russian and Syrian gov-ernment disinformation campaign claiming that they fabricated docu-mentation of war crimes and supported radical Islamist rebels (Levinger 2018). In this case, though, the sources were happy to talk once they learned that Geert could help them reach a new national audience, given that they were on a fundraising campaign seeking support from European governments.

Karim arranged and translated a Skype teleconference call with a couple of White Helmet volunteers, sitting beside Geert in the latter's apartment. The interviewees wanted to talk big picture politics, but Geert steered them instead toward personal accounts of racing to the scene of explosions and searching for survivors beneath rubble. Geert asserted **frame control** by choosing to focus on these personal experi-ences rather than on political slogans or lists of the Syrian govern-ment's human rights violations.

Geert had to depend on those activists for access to information from inside Syria. To fully adopt their sensemaking, though, to hand over control of the story's overall frame to them and focus on Assad government war crimes and the righteousness of the rebel cause, would have offended Geert's sense of professional autonomy. The compromise that satisfied both the activists and the reporter was the personal-ization of the story.

The story still aligned with the White Helmets' and Syria Campaign's politics as far as who figured as a hero and who as a villain. After all, it was the Syrian government bombing and shelling the civilians whom the White Helmets were rescuing or unearthing.

When journalists talk and teach about their craft, they tend to stress the literary and empathy-provoking benefits of personal stories. They may be right about the power of focusing audiences in on individuals rather than discussing political or cultural conflicts in more abstract terms. Yet personalization can also be journalists' compromise with the competing aims of activists and sources, a compromise that protects the author's status within journalism from accusations of co-optation. Savvy activists and publicists play along with this personalization because it allows them to claim that they are not shoving their political agenda down journalists' throats, thus earning them greater trust among, and access to, media outlets that they need to reach a wide audience.

To rise in status within journalism, informal recognition among insider peers is key, as when Burcu went from "local staff" to "Turkey producer" in her foreign colleagues' eyes. But even nominal labels that insiders informally refuse to recognize can convince outsiders such as state authorities of a news contributor's professional legitimacy.

After a few months and stories for DDT on migrant smuggling and Germans in Syria, the channel offered Karim a full-time producer contract. For the TV channel, the contract was foremost an exclusivity deal, a way to keep Karim to themselves and away from competitors. Karim may have been a "bureau producer" on paper, but they went on referring to him as their fixer.

Karim readily accepted their offer, the stable income, and the press card that they helped him obtain. Even if he was in practice considered a fixer, Karim found that his official status and especially his new press card helped him avoid problems when traveling inside Turkey.

By this time, the Turkish government had started providing Syrians with *geçici koruma kimlik belgeleri* – temporary protection identity cards, which Syrians knew as *kimlik* – that entitled them to free healthcare and education. The problem was that each *kimlik* was location specific. If a Syrian wanted to relocate within Turkey, they had to inform authorities in advance, then re-register for another *kimlik* in their new location, a lengthy process. Sometimes Turkish officials and companies interpreted the complex and unclear rules to mean that Syrians were not entitled to travel around the country, which could create problems for fixers who needed to board a bus or a plane for work (İneli-Ciğer 2015; Baban et al. 2016; Bellamy et al. 2017). In this context, Karim's press card was valuable as official accreditation from the Turkish Prime Minister's Directorate General of Press and Information that he was producer and representative of the international media, a trump card to play when facing an intransigent gendarme at a checkpoint or sales agent at a ticket counter.

Karim had also grown pessimistic about prospects of a democratic revolution or peaceful near future in Syria. He expected to one day seek asylum in Europe or North America. Documentation of an official position at a foreign news organization would help convince the UNHCR that he could not safely return to Syria.

In addition to refugees and smuggling, Karim's colleagues at DDT were interested in high-adrenaline trips into Syria to report from the front lines. Karim was still wary of returning to his home country, given the circumstances of his departure and threats he had faced from ISIS even within Turkey, but he assisted the German channel as a remote meta-fixer. Expanding his network from his days with revolutionary coordinating committees, Karim was able to establish working relationships with sub-fixers inside Syria and with rebel commanders to secure safe passage for the visits he coordinated from Istanbul.

Then ISIS rose from a bit player in the civil war to a nation-shattering "caliphate" larger than neighboring Jordan. The self-proclaimed Islamic State grabbed international attention while also making it more difficult for foreign reporters to themselves travel to Syria. DDT stopped sending correspondents into the country and began to rely more on content from people they called activists or citizen journalists. Karim helped organize the recruitment of Syrians inside ISIS territory, whom DDT paid thousands of euros for footage smuggled to Turkey at risk of gruesome punishment.[2]

---

[2] On other cases of news organizations outsourcing/subcontracting risk to local contributors, see Pendry (2011) and Seo (2019).

# Nur and İsmet

In her first year after university graduation, working as a fixer in the Kurdish-majority city of Diyarbakır, Nur more or less followed the formula of her first fixing adventure with Alison. She would introduce visiting reporters and academics to her friends, to Kurdish Movement activists and intellectuals and cultural revivalists, to people she wanted to talk with herself. Her clients were also interested in talking to these people but considered her more of an activist than a professional fixer. She would often end up surprised and disappointed to find articles that reporters had published without showing her a draft or sending her a link, articles that went against her guidance and understanding of an issue.

Nur was especially likely to be labeled an activist – useful but with an allegiance that trumped journalism – when it came to stories covering labor because she also worked part-time for a workers' rights organization. She assisted the NGO with public relations and even shot some promotional videos for them using skills she was learning from her work with TV crews and documentarians. When foreign reporters invited her to suggest story ideas, Nur would reliably pitch something labor related. Clients would sometimes contact her to first function as an interviewee and second connect them with other NGO representatives as a public relations duty (for which contributions reporters did not expect to pay).

Her ideas about the proper relationship between her NGO and journalism work changed, however, under the influence of a producer named İsmet. Nur met İsmet while covering *Newroz*, the spring equinox new year that is an important holiday for Kurds, Alevis, Iranians, and Central Asians (less so for Sunni Turks). *Newroz* celebrations were in previous (and future) years newsworthy because they were predictably a time for clashes between militarized police and Kurdish protesters in southeastern Turkey, and so late March was typically a busy season for Diyarbakır fixers.[1]

That year, 2013, the holiday was newsworthy for a different reason. Reciprocating government gestures toward greater cultural and political tolerance of the country's largest minority known as the "Kurdish Opening," imprisoned PKK leader Abdullah Öcalan declared peace. He ordered guerrilla fighters to withdraw from Turkish soil and announced the start of a new era of non-violent democratic struggle in a letter read aloud to the cheers of a Diyarbakır crowd waving the flag of Kurdistan.

Nur and İsmet were both in the press corps covering the celebrations. İsmet stood out from the rest for his tailored and buttoned-down style, looking behind his dark sunglasses like he ought to be lounging on a yacht far from the sweaty, crowded jubilation. Though a Kurd from the southeast himself, he also stood out from the other local news workers for his neutral, businesslike comportment and apparent emotional distance from the event.

İsmet was two decades Nur's senior and had grown up in a village near Diyarbakır. His family farmed and ran the local tea shop in the winter. From a young age he had wanted to escape the poverty and claustrophobic insularity of village life, not to mention his bullying big brothers. Foreign languages seemed the best way to get out of the village and into the world. He learned Arabic at religious school and taught himself English and German by brute force – up to fourteen hours a day in his teenage years, he claimed.

His English became good enough for a job as a private-school language teacher, then as an interpreter for an army general during his mandatory military service, then in tourism both in the southeast and along the beaches of western Turkey. Diyarbakır hotels would refer visiting reporters to İsmet, and in international journalism he finally discovered his ticket to the world.

İsmet built a reputation in the late 1990s for delivering on difficult stories about the PKK conflict both in Turkey and across its southern borders. When İsmet told me about fixing in those days, he provided a

---

[1] Yanik (2006) provides an explanation of the evolving politics of *Newroz/Nevruz* in Turkey.

string of examples of the ways tasks formerly assigned to fixers can now be delegated to machines:

I used to work in northern Iraq, Iraqi Kurdistan. ...To make a phone call, you are traveling six hours, just for a phone call, from Erbil to Turkish border. There was not any land lines. There was only a satellite phone. It was not working properly and it was very expensive. I'm not sure but as I remember, one minute was between five and ten dollars. One minute, yeah. We don't have laptops to write our story. We have to write notes and tell on the phone, and they write it. And it takes a long time. So it cost a big money. So we have to – if it's not urgent – travel six hours to border and make phone call and then go back. We don't have any equipment to transmit our materials like pictures, like video. ... For example, there was not digital camera. We were using manual cameras with films. We sent films; we traveled six hours to the border, and from border four hours to Diyarbakır. We send our films and then they wash it and print it. And they send it Istanbul. It was so difficult.

The label **fixer** became standard journo lingo in the early 1990s, but the associated job description has since been in continual flux. It was once a major part of a fixer's job to handle the logistics of phone calls and film processing. Reporters now handle these tasks themselves with the assistance of internet and cellular services and do not even think of the transmission of text or images as a problem requiring a local *in*.[2] Except for a brief moment of conspicuousness when they are brand new, machines and infrastructures are the lowest profile of brokers (Latour 1988a; Larkin 2013).

İsmet went on to cover the 2003 American invasion of Iraq from the country's northern Kurdish provinces. Gradually, his foreign colleagues began to see him not just as their man in Kurdistan, but as a professional who could be trusted to report beyond a regional bailiwick. When a posting opened up in Russia in the mid-2000s, İsmet seized the opportunity to prove that he was now a Global, not just a Local. İsmet clawed his way up journalism's hierarchy and was a TV producer, based in a Gulf Arab country and jetting all around Eurasia, when he and Nur met.

They chatted on the sidelines of the *Newroz* rally and then at a café before İsmet departed Diyarbakır. Nur wanted to hear about İsmet's

---

[2]  See also Tüfekçi's (2017: 34–36) discussion of the process of broadcasting imagery from Turkey's southeast in 1996 as compared to 2011.

career path, and he was not shy to play the self-improvement guru, coaching her on how to earn the respect of foreign news organizations. Once he began sending reporters Nur's way when he could not make it to southeastern Turkey himself, he was not shy about criticizing her work, either.

If she wanted to be taken seriously as more than just a translator or activist, Nur could not come off as one-sided, as only introducing them to her own people, İsmet counseled. A reputation for being an activist would only reduce her control over news stories because reporters would not trust her. He had the charisma, as one who appeared to have mastered the strange world of international media, to hold role-model appeal and convince Nur that she should in fact aspire to be more than a translator or activist. Sometimes meta- and sub-fixer relationships are more like apprenticeships than outsourcing.

Nur found İsmet's guidance persuasive, but was unwilling to abandon her personal allegiance to workers' rights or to the Kurdish Movement. Unlike him, she had not gotten into fixing to escape, but to serve causes in which she believed. Nur's compromise between outsider and insider values was a resolution that if she were to be a professional fixer, she had to split her fixing self off from her activist self.

Henceforth, if offered payment for a story about workers' rights, she would refuse it and tell reporters that she was helping them as a representative of her NGO, not as a fixer. She also worked to expand her contact list to include even sources she personally hated and distrusted, the better to provide discerning clients with a range of perspectives.

Geert, the Belgian reporter, found Nur through the foreign press club's fixer list and worked with her on a story about political conflict within the Kurdish community. Among others, he wanted to talk with representatives of the Free Cause Party, the political wing of Kurdish Hizbullah known by the abbreviation Hüda-Par (which like Hizbullah means "Party of God"). Sunni Islamist Hizbullah members had murdered numerous journalists and, Nur believed, her brother's high school teacher. They also threw acid on the faces of women or strangled them for failing to observe Islamic modesty rules (Kurt 2017: 27).

Nur called up a Hüda-Par politician whom she had cultivated as a source and, as a woman wearing a leather jacket and no headscarf in a meeting room with Geert and a group of men who thought the proper place for a woman was in the home, acted nothing but polite and even-handed as she translated (at least as far as Geert, who did not speak Turkish or Kurdish, could understand).

She waited until they were in a taxi after the interview, Geert later recollected to me with a chuckle, to explode with counterarguments and refutations of all the lies she said the Hüda-Par representatives had told. Her activist, leftist, feminist self was not gone, just checked at the interview door for her performance of neutrality.

Geert liked working with Nur precisely because of this ability to intuit the appropriate time and place to shift between behaving as a disinterested professional and behaving as an insider with her own views. They spent the evening after the Hüda-Par interview drinking local Assyrian wine and smoking pot with Nur's scruffy anarcho-syndicalist friends.

It is tempting and would be tidy to plot Nur's fixing career along a clear one-directional narrative and to take her and İsmet's claims about her transformation from activist to fixer at face value. But as I heard from others who worked with her, it occurred to me that her neutrality might be more a matter of optics than an unwavering allegiance to outsider values of objectivity and balance.

What it took to successfully pull off a performance of neutrality might depend on her audience. It might depend on the exigencies of the situation. Convincing a veteran Turkey correspondent like Geert of her professionalism required a different performance than convincing a reporter with less local knowledge.

Back in Istanbul, I brunched with a London-based journalist who was passing through after a brief trip to report from Diyarbakır, his first time in the city. He had worked with Nur and been very impressed with her and commented to me that it was fascinating how "on the same page" everyone over there was in support of the Kurdish Cause. He was surprised when I told him about recent violence in Diyarbakır between Kurdish leftist and religious factions.

Nur's growing expertise was in reading clients more than it was in transcending to an enduring state of unbiased objectivity. She used her ability to control the British reporter's information about local politics – facilitated by his lack of foreknowledge with which to assess her contributions – and guide him to a view that the Kurdish Left was the only representative of the Turkish Kurds while maintaining the impression of dispassionate professionalism. No need to give Hüda-Par or other right-wingers a chance to sell their views to a client, when that client did not even know they existed.

# *Habib*

For Habib, fixing remained a side hustle to his job as an interpreter for an NGO called Civic Aid that assisted Persian- and Pashto-speaking asylum seekers. He did not think of himself as a journalist or distinguish fixing from other projects in which he functioned as an intercultural broker, as when academics hired him as a research assistant.

Habib was young and ambitious, possessing a self-discipline correlated to the years of martial arts training that left him with a solid build and erect posture. He was eager to please all those clients, to build himself a prestigious international network. Pleasing clients meant providing them with a steady stream of Afghan emigrants to interview.

As violence against civilians rose in the Afghan conflict during the 2010s, the exodus to Europe accelerated. In Istanbul's Zeytinburnu neighborhood, long-distance call shops sprang up that also arranged money transfers to and from Afghanistan and coordinated boats smuggling asylum seekers to Greece. Hawkers of camping gear and unreliable life jackets did a brisk business. Afghan restaurants catered to newly arrived consumers, and textile sweatshops took advantage of the influx of cheap, undocumented labor.[1]

The call shops were easy places to find sources. At the height of Mediterranean migration in 2015, long queues of Afghans lined up daily outside the shops with backpacks, waiting to board buses that would take them to the coast. Habib quickly learned, however, that there was an order to things in Zeytinburnu. It was most prudent to seek smugglers' approval and help recruiting sources instead of circumventing them.

The fixing routines Habib developed took advantage of his other role, as a Civic Aid interpreter. Habib was less concerned about status

---

[1] There was some overlap in workplaces and smuggling networks between Afghans and Syrians, but the latter transit community in Istanbul was centered in the neighborhood of Aksaray, a long-standing hub of Middle Eastern and African migration.

among journalists than Elif, Burcu, or Nur, less intent on walling off a professional fixer self from the Habib that played in other fields. If anything, he worried about his fixer self contaminating his professional status in the NGO world. He avoided recruiting news sources among the asylum seekers he assisted at Civic Aid, but would highlight his refugee assistance work when introducing himself to news sources he found elsewhere.

I hired Habib to assist me for a report I was writing on Afghan migrants in Istanbul. On one of my visits to Zeytinburnu, Habib took me to a safehouse rented by a smuggler who served as Habib's sub-fixer in exchange for favors from Civic Aid. The smuggler assembled a family of Europe-bound Afghans in the dingy apartment's living room. I recorded Habib introducing himself in Persian to our prospective sources like this:

"I work for the UN in the refugees' affairs section. When some friends come from other countries, they approach me to help them on refugee-related matters." The United Nations part was a stretch – Habib was a part-time interpreter for an NGO that helped asylum seekers with paperwork for the UNHCR. He followed that introduction up with a statement that our interview "does not harm you nor can it have a direct passive benefit for you," but it seemed to me that phrasing this caveat in the style of a UN bureaucrat only furthered our sources' impression of the formality of our conversation.

Habib's performance of officialese worked. The family consented to speak with me, to the extent that anyone in their situation could provide voluntary and informed consent.

Habib could not have introduced himself to those prospective sources as a fixer. There is no direct translation for "fixer" in Persian (or Turkish), and at any rate the concept is foreign to most people without experience in journalism. Habib had to figure out another way to help them make sense of who he and I were and why we wanted to talk. His choice of self-presentation was strategic.

Habib chose to use his alternative label of NGO interpreter (stretched to "work[ing] for the UN") to encourage the asylum seekers to talk and to classify him and the foreigner asking them questions within familiar categories. Asylum seekers expect to be confronted by bureaucrats demanding information. And labeling clients like me as "friends" left our status ambiguous enough that interviewees might think their asylum cases would be helped by their cooperation.

Purity-oriented journalists like to think of journalism as separate from other fields like humanitarian or intelligence work. Hence all the boundary-work; hence the trust in colleagues who are farthest from the contaminating influences of other fields as the truest, most objective journalists. But others do not make such fine-grained distinctions.

Refugees and asylum seekers tend to see journalists as part of a larger system of international organizations that surveil, classify, and provide resources to them. Their view is more realistic than that of purist journalists. The UNHCR weighs clippings of news articles that confirm an asylum seeker's story as evidence when considering them for refugee status. Positive news coverage can even secure individuals support from foreign philanthropists.[2]

Reporters benefit from sources' association of them with other international organizations and from sharing personnel like Habib with those organizations. Acknowledging that association, though, would be a threat to their claims of professional independence.[3]

[2] For example, a *New York Times* article (Nordland 2014a) about an Afghan "Romeo and Juliet" on the run for their forbidden love captured the sympathy of an American billionaire who gave the couple money and used her connections to the US ambassador to the United Nations and the president of Rwanda to secure them an offer of asylum (Boteach 2015). Reporter Rod Nordland did not acknowledge, in follow-up coverage describing the philanthropist's intervention or a "story behind the story" piece discussing how he obtained consent from his sources, that his reporting directly benefited them or that the only reason the billionaire became interested in the couple's case was because of his article (Nordland 2014b, 2014c).

[3] The same argument, that authors must turn a blind eye to the complex positionality of the brokers who secure them access to information in order to preserve the impression of their own ethical purity, can be applied to social scientific research (Sanjek 1993; Clifford 1997: 17–47). Habib assisted multiple large-scale survey- and interview-based research projects using the same methods for recruiting participants. While ethnographic researchers often adopt reflexive approaches to discussing and acknowledging problems with the consent process, quantitative studies including those Habib contributed to do not commonly acknowledge such complications.

# The Fixer's Paradox

When international journalists talk publicly about their work, they often succumb to the temptation to present themselves as charismatic adventurers all alone in foreign lands (Murrell 2015: 32). Yet reporters, though often credited as sole authors, are just one link in a chain of contributors assembled to create news stories. Sources, publicists, activists, translators, fixers, and producers also act as information brokers between local events and foreign editors.[1] And the process does not end with editors. Search engine optimizers, marketers, news corporation executives, and social media influencers all shape the content and reception of the news in turn (Lohr 2006; Dick 2011; Gürsel 2016: 68–77).[2] Even that list leaves out the non-human mediators in that chain, such as the social media platforms that helped José find sources or the cellular networks that let İsmet's clients more easily transmit stories to editors. Why so many intermediaries? And who among them should count as a journalist?

Labels like **fixer** or **producer** function as indicators of social positions, access and sensemaking responsibilities and capacities, and moral

---

[1] Even the people who get labeled as sources are themselves information brokers in the chain of news contributors (Soley 1992; Carlson 2016). This is particularly clear in the case of experts and pundits who provide soundbites distilled to fit journalists' frames. But even vox pop, Temel-Q.-Public sources are information brokers. News stories need to be about more than individuals' stories to draw interest beyond their immediate community – hence the importance of a "nut graf" telling readers in a print article's second paragraph that the anecdote or quotation of the "lede" paragraph reflects a larger issue. Stories must address abstractions like Islamism or democracy or class struggle or American interests that can only be accessed indirectly through the mediation of sources, who are often aware that journalists are using them to simulate access to a wide swath of society.

[2] The editor is yet another link in the chain of brokers, rather than the ultimate decision-making authority in journalism. Editors are constrained in their actions and worry about threats to their professional purity like everyone else. Although the editor is far removed from the status threat of local bias, the influence of the corporate side of the industry threatens the editor's professional purity (Berkowitz et al. 1996; Anderson 2011).

94

dispositions. When it comes to social position, we can roughly sort, if not neatly delineate, news contributors into a chain based on who interacts with them. Elif was never in direct communication with editors to whom José pitched stories; José was never in contact with the design or marketing teams of the news outlets that published his freelance work.

Sometimes the chain has fewer links, as when a reporter contacts a source independently of a fixer or a public relations representative directly provides an editor with content to publish as news.[3] When brokers catalyze new relationships rather than serving as permanent buffer, or when they take on an extra task themselves instead of delegating it, they shorten the length of the chain. Long or short, the sequence of interaction maintains a consistent order. Editors do not call translators to ask if they approve of the way a producer framed events. Publicists do not ask reporters to forward press releases along to fixers.

Information that becomes news travels from left to right along the chain of news production represented in Figure 2.2. The focus of this

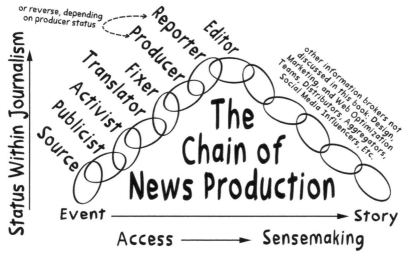

Figure 2.2 The chain of news production[4]

---

[3] See Davies (2009) on "churnalism": the practice of repackaging content provided by corporate and government public relations machines as news.
[4] McNelly (1959), Bass (1969), and Shoemaker and Vos (2009: 11–21) have proposed similar models for newsmaking as being controlled by a series of

book is the fixing that takes place between sources and reporters. Even within that segment of the chain, there is a spectrum of roles and positions.

First, there are local insiders closest to sources, such as publicists whose job it is to shape stories according to sources' interests (Lippmann 1922: 344–345), or impromptu translators like the friendly atheists who helped José on his first story. Farther along the chain, we find brokers with closer cultural, financial, and professional ties to foreign reporters: fixers and producers. Fixers broker information to producers and reporters, who transform information into news narratives or story pitches that they transmit to editors (Murrell 2015; Palmer 2019).[5]

At each moment in this process, contributors rely on whoever is on their immediate left in the assembly for access to information from those closer to the events they are covering. They translate that information into a form that makes sense to whoever is on their immediate right so that it can become a news story.

Among the sources, activists, publicists, translators, fixers, and producers engaged in fixing, there is a status hierarchy within the field of journalism. Higher-status labels (toward the center of the chain) correspond to social distance from sources and social proximity to news organizations, the bases of objectivity and professionalism.[6]

---

gatekeepers, though none included fixers in their analyses. I favor **broker** or **mediator** over the term **gatekeeper** because the latter metaphor does not capture the full extent of what news contributors do: at first blush, the job of gatekeepers would seem to be simply to either let things through or block their passage. Gatekeeping Theorists are forced to constantly remind us that their metaphorical gatekeepers not only select what content gets through to publication but also transform that content along the way (e.g. Chibnall 1977; Shoemaker and Vos 2009).

[5] The "editor" role may be further decomposed into a chain of contributors. See, for example, Boyer's (2013: 13–46) study of coordinating editors known as "slotters" who mediate the flow of incoming breaking news reports to wire agencies, constituting a link between agency reporters and the editors of client outlets acquiring wire reports.

[6] Scholars of journalism have in the past couple of decades challenged the easy equation of objectivity and professionalism (Schudson and Anderson 2009). Some have argued that in non-Anglo-American traditions, reporting that expresses political values and allegiances rather than presenting the journalist as disinterested is the norm, and journalists nonetheless have developed standards of professionalism (Hallin and Mancini 2004). But remember that I am putting my own twist on the definition of objectivity, using the term to

Journalism purists consider publicists and activists to be outside of their field and potentially dangerous sources of corruption (Schudson 2003; Carlson 2016). People who are less trusted than fixers but not quite as biased insiders as activists or publicists are labeled according to the ostensibly mechanical task that they are expected to carry out without otherwise contributing to the story: **translator** or **driver**.[7]

Fixers are in a more ambiguous and negotiable position. Producers, reporters, and editors hem and haw over whether they should be considered journalists. Fixers are tainted by the ties that enchain them to local societies, but less so than activists and publicists. Their work requires more sensemaking skills and objectivity than that of translators or drivers, but they are still less worthy of frame control than producers.[8]

Labels like **journalist** or **fixer** are simultaneously 1) descriptions of people, and 2) discourses that exercise power by justifying hierarchies among those people and among different ways of seeing the world (Hall 1997). When a person is introduced as a producer, their colleagues delegate different tasks to them than if they are introduced as a translator. Fixers rely heavily on word-of-mouth referrals from reporters and other meta-fixers, and the initial orientation a new client gets – *Try calling Nur; she's a translator and activist with good contacts in the Kurdish Movement* – will shape the reporter–fixer relationship that subsequently unfolds and constrain the divisions of labor and frame control. Because labels function as user guides, the stakes are high to secure a good one for yourself.

---

mean *the ability to objectify in order to transform into a newsworthy object.* All journalists, whether or not they adopt a norm of disinterest and political balance, must objectify local events, converting them into objects of interest to the audiences they address. To be a producer or high-level fixer capable of suggesting sources and story ideas based on an understanding of client needs, this form of objectivity is required.

[7] Palmer (2019: 61–87) and Bishara (2013: 136–166) demonstrate how even the seemingly noneditorial task of managing logistics can require a high level of skill and impact the news.

[8] See Palmer (2019: 35–60) and Plaut and Klein (2019b) for examples from around the world of conflicts between foreign journalists and fixers over frame control.

The claim we have heard from characters like Burcu and Orhan about the superior capacity of producers over fixers and fixers over translators might have been self-serving, even snobbish, acts of boundary-work, but we should not dismiss them out of hand. The ability to accurately imagine multiple perspectives and calibrate communication accordingly is both difficult to master and essential for mediating between disparate groups (like Turkish sources and Arkansan viewers).

But are differences in fixing capacities just a matter of cultivated expertise? Or do they reflect limitations and opportunities inherent in a person's social position as insider or outsider? Take the attributes of shamelessness and fearlessness, of being able to override local social norms to get a story. When I asked Geert, the Belgian reporter, what he looked for in a good fixer, he responded, "They have no shame, and they have no fears. ...They're able to bludgeon their way into things, whereas non-fixer[s], just translators, are always going to be inhibited."

So shamelessness and fearlessness are desirable, but are they skills or just the effects of social distance? Shame is for insiders, a discomfort at standing out from one's own moral community (Katz 1999: 319–320) – for example, by bothering its members on behalf of a meddling foreigner. The insider, though they have access to the community, is inhibited from using that access. The outsider is freer to be shameless, but less likely to have access in the first place.

The **Fixer's Paradox** is that both their greatest asset and their greatest liability is local connection (Burt 2007: 95–97; Stovel 2013). Being socially, emotionally, and physically close to sources makes fixers useful but simultaneously limits their ability to claim higher-status journalism labels like **producer**.[9]

---

[9] Bunce (2010: 522) found these same tensions in the Nairobi newsroom of Reuters, where a mix of local and foreign staff worked, with insider-ness serving as both a point of pride and differentiation from more superficial short-term visiting journalists and as a threat to objectivity claims:

*Reuters* occupies an ambiguous space between "insider" and "outsider" in Nairobi, reflecting the divergent positionalities of the journalists themselves. At certain times, journalists emphasised their insider status, especially in contrast to temporary "parachute" journalists; this was proudly displayed as giving privileged access to local knowledge and contacts. At other times, however, especially in the middle of the crisis, to be too deeply embedded was clearly both personally difficult and a journalistic liability.

Meta-fixing is one response to the paradox. Meta-fixers actively establish new, protective links down-chain of themselves: sub-fixers between themselves and sources. They secure access without becoming insiders. Meta-fixers insulate both themselves and their news organizations from near-sightedness, bias, and inhibition by acting as a buffer against unwelcome contributions from insider sources and sub-fixers.[10] They vet, filter, and translate information, keeping the signal and blocking the noise.

Remember how Burcu liked Elif's tears because they mirrored the emotion of mining disaster victims' relatives but disliked Elif's quotation because it mirrored the perspective of an opposition political faction? Burcu's job as meta-fixer was to manage and filter her sub-fixer Elif's insider-ness, letting through the useful bits and excising the dangerous bits that might threaten channel XYZ's claim to balance and objectivity.

Another response to the Fixer's Paradox is splitting oneself into multiple personalities in order to exist as both insider and outsider.[11] Nur's shifts between fixer and activist selves allowed her to earn a reputation as a diligent professional without sacrificing her allegiance to local causes. Burcu claimed that she could be objective because she split her producer and citizen selves: "I'm extremely opinionated; obviously I vote. I know who I like, who I don't like – but it doesn't affect my job."[12]

---

    Analogous insider vs. outsider tensions and hierarchies can also be found among domestic press journalists in the United States. Gans ([1979] 2004: 133–141) observed differences between beat/local reporters and generalist/national reporters that corresponded to their different positions along the insider-to-outsider spectrum. Insider beat reporters had objectivity problems; outsider national reporters had access problems.

[10] Analogies can be found in many corners of the world. Doormen manage the disorder and uncertainty of the street so that residents don't have to. Professional "fences" – sellers of stolen goods – provide the service of insulating buyers of hot merchandise from the criminal underworld (Klockars 1974; Bearman 2005).

[11] On the signaling of professional objectivity through insider-outsider performances of self in the cognate field of anthropology, see Clifford (1997: 64–76). See also Fanon (1967) on self-splitting as a survival strategy among colonized and racialized subjects.

[12] Part of being a professional of any kind is acting in certain situations not as a whole person but as a limited functionary. For example, romantic advances in the workplace are unprofessional because the ethos of professionalism prescribes that we check our sexual selves at the office door. Professionalism is subtractive as much as it is additive.

Neither meta-fixing nor self-splitting is easy. Meta-fixers must find and manage sub-fixers, taking care that the latter does not sully their own professional reputation or label in foreign clients' eyes (the way Jimmy got Orhan into trouble by introducing him and Alison to sex workers instead of Syrian wives). Convincingly splitting yourself requires the discipline to behave contrary to your own values – for example, by politely allowing interviewees you hate to lie to your face and espouse ideas you abhor to your client.

The practice of splitting your fixer self from your other selves contains its own paradoxical tension when those other selves are what gain you entrée in the first place. For this reason, fixers are inconsistent in their performances of self. They send different signals about who they are and what they are doing to different audiences. Burcu, the high-status producer, downplayed her status when fielding angry sources' phone calls over XYZ's reporting. Habib highlighted his NGO–interpreter self to secure sources' consent to be interviewed.

When their audience is a foreign journalist, a fixer is more likely to perform outsider impartiality in order to lay claim to professional status and trustworthiness. Nur performed journalistic balance in introducing clients to radical Islamists and not only sources who shared her left-leaning personal worldview. She only did so, however, when she gauged a particular client was knowledgeable enough to question her objectivity and pejoratively label her as an activist if she did otherwise.

Journalism's labels are linked to professional duties and capacities, but only loosely so. There is no rigid and regulated division of labor in journalism that corresponds neatly to labels like **activist, translator, fixer,** or **producer** the way there is, for example, in medicine. A hospital orderly does not administer medication; a nurse does not to perform surgery. But an activist might translate for a reporter; a translator might suggest a story idea; a fixer might conduct an interview on their own; a producer might capture footage with a hidden camera. A person doing one of those tasks might be called an activist one day and a fixer the next.

And so there exists a constant struggle to claim and redefine labels, to delineate others' and one's own proper position and role in news production. That struggle not only determines who controls which aspects of reporting, but is also itself constitutive of the process of reporting. Every choice a contributor makes – how to convince a source to talk, how to explain a situation to a reporter, how to translate and compress long interviews into soundbites – contributes to their interlocutors' impressions of who they are, how they should be labeled, and what they can be trusted to contribute to the news. Each contributor accordingly acts with an eye to impression management, and when finally published, a news story is the amalgamated artifact of all such choices along the production chain.

# PART III

# Moral Worlds of Ambivalence and Bias

# A Fragmented World

The term **ambivalence** is only a century old. Swiss psychiatrist Eugen Bleuler coined the word at a time when social scientists were grappling with the rapid societal change of modernization. In the new metropolis, millions of people could move among disparate social worlds and take on multiple roles with far greater ease and speed than in the village (Simmel [1903] 1971; Bauman 1991: 60–63; Bernet 2006). Some feared that society's moral order would come crashing down because people were faced with a splintering of culture and morality as they moved from work to home to recreational life. They could no longer abide by a simple, unified moral world. Taking on a multitude of roles and being exposed to a multitude of different expectations could – social scientists, theologians, and cultural commentators worried – free people to do whatever they wanted with no unified moral code to regulate their actions, or render people ambivalent to the point of moral paralysis or psychological breakdown. Taken to extremes, ambivalence was a component of the pathological fragmentation of thought, feeling, and intention for which Bleuler coined the term **schizophrenia**, from Greek words for "splitting" and "spirit" (Bernet 2006; Ashkok et al. 2012).

Since Bleuler's day, humanity's aggregate ambivalence has increased with societies' growing heterogeneity and the extension of our communicative reach (Park 1928; Bauman 1991). In this disunified but connected social world, intermediaries like fixers find their purpose. They also find themselves caught in the contradictions between the different cultures and moral worlds that they bridge.

Morality might seem a lofty concept embodied in philosophical treatises, legal codes, religious doctrine, and brain chemistry, but it is grounded in the everyday expectations of those around us (Abu-Lughod [1986] 2016: 237–238). For our purposes, morality is practical: not about what is inherently right or wrong, but about what people understand and signal to be the right or wrong thing to do in a given situation. Moral codes, which I will also call **norms** when relatively stable over time, are **scripts** for what should be done, how, and when.

At every moment of social interaction, we prescribe behaviors for ourselves and each other and feel accountable to the scripts of those around us. **Prescriptions** may not even be expressed in conscious ideas or explicit judgments, but we can detect them when they are **breached**: through awkwardness, discomfort, annoyance, impatience, guilt, or shame.[1] Some prescriptions are immediate and external (*do this or you are fired!*), while others are cultivated internally over years of learning to link values and actions (*what would Jesus do?*).

A person's **moral world** can be defined as the weighted sum of the prescriptions for what they should and should not do at a particular moment. A moral world may be shared or lonely, depending on whether those around a person are faced with the same prescriptions. A moral world is the product of continual negotiation among conflicting expectations within a person's evolving network of social relations, and so a person's moral world is a hybrid between the moral worlds of the different people with whom they connect.

The **moral world** concept is a way to link together the culture and politics that shape expectations with the individual interests that add weight to some expectations over others. It is also a way of circumventing the commonplace but questionable distinction between rational and emotional responses – both are triggered by demands that a person act one way or another and can be the expression of ambivalence between conflicting expectations (Lutz 1988; Katz 1999).

We usually define ambivalence *psychologically* as the experience of mutually contradictory thoughts and feelings (as when I love-hate my frenemy Temel). Robert K. Merton's concept of **sociological ambivalence**, though, takes us beyond the individual mind to social relationships. Sociological ambivalence occurs when conflicting normative prescriptions are directed toward a single person due to their position in society (Merton 1976: 6–12).

There are, Merton argued, two kinds of sociological ambivalence. The more easily managed: a person performs multiple roles, each

---

[1] I use **prescription** following Latour's (1988a: 305–306) definition: "whatever a scene presupposes from its *transcribed* actors." In the quotation, "transcribed" means primed to behave according to a script that, if followed, allows a scene of social interaction to unfold with minimal conflict and effort.

subject to its own moral norms that conflict with the norms of that person's other roles.

People learn to compartmentalizing the self into different personas for different moral worlds to manage such multiple-role ambivalence, as we already have seen Nur do by separating her fixer self from her activist self. But compartmentalization can come at a cost. Ambivalence spawned from holding multiple roles is associated with stress, identity crises, and leakage of work personas into private relationships. Self-splitting can be an effective strategy, but it can also be a mental disorder (Fanon 1967; Bateson 1972: 201–243; Ashkok et al. 2012). Attempts to split the self can also test limits of time and space: a businessperson might stay late at the office, violating the family prescription to be home for dinner by following corporate norms.[2]

Organizations often attempt to pull members into the organizations' own moral worlds, away from the norms of other roles. Employers, institutions like hospitals and prisons, and even social clubs encourage close ties among their members by educating them, overseeing rituals meant to create and reinforce organizational identities, and separating members from the rest of society. A "total institution" fully strips people of their old identities and molds them into obedience to a new, unified script prescribed by the institution itself: a **unified moral world** (Goffman 1968).

Journalism is not a total institution. If news organizations sought to fully socialize fixers and segregate them from local populations, it would defeat the purpose of hiring the fixer in the first place: to bridge the respective moral worlds of clients and sub-fixers/sources.[3] Fixing inherently exposes a person to multiple, disparate groups with divergent prescriptions for behavior, what Merton and his contemporaries called "role strain" (Goode 1960). This exposure to a chaotic clash of norms places fixers in an **ambivalent moral world.**[4]

---

[2] See Jackall (1988) and Zaloom (2006) on further cases of self-splitting from the business world.

[3] Client reporters do not exist in a unified moral world of journalism, nor do all sources and sub-fixers exist in a unified moral world of local society. If we take a bird's-eye view of the chain of news production, we can see ambivalence at all links. But if we take the perspective of any one broker in that chain, their immediate interlocutors look like representatives of the networks and moral worlds behind them along the chain.

[4] In Actor-Network Theory as developed by Bruno Latour and others, everyone and everything operates in an ambivalent moral world. Latour criticizes other

Merton's second form of ambivalence emerges when a single role is inherently subject to multiple, conflicting norms. Single-role ambivalence resists compartmentalization as a solution, especially when contradictory moral obligations apply in the same moment of face-to-face interaction. Fixers cannot simultaneously perform their professional and local selves, and they cannot keep the worlds of reporters and sources neatly segregated.

News organizations and client reporters have goals, professional cultures, rhythms to their work, and ways of communicating that clash with sources' scripts.[5] I will discuss various subcategories of moral conflict as **strategic, coding, rhythmic,** and **reciprocity conflicts** in the chapters that follow. Both clients and sources expect – and try to force or convince – fixers to take their side when a conflict arises in the reporter–fixer–source **triad** (Simmel 1950).[6]

Fixers learn to manage the strain of sociological ambivalence and strike compromises that require expertise and cause stress.[7] They coach both sources and clients to follow one another's prescriptions: to ask the right question, to phrase a response the right way, to focus on a nondivisive subject (Palmer 2019: 88–113). They control reporters' and sources' exposure to one another. They balance the expectations of others against personal dispositions that they refuse to betray. And when conflict cannot be contained, they perform neutrality or invisibility.

---

social scientists for reifying concepts like "structure" and "institutions," when in fact every member of any group is not subject to some unified corporate norm, but rather mediates between those humans and non-humans with whom they are in immediate contact (Latour 2005b). Thus, everyone is exposed to the stickier ambivalence and exists in their own atomized moral world. I would argue, however, that an ambivalent moral world emerges from specific social circumstances just like a total moral world; moral worlds are sometimes more atomized and at other times more shared.

[5] See also Moon's (2019) study of Rwandan journalists reporting for the international media and caught 1) between their foreign colleagues' and trainers' expectations that they practice independent, critical journalism, and 2) the Rwandan government's expectation that they provide positive coverage and avoid politically sensitive topics.

[6] **Dyad:** a group of two; **Triad:** a group of three; **Tetrad:** a group of four

[7] See also Goode's (1960) discussion of "role bargains" that resolve role strain.

# Noah

In 2016, I expanded my research methods from interviewing and observing reporters and fixers to working in both roles myself.[1] Becoming a freelance reporter was as simple as pitching a story idea to a news outlet and hiring one of the fixers I knew to help me. I recruited multiple fixers for each story I reported so that I could compare how a change of brokers might lead me in a different direction. This was a luxury few reporters can afford. I was lucky to have my journalism subsidized by research funds from Columbia University and the National Science Foundation, because I lost money on every story I wrote.

To become a fixer, I added my name and qualifications to a "Fixer and Translator List" that the Istanbul Foreign Press Club circulated. I also advertised on a private Facebook group for international journalists. I offered my services at a bargain price with the caveat that my clients agree that I could use our experience as fodder for my study. Emails began trickling in from reporters who had seen my advertisements and later from those referred by my previous clients or other research participants.

As a rookie fixer, I found myself in the ambivalent middle of conflicts both mundane and profound. Before finding my first reporter client, I worried most that I would lack the Turkish vocabulary for reporting on specialized topics as a non-native speaker. In practice, the hardest part was not the word-for-word conversion of Turkish into English but everything that took place around it.

Some of my early blunders were specific to the client's medium: radio, television, or print. On my first radio job, my reporter client repeatedly corrected my back-channeling: the feedback of "hmm,"

---

[1] Fishman (1980: 23–24) and Bishara (2013: 13–16) previously demonstrated how working as a journalist could help a researcher understand the process of news production.

"right," "really?" that I fed interviewees as they spoke. She needed a clean audio signal, and my little noises would complicate editing. I had been socialized into the scripts of ordinary conversation, wherein back-channeling communicates attentive listening. Faced with the reporter's competing demand for silence, I was forced to somehow satisfy both prescriptions or risk impoliteness to the source. This conflict over how to encode communication was an easy one to resolve: like any radio journalist, I learned to back-channel visually with nods and eye contact.

That first client also had to remind me more than once to push the audio recorder close enough to our source's face (I held the recorder so that her hands were free to write notes – a higher-level sensemaking task). There was a lot of background noise as we were on the sidelines of a protest over the prosecution of political dissidents, and the reporter wanted the microphone almost touching the source's mouth despite the latter's evident discomfort. I would have been uncomfortable violating a stranger's personal space like this in a casual conversation, let alone while they emotionally discussed a family member's imprisonment on scant evidence.

A more jaded fixer might have felt less ambivalent about this predicament. Given that our source was no one with whom I needed to maintain a relationship beyond that one interview, they might have simply discounted the source's discomfort and aligned with the client's prescription. Or a more experienced fixer might have used their extensive social network to avoid conflict altogether by finding a veteran interviewee accustomed to speaking into microphones.

Another challenge of audio and video reporting was prompting sources to say what my clients needed in a pithy soundbite. TV journalists especially prefer shorter clips and have limited flexibility to edit together sentence fragments. This directive was no problem when interviewing politicians used to speaking in punchy broad language and cognizant of what the team was after. Public intellectuals were likewise media savvy and usually preferred to speak directly with the correspondent in English and craft their own soundbites. But the pursuit of soundbites could be frustrating with man-on-the-street vox pop interviews.

One TV channel for whom I fixed had already established a vox pop sourcing protocol: which Istanbul neighborhood to visit for which soundbite. Karaköy, with its attractive backdrop of a bridge, ferry station, and view of the Old City, for a range of views to balance against one another; Beşiktaş for secularist voices in a bustling downtown setting; Fatih for Islamist ones with an Ottoman architectural background. These neighborhoods were close and accessible enough to visit in a single day, avoiding conflict with the channel's tight daily deadlines.

Yet even when we found someone to express the view the channel needed, the source would often speak in convoluted sentences or reference people and events indirectly. Such prolixity is characteristic of political talk in Turkey, as I had learned in my own years-long struggle to interpret the allusions and ellipses of national newspaper columnists.

It was my job not only to translate from Turkish to English, but to transcode Turkish-style political discourse into a form comprehensible to an American audience and expressed within a few seconds. I would rephrase questions and beg for specificity until sources contributed the requisite soundbite. Sources often found this obnoxious. What I never mastered, but did observe among more expert fixers, was the art of subtly coaching sources on a moment-by-moment basis, of coaxing rephrased statements without seeming repetitive.

Print journalism comes with its own strange norms for communication. Reporters writing long-form print stories prescribe that sources contribute rambling accounts which they can selectively quote and remix with other sources' quotations into their own creative, narrative pastiche. For many sources, being asked to contribute longwinded, detailed accounts can violate their norms for polite talk: troubling issues should be allowed to slide by with the lubrication of a stock truism, proverb, or political slogan; conversation should be a back-and-forth exchange of views rather than a monologue. Some of my reporter clients, though, prescribed a rhythm of asking questions and then immediately moving on without reciprocating with their own stories and viewpoints. Reporters of whatever media format, when faced by deadline pressure, press fixers to press sources. Skip tea and pleasantries; extract information and move on.[2]

---

[2] See Palmer (2019: 64–87) for further examples of fixers reconciling rhythmic conflicts between journalists and sources.

When it came to spoken interpretation between reporter and source, I was caught in a basic but stressful conflict of **coding**.[3] Reporters expected information encoded in English and sources expected it encoded in Turkish. Neither enjoyed being excluded from a monolingual conversation that made no sense to them. A source might not yet have reached their main point when my client would telegraph *Time's up* by making little frustrated noises, tapping a foot or pen and looking pointedly at me. Not understanding Turkish, they might surmise that the source was veering off on a tangent and want me to translate so that they could interject and redirect the interview.

I also felt myself pulled in two directions by the prescription for accurate translation and the prescription that I maintain the pattern of reporter → fixer → source → fixer → reporter speaking turn order, which kept the reporter in the driver's seat of the conversation.[4] Nothing seemed to annoy a client so much as when I asked a clarifying question of a source in order to translate accurately, leaving the reporter sidelined from what was now a private exchange in Turkish. Worse still, a source might take my clarifying question to mean that the implicit conch shell of speaking turn order had been handed back to them and segue into an altogether new statement, expanding my backlog of words to translate.

Depending on the medium, such microlevel conflicts of conversational rhythm can be overcome through expertise. I discussed my consecutive interpretation woes with veteran producer Burcu, who told me that when she used to work in print, she had the same problem until she mastered the art of simultaneously listening to sources speak while whispering translations to correspondents. This technique worked well for print. For radio and TV, though, depending on the microphone and its positioning, on the need for clean audio of sources' responses or reaction shots of foreign correspondents nodding without anyone whispering in their ear, even Burcu was caught in the **rhythmic**

---

[3] I use code in a broad sense to mean any system of rules governing the symbols that represent messages. Code in this sense includes rules governing the meaning of phoneme combinations (i.e. language), as well with social rules in which symbolic behaviors send messages of respect or disrespect, superiority or subordination, and so on (e.g. the "code of the streets" detailed by Anderson 1994).

[4] There is also a conflict over the proper interaction order when a source talks to the fixer but the reporter thinks the source should be talking to them *through* the fixer (Goffman 1983).

**ambivalence** of consecutive interpretation. To deal with this problem, she developed an expert feel for timing interruptions. She would anticipate clients' prescription of prompt translation and jump in to translate at the end of what she had learned to identify as a useful soundbite, all without offending the source.

The very discomfort of thinking in two languages simultaneously or in quick succession indicates that face-to-face translation is an inherently conflictual undertaking. Inexperienced fixers, including me, despite being comfortable speaking either of two languages for long stretches, find it exhausting to translate between them for extended periods. People often used metaphors like "brain melt" or "brain fry" when talking about the effects of a long day of translating.[5]

However, it does seem possible to build up code-switching expertise and stamina with time and practice. Some people's backgrounds better prepare them for code-switching. Elif, who grew up between Turkey and the United States and hung out with expats in Istanbul long before she became a fixer, told me that upon starting the job, she realized that the translation part of fixing was something she was already routinely doing for her friends and romantic partner.

When it came to the most awkward of interviews, the on-camera confrontation for a vox pop soundbite, I often did not even get as far as having to worry about the subtleties of socially sensitive translation. Only a small minority of passersby in places like ferry docks would talk to me at all if I introduced myself as a journalist seeking comment on some political controversy, let alone remain polite as I pressured them into a soundbite. Sometimes the young and politically active would stop to provide me with a slogan or stock phrase. But older people tended to steer away as if my microphone was a cattle prod.

A larger conflict between press and populace underlay sources' hesitance to speak with me. These were dangerous, uncertain days, Turkish politics an opaque and shifting power struggle.

The alliance between Recep Tayyip Erdoğan and Pennsylvania-based cleric Fethullah Gülen's network of followers had collapsed.

---

[5] In linguistics and professional language services literatures, "translation" is commonly defined as written and "interpretation" as spoken. I am less careful. I use "translation" for the transcoding of both written and spoken signals, and occasionally "simultaneous" or "consecutive interpretation" to underline a fixer's strategy for managing rhythmic and coding ambivalence.

Explanations (depending on whom you asked and when) and/or symptoms of the mysterious schism included Gülen's opposition to the Kurdish peace process, government closure of Gülen Movement schools, Erdoğan's authoritarian response to the Gezi Park protests, and a high-level corruption scandal that allegedly Gülenist police and prosecutors brought to light (Karaveli 2012; Hakyemez 2017; George 2018). After a brief moment when it seemed the corruption scandal might bring down the government, Erdoğan gained the upper hand and began to purge suspected Gülenists from the state and other influential positions in society.

Erdoğan and his allies accused Gülen and other rivals of anti-democratic conspiracy. A mysterious Twitter whistleblower calling themselves Fuat Avni warned, sometimes prophetically, about now-President Erdoğan taking measures to seize absolute power. My friends speculated about which Turkish news outlet would be raided and which government official would be purged next. The AKP's own prime minister, Ahmet Davutoğlu, a voice of relative and toothless moderation within the party, abruptly resigned. Davutoğlu was replaced by Erdoğan loyalist Binali Yıldırım, who as transport and communications minister had previously overseen the expansion of internet censorship and surveillance (Yeşil 2016: 114–123). Yıldırım's main platform as prime minister was the abolishment of his own position in favor of a strengthened presidency.

Social media had been a largely free space for dissent without serious consequences before the Gezi Park protests. In the ensuing years, though, the government ramped up the prosecution of social media users for tweets and Facebook or Instagram posts on grounds of insulting public officials or spreading terrorist propaganda (e.g. Johnson 2016). Loose talk in any public venue could now get you into trouble.

As President Erdoğan embraced a nationalistic strongman image, he scored political points by confronting the foreign press and spinning tales of international plots against him. He denounced the *New York Times* as a "rag" connected to the "Armenian lobby" and colluding with Fethullah Gülen to a cheering crowd at a rally commemorating the Ottoman conquest of Constantinople (*Cumhuriyet* 2015). Government supporters took the xenophobic cue and grew more hostile toward American and European journalists.

Visible markers of Western-ness became impediments to access, stigmas that inherently sullied journalists in pro-government sources' moral judgment.[6] Marie, a French woman who had lived in Turkey for years and worked as a fixer, recounted covering an AK Party rally during the June 2015 parliamentary election campaign. Erdoğan gave a rousing speech (despite a constitutional requirement that sitting presidents be unaffiliated with any political party) and then Marie walked around asking opinions of the dispersing crowd in her French-accented Turkish.

She found herself backing away from one group after another in the face of angry stares. One old man hit her over the head with a party flag. Marie finally found a quiet spot and a young woman, a law student, willing to answer her questions. Part way through the conversation, the student paused. She stared at the tattoos that poked out from Marie's short sleeves. The student told Marie that she did not want to be rude, but felt she ought to let Marie know that she was aware that Marie was a servant of Satan. The student aspired to become a prosecutor so that she could help punish the immorality that people like Marie spread. There is only so much a visibly foreign journalist can do to build rapport when national opinion leaders have literally demonized the foreign press.

Across much of the Turkish political spectrum, people believed that the United States was the secret power behind whomever they considered the enemy: the AKP, ISIS, the Gülen Movement, the PKK, the Armenians, the Syrian state or the rebels fighting it. Few bought into the idea of an objective and independent media. Indeed, it was logical to extrapolate from a Turkish domestic press closely aligned to political and business interests to an assumption that the American press was simply a mouthpiece for American political and economic interests (White 2013).

According to Burcu, the TV producer, skepticism about foreign journalists' claims to objectivity and government prescriptions for the proper role of the press made Turkey a difficult place to work.

[There is] a large misunderstanding between members of the media and the government. Because the government is not used to an open free press with the standards that we're used to in the States, France maybe, Australia,

---

[6] A **stigma** is a disqualifying signal that is difficult to hide (Goffman 1963). Stigmas are relational, meaning that whether they hurt your ability to be seen the way you desire depends on the audience with whom you are interacting. Markers that bestow privilege in some or most situations can be stigmatizing in other cases.

England, what-have-you. So they react in some cases understandably to what they perceive as tremendous bias on behalf of the media.[7]

The government, as she saw it, thought in terms of positive and negative coverage rather than true or false reporting, and criticized journalists accordingly:

Journalism in this country is almost like – it's opinion. You're either for or against and there's nothing really in between. . . . [Y]ou have to be affiliated with one camp. And that's what I mean by like there's this misunderstanding because there's no real – whatever that is – journalism practice, so the government reacts to that, because they don't know what real journalism is.

News organizations expect to do "real journalism," however they define it. Sources, whether government officials or people approached on the street, expect the press to serve the interests of their political camp. They perceive a fundamental **strategic conflict** with foreign journalists who they believe are working against their – or their country's or party's – interests.

All of this is to say that, in Turkey, in spring 2016, people were hesitant to talk to the press, especially the American and European press. If they were pro-government, they were suspicious of foreign journalists' honesty and intentions. If they were anti-government, they held similar suspicions but also worried that expressing their views to journalists could get them into legal trouble. This perceived strategic conflict trickled down to the microlevel of reporters' and fixers' everyday interactions with prospective sources. When I approached one young kiosk worker near the Karaköy ferry station on a vox pop hunt, he scowled, asked me what country I was reporting for, then shook his head as soon as he heard America and refused to engage further.

There is only a slight difference for fixers' practical concerns between a real and perceived strategic conflict. I faced hostility whether or not I was going to use the interview for nefarious ends. We can thus set aside the question of whether sources and government officials are

---

[7] Whether the attitudes of American government officials toward press freedom were then or are now different from those of their Turkish counterparts is not relevant to my argument, except insofar as the lessons about hostility toward journalists from 2010s Turkey might actually be more applicable to 2020s America than Burcu's statement suggests.

correct that the American press is a propaganda machine.[8] The pre-scription for managing both real and perceived conflict is the same: a fixer must signal that they are actually on the source's side in the conflict, give the source a reason to talk that outweighs their fear or hostility, or convince them that no conflict exists after all.[9]

How did I manage conflict between prospective interviewees on the Karaköy pier who did not want to talk and clients who demanded I convince them to talk? Mainly I roped in sources by foisting countervailing scripts on them. Fixers not only receive but also apply moral pressure.

Initially, I led by saying we wanted to learn their views on the latest political controversy, but over the course of my first day shortened my opener to "Hello, do you have a bit of time?" following the example of the NGO fundraisers in colorful vests who had accosted me on many a walk down İstiklal Boulevard. I kept my microphone down at my side or behind my back. Most still said no and kept walking, but I had more success with those who stopped. By that point it would be awkward –a breach of politeness code – for them to just walk away instead of answering a question.

"We have to pretend as if like I am their sister or something," is how Elif described her technique for persuading people to talk. "I have to get into their life in order to get the words from their mouth. It takes a little bit of acting."

When it came to convincing sources that I was on their side, I had the advantage over my French counterpart Marie that I did not look foreign, with my half-Persian features. I would identify as Iranian rather than American when expedient (I am a dual citizen). Sometimes being Iranian served to convince people I was not one of *those* journalists, the imperialist CIA-affiliated ones. I would do my best to signal, through word and gesture, empathy or at least openness

---

[8] Critics of American journalism (e.g. Said 1981; Herman and Chomsky 1988; Knightley 2004) would contend that the assumption that the US foreign news mirrors and justifies the interests of powerful state and commercial actors is more accurate than the assumption that journalists will report honestly and independently on the rest of the world.

[9] As we will see in subsequent stories, the more violent the situation and the less time for explanation and long-term trust-building interactions that allow the reporter–fixer–source triad to feel one another out instead of relying on assumptions and stereotypes, the bigger the problem of perceived conflict becomes. See also Shin and Cameron (2005: 322) on "false dissensus" between journalists and sources.

to whatever cause I thought they supported. The latter strategy was less successful, though: I got the feeling many sources correctly viewed me as playing a confidence game for their trust.[10]

In each case I have described, if my client reporter shared a language with and had been able to interview sources alone, they would have had to struggle with these same problems. Any reporter worth their salt learns to manage the discrepancy between their expectations and what sources are prepared to contribute. Outsourcing interaction with sources to fixers makes reporters' work easier in two ways, though.

First, it turns a large task of expertise into a small one of delegation (Latour 1988a). Instead of learning to speak a foreign language, to interpret an unfamiliar discursive style, to find sources, to convince sources to talk by developing a time-place-and-culture-specific set of signals, a reporter can simply hire someone in those capacities. Second, the presence of the fixer shifts the burden of ambivalence. The reporter experiences less ambivalence because the fixer mediates conflicting local norms, reconciling them with the reporter's prescriptions.

Only when I was incompetent as a fixer, holding a microphone too far from a source's mouth or failing to break a source's speech up into useful soundbites, did my client reporter suffer the moral discomfort of inter- rupting or otherwise offending the source. In moments of unbuffered reporter–source dyadic interaction, the burden of the conflict shifts. The reporter is now ambivalently caught between the source and the report- er's own employer and profession. If a fixer holds their position in the center of the triad, though, the reporter can be less ambivalent, pulled only between their news organization and their fixer. The moral distance between reporter and fixer is less than that between reporter and source.

Chains of news contributors are sometimes longer, sometimes shorter. A shorter chain depends more on the resource of time, the capacity to absorb stress, and expertise (the collection of little tactics, like nodding instead of vocally back-channeling, that can be routinely deployed). Each added link reduces the need for these resources at any one link in the chain, the moral gap between adjacent links, and so the ambivalence of each news contributor.

---

[10] See Goffman (1969: 14–22) on the parry and riposte of "control moves," in which you factor in your opponent's strategy and perspective when interpreting their actions and deciding on your own.

# *Burcu*

Fixers are not always ambivalent. Sometimes one side of the triad holds greater sway over the broker, who is accordingly biased in their favor. That sway may be strengthened by one brokered party's threat of immediate sticks or promise of immediate carrots to the fixer. Or a fixer's allegiance may be swayed because of the longer-term alignment of their dispositions with either reporter or source, based on the fixer's socialization and aspirations for the future.[1] Fixers are not just reeds leaning in whichever direction the wind is currently blowing. Their deep-rooted dispositions both transcend and inform their responses to particular moments of source–reporter interaction (Bourdieu 1977: 81). These dispositions are built from personal experiences that are often part of larger trends: political movements, economic changes, mass migrations, and so forth.

I am defining **bias** more completely than journalists do. For journalists, bias means partiality toward local interests. Yet we can also think about fixers being biased in favor of journalism and against locals when they follow the prescriptions of clients even when they conflict with local prescriptions. Both insiders and outsiders are biased, just toward different scripts.[2]

Take the trajectory of Burcu, Elif's mentor at XYZ. Before she became the channel's producer, Burcu had attended an elite

---

[1] I use the term **disposition** following Pierre Bourdieu (2002: 27–29) to refer to "schemes or schemata or structures of perception, conception and action" that guide people's responses to new situations as they arise. Bourdieu refers to a person's collection of interrelated dispositions as their "habitus." Although a habitus is the product of a long period of development and often relatively static because of relatively static social conditions of that person's life, dispositions do evolve alongside changes in society and the person's place within it.

[2] On the far outsider-biased end of the spectrum, see Dabashi's (2011: 12–13) discussion of the "native informer" who assists outsiders, whether anthropologists or imperial invaders, in dominating the informer's own homeland.

English-language university in Ankara. She then lived in the United States for several years and found an entry-level editorial position at a TV news channel there in the late 1990s. She returned to Turkey fluent in English and qualified for a producer job at a Turkish TV foreign news desk. Parallel to this career, Burcu freelanced as a hobbyist fixer, not only for TV but also for radio and print clients.

Given that Burcu fixed only part-time and held a well-paid day job, foreign clients did not have much leverage to force her into siding with them when, for instance, they wanted to discuss one subject and a source wanted to discuss a different one. Nor did Burcu have much sway over her clients, as her position in Turkish TV did not automatically translate into high status or respect among foreign journalists.

Burcu recounted working with a young, ambitious reporter named Lydia on a story about domestic violence and marital rape. In an interview with one victim, Lydia probed for graphic details. She was asking, Burcu felt, the source to relive her trauma. Burcu told Lydia that she thought the interviewee was in a fragile state and that they should take it easy on such explicit questions.

"I don't need a lecture!" Lydia yelled in response. Lydia also wanted to use the interviewee's real name and an image of her in the story. Burcu had no qualms about siding with her source against her reporter. After a long argument, Burcu convinced Lydia that identifying the woman could put her in danger of "honor killing" and that the benefit to the story was not worth this risk.

After that interview, Lydia pressed Burcu to secure her access inside a women's shelter. Burcu had women's rights NGO contacts who might have given them such access, she but told Lydia it would be impossible and illegal.

"Reporters come in like a storm," Burcu told me, and leave problems in their wake for fixers to sort.

In some cases, Burcu was not much swayed by the local side of the triad, either. There were plenty of Turkish people to whom Burcu was not enchained by close social ties, a shared worldview, or much sympathy. Burcu sometimes felt detached from both client and source, tethered to the triad only by the short-term carrots and sticks of money and etiquette and a general desire to be good at her job. This configuration of relations was a recipe for stories that Burcu was later embarrassed to remember.

On one occasion, a "parachutist" (in Burcu's words) reporter named Fred dropped into Turkey knowing he wanted to do a story about Kurdish language usage. This was indeed an area of controversy: an element of Erdoğan's "Kurdish Opening" outreach to the Kurds was support for limited mother-tongue education initiatives and Kurdish language broadcasts on public TV and radio (Zeydanlıoğlu 2012). Official use of Kurdish letters was part of the debate. The letters X, Q, and W are part of Latin-alphabet Kurmanji Kurdish but not Turkish. At the time, a 1928 law making their usage illegal was still on the books, though the government planned to lift that ban.

Burcu thought it a worthy overall topic. But Fred was stubbornly resistant to Burcu's attempts to explain nuanced but important distinctions between *speaking* Kurmanji – which had been illegal until 1991 but was no longer controversial – and *official usage* of the language in election campaigns, public signage, and education.[3] Fred insisted, based on his reading of other English-language news stories before arriving in Turkey, that many Turks thought that Kurmanji should not even be spoken. He wanted to include someone saying this for his piece to "balance" the pro-Kurdish voices that Burcu found for him.

They visited several neighborhoods Burcu knew for their Turkish nationalist reputations but could not find anyone who would say they opposed fellow citizens speaking Kurdish. What Fred lacked in sway over Burcu's opinions and sympathies, he made up for with annoying persistence. Fred continued to pressure Burcu to find a source to balance the story until, with resignation, she arranged a visit to a local "Idealist Hearth" (Ülkü Ocağı), a social club for Grey Wolves. The Grey Wolves are a neo-fascist militant group connected to Turkey's Nationalist Action Party and implicated in a great deal of political violence against Kurds, Alevis, and leftists since the 1970s. Burcu used Fred's phone to call the Idealist Hearth because she did not want them to have her number. Burcu was not afraid of them personally; rather, she knew that if they got her number, they would start calling her up to make unwanted advances.

---

[3] On controversy around and perceptions of official Kurdish language use, see also White (2013: loc. 330–442) and Aydın and Özfidan (2014).

When Burcu and Fred arrived outside the club, he recognized the Grey Wolf logo on the door with surprise and asked Burcu, *Wait, are these the people who shot the pope?*

*Yes they are,* she told him. Even when a fixer lacks sway over her client, she might convince him to modify his expectations simply by showing him that his ideas conflict with reality. If Fred did not believe Burcu, she would show him that they had to visit a fringe militant group to find the opinion that he insisted was mainstream.

As it turned out, even the club members gathered were not as extreme as Fred had hoped. They agreed that it was fine to speak Kurdish privately, just not in official communications. But when pressed, one of the men did oblige with a soundbite that using Kurmanji letters was a kind of separatism and should be prosecuted. Fred was finally convinced to adjust the story's frame to focus on legalization of the controversial letters X, Q, and W.

After that interview, Fred called the Idealist Hearth number saved on his phone to follow up on details for the story. They had difficulty communicating given club members' limited English, so Fred gave them Burcu's phone number to be in touch in Turkish. As predicted, Burcu ended up getting flirtatious calls and text messages from lonely Grey Wolves.

Burcu's fixing experience, whatever its tribulations, put her on the foreign media's radar and eventually landed her a producer job in XYZ's Istanbul bureau. Her background in Turkish television, though no guarantee of status in the international press, provided her with some of the same skills and dispositions that XYZ sought, from understanding the operation of Satellite News Gathering equipment used for live broadcasts to intuiting the components of a strong soundbite.

\* \* \*

As she rose in status from a freelance fixer in the early 2000s to an XYZ staff producer in the 2010s, Burcu grew more morally disposed toward American news TV's modus operandi and worldview. Burcu became biased in favor of the norms of international journalism, which is another way of saying that she was rising in professional status and purity. As she fell into step with her foreign colleagues, Burcu also gained their trust, and with it, greater sway over what to report and how to report it. With Burcu in charge of XYZ's Turkey bureau, the channel would never run a story like Fred's Kurdish language piece.

As she went from working in the field to working in the office, Burcu was better able to avoid altogether the mini-conflicts of soundbite production and politeness that so preoccupied me as a rookie fixer. She no longer routinely dealt with sources who lacked experience with the foreign press. When Burcu arranged interviews for XYZ correspondents with politicians, technocrats, and pundits, those sources spoke soundbite-friendly English or at least were accustomed to the rhythms of consecutively interpreted conversation. They were used to cameras and microphones pointed at them. These elite sources took on the task of spinning information into conformity with foreign reporters' prescriptions and criteria for relevance and clarity, so Burcu did not need to do so herself. Given this relative harmony, Burcu could act more as catalyst than buffer.

A fixer's job is much easier when conflicts among parties can be avoided in the first place. Ideally, sources and reporters' expectations and fixers' dispositions are all pre-aligned. Good matchmaking allows everyone to behave according to mutually prescribed scripts. In that moment, the three share a moral world. The more expansive a fixer's social network and the more accurate their understanding of what clients want to take and what sources want to give, the better they can align worlds before parties ever meet.

Burcu told me that correspondents trusted her to choose sources because they knew her talent for understanding "who would give you the best quote in the smallest amount of time." It can be strategic for fixers to use the same sources repeatedly because they know what to expect from them and how to approach them for a smoothly predictable reporting process.

When her job went so smoothly that she became invisible to the parties she brokered, Burcu was a **non-person**. A non-person may be physically present but is socially absent/dead, even if they perform a role and follow the instruction of the people present (Goffman 1959: 151–153; Wadensjö 1998: 66–67; Bearman 2005: 7–11). Servants are a classic example: you need not be polite or ashamed (for example, of not being fully dressed) in front of them, and they are expected to refrain from exhibiting personal characteristics or participating in your conversations. A non-person may carry out a mechanical task but need not be scrutinized for their bias or pressured morally, because they lack agency to affect the interactions that they background.[4]

Appearance can signal non-personhood, for instance, by way of the uniform and neutral affect that turn the ideal butler, maid, doorman, or bodyguard from a distinct individual into a generic servant. Language can accomplish the same social disappearing act, as when a translator adopts another speaker's linguistic subject position (Wadensjö 1998: 111–118). As a fixer, I frequently made the mistake of inserting myself as a person at the wrong moments of interviews by adding asides like "I think he's claiming that . . ." instead of translating directly and using "I" to mean the source.

In Burcu's early fixing days, non-VIP sources she met in the field treated her as a person; they would remember her name and ask her even years later why she never came around their neighborhood anymore. But once Burcu became a producer and shifted to brokering for government officials, Burcu became a non-person by default. The process of reporting was routine enough to all parties involved that she was overlooked with little thought. Media-trained officials and clients would simply address one another through Burcu's translation, unbothered by her as a third party to their interaction.

Another broker's paradox: when there is harmony between brokered parties, it is easiest for the broker to be overlooked as a non-person because communication can proceed smoothly. Yet in these moments, it enhances the broker's prestige to be visible as a person. Burcu confessed to me that if she had any aspiration to power, it was the power of being seen as a connector between influential people inside and outside of Turkey, as someone you needed to know. She wanted status and credit, which non-persons do not get.

When conflict erupts between brokered parties, though, non-personhood is safest. Non-persons earn no credit, but neither do they receive blame. Yet in these moments of conflict, for parties who had in times of harmony been happy to keep the credit for themselves and ignore the broker, it suddenly becomes advantageous to drag the

---

[4] Personhood and non-personhood signaling are aimed at convincing your audience that you are carrying out a buffer or catalyst role, respectively. When the audience is yourself, personhood and non-personhood, respectively, correspond to what Boyer (2013: 42–45) calls "praxiological" and "mediological" self-understandings. See also Palmer (2019: 112) for an example of a fixer in Bahrain playing the non-person to avoid government trouble.

broker back into the spotlight as a person and expected ally against their adversary. So Burcu still felt the contradictory pulls of ambivalence at moments of immanent conflict between the government and XYZ.

She saw herself as taking a more measured view of the government and its alleged misdeeds from her vantage point at the channel's bureau than did fixers and foreign correspondents in the field. She sometimes acted as a moderating force, as when she intervened to re-edit Elif's video package that included speculations about electoral fraud.

Back at her university in Ankara, a feeder school for the technocratic elite, Burcu had gotten to know many future high-level bureaucrats and influential pro-government columnists. As she put it, "My classmates now are in the ruling circle." Burcu's long-standing social ties to these people were part of what made her valuable at XYZ: she could arrange interviews with senior government officials and understood their perspectives.

These government-affiliated elites might have been comfortable with the codes and rhythms of journalistic communication, but they were at odds with XYZ at the strategic level. The two sides often disagreed about how an issue ought to be framed and what information ought to be transmitted to news audiences. This conflict waxed and waned with the Turkish state's foreign relations, the election cycle, and the rise and fall of opposition movements. When conflict erupted and government officials looked for a point at which to apply pressure to XYZ, Burcu was thrust back into unwelcome visibility as a person, a recognized mediator. Government officials had more leverage over her than over her foreign colleagues.

During the 2013 Gezi Park protests, the government thought that the foreign media should follow the example of the pro-government Turkish press: either ignore the movement or balance protester-as-hero and police brutality stories with news about protesters' disorderliness and provocations. Burcu remembered a call from one of Erdoğan's close advisors protesting XYZ's coverage of the Gezi protests. "He said, 'Okay [Burcu], I'm very disappointed with you, because we were good friends back then [in university].'... At those times, they were seeing the foreign press as enemies."

Burcu recognized that such officials could punish her by revoking her privileged access to the ruling circle. She also found their complaints to be justified at times. She gave the example of a cameraperson who wanted an XYZ report to include extensive footage of police charging and beating Gezi protesters, but no footage of protesters throwing glass bottles at the police minutes earlier.

Burcu could reconcile conflicts to some extent. On the one side, she could shape XYZ coverage to be fairer (to government eyes), for example, by overruling the cameraperson about which footage would comprise the video package they sent to headquarters. On the other side, she could try to explain XYZ's position to her old schoolmates, in the hope that it would resolve the "large misunderstanding" they had about what constituted proper journalism and so change their normative prescriptions for her.

But Burcu could not reconcile conflict altogether, and when all else failed and a government contact remained angry, she would retreat into a non-person shell and say that she was "just the translator." Or she might **code-switch** and send different signals to her two audiences, so long as she could keep them linguistically and socially segregated. She might tell her source in Turkish that she agreed that her foreign colleagues had been unfair, then tell those foreign colleagues in English that her source was complaining unreasonably again.[5]

---

[5] See Goffman's (1959: 135–140) and Merton's (1976: 8, 17–19) discussions of polyvocal strategies for managing conflicting expectations.

# *Elif*

A year into her fixing career, Elif guiltily felt like her job was to *use* people, to subject them to journalists' interrogations and dehumanize them as mere bits of information. She felt exploitative in a general way when pressuring strangers into talking with her clients, but experienced a particularly knotted anxiety when introducing foreign reporters to people she knew and cared for.

Elif's moral qualms coincided with practical concerns about precious **social capital**. A person's social capital consists of their ties to others that can be used for professional or personal ends. There is little social cost to a fixer in bothering or alienating a stranger on the street; strangers are in plentiful supply and the fixer has not invested time or effort into building ties with them. Pressuring an acquaintance into contributing to a story, however, puts social capital at risk.

Scholars who study social capital have mainly focused on the ways people *accumulate* it (e.g. Bourdieu [1986] 2011: 86–88; Burt 2007), but social capital can also be *expended*. Sometimes Elif got the matchmaking just right and paired an acquaintance with a reporter, the two hit it off, and both were happy with the resultant news story. The acquaintance might even consider Elif to have done a favor by introducing them to her client.[1] But just as often, it felt like Elif was *calling in* a favor, especially when there was friction between reporter and source. If the source did not enjoy talking with her client or disapproved of the story, if Elif kept asking for their help and offering nothing in return, she could only call them so many times before they would stop answering.[2]

---

[1] See also Mears (2015: 1107–1114) on the efforts of another kind of broker, VIP party promoters, to convince attractive women that party attendance is a desirable leisure activity (a favor by the promoter) rather than unpaid sexual labor (a favor by or exploitation of the women).

[2] As a researcher, I was not above such concerns about reciprocity, about providing something of value in exchange for my subjects' participation in the

How many times Elif could call and how large a favor she could ask depended on the strength of her tie with an acquaintance. She might have only one chance to get it right with a bigshot she barely knew. In the case of her closest friends and family members, though, she might even ask for their ethically dubious collusion to make up for other gaps in her social network.

One of Elif's first gigs after her Gezi Protest initiation into fixing was for a Scandinavian lifestyle magazine. She recalled the project with embarrassed laughter. The team had written to her a few days before they arrived in Istanbul with a very specific list of demands for a story on Turkish women: Elif should find them a Kurdish intellectual lesbian, a female DJ living in poverty, and a bourgeois headscarf-wearing mother.

Demographically speaking, the third on the list was in the most plentiful supply, but in Elif's case, with her personal history and position in Turkish society and politics, that request proved the most difficult to fulfill. She located a Kurdish intellectual lesbian through activists she had met during the Gezi Park occupation and personally knew a female DJ who had at least a messy apartment. But Elif came up short on the bourgeois headscarved mom.

The magazine crew touched down at the airport and Elif panicked. She called her aunt, who was a bourgeois mother but did not ordinarily cover her hair, and asked her to play the part. When Elif arrived with the clients (none spoke a word of Turkish) at her aunt's apartment, her uncle was home and let them in, but then left before Elif's aunt arrived for the interview. While the reporting team waited in the living room, Elif began out of habit and nerves to look through the refrigerator and kitchen cupboards, helping herself to a snack. The Scandinavians were shocked at this behavior and asked if it was normal to rummage

study and losing social capital if I did not. It was a relief whenever my social ties proved to be useful to fixers working on tight deadlines. On one occasion, Elif called to say she was working with a crew from XYZ that wanted the views of Americans living in Istanbul. I referred her to a comedy troupe consisting mostly of expats, thinking that they would be more interesting than the usual tourists standing in front of the Hagia Sophia. I also hoped that the troupe would see a benefit to getting TV exposure. In the end, and after Elif coordinated with the troupe, XYZ dropped the story. I nonetheless acquired social capital for my sub-fixing: Elif was apologetic on behalf of the channel for wasting everyone's time and, I think, felt that she now *owed me* a favor. As Elif took the blame for the failure, I felt that I came out with my ties to the comedians intact as well.

through a stranger's kitchen. Elif told them *Of course! Turkish hospitality*. They were impressed. Elif's aunt eventually arrived tidily head-scarved, posed for a photo shoot, and provided the Scandinavians with responses about the reconciliation of Islam with modernity and capitalism that she and Elif had rehearsed beforehand.

In this case, Elif was able to make up for her lack of social capital (ties to a large section of Turkish society) by exploiting a strong tie to her aunt, who was willing to satisfy to Elif's prescriptions even to the point of fraud. This was just a stop-gap measure, though; Elif's ploy would breach her clients' journalistic norms if detected. Elif had to repair any fissures between the reporters' scripts and the experience that she choreographed for them. Her aunt had to be coached to satisfy the Scandinavians' expectations for a representative of the Islamic Modernist Turkish Bourgeoisie that everyone was talking about back in Northern Europe. Elif had to cover up the incongruity of her raiding the kitchen by fitting the occurrence into an Orientalist trope about hospitality in the House of Islam.

To reduce her dependence on friends and family, to increase the likelihood that she had a contact at the ready who could satisfy any client's prescription without trickery, Elif hustled to expand her social network. Whether she was rolling out her yoga mat before a class or sipping wine and half-listening to an artist friend's critique at a gallery opening, Elif was on the lookout. When she did find a prospective source, her approach mirrored a romantic seduction: appear interested but not desperate, hint at offering something they want without vulgar transactionalism, get their phone number.

The downside to her vigilance, Elif felt, was that she increasingly thought of people as sources of information: *friends* were turning into *contacts*. Her ears perked up at the mention of a potentially valuable source, and she could never quite turn off that objectifying gaze, even when she was not working on a story. Elif was ambivalently caught between two ways of considering others: as whole people or as information packets.[3]

---

[3] Malcolm (1990: 32–33) argues that every journalist-cum-artist in the business of transforming people into stories engages in a similar guilt-inducing objectification:

The look that one directs at things, both outward and inward, as an artist, is not the same as that with which one would regard the same as a man, but at once colder and more passionate. As a man, you might be well-disposed, patient,

As the strength of Elif's ties to these new contacts grew, so too did her anxieties over introducing them to client reporters. The norms of friendship increasingly tugged on her. Even if she first met someone in the course of reporting, they might go from source to friend. She might begin to feel protective of them.

Convincing a source that participation is worthwhile, only to have a reporter fail to engage, is a risk that fixers learn to consider when matchmaking. Elif's clients would sometimes ask her to contact a prospective source but then not follow through because they changed their mind or mismanaged their schedule or decided they already had enough material for the story. When this happened, Elif felt cheated. She had called in a favor, perhaps convinced the source that they would benefit from the coverage, only for the reporter to fail to uphold their end of a bargain she had so painstakingly brokered. Foreign reporters more readily cancel interviews than fixers because the former have invested less of their own effort and social capital into the pre-production work of finding and seducing sources.

Worse yet, some clients offended sources or exploited them. (Where Elif drew the line between good journalism and exploitation depended on her evolving dispositions toward journalism and toward the source in question.) One of Elif's clients, Chad, had never been to Turkey but reported on the whole world remotely from the United States. Elif would connect him with English-speaking sources to interview via telephone or Skype.

"I don't think he knows how to empathize with people," Elif told me. "It's a very awkward conversation." Chad asked obtuse, insensitive questions, and his personal social awkwardness was enhanced by his physical and moral distance from sources. Chad lived in a very different world from sources and was not exposed to the sights, sounds, and smells any reporter on the ground confronts in the course of living in a country and traveling to meet sources. Such sensory data provide reporters with a more nuanced understanding of the world of the source and bring the former into greater alignment with locals, at

loving, positive, and have a wholly uncritical inclination to look upon everything as all right, but as artist your daemon constrains you to "observe," to take note, lightning fast and with hurtful malice, of every detail that in the literary sense would be characteristic, distinctive, significant, opening insights, typifying the race, the social or the psychological mode, recording all as mercilessly as though you had no human relationship to the observed object whatever.

least on the basic level of shared perception of what is happening around them.[4] The physical distance between Chad and sources also meant that they depended on unreliable communication technology, whose spotty and often-desynchronized audio served to exacerbate misunderstandings and microlevel breaches of coding and rhythmic norms of conversation.

In one instance, Chad did not log on to Skype for an interview with a source in Diyarbakır who waited for him to call amid violent clashes between police and protesters. In the end Elif told the source, *Never mind, let's cancel, go home and stay safe.* In other cases, the way Chad conducted interviews or wrote stories drew the ire of sources. Chad's actions degraded the value of her word in vouchsafing future clients to those sources.

"After [one interview] I was like, 'I don't really wanna give my contacts to someone who I don't know [to be] a decent interviewer, because this [Chad] guy . . . like oh my God I want to punch him.'" Elif also adopted the strategy of inserting herself as a buffer between Chad and sensitive or valuable sources in order to limit the damage he could do. When it came to the best friend of the victim of a terrorist bombing, for example, Elif neglected to inform Chad that the girl could speak English. That way, Elif was the one who conducted the phone interview, providing a selective translation of responses for Chad's write-up of the story.

I'm so glad he didn't speak to that girl . . . because she, she needed – we both needed a very soft conversation. Like, I wasn't asking questions, I was just – she was just talking and I was just, you know, listening. If it were like, QUESTIONS, I think she would have freaked out.

The moral dimension of protecting sources cannot be reduced to immediate concerns for social capital: that girl would not likely be a valuable source for future stories. Rather, Elif's broader moral disposition induced feelings of protectiveness. Like anyone living in Turkey at the time, Elif feared that she or a loved one would be among the random victims of one of the increasingly frequent

---

[4] Reflecting on her first days in Istanbul, American journalist Suzy Hansen (2017: 34) noted the importance of sensory exposure for making sense of people and places: "The impact of merely seeing foreign things with my own eyes was the equivalent of reading a thousand history books. I found that I was watching life more carefully, that every nerve was alive to my environment."

terrorism attacks rocking the country. She could imagine herself in the girl's shoes but thought Chad, safe at his home office in America, lacked this capacity.

Another potential source whom Elif shielded from Chad was Rakel Dink, the widow of Hrant Dink, a prominent Armenian-Turkish journalist murdered in 2007. At that time, Hrant Dink had been on trial for "insulting Turkishness" by discussing the Armenian Genocide, and his assassination was emblematic of Turkish hardline nationalists' continued hostility toward the country's Christian minority. Elif had gotten to know Rakel at an art event, but came away deeming the latter too vulnerable and too valuable to connect with Chad:

She has this weird smile, it's like – she's lived through a lot, you know? It's very, I don't know, you can see pain on her ... I wouldn't approach her for anything that's not, that I don't – I don't think that I would approach her for anything, really. You know, if it was like a long-form documentary ... maybe then. Yeah. But these wounds are really, really deep. [I wouldn't approach her for] a two-minute story.

For routine stories, Elif learned to direct clients like Chad to local journalists as interviewees because, she said, at least the latter knew the game. She protected her friends and valuable contacts like Rakel Dink. Or in a less generous interpretation, she held them in reserve: social capital in the bank for a special project like a long-form documentary.

Elif had to balance social capital among sources with social capital among journalists. Freelance fixers like Elif are dependent on reputation, referrals, and repeat customers (Plaut and Klein 2019b: 1706). Elif risked losing or halting the growth of her social capital within the field of journalism whenever she disappointed a reporter by failing to connect them with desired sources.[5]

Fixers conceive hierarchies of sources by value and of clients by trustworthiness and prestige, pairing only trustworthy reporters with valued sources. When a reporter has no history of working with a fixer or arrives

[5] Moon (2019) provides a case study of Rwandan journalists working in the international media similarly caught in a bind between the prescriptions of their employers and of the state. Some of these journalists sacrificed social capital locally for cultural capital in the field of international journalism by reporting critically in ways that burned bridges with government sources but secured their reputations among foreign colleagues.

without a solid colleague referral, an experienced fixer will hesitate. They profile the client, factoring in both the news organization's reputation and stereotypes of reporter types: the clueless parachutist, the cut-throat young freelancer, the sleazy tele-tabloid producer, the warzone adrenaline junkie. The fixer will not stick their neck out by introducing a valued source to an unknown client reporting for a minor outlet who fits the wrong stereotype. (The same goes for a valued sub-fixer.)

\* \* \*

Even when Elif aligned dispositionally with client reporters, even when she did not particularly empathize with locals, she could be forced into temporary ambivalence by the latter's immediate coercive power. Elif' first experience with police interrogation was a clear case.

After the Soma mining disaster, Elif worked mostly for XYZ under Burcu's guidance, but she continued freelancing for others and farther afield. In summer 2014, she traveled to Kurdish-majority southeastern Turkey for the first time to assist with a documentary film.

A few months earlier, Elif had met Mahmut when reporting on the trend of young nationalist Turks getting tattoos bearing the signature of Mustafa Kemal Atatürk, founder of the Republic of Turkey. Mahmut was originally from a Kurdish village near the Iraq border, but now worked as a tattoo artist in Istanbul's swank Kadıköy district, where he found himself inking clients with a symbol, to his eyes, of ethnic Turkish chauvinism. Mahmut and Elif got along well, and she made note that he had an interesting life story and filled a gap in her social network.

When Brigitte, a French filmmaker, got in touch to ask Elif for help on a documentary about perceptions of the Turkish-PKK peace process in the Kurdish heartland, Elif thought of Mahmut. Elif first vetted Brigitte, looking up her previous work and inviting her to coffee. Brigitte may have thought that Elif just wanted more details about her project, but Elif was more broadly gauging Brigitte's understanding of the region, her cultural sensitivity, and her humility about the limits of her knowledge. Brigitte passed the test, and Elif contacted Mahmut to introduce him to Brigitte and ask if he might help arrange a trip to his home region. Elif would function as meta-fixer and English-Turkish translator; Mahmut would accompany the team as (unpaid) sub-fixer, Turkish-Kurdish translator when needed, and source.

Mid-2014 was the apex of the Turkish-Kurdish peace process. Hope was high and violence low in the southeast, though the peace process was still on shaky ground. Conciliatory rhetoric and gestures between the Turkish government and imprisoned PKK leader Abdullah Öcalan had yet to be backed by legislation or any official accord (Tezcür and Besaw 2016; Hakyemez 2017).

In this environment of tense and tentative optimism, Brigitte, Elif, and Mahmut traveled to Şırnak Province. The area, bordered by both Syria and Iraq, had often been a hotspot of conflict. Security forces still had a heavy presence. The team interviewed pro-government Kurdish village guards, PKK supporters, and children who had grown up with a slow-burning insurgency always in the background. They asked about the peace process and about the upcoming presidential election, in which charismatic young Kurdish candidate Selahattin Demirtaş was running but posed little threat to Erdoğan (who went on to win the presidency in August).

They were chatting with village kids and taking photos when police approached and invited them to their station for a chat. Unbeknownst to the team, who thought they were just capturing the beautifully rugged landscape in the background of their selfies, there was a gendarmerie installation in the distance that they now stood accused of illegally photographing.

The police demanded to see photos and footage. Brigitte had thankfully had the foresight to transfer footage of pro-PKK interviewees to a hard drive left in their hotel room, so there was nothing to get them in trouble on her camera's memory card. These officers were not sources per se, but Elif nonetheless found herself as a buffer between them and Brigitte, if not a puppet through whom they spoke to the French documentarian as ventriloquists.

"[T]hey focused on [Brigitte] because [she]'s foreign, you know? And they were very – it was very peculiar. I mean, they said very strange things. ... They asked [her] – and I have to translate this ... the police were saying these very bizarre things like, 'Are you a spy?' And I would have to say, like, '[Brigitte] are you a spy?'" Elif laughed and face-palmed remembering it. They also lectured Brigitte about PKK terrorism and, while at it, European heartlessness toward Syrian refugees, with Elif serving uncomfortably as translator.

I had to translate and it felt so gross for those words to be coming out of my mouth, because they were saying, "You know, these terrorists," talking about the PKK. ... He was kind of equating ISIS to the PKK. And it was just [a] bizarre kind of train of thought in this mentality, [so] it was kind of weird coming from my mouth, I guess. Apparently I wasn't very good at hiding my expressions while they were saying this, 'cause [Brigitte] was like "You, you just look shocked." And I *was* shocked! I was like "*What*?!"

Elif was not *psychologically* ambivalent. In her mind, she was on Brigitte's side: she saw the trip to the police station as a waste of time and viewed their interrogator's questions about the refugee crisis and accusations of Brigitte's espionage as respectively irrelevant and ludicrous. Elif was nonetheless *sociologically* ambivalent: pulled in one direction by her understanding of the world but in a different one by the power of the police. She felt compelled in the situation to function as an avatar for the police and speak their words with her own mouth: *terrorist, spy.*

Elif nonetheless reflexively adopted a behavior that served to salvage her moral standing in Brigitte's eyes. Her look of shock signaled, intentionally or not, to Brigitte that Elif was in no danger of taking their interrogators' side, of wondering herself whether Brigitte was a spy. Such tactics for managing sociological ambivalence are not necessarily cold-bloodedly calculated or even conscious. Rather, a person's immediate, improvised reaction to a novel situation is patterned by their longer-term dispositions, which provide them with cultural and emotional tools to confront threats to their moral standing (Swidler 1986; Bourdieu 2002: 30–31).[6] Elif's dispositions conditioned her to automatically find a middle ground between competing prescriptions: translate the words of the police, but look shocked while so doing.[7]

Ultimately, the police treated them to colas and let them go. "Yeah. It's nice to be non-threatening, white-complexion female," Elif reflected with another laugh. Kurdish, dark-complexion male Mahmut was interrogated separately and more sternly.

---

[6] "Moral standing" here is synonymous with "face" in Goffman's (1967) writing.
[7] See also Katz (1999) on how emotional responses like tears or spikes of rage, though they may feel to us as if they are acting on us as an outside force, can strategically serve to protect us from various threats to our own and others' sense of our worth and membership in a community. We generally think of strategy as based on intention, which makes it difficult to discuss emotive signaling as wholly strategic. If we redefine **strategy** simply as action that efficiently completes a task, though, we can discuss our characters' behaviors without assumptions about intention and agency.

# Nur

For Elif, a police interrogation was a frightening new experience. But Nur and other Kurdish fixers in the southeast considered state security forces as a fourth party ever in the background of their interactions with reporters and sources. No mere dyad or triad but a **tetrad** of fraught relations complicated Nur's moral world.

She complained to me that journalists who failed to consider that her phone was likely tapped would call and ask stupid things like, *Do you know protest organizers?* or *Do you know people in Qandil?*[1] Nur had those contacts but would never admit as much over the phone. Her response would balance reporters' expectations against the danger of incriminating herself: *No, I don't know such people, but maybe if we walk around we might run into them.* They would discuss sources further in person.

Nur was not paranoid. Evidence of contact with the PKK was used during the 2010s in the prosecution of Kurdish domestic press journalists on charges of membership in a terrorist organization. Rights advocates and the defendant journalists argued that evidence drawn from wiretaps and intercepted emails showed nothing more than journalistic work: they had contacted PKK affiliates as news sources (HRW 2011; Karakaş 2019). The panoptic state prescribed that locals, journalists or not, avoid connection to the PKK and enforced that prescription through surveillance and prosecution. That expectation clashed with clients' script to prearrange reporting by phone before arrival in Diyarbakır.

When walking around town and talking face-to-face, Nur still had to balance reporters' desires against the prospect of state surveillance. Clients, especially television reporters for whom visual background was important, liked talking to people in the street and alongside events like political rallies. The sight of a foreign journalist or TV crew

---

[1] The Qandil Mountains in Iraqi Kurdistan are the site of the PKK's headquarters.

conducting an interview would draw a crowd, which could attract the attention of the plainclothes police and intelligence officers who monitored Diyarbakır's public spaces. Nur tried to offer advantageous alternatives to the street, more private spots to meet interviewees that still satisfied her clients' need to present themselves to foreign viewers in an adventurous setting, such as a sixteenth-century caravanserai inn or the Dengbêj House of Kurdish balladry.

Beyond Diyarbakır, Nur frequently reported from nearby towns that had taken in large numbers of Syrian refugees. In the settings of both rural towns and urban slums, Nur also had to manage the decentralized, nothing-better-to-do surveillance of the suspicious elderly and the mischievous young. These fourth parties were, at least, easier to align to her interests than was the Turkish state.

When Nur led a client through a dodgy area, a posse of boys would often follow them. Nur learned that the best solution was to call over the biggest one and appoint him her team's security guard, thus co-opting a group who might otherwise have started throwing rocks at the foreigner for sport. Sometimes Nur paid the bully in candy; other times a grown-up granting the boy the dizzying authority to cow his peers into obedience was payment enough.

When covering fast-paced and large-scale events, co-optation was not an option. Equally impractical were strategies of audience segregation or non-personhood signaling. Nur's usual strategy was to instead signal neutrality.

At political demonstrations, for instance, protesters would cluster together in a mass, a stone's throw from a phalanx of riot police. Nur learned to position herself and her clients in the middle between the police side and, in her words, "society's side." Nur *had* to stand somewhere; she could not be a non-person in a situation where the location of one's body signaled membership in one faction or the other, and she could not send discrete signals to protestors and to police as they faced off in a public square.

When Nur positioned her team in the middle, demonstrators would not think they were associating with the police (as opposed to journalists from the Turkish national media who stood behind the police phalanx). The police would not think her team was part of the rally when they moved in shield formation to disperse the crowd with batons. The downside of being in the middle was that gas canisters, paintballs (to later identify troublemakers), and rubber bullets would whizz past Nur and her clients in one direction and bottles and rocks in the other. Not picking a side is dangerous.

She ran into less trouble shepherding foreign reporters when they came alone than when they were accompanied by ethnic Turkish colleagues. On one occasion, a TV crew arrived with a Turkish cameraperson who looked like a cop behind his aviator sunglasses. Some demonstrators noticed him discretely filming them, beat him up, and smashed his camera before Nur came to his rescue. She managed to convince the attackers, whom she addressed in Kurdish as *"hevalên"* (comrades), that the cameraperson was helping her get the Kurdish Movement's message out to the world.

Conflict does not always amplify steadily along the spectrum from local to global. Turkish journalists were more local than their foreign counterparts, but many Kurdish sources were more hostile to local enemies than to foreign guests, particularly once the United States and some European governments began to support their Kurdish comrades in Syria against ISIS.

Nur's Kurmanji (the Kurdish dialect primarily spoken in Turkey and Syria) abilities were key to mollifying suspicious Kurdish nationalists. She spoke with self-conscious purity – sophisticated grammar and minimal Turkish borrow words – that functioned as a shibboleth for her membership in the Kurdish community.[2]

One of Nur's clients even remembered a source apologizing, embarrassed but admiring, that their Kurmanji could not keep up with hers. They asked to continue the interview in Turkish. If Nur's intention was merely to facilitate communication, it would seem odd for her to speak Kurdish to sources who had been educated in Turkish schools and were better able to address complex topics in that language. But Nur was not just communicating the messages her clients wanted translated; she was also signaling her consummate membership in the sources' ethnic group.

\*\*\*

---

[2] A **shibboleth** is the opposite of a stigma: a qualifying signal that is difficult to mimic. The word "shibboleth" has a biblical origin in a story (to today's reader, about murdering refugees for not assimilating culturally) in which Gileadites made suspected Ephraimites say the word "shibboleth," Hebrew for an ear of corn, and killed them if they mispronounced it. (Judges 12:6). The difficulty anyone who was not born and raised Gileadite typically had pronouncing the word made it a valuable signal to evaluate who was really on their side and who was a mimic. See also Gambetta and Hamill (2005) on signaling and mimicry.

In the first half of 2014, the self-proclaimed Islamic State shocked the world with a blitz that captured Raqqa in Syria and Fallujah, Mosul, and Tikrit in Iraq. In September, now equipped with American-made heavy weaponry and armor captured when the Iraqi National Army fled Mosul without a fight, ISIS launched a major offensive against the Syrian-Kurdish enclave of Rojava. The region had been under the control of the Democratic Unity Party (abbreviated PYD from *Partiya Yekîtiya Demokrat*) since 2012 in an uneasy and inconsistent ceasefire with both the Assad regime and other Syrian rebel groups. Turkish officials justifiably regarded the PYD and its militias, the People's Protection Units (YPG) and all-female Women's Protection Units (YPJ), as the Syrian wing of the PKK.[3]

The Turkish government worried that an autonomous Rojava would be a haven for the PKK and inspire further separatism among Turkey's own Kurdish population (Catar 2015). When ISIS gained ground in Rojava and launched a large-scale offensive against the small border city of Kobani in September, the PKK rushed to send reinforcements from Turkey and northern Iraq to their Syrian comrades while Turkish forces stationed along the border stood by, watching the siege unfold. The Kurds widely believed Turkey to be supporting ISIS, an accusation lent credence by reports that Turkish guards were giving a harder time at the border to Kurds crossing to fight or provide aid in Kobani than to Syrian and foreign jihadists crossing to join ISIS (Filkins 2014; Letsch 2014; Stein 2014). Turkish–Kurdish relations were intertwined now more than ever with events in Syria.

In Suruç, the Turkish town just across the border from besieged Kobani, Nur had her first extended experience with pack journalism. Journalists both foreign and domestic clustered in the town and often went out in groups to report. İsmet, Nur's mentor, flew in from the Persian Gulf to cover the battle. When the United States came to the beleaguered Kurds' aid with airstrikes, yet more journalists arrived in Suruç.

With so many journalists in town, fixers from across the country had the opportunity to meet, establish new meta- and sub-fixer relationships, and even develop group solidarity. Nur and İsmet joined with other fixers to organize an ad hoc charity to share some of their

---

[3] The YPG-YPJ would become the main component of the Syrian Democratic Forces (SDF) with the inclusion of some allied militias.

earnings with refugees. The fixers also compared notes about which foreign reporters were knowledgeable or ignorant, ethical or exploitative, generous or petty, giving them nicknames like Cheapo or Sleazeball.

Nigel, a British photographer who hired Nur, was Sleazeball. He was a freelancer and, Nur told me, ruthlessly ambitious. He wanted to use Nur's connections to sneak them into Kobani, but Nur refused, worried that the Turkish authorities would treat her as a YPJ fighter if they were caught crossing the border in either direction.

Then Nigel had the idea of giving inexpensive cameras to Kurdish youths who were sneaking back and forth across the border, smuggling aid into Kobani. They would document life near the front lines and bring pictures back to him to forward to publications. Nigel earned around £500 (then about US$800) per image, but initially paid the actual photographers nothing. Nur argued with him, and he grudgingly agreed to pay them a pittance, around 50 Turkish liras (then about US$20) per published image. In Nur's view, these kids were doing Nigel's job for him. Nigel maintained that because they were citizen journalists and activists, not professional photographers, the money he finally gave them was just charity.

"He was so disgusting. So, so disgusting," Nur told me. After that, Nur refused to work with Nigel, and she and other fixers warned sources to avoid him. They saw it as a moral mandate to act in the local interest against the nefarious outsider.

# *Elif*

Elif spent a few days covering the siege of Kobani from Suruç, where, she admitted, "I felt totally like a stranger." She traveled to the border with a TV crew from XYZ, which had become her main employer. It was Elif's first Syria-related story and just her second time in Turkey's southeast.

Although most Kurdish citizens of Turkey speak Turkish as a first or second language, the Syrian Kurds escaping the battle spoke Kurmanji alongside Arabic. Elif was unable to communicate with them directly unless they spoke English.

She recruited as her sub-fixer an enterprising Syrian-Kurdish refugee with passable English who had fled ISIS's advance (and whose future self we met in Part II trying to pass sex workers off as Syrian second wives). He called himself "Jimmy" – Elif never learned his real name – and frequented a hill outside Suruç that drew crowds for its view of Rojava. Jimmy made the rounds offering his services to the TV crews that vied for a good spot. A news network he had worked with the previous week referred him to XYZ's producer Burcu, who in turn gave Elif his phone number before the team arrived.

Every day on the hill with the view, side by side with locals watching the battle through binoculars, XYZ's correspondent did a "standup" explaining the latest developments and the cameraperson captured B-roll footage of explosions in Kobani with a telephoto lens. The daily filming routine also included shots of Turkish armored vehicles parked impassively along the border and of evacuees looking desperate behind barbed wire or among rows of identical tents or in line for a meal.

The correspondent asked Elif and Jimmy to find an interesting refugee to interview for a special feature. Elif's utility in this case was not as a translator: Jimmy spoke English and prospective sources did not speak Turkish. Rather, the correspondent trusted Elif over Jimmy to gauge newsworthiness and pre-align sources to XYZ's prescriptions.

Elif and Jimmy walked around a neighborhood that Jimmy knew had taken in many Kobani evacuees, peeking into windows and yards. Through an ajar door, they found a family seated on floor pillows speaking Kurmanji and invited themselves in. The family had just come from Kobani and, as a huge bonus, one of the daughters had been a YPJ fighter and was recovering from a battle wound.

It took some time to convince the family to allow them to return with a correspondent, producer, and cameraperson to interview the young woman. As Jimmy mediated between the family and Elif, she grew increasingly irritated with him.

ELIF:     We were like sitting with the family, trying to convince them, and you know he wasn't listening to me. He had this like arrogance.

NOAH:    [Jimmy] wasn't listening?

ELIF:     Yeah. He had this like very patronizing style towards this family as well. I was really uncomfortable with [the situation]. I don't think he was translating properly. But somehow we got the interview.

NOAH:    What gave you the feeling – do you remember? – that he wasn't translating properly?

ELIF:     Just the way he sat. It was very – like when I'm in that room as a [stranger], you know, I don't want to impose. I'll make myself as quiet and respectful as possible. But he was just kind of lounging and like, you know, Kurdish Man. And maybe it's a male thing. ... Me and [the young YPJ fighter], we were like always very quiet. And it was important for me for her to be comfortable with me. And she was.

This sit-down with the family was not only meant to secure consent, but also functioned as a "pre-interview." The pre-interview is a staple of TV and some radio journalism, which demand brief soundbites that summarize issues to unfamiliar foreign audiences and often feature high-status hosts who do not dally long with sources. Fixers and producers familiarize sources with the rhythms and informational prescriptions of journalism, coach them on how to encode their answers as soundbites, and figure out what they can offer to fit the story's frame.[1] After Elif pre-interviewed the family, she consulted with

---

[1]  To use vocabulary that will be clarified in Part IV, the pre-interview is a technique of efficiency, boosting sources' signal-to-noise ratios to ensure that they will transmit information that fits the news organization's frame. As with other techniques that enhance signal as defined by reporters' preexisting scripts, the

her foreign correspondent, coaching him on what to ask and how to ask it in order to elicit the most newsworthy responses.

When it came to the actual interview with the correspondent the next day, Elif again grew frustrated with Jimmy's performance. Rather than playing the non-person, minimizing his presence to maximize the impression of direct communication between the correspondent and the family, Jimmy inserted himself into the conversation. He spoke and carried himself as a person, against his prescribed role as sub-fixer.

[The fighter] was very timid until we asked her about what it means to be a female fighter for the YPG [*sic*], what it means for Kurds, and she gave us her standard, doctrinized answer that was very strong, and that was interesting. So I was kind of sitting outside the ... room, and [Jimmy] was sitting to the side. And ... he was interrupting her. But you, you shouldn't interrupt, right? 'Cause you need the soundbite. So then we told him, "Shh, don't interrupt, and just give us a summary later."

Elif and the correspondent privately agreed that they did not trust Jimmy's translation. XYZ paid another Kurdish translator to check his work. They distrusted Jimmy not because they understood any Kurdish or because his translations seemed inconsistent or incoherent, but because of his style of interruption and his body language. When a fixer jumps in smoothly at the end of a soundbite to translate, their intervention is less visible. Fixers interrupted sources routinely and necessarily in every bilingual interview that I transcribed during the observational portion of my research. Jimmy did not breach protocol by interrupting per se, but by doing so artlessly, violating the prescription for the capture of audio amenable to a clean edit.

Jimmy made himself visible through the rhythms of his speech. Not only that, Jimmy *lounged* and imposed himself physically as the center of attention, asserting his presence and personhood in the interaction,

cost of the pre-interview is that it eliminates the "noise" of unrehearsed and surprising responses that might productively lead reporters in new directions. Latour (1988a: 307–308) refers to such work, priming actors to behave in prescribed ways before they come into interaction, as "pre-inscription." Alignment through pre-inscription minimizes conflict among participants and decreases their awareness of the brokerage process altogether.

as well as his insider status as a member of the Syrian-Kurdish family's community. Elif feared that Jimmy was pushing their journalism in a propagandistic direction as he translated their source's replies to be well-worn YPJ slogans. As the second translator later confirmed, though, the young fighter did not need Jimmy's help; she was indeed toeing the party line in her original responses.

# *José and Zeynep*

José also covered the siege of Kobani. The young reporter was now a stringer: he had an informal agreement to regularly provide content to an American news website, which even provided him a modest travel and expense budget when the story was big enough. The Kobani story was huge, and in October José headed to the border with an Istanbul fixer named Zeynep. Elif was his first choice, but she was already engaged by XYZ. The channel paid her more than José could dream to. José chose Zeynep next because, though not Kurdish herself, she was a leftist grad student activist who seemed to strike the right insider-outsider balance for the story. When the two had previously collaborated, Zeynep had demonstrated an educated fluency in engaging with Kurdish Movement sources and deciphering their codes and allusions for José, while still adopting a critical distance when she and José discussed the PKK conflict. By contrast, José complained to me, others of his growing stable of novice and budget fixers lacked the sensitivity and even self-awareness to assist him on Kurdish issues.

On one occasion, he interviewed a Kurdish writer who had spent time imprisoned on terrorism charges. José called the source using Skype, with a journalism student named Pınar beside him as translator. During the interview, José noticed the Kurdish writer bristle when asked about the PKK, and from there on the answers seemed terser and stiffer. After they hung up, Pınar apologized to José. She confessed that she had pronounced PKK as *pekaka* out of force of habit and kept failing to catch herself doing so despite noticing the interviewee's reaction.

There is no politically neutral pronunciation for the acronym PKK in Turkish.[1] *Pekeke* is the respectful way to pronounce the acronym;

---

[1] One could also say that the neutrality of political terms' pronunciation is in the ideology of the listener (Hall 1981). If a fixer uses the pronunciation *pekeke* to refer to the Kurdish militant organization, the phonemes might pass through the ear of a Kurdish interviewee unnoticed as a neutral signifier, but a Turkish

*pek̲ak̲a* includes the sound *kaka*, as in excrement, as a petty deroga-
tion, and more importantly is the favored pronunciation of the ethno-
nationalist Turkish state. *Pek̲ak̲a* was how Pýnar had learned to say it
in public school, and she had trouble breaking that ingrained coding
bias, which the interviewee interpreted as reflecting a political bias.[2]

When José invited Zeynep to accompany him to Suruç, she enthu-
siastically assented. She wanted to see for herself what seemed a heroic
last stand. Zeynep's leftist and anti-nationalist political disposition
corresponded to a sympathy for the Kurdish cause, particularly as
the PYD was branding its Rojava canton as a radical experiment in
grassroots "democratic confederalism."[3] It was also easy to root
against ISIS.

Whatever her enthusiasm, Zeynep did not speak Kurmanji or
Arabic. Before she and José flew to Antep, the largest nearby city,
Zeynep contacted the local office of the HDP, a Kurdish-leftist political
party considered by Turkish nationalists to be a PKK front. She asked
if they could recommend a driver who spoke good Kurmanji. Zeynep
had learned from previous experience that the HDP, eager for international sympathy, was the most responsive of Turkey's political
parties to the foreign press. She spoke to three drivers that the party
had recommended and selected the one who she intuited was the most
politically connected and who spoke in what she recognized as PKK
lingo. She hoped that having a Kurdish Movement insider with her
would help open new doors.

Zeynep proudly recalled to me that they were able to get far better
access in Suruç than the Turkish domestic news teams (excepting
Turkish-Kurdish news outlets), whom the locals viewed as anti-
Kurdish propagandists. After several days of asking around, Zeynep

---

nationalist would mark that same pronunciation as a signal of
terrorist sympathies.
[2] The Syrian Civil War gave rise to similar shibboleths and litmus tests. Syrian-
American reporter Nour Malas (2019: 85) notes, "Only a straight-up rebel
supporter, some would say, would still refer to the conflict as a 'revolution.'
Regime backers tended to call it 'the war,' while those in the hazy area between
the regime and its opponents reverted to the conspicuously broad term 'the
events.'"
[3] Reports on PYD/SDF intolerance of dissent and expulsions of local Arabs have
suggested a gap between claims of a radical experiment in pluralist democracy
and "libertarian municipalism" to international audiences and a more
authoritarian reality on the ground (Amnesty International 2015; Yassin-Kassab
and Al-Shami 2016: 73–75; Gutman 2017a, 2017b).

and the driver were able to find a young Turkish-Kurdish man planning to sneak across the border to join the YPG and fight ISIS. She let the driver do the convincing. He addressed the fighter as *comrade* and stressed that the HDP had endorsed their reporting trip. The fighter agreed to an interview.

At this point, Zeynep took over and arranged a meeting with José in the latter's hotel room. With just José and her present, she reasoned, their source would feel less pressure to stick to Kurdish Movement orthodoxy than if the driver were present as an HDP minder (one danger of employing an insider broker). Nonetheless, it took some time to get the fighter past sloganeering. Zeynep had heard the stock phrases before from leftist media and Kurdish friends, and so could tell José when they needed to push further to get something original. José gladly allowed Zeynep to ask her own questions as well, and she directed the interview to the young man's family life, his hopes and fears.

This change of direction, from the big-picture political to the intimately personal, reconciled a tacit conflict. José wanted a fresh and detailed take on the YPG, while the fighter wanted to ritually reaffirm the YPG's official narrative. By personalizing the interview, Zeynep found less contentious ground for interaction, a trading zone where the fighter could provide something that José would accept as story material.

José's Turkish had come along to the point where he could roughly follow exchanges between Zeynep and the fighter. He was pleased to note that Zeynep always pronounced PKK as *pekeke* to signal solidarity with their source.

Reporters are not necessarily naïve to the utility of fixers presenting themselves as sources' allies, even against the fixers' own clients. Reporters and fixers can form teams in something resembling a good-cop-bad-cop routine. The fixer is the good cop, encouraging the source as a friend to tell their side of the story; the reporter is the bad cop, pressing for information but placable if the source cooperates with the fixer.[4]

---

[4] I use the **teams** in the sense introduced by Goffman (1959: 77–105). Murrell (2015) describes similar phenomena as reporter and fixer team members borrowing one another's cultural and embodied capital. Teaming up in this way is particularly demanding of trust between reporter and fixer. Fixers can unwittingly play good cop, convincing a source to engage and then feel betrayed or guilty if a story is published that breaches the source's strategic prescription.

The fighter left for Kobani soon thereafter but clandestinely crossed back into Suruç several times while Zeynep and José were in town. He would give them updates on the battle while charging his phone batteries in her hotel room.

José's story about the young fighter attracted approving attention from other members of the foreign press in Suruç. One foreign journalist approached Zeynep to ask, in a friendly but pushy way, very detailed questions about the smuggling routes the YPG was using to cross the border at night. Zeynep said she had no idea, though she thought that her YPG fighter had come to trust her enough to show her those routes if she asked. Much as she dismissed widespread conspiracy theories about foreign journalists being spies, this "journalist" (she air-quoted as she recounted) raised her suspicions, and she felt protective of her source.

José and Zeynep returned to Istanbul after a couple of weeks. Once ISIS was finally driven back from Kobani in late January 2015 after months of grueling urban warfare, the young fighter likewise returned home. Having resumed life as an ordinary citizen, he was no longer a particularly valuable source, but he continued to send Zeynep messages on her phone and on social media, a mix of pro-Kurdish propaganda that he asked her to forward along to the international media and *where-are-you-what-are-you-doing?* messages that she found tiresome. She felt obliged to respond, though she gradually receded from him over the next year. "If I don't stay in touch with people I'm doing good stories with," Zeynep told me, "it's like I'm *using* them."

When it comes to the rhythms of social life as measured in months and years, yet again we find fixers managing asynchrony between foreign journalists and sources. Sources often prescribe a continuously flowing legato rhythm of interaction, the kind we are used to with personal friendships. For reporters, on the other hand, interactions with sources should either be one-offs or follow a staccato rhythm: a beat here, a beat there, another beat maybe months or years later when they next have a use for the source. Reporters covering expansive geographic and thematic beats do not have time to be constantly in touch with all their sources.

Fixers synchronize these social rhythms by keeping more regular contact with sources to smooth over client reporters' sudden appearances and disappearances. Fixers may keep in touch with sources in a conscious calculation that they will be useful in the future, but also experience a sense of moral obligation to do so.[5] Zeynep kept in touch with the YPG fighter on social media even when she was not contacting him on behalf of José or other clients. That sense of obligation did eventually fade, however. As the fighter returned to civilian life and his value as a source diminished, so did his moral sway over Zeynep.

---

[5] See also MacFarquhar and Barnard's (2016) account of *New York Times* Beirut news assistant Hwaida Saad's late-night conversations with sources in Syria ranging from government officials to Islamist fighters:

Sometimes, she feels badly about living comfortably in Beirut while her interlocutors are mired in an intractable war, but the hours online are transporting. "You live through their experiences," she said. "I do not want to be rude to them, ever – some of them have risked their lives to help me."

# *Nur*

Nur's services were in even higher demand in 2015. Perhaps the deepest ambivalence of fixers: thriving business is correlated to calamity. Reporters are drawn to events that destroy sources' lives. It can be hard to keep up a performance of objectivity and professionalism for clients while sharing sources' experience of suffering.

A parliamentary election was scheduled for June, and the Kurdish-leftist HDP was on the ascent. The party gambled on a new big-tent strategy of drawing votes from Kurdish conservatives, non-Kurdish progressives like environmentalists and LGBT voters, and other minorities including Alevis and Christians. If successful, the HDP would not only enjoy larger parliamentary representation, but also prevent the AKP from winning the majority needed for one-party rule. The loss of an AKP majority could interfere with Erdoğan's push for "reforms" meant to increase his presidential powers.

Tensions between the AKP's Syrian policies and the Kurdish–Turkish peace process had been laid bare during the siege of Kobani, as Turkish government hostility to the Kurdish YPG-YPJ seemed to trump opposition to ISIS. Now the HDP's electoral threat further reduced the government's interest in the peace process, which seemed to be bolstering HDP popularity. Erdoğan cut off talks with imprisoned PKK leader Abdullah Öcalan and returned him to solitary confinement (George 2018). Multiple HDP rallies and offices were targeted in arson, bombing, and gun attacks during the campaign season. Perpetrators were never caught or, HDP supporters argued, even seriously pursued.

In addition to this emergent conflict, commemoration of past violence occupied much of Nur's schedule. 2015 marked the 100th anniversary of the Armenian Genocide, perpetrated mainly in what is now eastern Turkey by Ottoman troops and Kurdish auxiliaries during World War I against the empire's largest Christian minority (Akçam [1999] 2006).

Nur was unceasingly busy reporting on southeastern Turkey's hopes, fears, and memories. There were few other well-reputed fixers with extensive regional contacts. One competitor would tweet moderately in English but then rant in Turkish about his clients being *fucking Jews and Christians and spies*. Code-switching on Twitter to segregate audiences was ineffective: meta-fixers in Istanbul and Ankara read those Turkish tweets and avoided sending clients his way, and even monolingual foreign reporters could get the gist of his messages through automated translation.

When foreign reporters travel outside of Istanbul, they like to maximize their story-to-cost efficiency. Clients visiting Diyarbakır would ask Nur to help them cover the election campaign, genocide anniversary, and Syrian refugee crisis all in the space of a few days. Nur maximized her own efficiency by returning repeatedly to the same sources.

Reporters do not necessarily mind fixers recycling contacts. On the one hand, it challenges the reporters' sense of adventure into the unknown and their public claim to provide unique information. On the other hand, it can make their work easier.

Alison, the American journalist who first recruited Nur as a fixer four years earlier, returned to Diyarbakır that spring. Nur matched her to a source who was investigating his Armenian heritage. A taboo-breaking trend was on the rise of citizens opening up about or exploring their politically fraught ancestries. During the genocide, families hid their Armenian identity to survive; Armenian orphans were adopted and raised Muslim (Çetin 2012).

Nur's source had pieced together bloodlines from archival records and found long-lost Armenian relatives online. Nur had interviewed him enough times to be familiar with his story and to address him as a friend. Alison was aware that he had already appeared in the stories of major American and British news outlets, but, she told me, "It was fine, because every story had a different flavor." Alison was interested in a personal profile, whereas previous reporters had taken a more explicitly political angle.

In fact, Alison found Nur's familiarity with the source to be an asset: "[She] was really comfortable and knew what to ask, knew how to ask it, and was like, 'Hey hey hey, explain this thing. … This thing that I already know about.' Like, 'Hey, this is a good … story; why don't you tell [Alison] about this?'"

Nur's repeated contact with sources, Alison told me, provided the team with the advantages of longer-term reporting even though she was only in town a few days:

I've interviewed people more than once for the same story and knew much better what to ask the second time around or the third time around. ... It could shape stuff, yeah. Because maybe I would have never learned this thing about [the source], had [Nur] not been like – had [she] not known about it already. Maybe it would never have come up in our conversation.

Even as she acknowledged the benefits, Alison was ambivalent about the way Nur recycled some other sources. It quickly became apparent to Alison that the effects of overwork were catching up with her fixer. Alison had found it a delight to work with Nur on previous Diyarbakır visits, but now Nur seemed to be almost on autopilot.

"[Nur is] like, 'Okay, I'm burning out. These are the story ideas I have. Let's go.' And it doesn't work for everyone. And having the same story over and over and over in the media is also not necessarily a good idea." It was one thing to revisit familiar sources to produce new stories with new flavors, but the very pace of Nur's work, Alison worried, was homogenizing coverage of the region.

When Nur took Alison to meet a Syrian-Armenian refugee who spoke Kurmanji, Alison got the uncomfortable impression that Nur had been using and re-using the woman to the point of exploitation:

It sounded like she had been interviewed, like [Nur] had taken a few people to interview her. But [the refugee woman] was just exhausted. She was hopeless. Like her kids – one of her kids didn't remember how to read. She was just really desperate to get out. And so she had come, like [Nur] had arranged us to interview her, and it was like – I'm looking at her, and I'm like, "I don't want to interview her. This woman just needs help at this point."

Fixers are not always the ones to sway in favor of sources. Fixers may feel less empathy toward sources than do client reporters, particularly when acting as catalysts who bring parties together into direct inter-action. Alison spoke enough Arabic that she could communicate dir-ectly with their source. Meeting face-to-face, she could also read the refugee's body language, see her fatigue and struggle to care for her children. Alison, in her own moral world of competing values, weighed protecting the source more heavily than producing a story.

The pressures of overwork led Nur to shift from artisanal to mass production, cranking out an identical product for every foreign reporter who came her way. With less time to carefully assess either her client's or her source's perspectives or expectations, Nur ended up putting both into an uncomfortable situation.

\* \* \*

The HDP tallied a short-lived victory in the June 2015 general election. They received over 13 percent of the vote, and a hung parliament resulted. After the AKP failed to form a governing coalition with any of the three opposition parties, Erdoğan called for November snap elections.

On July 20, a Turkish-Kurdish ISIS suicide bomber murdered thirty-two young volunteers in Suruç on their way to assist Kobani's reconstruction. Two days later, two police officers were found dead in the nearby town of Ceylanpınar. The government blamed the PKK.[1] The ceasefire and peace process collapsed. Erdoğan ramped up hardline rhetoric and blamed the HDP for PKK terrorism, courting rightwing Nationalist Action Party voters and undermining the HDP's cross-ethnic and conservative Kurdish support. The strategy paid off: the AKP would go on to regain its parliamentary majority in November.

Geert, the Belgian reporter, returned to Diyarbakır to do a story with Nur on resurgent violence and the PKK's connections with the Syrian Kurds. The latter subject was a touchy one, as the United States had adopted the YPG and YPJ militias as proxies to fight ISIS in Syria and Europe powers were flirting with the idea of following suit, even as the PKK remained on the US State Department's and European Union's lists of terrorist organizations. The Syrian Kurds and Americans were at pains to represent the Turkish PKK and Syrian YPG-YPJ as separate, while Turkey demanded its NATO ally stop providing support for what it considered a single Kurdish terror group. This contradiction became an even larger problem for international relations when fighting renewed between the PKK and the Turkish state.

---

[1] The circumstances of the Ceylanpınar murders remain mysterious. Different branches of the PKK issued contradictory statements as to whether the killings were authorized retaliations for the Suruç bombing. Nine Kurdish suspects were acquitted for lack of evidence in 2019, fanning the flames of speculation that the murders were part of a conspiracy by ISIS and/or elements within the Turkish state to sabotage the Turkish–Kurdish peace process (Hoffman 2019).

Geert had worked with Nur in the past and admired her profession-alism. But the collapse of peace was evidently striking a nerve with Nur that was perhaps all the rawer because of the exhausting schedule that she had maintained for months. Geert still appreciated her ability to make Kurdish Movement sources comfortable, but he was concerned that she was acting *too* close to them. He began to lose trust that Nur could restrain her activist self when the stakes were so high.

Geert recounted interviewing a woman who ran an organization that commemorated PKK "martyrs." A strategic and framing conflict quickly became apparent: the source wanted to focus on the plight of the Kurdish people and righteousness of the PKK's cause, but Geert wanted to know about overlap between the PKK and Syrian Kurdish militias.

I was like, "How many martyrs do you have from the YPG-YPJ?" I wanted to know, "Out of your family of martyrs, how many are ... PKK martyrs, and how many of them are YPG-YPJ?" And she didn't want to answer that question. But I'm used to having people offended by my questions. So I reformulate and I come at it from different angles.

The question was an extremely sensitive one because admitting that this Turkish-Kurdish organization was linked to Kurdish fighters in Syria would belie the claim that the YPG-YPJ was a separate entity from the PKK and so eligible for American and European military aid.

Nur sided with the source more than Geert liked. Geert remembered that Nur started making dramatic faces at him as she translated back and forth:

"Like, '*Why* are you asking these questions five different ways? She clearly is not going – she doesn't want to answer it, and it's not correct to keep pushing.' And, you know, [Nur] felt upset that I kept pushing. And I was like, 'Just ask her, tell her I don't need to source it to her ... just like a ballpark figure ... give me a spectrum that I can work in.' Finally, what I got was that these two notebooks, these two fat note-books were full of YPG-YPJ names. That was all I could get. I had to ask eight times and [Nur] was just like," Geert imitated a petulant voice with a laugh, "'Very rude!' I'm like, 'Sorry, I'm not here to make everyone happy. Sometimes our work has to be a bit confrontational.' You're not going to be buddy-buddy with everyone you interview."

As far as Geert was concerned, it was up to him to decide what questions to ask and whether the interview was confrontational. Nur's pointed looks and side comments were an uninvited challenge to Geert's control over the conversation's framing.

In a face-to-face interview, Nur had little ability to segregate her reporter and source audiences in order to manage conflict between the two. When Geert refused to accept evasive answers, instead pressing repeatedly for information that the PKK martyr organization representative was unwilling to provide, it was impossible for Nur to simultaneously be polite with the source and satisfy Geert.

Face-to-face reporting also meant that Nur could not code-switch in her emotive signaling to convince both sources and Geert that she was on their respective sides. Later that week, when talking to the families of those killed in the most recent fighting, Geert found his work impeded by Nur's personal emotional involvement:

[Nur] gets very emotionally affected. . . . [She's] kind of on the edge of tears whenever you're working, because it's [her] people so [she]'s upset. So then in that context [she]'ll be very protective of the people who are in mourning and like, 'Don't ask them too many questions.' Or, 'Don't bother them for too long.' . . . [She]'s usually very good with the translating, but in these kind of like raw moments, [her] translations go to shit, and it's really shitty because you're like, 'I kind of need to know: is it the father or the uncle that got killed? Can we ask again?' And [she]'s just like . . .

Geert imitated Nur holding back tears. Those tears were a signal of insider-ness to the war-torn community that Nur failed to hide from Geert, and he accordingly downgraded his view of her professionalism.

\* \* \*

I was in Diyarbakır around this time, summer 2015. It was before the PKK's urban youth wing dug trenches, constructed barricades, and declared Diyarbakır's Old City an autonomous zone, and before Turkish security forces crushed the uprising and much of the district in the process, its ancient city walls offering little protection from modern siegecraft (ICG 2016a). The closest thing to combat I witnessed was teenagers throwing fireworks at a police station and then escaping down side streets when an armored vehicle gave chase. It was still safe enough to stroll the Old City in the evening and eat at street-corner grills, though every night after I returned to my hotel I would hear and smell fireworks and teargas.

I asked around at hotels, local news outlets, and the HDP mayor's office about fixers, looking to recruit new participants to my study.

One young man with a low-level municipal job said that he knew of a French journalist in town and offered to take me to a café that she frequented.

As we walked, he told me that to complete my education as a sociologist I really needed to read the books of Abdullah Öcalan and Murray Bookchin, an anarchist-communalist philosopher from whom the imprisoned PKK leader had drawn inspiration. He also confided that he was sure this French woman was a spy. Why else would she be going around asking so many questions? We got to the cafe, a leftie-intellectual hangout by the décor. It turned out that the "French" journalist-spy was none other than Nur, who at any rate was too busy for another interview with me. Even as Geert viewed Nur as too aligned with the Kurdish Movement, local Kurdish Movement sympathizers were lumping her in, nationality-wise, with her foreign clients.

A few days later, the police showed up to my hotel while I was out to inquire about a list of persons of interest that included my name. I left soon thereafter. Contact with the police, I was worried, could not only be personally unpleasant but also compromise or cut short my research.

Shortly thereafter, two British *Vice News* reporters were detained in Diyarbakır and deported. Their fixer Mohammed Rasool, an Iraqi Kurd who had attended a Gülen Movement–affiliated university, remained in detention for far longer (*Evrensel* 2017). Dutch journalist Fréderike Geerdink, the only foreign correspondent based in Diyarbakır, was detained the next week and later deported (CPJ 2015). A few months after that, American journalist David Lepeska was denied reentry into Turkey after reporting on the destruction of Diyarbakır's Old City (Lepeska 2016).

When I returned to Turkey the next spring, the east of the country was still violent and militarized enough that I decided to stay in Istanbul. That is why there will not be a Nur chapter in Part IV of this book.

# *Aziz*

Conflict between the respective interests of journalists and locals is clearest when people on whom journalists want to report would rather kill or ransom them. Between 2012 and 2014, numerous journalists were targeted by militants in Syria. Some ended up in ISIS custody. Initially, there was a blackout on media coverage of these abductions, in a later-controversial consensus that reportage could compromise negotiations for release. But in 2014, ISIS released beheading videos of freelance reporters James Foley and Steven Sotloff, which made headlines around the world (Simon 2014).

By 2015, more than eighty journalists, local and foreign, had been killed in Syria and an even larger number abducted (Mahoney 2015). The number then declined, not because Syria was getting safer, but because international news organizations had ceased sending people into the country and because so many Syrian journalists had already fled (Beiser 2015).

A year into their stay in Turkey, Leyla and her husband, Aziz, were broke. They felt obliged to support other family members stranded in Turkey but could barely afford their own living expenses. The continued influx of Syrians allowed landlords to hike apartment rents in Antep, and Leyla and Aziz needed to stay in the city for their NGO work. Aziz even took occasional under-the-table jobs as an unskilled laborer alongside other Syrians with advanced degrees and white-collar pasts.

The couple's income from helping Geert and Orhan with stories on Syrians in Turkey and long-distance reports on events within Syria helped keep them afloat. For a long time, they turned down requests from other journalists to cross the border with them for reporting trips. But eventually, ground down by manual labor and financial stress, yet also equipped with increasingly serviceable English, Aziz decided a border crossing would be worth the risk. He agreed to bring a group of reporters to Aleppo, in northern Syria, to cover the ever-grimmer regime siege of the rebel-held side of the city.

"I have good connection with Free Syrian Army," Aziz later recounted to me. "So I asked some of leaders there that like, 'A journalist want to get inside and work.' And these people I have asked, I 100% trust. So they said, 'We can provide you with a permission if you want, just for you because you are a friend of us.'"

Although Aziz described his contacts to me as from the secular FSA (managing my perceptions as he did his clients'), they were actually from an explicitly Islamist militia that intermittently cooperated and fought with the FSA and with other radical factions. A high-ranked commander wrote Aziz a letter of safe passage and offered an escort of armed fighters, which Aziz would later regret declining. Leyla stayed behind in Turkey.

The Turkey–Syria border could no longer be crossed as easily as when Leyla and Aziz had fled the previous year. Aziz's rebel/activist (the boundary was blurry) contacts referred him to a reliable smuggler who got them across the border. It was a predawn hike of four hours through the mountains until Aziz and his clients rendezvoused with their driver. The friendly commander had lent them the driver, who could navigate the front lines of Aleppo and serve as a sub-fixer guide. On the drive to the city, the team passed through frequent rebel checkpoints without problem. In the city, they stayed with a relative of Aziz still living in what he called the "liberated zone" of eastern Aleppo, dining on Syrian home cooking and smoking hookah together.

The next day, they began to drive around the city to visit places of interest that the reporters had selected from the menu Aziz and the driver put on offer. All was going well until a black van cut them off in the street. Armed men wearing black piled out and grabbed them.

"They appeared like they are kind of ISIS," Aziz remembered, estimating that it took about ten seconds for them all to be stuffed into the van with bags over their heads. "They put a knife on my neck here, and Kalashnikov like here, just here, try to scaring me," Aziz indicated a gun barrel against the side of his head.

After a long drive, the group was herded into a basement, where their captors said they would kill them all. The abductors showed no interest in Aziz's protestations that they were under the rebel commander's protection. After a few hours, the foreigners were taken in one direction and Aziz and the driver in another.

"I felt like some guilt because of my friends," Aziz later told me. "They put their trust on me, so I was very sad in that situation."

The militants released the driver after a few days, but Aziz remained behind the bars of a homemade prison cell. Initially, Aziz feared that ISIS had kidnapped them and they would all be gruesomely executed on video, if his clients had not been already. However, when his captors provided Aziz with some religious books to read, he noted that they were stamped with the logo of Jabhat al-Nusra ("The Victory Front"), Al Qaeda's affiliate in Syria.[1] This was a slightly better predicament than being held by ISIS.

AZIZ:    Nusra Front told me that I am a bad person because I – these
         journalists are enemies and I support them, which means like
         I'm a bad guy. I'm against Syria or something like this.
NOAH:    And what did you ... say to them?
AZIZ:    I said, "We are journalists. We show the people – like, other media
         inside are focusing on ISIS, on – we know that ISIS is very bad,
         but we have to focus about what Syrian regime is doing,
         bombing the Syrian people. So we have to show the world ...
         how Syrian regime bombing, how the situation is so bad. Because
         we have to show the people the truth." But they didn't believe me
         and they didn't respect.

A Nusra judge began visiting Aziz in his cell, just for a few minutes every week or so. He rejected Aziz's claims that the foreigners were journalists, saying that they were intelligence agents, and asked Aziz where exactly they had been snooping.

When reporters and locals (in this case, local captors) disagree about even the reporters' basic intentions and the kind of information they will share – a news report versus an intelligence briefing – relations turn ugly. Aziz faced judgment, in the most literal sense, as a traitor for his very association with international journalism.[2] For his part, Aziz did his best to convince the judge that his team's strategic goal aligned with those of the rebel faction: they sought to share information about the Syrian regime's war crimes.

---

[1]  The Nusra Front would in 2016 rebrand as Jabhat Fateh al-Sham and claim to
     cut ties with Al Qaeda in an effort to rehabilitate its international image.
[2]  See Smith (2019: 137–142) for the story of a fixer whom ISIS killed for "sedition"
     based on his work with foreign reporters.

The judge eventually softened his accusation. First, he allowed that Aziz was an unwitting collaborator, then that he had committed no crime. They needed to hold him in custody for a time nonetheless so that he could not talk to anyone, perhaps because of hostage negotiations taking place over the foreigners. Jabhat al-Nusra did take decent care of Aziz and prescribed him good medicine, he said: antidepressants.

After many weeks, and to his surprise, Aziz was released. They brought Aziz to a large holding cell with a mix of prisoners from the FSA, the Assad regime, and ISIS, then put him in a car and dropped him off on the shoulder of a remote highway with instructions to return directly to Turkey without talking to anyone.

Aziz hitchhiked back to Aleppo and complained to the commander who had granted his team safe passage, who Aziz said was furious at the Nusra Front. It was only later, though, that the foreign reporters' release was secured by negotiations involving multiple governments and multimillion-dollar ransoms. As far as he knew and for better or worse, Aziz's freedom was never raised as a point of interest in these negotiations.

Back in Turkey, Leyla had desperately sought to find out what happened after she lost touch with Aziz. When the driver was released, she learned the story from him and posted about it on Facebook. She received a barrage of questions from journalists, particularly from the abducted reporters' countries. Apart from reporters who already knew the couple, most foreign journalists who interviewed Leyla in these months focused on Aziz's kidnapped clients and were primarily interested in her husband insofar as they probed whether Aziz might have betrayed his clients.

There are two kinds of expectations at play when we describe fixers' moral worlds: prescriptions and predictions. **Prescriptions** are expectations of what *should* be done, what people *want* to happen. But **predictions** of what *will* happen also matter.

A fixer's prediction of whether a news organization or government will pay their ransom affects what they are willing to do for their clients. Before the Aleppo trip, Aziz had not considered that he would enjoy less international support than the reporters if something went wrong. He adjusted his expectations with experience. After he returned to Turkey, Aziz never brought another client to Syria. He and Leyla became more selective about whom they worked with, despite continued economic hardship.

The informal nature of fixing means that many of Aziz and Leyla's counterparts share a similar sense of precarity, and with it distrust. Burcu, the channel XYZ producer, understood why freelance fixers she hired would hedge their bets, not doing everything XYZ's foreign correspondents asked of them, especially in potentially violent situations. Frankly, Burcu herself did not know if the organization had those freelancers' backs.[3] The channel's Turkey bureau had yet to see a freelance fixer injured, arrested, or abducted while in their employ, but if it did happen, Burcu suspected that XYZ would offer less support than its salaried staff would enjoy.

Burcu at least made sure that fixers always got the same safety equipment as foreign correspondents: if a situation was dangerous enough that an American ought to wear a flak jacket and helmet, it was dangerous enough for a Turk or Syrian to wear them as well. She saw discrepancies in these basic provisions as unfair and criticized how news organizations treated freelance fixers.

"They're asking you to be part of the team," Burcu told me, but without providing personal injury protection or hostile environment training, as she advocated XYZ provide its fixers. She reasoned that if XYZ mitigated fixers' exposure to risk, they would trust the organization more and ultimately do better work (i.e. work that better satisfied their correspondents' and producers' prescriptions).

Burcu's advocacy of more formalized employment with greater benefits and protections for fixers aimed to increase their bias toward XYZ. Giving fixers pensions, insurance, and assurance that the company would be their ally in case of trouble would make their futures more predictable, and more closely synchronized to the organization.

---

[3] See also Pedelty's (1995: 203–207) discussion of the well-founded cautiousness of Salvadorans working for the foreign press during their country's civil war.

# Karim

When we assess risk and weigh moral pressures, we reference (consciously or not) **time maps** that chart our remembered past and predicted future (Snyder 2016: 15–17). When we consider ourselves ahead or behind on a known path based on a narrative of success that we share with our peers, we are tracing our movement through a time map. When a company standardizes a career trajectory, promising employees a path from entry level to seniority with standard salary increases and pension contributions along the way, it creates a time map for those employees. That map aligns employees to the company's moral world by making their long-term relationship with it predictable. Other time maps do not assure safe predictability but warn of dangers along the way or display terrifyingly uncharted future territory.

Reporters' and fixers' moral worlds misalign when their time maps diverge, both in long-term trajectories and in the short-term rhythms of life. Many foreign reporters follow a time map in which they depart cities within days, countries within months, regions within years. Geert's willingness to cause discomfort in Diyarbakır was influenced by his prediction that he would soon be back home in Istanbul and likely never speak to that particular source again.[1] Nur, by contrast, expected to stay in Diyarbakır and continue working as a fixer, which influenced her own discomfort with Geert's questions and protectiveness of their source. When a fixer lives on a time map that intersects only briefly with their client's, it is no surprise if the two disagree about what is right and wrong and worth the trouble.

Karim's time map, and with it his disposition toward journalism, transformed after he parted ways with German TV. Even though he

---

[1] Much criticism of journalists acting as propagandists even in the absence of overt censorship centers on their time maps. Journalists trade favorable coverage of the powerful for the future access they predict they will need to have successful careers (Herman and Chomsky 1988: 18–25).

162

was technically a staff producer, Karim's treatment by his German employers had been straightforwardly transactional and focused on the short term. He gave them Syrian content and they gave him money without asking too many questions. Journalism was a gig, not a vocation.

Then he met Sally, a Canadian print reporter who operated differently. Karim was still a regular at parties in boho-chic apartments or on Bosphorus rental yachts attended by European and North American reporters, aid workers, and a select few fixers with the right cosmopolitan dispositions (Elif was another frequent invitee). Gossip about romantic trysts flowed into arguments about politics and shop-talk about colleagues' reporting. A conversation with Sally at one these parties made Karim rethink his work with channel DDT. He confided to Sally about the hidden camera and cash-for-footage tactics of his channel, and she told him bluntly that shit like that got people killed and ruined other journalists' relationships with sources.

Sally had moved to Istanbul a year earlier after spending several years in Syria, Lebanon, and Iraq. She was committed to reporting on the Syrian civil war for the foreseeable future. She thought longer term about her relationships with both sources and fixers. When Karim left DDT and the two of them began to collaborate, Sally viewed their work as a partnership rather than a series of transactions.

Fixers ordinarily intend to stay put after journalists leave, but in this case, Sally and Karim, with little optimism about an end to the Syrian civil war, predicted that Karim would eventually move to North America or Europe as a refugee. In the meantime, Sally expected not merely to extract story content from Karim, but also to help prepare him for a career as a reporter in his own right. This predicted future tied Karim more closely to journalism and disposed him toward Sally's scripts. Karim reflected to me, "You know, when I start working with [Sally's publication], I wasn't journalist. I was fixer. But . . . [she] made me a journalist."

Sally's policy was to always inform sources: we are journalists; this is the story we are reporting; we cannot pay you. Her moral disposition swam against the tide of media money washing over the Turkey–Syria border. In 2014, journalists, including well-heeled TV crews, flooded in to report on ISIS and transformed the news economy. A new wave of fixers arose who operated on the border in à la carte fashion, charging journalists not a set day rate but a negotiated finder's fee based on the value of the source. Sally described them as "all these weird middlemen who want to be paid thousands of dollars just for like a very simple introduction."

By late 2014 and early 2015, what became Eurocentrically known as the European Refugee Crisis had become a top story, bringing more international media attention to Syrians in Turkey. Not just middlemen but also sources increasingly expected payment for their time. The explanation, according to Sally, was twofold: parachutists changed the scripts of interaction by injecting money into reporting, and asylum seekers tired of talking to journalists without seeing any evidence that coverage helped them. "By that point, it was like the refugees were asking for money, people just sitting in camps. . . . [T]hey were just like, 'This is the eighth interview that I've given, and why would I bother my time? And I really need money because, you know, I need to feed my family.'"

After the weak moral pressure to be polite has worn thin, why should anyone sacrifice their time and take the risk of allowing a stranger into their lives? What do sources get in return for engaging with journalists?

If journalists had it their way, the abstract benefit of disseminating knowledge to the world would always suffice. But sources prescribe more concrete forms of reciprocity.

Sometimes, journalists are lucky enough that chatting with an exotic foreign journalist is an adventurous reward in itself for a source or even for an ad hoc fixer. Interaction with a journalist can be a welcome disruption of the monotonous order of life. José recounted to me a trip he made to a refugee camp, during which he happened on a former English teacher who was eager to engage with him out of sheer boredom. The man spoke with José at length and then acted as an impromptu fixer. He showed José around, translated, introduced other bored refugees to his new reporter friend from America, and then refused José's offers to pay him.

What a source gets in return might also be positive coverage of them as individuals or propaganda for their cause. Some reporters and fixers explicitly promise benefits to sources. One client I fixed for made me uncomfortable by telling every source we interviewed that her story might help them personally or their cause in some way. Such a strategy of hollow promises may work for journalists when they have access to a continuous supply of new sources who never communicate with one another. It may work when a reporter's time map plots a rapid course on to the next story or the next country, and so burning bridges for themselves or their fixers costs the reporter little. But trust is built or lost over the course of repeated interactions, whether between individuals or between groups.

During the early days of the Syrian exodus, journalists promised that coverage would help. When coverage failed to deliver either a military intervention against the Assad regime or a sufficient outpouring of humanitarian support, many Syrians' trust in the foreign media broke down. They failed to see how international journalism was helping them or why they should contribute to it.

In the absence of trust, money is the universal medium of exchange for time, effort, and risk. People use money to give their prescriptions greater moral weight. Money is, after all, an important element of the reciprocal relationship between fixers and reporters. Reporters pay fixers, and in exchange, fixers provide access and sensemaking services. But in the case of brokers farther down the chain – activists, militants, or sources – exchanging money for information is considered a breach of journalistic ethics (Malas 2019: 93–96).

Caught in these **conflicts of reciprocity**, fixers get creative. Simply changing the mode and time of giving can almost magically resolve the conflict. After Elif and Jimmy interviewed the Syrian-Kurdish fighter and her refugee family in Suruç, Elif remembered,

[T]hey were like ... "Maybe you can contribute something?" So ... we went shopping. We went and bought her a nice jacket, bought them a lot of food, like lentils and rice and blahblahblah ... and it was very embarrassing. ... They were embarrassed; we were embarrassed. ... We just like walk in with all this – but I mean everyone needs food so, it's not like, you know, giving cash. You can't give cash anyway. But, you know, we did appreciate their – I mean it's not easy to – I don't understand why she would sit – like, I wouldn't ever sit down for an interview like that.

Elif was caught between two conflicting prescriptions to which she was sympathetic: "you can't give cash" vs. "maybe you can contribute something?" A gift of clothing and food *after* the interview was her way of defusing the reciprocity conflict.

The norm against checkbook journalism is not universally respected (Skjerdal 2020). European TV broadcasters routinely pay sources (Smith 2008: 134–138). The fact that they do so discretely and often delegate the task to fixers, though, demonstrates a recognition that payment breaches a professional norm.

Sally had some sympathy for the sources asking for renumeration, but not for the journalists and fixers who paid them. The influx of money impeded journalists who continued to follow the prescription to not pay sources. It also corrupted the stories produced by those who flouted the norm:

What [journalists] do is they come down [to the border] and they want like an ISIS defector. We did a story about that. They will tell the fixer that ... and the fixer will sometimes bring them a real defector for a price of, like, you know, five thousand dollars for an interview, I know one journalist paid. ... So when we were doing that story, we had a lot of wasted time. ... We always [insisted], "We're not going to pay, just so you know." And [sources would] say, "Yeah of course." [But] once we get into the interview, they're like, "Okay I'll tell you, but you have to pay." They think we're not serious.

The enormous demand for news stories about ISIS, combined with the enormous difficulty gaining access to a group whose press relations policy was murder, created perhaps the perfect storm to incentivize shoddy reporting. Karim told me that paying for interviews even led some fixers to invent in-demand sources when they had none to offer. In the case of a fixer who succeeded Karim at the German channel DDT,

"[DDT] ask him to interview a woman defected [from] ISIS. They were looking for a woman in [ISIS's all-female] Al-Khansaa Battalion. ... So this guy, he told [DDT], 'Yeah I can find this.' And he brought them his sister," Karim laughed, "and he covered her face. And he told them that she wants 500 dollar. And they said, 'Okay we'll pay her.' And they paid 500. He took the 500 and ... just ask people in ISIS region, 'Okay, what they do? Woman in Al-Khansaa Battalion, what they do usually?' And they say, 'Okay, they do this and this and this.' So he told his sister, 'You have to say this and this.' It's a true information, but yeah. And he got the money."

Syrian refugee-fixers in Turkey were, to be fair, living on time maps of extreme economic and political precarity. When news organizations cut deals with those fixers as one-off transactions without any promise of a future for them in journalism, when clients did not probe deeply into sources' stories or their relationships with fixers, it made sense for those fixers to extract as much immediate cash as possible and cut whatever corners they needed to along the way. Journalistic norms did not weigh heavily on fixers when their clients made audience segregation and information control easy for them, while expending little effort to train or develop lasting professional relationships with them.

Sally told me the problem of fabrication was widespread:

I can point you to any number of [stories] where – even [in] American TV media – where I know it's fake, and I know the fixer faked it. And I know it's because ... people just come, they tell the fixer to make all the contacts, and then they just do the interview and they leave, and in that story – I mean, you never see the fixer's name or anything.

My discussion of morality so far has presumed that reporters *want* the fixers they hire to adhere to their prescriptions for moral behavior. But viewed in a different light, fixers function as a useful corruption buffer to whom reporters delegate not only access and sensemaking but also the breach of journalistic norms. This arrangement is another way in which reporters and fixers can form collusive teams, not against sources but against journalistic ethics.

Reporters look the other way while fixers pay sources and recruit actors to play the parts that reporters want cast. In these cases, fixers are not under pressure to uphold ethical standards of journalism. Rather, clients hire fixers precisely *to* breach their moral scripts so that the clients do not have to get their own hands dirty.[2] Prominent reporters have built their careers on fixers' misconduct. Fixers reconcile conflicts between reporters' professed morals and sources' expressed prescriptions with lies. Reporters readily swallow the lies to avoid being confronted with fixers' misconduct and thrust into an ambivalence of their own: between a good story and an ethical one.[3]

[2] Journalism is not unique in outsourcing and subcontracting dirty work and danger (Hughes 1962; Örnebring and Conill 2016). Multinational corporations delegate the exploitation of labor to subcontractors overseas rather than running sweatshops themselves, in part because doing so affords them plausible deniability (i.e. moral purity) when scandals erupt (Phillips 2010). I discuss the analogous case of empires outsourcing brutality to local client rulers in Arjomand (2015).
[3] See also Beebee (2010) on the figure of the translator as *homo sacer*, a liminal figure to whom neither the ordinary rules nor the ordinary protections of the group apply but who nonetheless serves an essential social function.

The outsourcing of immorality also reinforces journalism's status hierarchy. A fixer with dirty hands is not producer or reporter material. The fixer's dirty hands justify their continued subordination, and the clean hands of their clients justify the latter's higher status and position as a buffer protecting the news organization from the moral threat that direct ties to the fixer would pose.

* * *

Karim and Sally were committed to following journalistic ethics, to respecting lines between who should *always* and who should *never* be paid for contributing to the news. The problem was, at least to the eyes of an outsider like me trying to understand their reasoning, those boundaries were blurry.

Prescriptions for who deserves which sort of reciprocation are linked to labels denoting who is inside and who is outside the field of journalism, who is a fixer and who a source. As discussed in Part II, these labels are ambiguous products of boundary-work that nonetheless have important consequences. A person's label determines whether payments to them are morally required or morally proscribed.

I asked Karim where he had gotten the idea for a story he had pitched to Sally and her editor. The story, discussed in greater detail in our exchange below, was about the experiences and futures of children born in the nascent "Islamic State" to foreign fighters. Karim wanted to report the story by interviewing the mothers of these children. It was apparent that Karim considered it a professional obligation to pay some contributors but a breach of professionalism to pay others for similar work.

KARIM:    My source in Germany [gave me the idea]. Because I always talk to him . . . just to say hi, just to keep in touch. . . . So I ask him once if he has any idea[s]. And he gave me this idea. He told me, "You have to write about this." And [then] I was with my source in Urfa and he . . . told me, "I know a woman." Because I always ask my sources [for] ideas. And he said, "I know a woman [widowed] from ISIS fighter." He came from France and she got married with him in Syria and he died. And [my source] said, "You can interview with woman." But the [overall] idea: ISIS, their future, the children future, it's my idea. He told me . . . "Only interview this woman, maybe you would be interested." So I told him, "Okay, yeah it's interesting to me if we found three more woman like her." And yeah he was trying to help me. He told me more than seven or eight woman but they're refusing to talk.

NOAH:     And these guys, your people who you talk to in Germany or in Urfa, do you ever hire them also?

KARIM:    No.

NOAH:     Like officially do they ever get paid, or they're just doing [it] because they're interested in getting the story?

KARIM:    No, [Sally's outlet] don't pay. I told you, I like [the outlet] because they are professional; they are really journalist.

It might seem obviously unethical and unprofessional to Karim to pay these men, but they were contributing to the story as his sub-fixers: he delegated the job of finding interviewees to them. Yet by labeling them as "sources" rather than "fixers" and by claiming the story idea in its overall frame to be his, Karim situated them outside the field of journalism. They were sources and not fixers, so reciprocating their help with money would have breached the news organization's norms of exchange. By contrast, it would have been unethical for the organization to *fail* to pay Karim for his professional services.

Because they did not pay sources or sub-fixers, Sally and Karim had to devote far more effort to earning their trust. It took a long time to sway those contributors to feel that Sally and Karim's favor was reward enough and/or to adopt the disposition that journalism was inherently worthwhile. "We have a reputation to be really honest," Sally told me, "and never paying for information and never lying, and never just doing any of the stuff that kind of starts to border the line with intelligence work."[4]

\* \* \*

The stigma against working for the foreign press that Aziz faced in Aleppo was based on an exaggerated, but not baseless, conflation of journalists with spies. Intelligence agencies court fixers, particularly in war zones, and blur the boundary between reporting and spying as a matter of strategy. The intersection of journalism with the field of espionage constitutes another moral threat to the Fourth Estate.

---

[4] At least this is the story Sally told me, though she should not necessarily be taken at her word. Journalists are more comfortable talking vaguely about building trust and mutual respect with sources, because that hides concrete and corrupting acts of reciprocity and so keeps their objectivity claims intact. In Sally and Karim's case, there may just have been forms of reciprocity at play that were invisible to me, which made their self-presentation as ethical journalists more convincing. I never was able to observe them at work, and my dependence on interview data in this section gave them greater information control than participants with whom I worked as a reporter or fixer.

In one case, a foreign journalist approached Karim, ostensibly to offer him a job as a translator at her country's embassy in Ankara:

First you know, she told me that, "Someone [who] works with [my] government wants to talk to you," and I told her "Why?" She said, "[The embassy worker] can help you; he can send your family to [our country]. You will work with them." And she told me that it's – she want me to work as translator in the embassy. ... So I told her "Yeah okay, so give him my number." And then, you know, I met him and ... that first meeting he said, "I'm from the government and we want you to work with us, and we'll send you the information, what we want from you. You can translate everything." And I told him okay. ... And then he send me email. He wants to find ... fighters [from his country that] came to Syria. So I sent him an email back, "Do you work with the government or with the intelligence or–? You offered me to work in the embassy."

The government man replied that tracking down nationals of his country who had joined ISIS was the work the embassy needed. "I told him 'Fuck off,' to be honest," Karim recounted.

The same journalist reached out to Karim again after he and Sally did a story about the smuggling of goods into ISIS-controlled regions. This time, he recounted, she attempted to recruit him into a scheme to put tracked cell phone SIM cards in the hands of ISIS members:

So after this article, the journalist who put me with [her country's] intelligence before, she spoke to me again and she told me that, "The guys spoke to me and they will pay you good salary if you start work with them. Just they want to know those smugglers, because they want to send SIM cards, like they give them iPhone and SIM. [They] put inside the iPhone [the] SIM card [and it] just gives them the location." So then I blocked her. I told her that if you try to reach me again, I will tell all journalists about you.

The reporter tried to sway Karim with a short-term monetary incentive but was thwarted by the stronger pull of his long-term aspirations in journalism. Developing a reputation for shadiness, for blurring boundaries between journalism and intelligence work (even by satisfying a client's demands), prevents a fixer from rising in status in the field. Karim sought to make a name for himself as a true professional journalist – more of a journalist than the reporter whom he threatened to shame before their mutual colleagues – and so was enraged at the attempt to corrupt him.

# Habib

As a specialist in stories about Afghans in Turkey, Habib had to reconcile his clients' prescription that sources freely and individually consent to interviews with the power that organized crime held over migrants. Human smugglers could make Habib's job harder or easier. They could secure or corrupt his reputation among reporters as a fixer for Turkey's Afghan community.

When I hired him to assist me with an article about Afghans in Istanbul, Habib relied on a network of smugglers to recruit sources. As we rode the bus together into Zeytinburnu neighborhood for a first round of interviews, I asked Habib if Afghan sources ever demanded money for interviews. He told me that some fixers would mark up their own day rates in order to give sources a cut, with foreign reporters none the wiser.

This practice followed the operating system that brokers and assistants to human smuggling had developed. A broker would tell migrants that he just wanted to help and would demand no money from them. The broker would then approach a smuggler with the offer to bring him paying clients if the smuggler would mark up his usual price for transit to Europe to provide for a finder's fee. With smugglers' assistants, the same payment was institutionalized as a commission per migrant client.

Habib, though, told me he was honest with his reporter clients and did not charge any hidden fees. Instead, he accessed sources by maintaining a symbiotic relationship with smugglers, particularly one I will call Wahid.

Habib had met Wahid years earlier on one of the first fixing gigs that Habib's big brother Abdullah arranged for him. Wahid was then a naïve, freshly undocumented migrant with asylum dreams in Europe, but had since spent his mid-20s rising through the ranks of organized smuggling in Istanbul. He now rented numerous apartments around the neighborhood to temporarily house migrants and

171

delegated day-to-day operations to several employees. Habib, unlike Wahid, had legal residency in Turkey, first on a student visa and then on a work permit for his day job as an interpreter for the NGO Civic Aid. Habib allowed Wahid to rent the first of those safehouse apartments in his name.

Habib was useful to Wahid and his colleagues not only for legal cover, but also as a broker to the field of international aid. When one asylum seeker developed gangrene on his foot after being injured on the rough hike across Turkey's eastern border with Iran, Habib secured healthcare for him with the help of a Civic Aid contact. When Habib visited Wahid's asylum-seeker customers, he would answer their questions about the refugee status designation process that awaited them once Wahid smuggled them into the European Union. Such ad hoc info sessions were reassurance to disoriented Afghans that they were in good hands with Wahid, on their way to Europe and not being swindled.

Habib and I met Wahid, a slight man about half the width of broad-shouldered Habib who never met my eyes, at a Zeytinburnu café on the second day of our reporting. Wahid was fasting for Ramadan, but Habib had a tea and cigarette. Wahid was wearing a brand-new smartwatch on his thin wrist that Habib reached over to play with while Wahid made calls to his employees to check who was in which apartment for us to interview. We walked together to a safehouse, making a detour on the way to pick up a baggy of hashish for Habib. I don't know if he paid or if it was another perk of his relationship with Wahid.

Turkey had recently signed a deal with the European Union to stop the passage of hundreds of thousands of migrants through Turkey into Greece, mostly by sea on unreliable boats that Wahid and other smugglers provided. The deal included provisions for the resettlement of Syrians but not of any other nationality (Collett 2016).

Many of the Afghans we interviewed in Wahid's apartments had been smuggled into the country since the Turkey–EU deal was signed and realistic prospects of them reaching Europe had vanished (except for the few who could pay extra to cross overland into Bulgaria under local mafia oversight). These migrants had little to no awareness of the deal and its implications for them. Smugglers in Kabul or Tehran had told them the route was still open, taken their money, and deposited them after an arduous journey in Istanbul, where they were housed by associate smugglers like Wahid and encouraged to find work in the neighborhood's booming textile sweatshop industry.[1]

At each safehouse, I went through the motions of explaining, through Habib's consecutive interpretation, informed consent and that they were free to refuse to talk with us (as discussed in Part II). But what truly informed consent would look like for people living illegally in a foreign country, under the eye of criminals who had endorsed the interview, and ignorant of basic legal and political facts of their situation, I do not know.

At the far end of the reciprocity spectrum is coercion, where it is the stick, not the carrot, brandished to incentivize engagement, where the promise of avoiding harm rather than of gaining benefit is what aligns sources. Coercion can be unwitting. Sources might fear the consequences of refusing to engage with journalists whom they associate with people or institutions holding power over them. During one interview I conducted with Habib, a family of Afghan asylum seekers asked midway through the conversation whether we worked for the United Nations.

Reporters can also outsource coercion to sub-fixers a link or two removed from them on the chain of intermediaries, keeping their own hands clean.[2] Under Wahid's effective control, the asylum seekers we interviewed likely feared negative repercussions if they defied Wahid's arrangement and failed to engage with us, whatever we told them about their participation being voluntary.

A blurrier case of coercion occurred whenever the head of a family consented on behalf of its other members. In these group interviews with Afghan migrants, once the father or eldest man said yes, everyone else would fall in line.

To describe sources' deference to authorities as coercion in all cases would be to assume that everyone shares the norm of individual freedom as an inalienable right that is violated whenever others make decisions for them (Mahmood 2004). Following a leader can, to the contrary, be experienced as altruism, as the right or the cool thing to do, as a way to reaffirm membership in a community and avoid the risks of unguided individual decision-making. What looks from the

---

[1] Many Afghans spent long periods in Iran before moving on to Turkey or the EU. See Arjomand (2016a) on these migration patterns.

[2] See also Wright (2018: 257) on local staff of international NGOs coercing people into participating in their media production.

outside like chains of bondage can feel on the inside like links of group solidarity, and vice versa.[3]

Habib was not the only fixer to face the problem of conflicting norms of consent. While reporting on the resurgence of violence in the southeast, Geert and Nur visited a Kurdish youth organization in Diyarbakır. Geert recounted,

With the youth … it was a bit hierarchical. So there was the top leader … until he came they didn't really want to talk. Once we interviewed him for like an hour and a half … we could see that he was in, like, I've-gotta-go mode, even though he was very friendly. He was like, "Is there anything else I can do?" I was like, "Do you mind if I hang out here for an extra half hour and talk to these kids?" Because I knew he was going to leave. And since he'd already talked to me, the kids would be relaxed. So he left and we talked to the kids, and then so we got all the nice quotes that really captured the story.

This tactic of using an authority figure as an informal sub-fixer is effective. Convincing people to talk becomes easier, and those people sometimes relax, once a superordinate signals that engagement with the journalists is permitted, if not prescribed.

The norm of group rather than individual consent nonetheless must be reconciled with foreign reporters' prescription for a performance of individual autonomy. Fixers must manage a conflict over what comprises the basic unit of social life that engages in reciprocal exchange: the group (as represented by leaders) or the individual. One way Habib reconciled these conflicting scripts was by recruiting sources through a smuggling network in which Wahid effectively consented for the group while Habib paid lip service to my journalistic/academic norms by informing sources that their participation was voluntary and asking for their individual consent.

Fixers also coach clients with **culture talk** (Mamdani 2004), highlighting and perhaps essentializing differences between East and West as they explain how things work in Their Culture. When Habib explained to me that fathers could speak for their families in Afghanistan, he was working to align me to the expectation of group consent. Depending on

[3] See also Foster and Minwalla's (2018) account of the interactions between Yazidi women survivors of ISIS and the international media. The authors found that aid workers and relatives pressured women into participating in interviews with foreign reporters, who asked the women to recount traumatic experiences in ways that further traumatized them.

how you look at it, a Western reporter's adoption of a group consent script is cultural sensitivity and/or a papering-over of coercion.

Habib was hesitant to ask Wahid himself for an interview with me. I pressured, and eventually the three of us did sit down together. Habib and I ate ice cream; Wahid fasted. I was curious about his transformation from a powerless migrant into a powerful smuggler, and so my first question was about when he first arrived in Istanbul. Had he also worked in a textile sweatshop like the migrants off whom he now lived? Rather than translate, Habib quietly told me that it would not be good to ask that question right now. Habib knew all about Wahid's past and would tell me later.

Habib recognized, I think, that this was a relatively unimportant question for me and not worth embarrassing Wahid over. Habib knew Wahid well enough to know that he did not want to discuss his lowly past and would rather be interviewed as a big-shot smuggler. Habib did not want to provoke breakdown in the interaction that would prevent me from getting the information for which Wahid was an essential source: the latest about the usage and cost of various smuggling routes. And so instead of translating my question, Habib talked back and coached me on how to approach our source, averting the conflict that my question would have opened.

Habib was happier to translate and Wahid seemingly blasé to answer questions about the effects of the Turkey–EU deal on his business and about his arrangements with associates from Baluchistan to Bulgaria. I noticed, though, that his shirt's underarms darkened with sweat as we talked. I wondered how voluntary *his* consent to be interviewed was. Habib had at least as much leverage over Wahid as Wahid had over Habib.

\* \* \*

Habib had not enjoyed such a functional relationship with smugglers a year earlier, when Geert had paid to fly him down to İzmir, on the Aegean coast, for a story on asylum seekers boarding boats to nearby Greek islands. Habib's connections in İzmir were yet to be cemented at that time, and so he arrived without prior contact with smugglers there. I asked Habib how he found Afghan asylum seekers.

"It's hard not to," he replied. "You just walk to Basmane Square and they're everywhere ... I don't know how ... [but] it just became the smuggling central."

Habib was familiar with the name Basmane Square[4] from Afghans in Istanbul: many planned to go down the coast to İzmir to cross into Greece. Others had already been down that path and then deported from Europe, only to attempt the journey again. Sure enough, when Habib and Geert arrived in the square, they were greeted by a multi-lingual cacophony of smuggling brokers and assistants:

They're like, "I work with a good smuggler," "My boats always make it," or "My boats are cheaper." Just like something to try to grab your attention. Or like, "Hey [brother] are you trying to make it to Europe?" Something like that. They tend to employ brokers of different nationalities so that they can reach to refugees of different nationalities and languages. So there's naturally ... Syrian Arabs, Syrian Kurds, Iraqis, Afghans.

They located some Afghans shopping for smugglers or waiting to board boats in the courtyard of a mosque on the square. As they tried to conduct interviews, a group of brokers – Afghan migrants them-selves, teenagers with red-rimmed eyes and PTSD in Habib's descrip-tion – gathered to heckle Habib in Persian. Whereas in Istanbul, Habib's connections to organized smuggling helped him recruit sources, in İzmir his lack of connection turned smugglers from allies into obstacles. The teenaged smuggling brokers mockingly asked Habib over and over if he thought his precious journalism was doing any good.

"They were like, 'You still believe in it? You really still believe in it? Are you that naïve? You really still believe in it?' And I was like, 'I don't see myself asking you any questions. This story's not about you. You don't like the media? You don't like me? No one's forcing you to be here.'" There was apparently no better sport to be had in the courtyard, though, and the brokers kept bothering them, which Habib found particularly obnoxious as they were interviewing asylum seekers about their experiences of violent trauma.

When Habib did not delegate reciprocity to a smuggler-as-sub-fixer, he had to worry more about his own direct reciprocal relationship with sources. Without Wahid as a buffer, Habib gave İzmir sources his own phone number, which gave them a longer-term means of exerting moral pressure over him.

---

[4] The square is, like many things in İzmir, officially named September Nine, after the 1922 recapture of the city from Greek forces in the Turkish War of Independence but draws its informal name from nearby Basmane train station.

One of the sources whom Habib and Geert managed to interview was an Afghan man who had recently attempted the voyage to a nearby Greek island with his family. Their boat had capsized and his companion family members drowned, though the man had been rescued by the Turkish coast guard. After that experience and after discussing his legal options with Habib, the man had decided to apply for asylum in Turkey instead of again hazarding the sea.

Geert recounted the man's tragedy in a magazine article he wrote, but the story was delayed by the editors. Breaking news from Europe took up more pages than expected, and they already had other refugee stories in line. The man had intended to use Geert's story, particularly its discussion of the dangers that forced his family to flee Afghanistan, as documentation in his asylum case. Given the massive backlog of asylum cases at the UNHCR, he was a long time away from an interview to determine whether he would be officially designated as a refugee, and so the delay of the article was probably not yet critical to his case. Nevertheless, the man felt he had been duped as the weeks dragged on without Habib sending him a link to Geert's article. He repeatedly called Habib to complain and demand to know when the story would be published. He also asserted that Habib ought to help him. He was struggling to get by in the central Anatolian town to which the UNHCR had assigned him to await status designation. Habib felt obliged to continue taking the man's calls. He offered consolation and eventually sent money, a good portion of what Geert had paid Habib.

# Unifying Worlds

Not all topics are politically contentious; not all cultural and linguistic barriers to communication are obstructively high; not all time maps are out of sync. Fixers' jobs are easiest when reporters and sources already agree about what information to exchange and how, when, and why to exchange it. Matchmaking compatible reporter–source pairings is an important part of fixers' jobs as catalysts, and fixers learn to expand their social networks to maximize pairing options. But perfect match-making is not always possible. Conflicts between journalists and locals arise, and fixers are caught in the middle. Expectations pull on them from both sides. The fact that additional parties – police, militants, spies, nosy neighbors – also surveil and pressure fixers adds to the complexity of their moral worlds.

Fixers may be ambivalent or may be biased toward one side. When they do find themselves threatened by ambivalence, fixers might try to prevent the parties they broker from realizing that their prescriptions conflict or steer the conversation toward less-contested grounds. Failing that, they might avoid being asked to take a side by signaling non-personhood or neutrality. If they can send discrete signals to segregated audiences, they might even perform allegiance to both sides.

Fixers are not free to send whatever signals they like. They have variable, but limited, control over brokered parties' access to information and to one another. Some signaling equipment, like languages, are expensive in time and effort to acquire; others, like facial features or skin color, are not easily changed. Hard-to-fake shibboleths, like Nur's fluent Kurdish, are valuable for signaling trustworthiness to a certain audience; hard-to-hide stigmas, like Marie's tattoos, can spoil a performance (Goffman 1968; Gambetta and Hamill 2005: 10–14).

Fixers' freedom of action is also limited by their dispositions: ingrained moral leanings and styles of acting. Dispositions are built out of past experiences and future aspirations. They are transposable from one situation to the next, guiding fixers' reactions to novel

178

circumstances (Bourdieu 1977: 72). Sometimes fixers' dispositions do not align with either locals' or foreigners' moral prescriptions but rather lead them to actions of which both brokered parties disapprove.

Rima was a Syrian-American fixer who had undergone a personal journey from devout, headscarved Muslim to privately professed atheist over the course of her country's increasingly sectarian civil war. She refused to wear a headscarf and was infuriated when a client reporter suggested she do so for an interview with an Islamist rebel commander. From the client's perspective, Rima should have facilitated the interaction with the commander by avoiding sartorial challenge to his religious prescriptions. Rima, by contrast, felt it important as a Syrian citizen in Turkey to assert, not minimize, her views that conflicted with other Syrians':

I think – and this is the part where that's my bias as someone who's local – where I feel the right to challenge perceptions, in the sense where like, "Sorry but Turkey is a secular country, and even if you just came out of [ISIS's capital] Raqqa that's not my problem. I'm not going to wear a burka for you. You don't want to talk to me, don't." You know? Now if I'm going into your home and you prefer me not to be – like I'm not gonna walk in in a tank top, you know? I'm gonna dress respectfully and in certain areas that are more conservative, like Urfa, I would wear longer sleeves ... I would wear a scarf to cover my chest area. I'm not an asshole about it. But I also like to stand my ground with it in just the sense where, like, "Sorry not sorry." This is a secular country.

Fixers' moral stands, especially as they conflict with both reporters' and sources' prescriptions, are connected to their positions in and aspirations across different fields, from journalism to Syrian politics. Rima's personal history – which intertwined with larger Syrian, American, and Turkish histories – led her to defy the prescription that she practice hijab.[1] Adventure-oriented foreign reporters can be more disposed than their fixers toward blending in, if not Going Native, according to their own social position and aspirations.

Rima went on, "I think it's really funny when like white journalists, female journalists, they're somewhere where you really don't need to wear hijab, like [Turkish cities] Gaziantep or Antakya, and they're like," she mimed dramatically flinging a headscarf over her shoulder

---

[1] See also Ehraim's (2019) reflections on the growing challenge of reporting inside Syria while asserting secular feminist values.

and imitated a posh British accent, "'*On the border of Syria.*' And then it's their Twitter photo or their Facebook photo, and I'm like, 'Calm down.'" Rima laughed. "It's kind of like if I was sent on assignment to the US and the first thing I bought was a baseball cap ... to blend in with the natives, you know?"

*Going* native holds exotic appeal to high-status foreign reporters, but *being* native is a status threat to fixers who aspire to rise in journalism. A fixer's aspiration to be a critical outsider to their own society, for instance by aligning with feminist values, can paradoxically conflict with their clients' desire for them to put on a performance of local authenticity.

On the other hand, turning a foreign client a bit more local, or a source a bit more global, can mitigate conflict. Fixers use their own moral leverage to align reporters to sources' norms or vice versa. Fixers coach reporters on how to be respectful, ask questions, interpret responses, and avoid trouble according to local realities and expectations. They pressure and co-opt sources through interruptions, arguments, and payments into providing reporters with newsworthy soundbites and testimonials.

Some sources and reporters welcome these alignment efforts; others do not. When Nur and Geert were interviewing the representative of the PKK martyrs' association in Diyarbakır, Nur sought to align Geert to the source with pointed looks and eventually side comments that his line of questioning was rude. She succeeded only in reducing Geert's confidence in her, as he took her efforts as a signal that she was source-biased and too close to the story.

When they fail, fixers lose clients or sources, status or trust. When they succeed, fixers unify, if only fleetingly and on limited terms, disparate moral worlds.[2] They assemble a new world, a trading zone in which knowledge can be exchanged (Galison 2010).

---

[2] See also Carey's ([1989] 2009) discussion of communication rituals as productive of social bonds.

# PART IV

# Translations

# Communication as Information

Any act of communication is both a social interaction and a means of transmitting information (Wadensjö 1998). Thus far, I have focused on communication as interaction: a means to signal identity, claim status, win or defuse conflicts. Yet communication among reporters, fixers, and sources also transmits the information that becomes news. We will now turn to the informatics of fixing with a close look at what is lost, gained, and transformed in translation from events in the world to stories in the media.

Engineers who study information transmission have developed a different set of vocabulary than have scholars who study social interaction.[1] I will preface these next chapters with a hypothetical scenario to introduce this new jargon, some of which is diagrammed in Figure 4.1.

Let's say that I was a reporter and contacted a Turkish fixer named Temel. In informatic terms, Temel's job was to act as a **transcoder**: the intermediate destination of a message, like my question to a source originally **encoded** in English. The transcoder converts the message into a new form (e.g. from English to Turkish) that the end receiver can **decode** and then relays the new message to that final destination. (I use the terms "translate," "transcode," "recode," "convert," and "transform" interchangeably.)

Temel's online profile claimed that he spoke English, but when we met, it turned out that the only word he seemed to know was "Hello!" Whether I asked him to explain his qualifications or what time it was, he just responded "Hello!" I became frustrated, thinking that I could not gain any **information** talking to Temel because he had no **freedom**

---

[1] Some communications engineering terms, like **signal, feedback,** and **code,** did make it into the social sciences, thanks to the interdisciplinary Cybernetics conferences of the late 1940s and early 1950s (Gleick 2011: 233–268), and later to Hall's ([1973] 2006) foundational work in Cultural Studies.

## Information Transmission Model of Communication

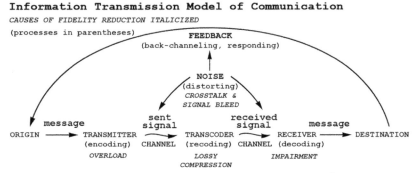

Figure 4.1 Information transmission model of communication[2]


**of choice**: When I asked a question, there was no uncertainty how he would answer, no possibility of surprise (Weaver [1949] 1964: 12–16).

But then I realized that he could not only say "Hello!" but also shrug his shoulders. He had two options and so had the **capacity** to send me one **bit** of information as often as he made a choice between those options. At any moment, I was uncertain whether he would next speak or shrug. The meaning of the word *hello* in English was irrelevant; in our communication it functioned simply as a binary opposition to a shrug. It would not matter if the content of his signals was instead *yes/no* or *0/1* (Bateson 1972: 399–420). We slowly developed a shared understanding of each combination of hellos and shrugs. This shared attribution of meanings to symbols was a language, a **channel** of communication that I called Temelçe (Turkish for "The Way of Temel"). For instance, *hello!-hello!-shrug-hello!-shrug-shrug* meant "turnip juice."

Temelçe had a capacity, measured in the bits of information that could be transmitted in a unit of time, far lower than English (time yourself conveying the message "turnip juice" in each language). Sometimes Temel would **overload** the channel by **transmitting** shrugs and hellos too quickly for me to decode. Other times, I would forget my glasses or hearing aide at home, which **impaired** my **reception** of his **signals** (Weaver [1949] 1964: 16–18).

---

[2] Adapted and expanded from Shannon ([1949] 1964: 34).

To deal with the problem that people could speak Turkish at a far higher bitrate than he could transmit Temelçe signals, Temel **compressed** the data he received from the sources we interviewed. He did not bother to transcode filler words, or even words he deemed non-essential for the point he wanted to make (**lossy** compression).

In addition to impairment and compression, another cause of **distortion**, also called **fidelity loss** and defined as inaccuracy in the reproduction or recoding of a message, was **noise**. Noise can be anything added to cause a difference between the sent signal and the received signal (Weaver [1949] 1964: 18–22; Clarke 2010: 162–164). It might take the form of random white noise, as when Temel would shout "Hello!" at me over the roar of a waterfall. I would have to subtract the roar in order to extract the signal he sent from the audio information I received. More vexing yet, the noise might be not random but patterned.

Temel insisted on walking around with a boombox on his shoulder, the noise of which was especially confusing when he played the Beatles' song "Hello, Goodbye." The lyrics would **bleed** into Temel's own utterances of "Hello!" and I would be unable to make out who was saying what in the **crosstalk**.

Signal and noise are both information; the difference is that signal is useful and noise is useless. I labeled Temel's words signal and the music noise because of which information I wanted to use (Serres 2007). But from the Beatles' perspective, their lyrics were the signal: I should be listening to them and reflecting on why I say goodbye. If we place the Beatles instead of Temel at the **origin** position of Figure 4.1, then Temel's words are the noise disrupting their message en route to its **destination** (me).

Signal and noise, like order and chaos, are in the eye of the beholder. But not all beholders have equal power to define a bit of information as signal or noise. This point brings us back to a distinction that will figure prominently in Part IV: between information control and frame control in newsmaking. **Information control** is power over access to information and grows as we get closer to the worlds that journalism describes. Reporters control editors' access; fixers control reporters' access; sources control fixers' access.

Frames, which I also call **templates**, structure news stories and so structure the behavior of news contributors. A **frame**, to expand on my previous explanation of the term, is a moral script for what information should and should not be transmitted. **Frame control** is the power to determine which information is signal and which is noise. There is a hierarchy of frame control among news contributors that runs along the familiar insider-to-outsider spectrum. An editor assigns a reporter to do a story on a topic; information about other topics is noise. The reporter tells their fixer how a story will be framed; information that fits the frame is signal and the rest is noise. The fixer coaches a source on how to frame their own experiences to satisfy that reporter's expectations; information that the fixer cannot use to satisfy their client is noise. Frame control constrains what information is a newsworthy signal.

Not only *what* information but also *whose* information counts as noise is a matter of perspective. Whether information from a contributor is signal or noise is a matter of moral judgment: Is that contributor a prescribed participant in the information exchange, an interloper, or a non-person who has risen above their station? If a news contributor is expected to act only as a non-person transcoder, relaying a message to a receiver with maximum fidelity, then any information they add is noise and any they subtract is signal loss. Yet, as we will see, sometimes such distortion is essential to make sense of information for brokered parties (a.k.a. origins and destinations) and to reconcile conflicts between them. To thus unify worlds, fixers must disguise their own contributions within translations or renegotiate their participation status in interactions with reporters and sources, oscillating between personhood and non-personhood.

Once Temel and I were confident in our shared understanding of Temelçe, we went to work reporting news stories. Interviewees would encode their messages in Turkish, and Temel would transcode those signals into Temelçe for me to decode. Sometimes his mind would wander, or he would decide to improve on what they said, and so the messages I received were quite distorted renditions of the messages transmitted. When I found a message particularly confusing, I might ask a follow-up question, which provided the interviewees with **feedback** about how their messages were being received (Gleick 2011: 238–239). When I did feel I understood, I would **back-channel** signals – nods, smiles, thumbs-up – that their message had been successfully transmitted.

Body language constituted an alternative or **redundant** channel of communication that circumvented Temel. I found that opening a direct channel, however limited in capacity, with an interviewee helped me correct for Temel's distortions (Gleick 2011: 230–231). Temel hated alternative channels because they reduced his information control and so his freedom of choice to transcode as creatively as he pleased without moral censure and within the constraints of Temelçe.

Setting the limitations of Temelçe aside for a moment and considering the languages that will be discussed in the following chapter – English and Turkish – it is worth stressing that word-for-word translation with perfect fidelity is an unattainable ideal. Differences in channel capacities between Turkish and English may add to the difficulty of translation. As Maureen Freely (2006: 146–147), who has translated many of Nobel laureate Orhan Pamuk's novels, puts it,

> The distance between Turkish and English is so great that literal translation is next to impossible. English, as we know, likes a linear logic. It has the soul of an examining magistrate. It wants to know who did what, and if at all possible, when, where and why. The word "is" lies at the heart of the equation, alongside the word "has." The road between subject and object is paved with prepositions. But Turkish is lean and double-jointed, arching effortlessly from active to passive voice, delighting in nuances, dispensing with definite articles, stringing suffix to suffix to create sparkling *mots justes* that would need eight or nine or even a dozen words in English, and offering up a tantalising array of clauses that do not link up until the sentence reaches its last syllable. It is interested in correspondences that cannot be reduced to equations, in games with time that tangle causes and effects.

The objective properties of Turkish make it more efficient to transmit some information, as with *mots justes* that would require more letters or sounds in English. Cultural scripts for using the two languages differ as well: English grammar enthusiasts disparage the passive voice as an evasive hallmark of poor communication, while the Turkish *edilgen* is respected as cleverly circumspect.

The larger reason for the impossibility of perfect, literal translation, though, is that words have not just dictionary definitions, but also shared meanings among cultural subgroups (Benjamin [1923] 1996). Words reference things without explicitly denoting them. Insider knowledge affects the meaning of the messages transmitted in verbal signals. Signals are never self-contained packets of meaning; the transmitters and receivers who respectively encode and decode signals add and subtract meaning. (Social scientists refer to decoding as interpretation to highlight the active role of the receiver). This meaning is easily lost in translation, as a signal does not carry its referents with it from one transceiver to the next. We utter words in situated interactional contexts but those words then travel into new contexts (Wadensjö 1998: 38–42; Bourdieu 1999: 221).

Temel and I ran into these problems when we interviewed two women about politics. The first described herself in Turkish as "*modern*," while the other described herself as "*çağdaş*." (I will use *italics* to indicate non-English-language speech throughout Part IV.) Temel translated both of these words into Temelçe as *shrug-shrug-hello!-hello!-shrug-hello!*, which I further decoded into English as "modern." The meaning of our sources' respective words that eluded me was that in Turkey, the term "*modern*" has been specifically embraced by Islamic modernists; the first woman was identifying herself with a particular political brand of modernism. The second woman, hearing the first call herself "*modern*," pointedly used the term "*çağdaş*," which referenced a Kemalist conception of contemporary civilization as a break from the past and from the reign of superstitious religiosity. The second woman's word choice identified her in defiant opposition to the "*modern*" woman (White 2013: loc. 1138–1163). Temel's translations were correct in a literal sense. He might have translated the second woman's self-characterization as *shrug-shrug-hello!-hello!-shrug-shrug* ("contemporary") to differentiate the two, but even this translation would obscure the cultural meaning and interactional usage of the word from me. The more fraught a word is with political subtext, the trickier and more powerful the act of its translation.

Novelist Elif Shafak (2006: 156) notes that in Turkish, "depending on the ideological camp you are attached to, e.g. Kemalists versus Islamists, you can use either an 'old' or a 'new' set of words." That statement is an oversimplification: There are not just two ideological camps but many, each with its own jargon and set of references that defy literal translation. The Gülen Movement, the Kurdish Left, and other factions each have their own ways of talking and attribute different meanings to key terms. Poor Temel also had to worry about *my* ideological camp and culture. He needed to know how I would decode English words like "modern" and "contemporary" and perhaps needed to nudge me to decode them the right way if he hoped for meaning to cross the gulf between our sources and me (Palmer 2019: 135–136).

Freely (2006: 147) writes of the translator's task, "You must choose what's important and leave the rest behind. More controversially, you must decide if your first allegiance is to the sentence or to the fictive world behind it."[3] If we replace "fictive" with "cultural," we have a good description of Temel's dilemma as he struggled to compress Turkish into Temelçe and to translate statements imbued with insider references like "*I am a çağdaş woman*." Temel's choices would simultaneously change the message and align the conversation to one participant's moral world over another's.

Fixers transcode statements and coach reporters in ways that can reveal, obscure, or change sources' meanings. No matter what choices fixer make, they shape the knowledge produced through interviews.

In the chapters that follow, I will walk you step by step through the process of reporting several news stories and show how chaotic swirls of signal and noise were transformed into coherent narratives about events in Turkey. Though my focus will be on information, the informational and interactional dimensions of the conversations I will recount were inseparable. Fixers distort the messages they transcode in order to manage moral conflicts thrust upon them in interactions with reporters and sources. What and how much they distort depends on the interactional expertise and dispositions they have cultivated, their positions in social hierarchies, and their personal and political aims. We cannot understand why particular information became a news story without considering the social context in which that information was transmitted from source to fixer to reporter.

---

[3] See also Benjamin's ([1923] 1996: 258) discussion of the "task of the translator" as "finding the particular intention toward the target language which produces in that language the echo of the original."

# Zeynep

Urban warfare raged across Turkey's southeast in early 2016 as security forces recaptured city centers from the PKK's youth wing. As the death toll mounted, it struck me as odd that foreign news reports about the conflict were still using the same estimate for the total death toll of the Turkish–Kurdish conflict – approximately 40,000 – that had appeared a decade earlier when I first started to follow the issue. I decided to write an article about where the estimate came from and why it seemed stuck at 40,000.

I hired Zeynep, the graduate student activist who had covered the siege of Kobani with José, as my fixer. She contacted government ministries and the armed forces, which were claiming high numbers of "neutralized" militants in the latest round of fighting, as well as NGOs that had kept independent tallies of combatant and civilian casualties over the years. Zeynep also had the idea of requesting court documentation from the trial of PKK leader Abdullah Öcalan, in which casualty counts were included as evidence of his alleged crimes against state and nation. Zeynep had little luck on the government side. The Interior Ministry directed her to the Armed Forces General Chief of Staff; the Armed Forces directed her back to the Interior Ministry. The court directed her to the Justice Ministry for Öcalan trial documentation; the Justice Ministry directed her back to the court.

When a reporter comes to a fixer with a story idea, the fixer's ability to fulfill the reporter's prescriptions depends in part on their social capital: the sum of their usable ties to other people. Social capital is thus a factor in a fixer's capacity to connect a reporter to a certain quantity of sought-after information per day or week.

Zeynep lacked social ties with state officials whom she could ask to sit down for an interview or to help us access official casualty counts. When formal public relations gatekeepers at the courts and ministries were not helpful, she lacked the capacity to provide me access to alternative sources in a timely fashion.

A political science grad student, Zeynep was at least adept at digging through public archives for official documents. She found the proceedings of a 2013 parliamentary commission that confirmed 35,576 dead, which would have to stand in for a human interviewee as the government side of the story.

Zeynep also managed to arrange an interview with Ümit Efe, a senior representative of the Human Rights Organization (İHD, *İnsan Hakları Derneği*), which publishes alternative death counts from the PKK conflict.[1] İHD is associated with the Kurdish Movement, and over a dozen members of their staff are counted among the thousands of unsolved murders connected to the counterinsurgency. Zeynep already knew Ümit, first through Zeynep's own political activism and then as a go-to source for reporters.

This selectivity of sources, based on the social ties that Zeynep possessed or lacked, shaped the content of my story before I even interviewed anyone. I would be relying on parliamentary documents and opposition voices for my information.[2]

I came to the interview seeking a quotation about why İHD counted casualties at all: Why were official numbers that state institutions published not reliable? I also hoped for information about İHD's methods for gathering data, which were poorly explained in the annual reports in which the organization published its counts.

Zeynep and Ümit greeted each other warmly when we met at the dingy-hip cafe next to İHD's Istanbul branch. I recorded the conversation on my phone.

---

[1] I am using the real names of sources and organizations already identified in my published articles.

[2] One way that fixers manage the conflict between clients' prescription to provide all sides of a story and the limitations of fixers' own social capital and dispositions is by making good faith, failed efforts to contact sources from whom the fixer is socially distant. When fixers can convince a reporter that one side in a conflict among locals is simply unresponsive (though they might have been responsive to a different fixer), the reporter is absolved of some responsibility for a failure of journalistic balance. In my and Zeynep's case, even though I only got the Kurdish opposition side of the story, I was covered against accusations of bias: I could write that the ministries, military, and court did not respond to my queries. So if my report was unbalanced, that was on them, not me.

From the start, Zeynep did her best to reconcile or pre-empt any potential conflict between Ümit and me. She introduced me in a way she predicted would be most amenable to Ümit: as an Iranian-American who spoke Persian. (Persian and Kurdish languages are close cousins, and in my experience and evidently Zeynep's, Persian is perceived as a kindred ethnicity among Kurds in Turkey.) As Zeynep explained our story-in-progress, Ümit volunteered she had been on a fact-finding mission to towns in the southeast that recent fighting had hit hardest. She asked if we were also covering the destruction of those towns.

*"I think we'll also include that,"* Zeynep told Ümit, despite me giving no indication in our previous discussions that I intended to do so. Zeynep's confirmation was interactionally oriented, giving a nod to Ümit's strategic prescriptions in order to encourage her engagement with us. Yet Zeynep's affirmation also shaped the informational content of the interview, as it authorized Ümit's repeated return to talking about her visit to the southeast throughout the interview.

Zeynep, though ethnically Turkish herself, was familiar enough with Kurdish-leftist coding norms to address Ümit with insider lingo, for instance calling PKK fighters *"guerillas"* whereas she had referred to *"terrorists"* in her communications with Turkish state institutions. In contemporary Turkey, the word *"guerilla"* is not neutral but signals sympathy with the cause. Even as Zeynep spoke in Kurdish-nationalist codes to Ümit, she softened Ümit's own Kurdish nationalist signals in her English-language translations. When Ümit said *"Kurdistan"* (a taboo word in the Turkish mainstream for the country's Kurdish-majority region), Zeynep transcoded it back to me as "the southeast" or as "Kurdish cities and areas." These translation choices served to present Ümit as a more neutral information source to an outsider like me.

Other distortions Zeynep made when transcoding words from Turkish into English had less to do with politics in general, and more to do with subtly converting Ümit's utterances into information that satisfied my prescriptions. When Ümit said the state *"never fully gave the names of soldiers"* who died, Zeynep translated it as "Government never gave all figures about the security forces." *"Names"* became "figures," because Zeynep knew that numbers killed were my interest. *"Soldiers"* turned into "security forces" because Zeynep knew the latter was the category used in the casualty statistics we had been perusing, even though security forces include not just soldiers but also police, gendarmes, and village guards.

It is irrelevant for our purposes whether these changes were consciously calculated or unintentional – perhaps in the course of our research I had gotten Zeynep thinking in terms of "figures" and "security forces" and so those words just automatically popped out. It is enough to note simply that neither *"name"* nor *"soldier"* is difficult to translate directly, nor does either carry an ambiguous meaning in Turkish, yet Zeynep did the extra work of distorting them to fit my line of inquiry.

Despite her efforts to unify the conversation, Zeynep found herself ambivalently caught between competing prescriptions for the interview's framing. Ümit and I had different ideas about how we should be discussing the PKK conflict. It soon became clear that Ümit was uninterested or unable to speak in any detail about İHD's methodology for figuring out, in the fog of insurgency, how many had died and who was a civilian. I shifted gears to asking what she thought about the media's loose use of casualty figures in an exchange transcribed below, from about 20 minutes into the interview. The passage shows the meandering route that information can take from asker to answerer and back and of how clarity can be lost and re-found as messages are translated back and forth.[3]

| Speaker | Content | Turn |
|---------|---------|------|
| Noah | I've seen a lot of different numbers in the media, both inside of Turkey and in the foreign media, that some reports say 30 thousand, sometimes 37 thousand, sometimes 40, sometimes 45 thousand. I wonder, does she know where those numbers come from and how reliable they are? | 1 |

[3] Although I understand Turkish, I did my best to ignore it during the interview and to base my field notes only on the English translations that Zeynep provided. I later (for this book, not my news story) went back to transcribe and translate passages from my audio recording. As the transcripts that follow demonstrate, I was only partially successful in turning off the Turkish side of my brain. I did not lie to the fixers I hired by telling them I did not speak Turkish, but I always spoke with them in English. Most of them did not know my level of Turkish comprehension. On one occasion, after translating for me all day, Orhan left me for alone with a source while he met with another reporter and came back to find us chatting in Turkish. "You have been laughing at me all day!" Orhan accused me, only half joking.

(*cont.*)

| Speaker | Content | Turn |
|---------|---------|------|
| Zeynep | *This of course – I feel this way; Nuh* (Noah's name in Middle Eastern languages) *also feels this way.* (inaudible) *the total figure from the beginning of the war is unclear;* (subject unclear) *says that it became 30, it became 35, then we passed 40, [then] they pulled it back to 35. Both from the domestic press, foreign media, as well as from institutions, from the state. Why is it like this?* | 2 |
| Ümit | *How do* **you** *feel?* | 3 |
| Zeynep | This is also (inaudible) – | 4 |
| Noah | No no no, **she** should answer the question this time. (Zeynep and Noah laugh) | 5 |
| Zeynep | *In* **your** *view –* | 6 |
| Noah | (interrupting) I interviewed [Zeynep] yesterday so – | 7 |
| Ümit | (talking over both me and Zeynep) *You mean civilians?* | 8 |
| Zeynep | *I did an interview too.* | 9 |
| Ümit | *The death of civilians?* | 10 |
| Zeynep | *No, the total number, like it changes –* | 11 |
| Ümit | *The total number –* | 12 |
| Zeynep | (talking over Ümit) *Reality –* | 13 |
| Ümit | *Because the state doesn't tell the realities. Actually* (inaudible) *psychological. But we know that, for instance in Nusaybin, they sent medicine to soldiers in need for mental depression and they sent a psychiatrist.* | 14 |
| Zeynep | *When?* | 15 |
| Ümit | *Two days ago. [Soldiers] began to submit petitions in large numbers to resign [or] to change postings. The state actually doesn't only perform a physical attack, it performs a psychological attack. And it does not provide true figures either about itself or about the other side. For that reason, the work of human rights organizations is very important; lawyers' [collection of] the people's testimonies is very important.* | 16 |
| Zeynep | First of all, it always have been a psychological war, so the government never gives the true figures. For example, and of the impact now in Nusaybin recently there's a spreading depression among the security forces and a psychiatrist was sent there. | 17 |

Chaos. The reality of interviews can be far noisier than the ideal *question → translation → answer → translation → question* organization of translated interviews when that order is not enforced and when coding and strategic conflicts exist (Wadensjö 1998: 104–106). Zeynep's question at Turn 2 apparently confused Ümit, who redirected it back to Zeynep at Turn 3 to answer instead of responding herself. Zeynep and I departed from the question–answer format to chat about my previous interview with Zeynep (as her activist self) in Turns 7 and 9. Ümit and Zeynep exchanged unclear sentence fragments from Turns 10–13 as Ümit tried to understand what we were asking. Everyone interrupted and talked over everyone else.

Yet from this messy exchange, full of crosstalk and confusion, I received information that I could turn into a straightforward quotation that satisfied my prescription for a line from someone with institutional authority about official figures being unreliable. My article ultimately read, "'Counts of the dead,' Ümit Efe told me, 'have always been a means of psychological warfare.'"

How in the actual interaction did we arrive at that information? After Ümit and Zeynep exchanged asides from Speaking Turns 8–13 that failed to clear up the initial question, Ümit offered a statement at Turn 14 about the psychological problems of soldiers in the southeast that seems to have little bearing on the question. Zeynep then asked *"when?"* at Turn 15, effectively abandoning the original line of questioning to align herself with the topic Ümit wanted to discuss. In Ümit's response to *"when?"*, however, an utterance fortuitously came that Zeynep could translate back into information that satisfied my broader informational prescriptions, even if it did not directly answer my last question. In Ümit's original utterance at Turn 16, it was unclear whether the *"psychological attack"* was related to the military's depressed and resigning troops or to the provision of false figures. Psychological warfare may just be a theme that ambiguously tied both of those issues together (to paraphrase Freely [2006]'s quotation about differences between Turkish and English: a correspondence that cannot be reduced to an equation). Yet Zeynep rendered the statement in Turn 17 as "it always have been a psychological war, so the government never gives the true figures." The word "so" provided me a clear causal link between psychological war and government figures. I scrawled Zeynep's Turn 17 translation into my notepad as "It's always been a psych war so govt never gives real figures." Zeynep

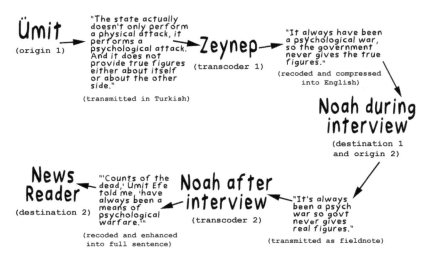

**Figure 4.2** Diagram of the transmission of information about PKK conflict death counts

also entirely dropped Ümit's final sentence about the importance of human rights organizations and lawyers – noise irrelevant to my line of inquiry.

Ümit's original statement was translated by Zeynep into nonfluent spoken English, then by me into handwritten shorthand. I distorted the signal one final time when I transcoded my fieldnote into a quotation that made the relation of psychological warfare to counts of the dead clearer still: "'Counts of the dead,' Ümit Efe told me, 'have always been a means of psychological warfare.'" The path of information from Ümit to the page of my story thus involved two rounds of transmission, transcoding, and reception, diagrammed in Figure 4.2.

The rest of the interview was more or less a conversation between Ümit and Zeynep (Ümit barely looked at me) about Ümit's fact-finding trip to the southeast, which Zeynep relayed to me in summarized form. Zeynep, having done her best to align Ümit to my informatic demands, now catered to Ümit's framing of the issue, giving her the opportunity to say her piece. She buffered me from the informational contamination of a source-directed conversation, translating just the bits and pieces that she judged might find a way into my script.

\* \* \*

---

```
News articles on the PKK conflict include boilerplate assertions

that it has cost 40,000 lives, but that figure is outdated.

According to_____, the number currently stands at_____.
            (state institution)                                (official count)
Even that figure is questionable because_____,
                                          (explanation of military propaganda system)
according to_____. The alternative tally of_____was
                (expert)                                  (unofficial count)
reached by _____. They arrived at that figure
            (research or advocacy organization)
by_____.
  (explanation of unofficial count methodology)
```

---

**Figure 4.3** Noah's framework for PKK story before Zeynep's fill-ins

Journalism is like a game of Mad Libs.[4] If you are not familiar with
phrasal template word games, they consist of an incomplete narrative
with blank spaces for the player to fill. Under each space is written a
general category of words to be filled in, but the player has the freedom
to choose what specific phrase to insert within that empty frame (I use
"frame," "template," "script," and "narrative" interchangeably).

I already had a script in place with basic elements of the article that
I wanted to write but needed Zeynep's help filling in those blanks. I did
not literally hand her a Mad Libs–style template like Figure 4.3 on a
piece of paper, but I made my expectations clear when we discussed my
story idea and potential interviewees and organizations to approach.[5]

---

[4] This Mad Libs metaphor is a variation on Kuhn's ([1962] 1970: 35–42)
metaphor of **normal science** as a puzzle of whose completed form "everything but
the most esoteric detail ... is known in advance." Just as news contributors are
prescribed to operate within the boundaries of frames outside of their control,
normal scientists operate within **paradigms**: frames for making sense of nature.
Like the tacit templates handed down to news contributors, paradigms both
produce and limit the scope of the questions that normal scientists ask (Kuhn
[1962] 1970: 13–15). Gans ([1979] 2004: 90–103) describes a similar process,
which he calls "buying, selling, and highlighting" of stories, along a chain of
reporters, writers, editors, and senior staff in the context of American TV news.

[5] Story templates are generally left tacit; as in many professional fields, making
prescriptions too explicit and detailed would insult participants' sense of
expertise and autonomy. Nonetheless, frames and blanks are more explicitly
recognized in some subfields of journalism (e.g. Czarniawska 2011: 38–42 on
newswire templates). In the case of TV stories, pre-production often includes the
drafting of a "shot list." This written list is a roughly defined sequence of images
and statements that will be filled in by specific captured footage. There is a
practical mandate for this routine: video is expensive to produce and unwieldy to

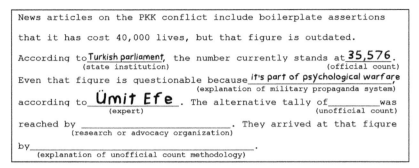

**Figure 4.4** Kurdish conflict story with Zeynep's fill-ins

Zeynep was to help me fill in the remaining blanks in the frame by brokering between me and sources.

It matters what and whose information fills in those blanks. For instance, while researching that same story, I found that Nedim Şener, a well-known Turkish nationalist journalist, had compiled and published his own estimate for how many had died in the conflict. Had Zeynep been of a different political disposition and connected me to Şener instead of Kurdish-leftist İHD, my article would have changed significantly, albeit within the confines of the same overall frame.

As it transpired, Zeynep and I filled in my script as seen in Figure 4.4. Zeynep failed to fill in all the blanks. She located archival documents to give me an official (albeit out-of-date) figure from a state institution. She transformed Ümit's signals into a fill-in about the unreliability of official figures. She was not, however, able to secure me an alternative tally from İHD or elsewhere.

I searched for alternative channels of information and devoted more of my own time to the story than I had planned. I ended up, independently of Zeynep and with the Internet as my fixer, discovering that the International Crisis Group and a political scientist in Florida were attempting their own independent tallies, but only of recent years' casualties. I was forced to revise my framing accordingly. Instead of providing a well-informed alternative count, I concluded that nobody

edit. Going into the field without a clear plan for what images and sounds should be captured would be inefficient.

really knew how many had been killed overall, and so it would be more credible for commentators on the conflict to limit themselves to referencing how many had been killed only in the recent upsurge of violence.

If we move up the chain of news contributors, I was in an analogous position to Zeynep. I was filling in details, albeit at a greater level of abstraction, in the frames of *editors*. Or at least I was supposed to.

Keeping with the Mad Libs metaphor, if reporters rely on fixers for help filling in blanks at the level of words and phrases, then editors are concerned with the overall shape and theme of paragraphs and delegate sentence-level fill-ins to reporters. Foreign news editors bring master narratives – rough outlines of what is going on in Turkey or Syria or wherever – to their judgments about which stories are newsworthy and how reports on those countries should be framed to best hang from the peg of a big event or important trend (Baker 2006: 78–83). These frames help editors to quickly make sense of events around the world and comparatively evaluate newsworthiness.[6]

Templates are more explicit when editors assign stories top-down to staff reporters or stringers. But even when reporters have their own ideas for stories, they must pitch editors, who will say *Yes, No*, or *Maybe if you do it this way* based on the pitched stories' compatibility with the editors' frames.

My article about PKK conflict death counts, though it addressed two topics of international media interest in summer 2016 – the Turkey–Kurdish conflict and fake news – did not fit into editors' templates. It offered an alternative approach to a well-covered issue, but for this very reason failed to resonate with editors. After all, editors' frameworks for how to report the conflict were based on the conventions that previous coverage had established. After failing to sell the piece to a half dozen outlets, I posted it on an online publishing platform without earning a dime (Arjomand 2016c).[7]

---

[6] Editors' narratives are not immaculately conceived, but based on their own experiences, preexisting cultural tropes, competing publications' work, the influence of agenda-setters like politicians and experts, and audience feedback (Said 1978, 1981; Gans [1979] 2004; Fishman 1980; Anderson 2011).

[7] My interpretation here may consequently be contaminated by personal bitterness, though I stand by it after five years to get over the slight of nobody buying my story.

# Solmaz

The Turkish government accelerated its crackdown on the Fethullah Gülen Movement, which had gone from Erdoğan's key ally to his bitterest foe. The police arrested members of its own force alongside judges, prosecutors, and journalists alleged to be Gülenist conspirators.

Just as Turkish business conglomerates and political parties directly or indirectly possess news organizations, so too were a collection of media outlets affiliated with the Gülen Movement. The government began to go after not just individual pro-Gülen journalists, but entire news organizations, successively seizing and transforming them into government mouthpieces. In March 2016, police dramatically took over the largest of the pro-Gülen news conglomerates, which included an English-language daily called *Today's Zaman*.

I decided to write a report about state pressure on opposition media, especially those affiliated with the Gülen Movement. I hired Solmaz, whom you might remember from this book's introduction. She spoke fluent English, was the product of an elite bicultural upbringing, and had just left a job as a reporter for *Today's Zaman*. This was her first fixing gig.

We met at a café and decided together whom to interview and what to ask. Solmaz was in the unusual position of being an insider-outsider to the field of Gülenist news media. She was, unlike many of her erstwhile colleagues, not personally an adherent to the Gülen Movement. Her experience working at *Today's Zaman* had left her both familiar with movement-affiliated journalists and critical of them.

Solmaz gave me the inside scoop on our sources' backgrounds and perspectives. She coached me that whereas adherents refer to the Gülen Movement as *Hizmet* (Service), outsiders use the mildly disparaging term *Cemaat* (The Flock). The government and its media allies had started using the acronym *FETÖ/PDY* (Fethullah-ist Terrorist Organization and Parallel State Structure). Solmaz cautioned me that her erstwhile colleagues were always secretive about their affiliation to *Hizmet*. She suggested that they would be more receptive to personal inquiries about how politics was affecting their family lives than about their connections to the Gülen Movement. She explained that one source was long winded and should be interrupted if I wanted to get a word in edgewise, one was a Twitter addict and might have interesting things to say about his social media usage, one had experienced legal troubles recently that he might reference or be guided to discuss. Solmaz's coaching pre-aligned me to make sense of what they would tell me and gave me tools to elicit the information I sought. She tuned me to the right frequency, in informatic terms.

Solmaz also talked generally about the atmosphere at the Gülen Movement–affiliated press. She believed she had enjoyed more freedom to write what she wanted at *Today's Zaman* than journalists did at many mainstream outlets. She just had to respect an obvious unspoken red line: Don't Criticize the Movement.

She described the recently seized media group as a bulletin board for the movement to talk to itself, with guests like her given a bit of space on the side to do their own reporting. I wrote in my daily notes, "[Solmaz] says *Zaman* when it started was more of a newsletter for a community than a newspaper."

I asked Solmaz to arrange interviews on her own phone – a way of buffering myself from the danger of direct connection to sources. Our interviewees' phones were very likely under surveillance, and I did not want to draw attention to myself, as I was on a tourist visa and without a press card.

Our first interview was at the office of *Özgür Düşünce* (Free Thought), a shoestring operation that had sprung up after its predecessor newspaper, *Bugün* (Today), was forcibly placed under state "trusteeship." Solmaz introduced me to Cihan Acar, a reporter on staff who used to work at *Zaman* (Time), the Gülen Movement's flagship paper that shared a building with Solmaz's English-language spinoff. He was happy to talk about *Özgür Düşünce*'s hardships and police violence in the takeover of *Bugün* and *Zaman*. Asking about their (widely known) affiliation with the Gülen Movement, though, was a game of cat and mouse.

Cihan repeatedly cited *Yarına Bakış* (Look to Tomorrow) and *Meydan* (Public Square), other movement-affiliated newspapers, as some of the few other "free" press organs, but when I asked about connections among the outlets and to the movement, he balked. Cihan would concede only that they happened to have similar editorial lines.

Cihan mentioned being *"transferred"* from *Zaman* to *Bugün*, but when I asked him if it was commonplace for reporters to transfer among *Hizmet* outlets owned by different companies, he quickly backtracked. He said he had just meant he had gotten a job at *Bugün* after working at *Zaman*. Solmaz, in a quiet aside, confirmed to me: Yes, it was commonplace for Gülen Movement publications to share and swap staff. She was also sure to highlight to me in a side comment that Cihan had used the movement insider's term *Hocaefendi* (Master Teacher) to refer to Fethullah Gülen.

I pointed out that demonstrators who came into the streets to respectively support *Zaman* and *Bugün* in the face of police seizures looked remarkably similar. Many were women in typical *Hizmet* garb of long dark coats and tidy flowered headscarves, unlike the scruffy inveterate protesters who came to other free press rallies equipped with gas masks and hard hats.

*"Those coming here,"* Cihan responded evasively, pointing to a photo on his computer screen from the day *Bugün* was seized, *"could be supporters of this movement. They could be democrats or [just] people passing by on the streets."*

I tried to approach the subject from an empathetic tack, inviting him to talk about oppression the Gülen Movement faced: "I notice you're avoiding saying anything – you're avoiding the word *Hizmet*; you're avoiding the [name] Gülen. Is it dangerous now even to talk about these things?" Cihan did not take the bait. He dodged again, saying that they were not a publicity or advertising agency for *Hizmet* and the work they did was entirely journalism.

That exchange is worth looking at in closer detail, as it illustrates the connection between a fixer's social position and the transmission of information. Solmaz's abilities and limitations as an interpreter, as well as her choices of how to translate, depended not just on raw linguistic skill, but also on her background and understanding of the parties she brokered.

| Speaker | Content | Turn |
|---|---|---|
| Noah | So I notice you're avoiding saying anything – you're avoiding the word *Hizmet*; you're avoiding the word *Gülen*. Is it dangerous now to even talk about these things? | 1 |
| Solmaz | *I am seeing that the words* Hizmet *and* Gülen *are not even coming out of your mouth* – | 2 |
| Cihan | (over her last words) *Because the work that we do* (Solmaz tries to interject) *is completely journalism.* | 3 |
| Solmaz | Because our job that we do is completely just journalism. | 4 |
| Cihan | *Our viewpoint, our situation* – (pauses) | 5 |
| Solmaz | Our point of view, our stance | 6 |
| Cihan | *A – we aren't a public relations agency.* | 7 |
| Solmaz | We're not a PR agency. | 8 |
| Cihan | *I mean we are not* (inaudible) *advertisement.* | 9 |
| Solmaz | We're not an advertising agency. | 10 |
| Cihan | *I mean we're not a committee doing the* Hizmet *Movement's publications.* | 11 |
| Solmaz | *Uh, not?* – (trails off) | 12 |
| Cihan | *Like, we are not a press* (inaudible) *of the* Hizmet *Movement.* | 13 |
| Solmaz | *You're not? You are like that [öylesiniz]* (ambiguous whether this is a question) | 14 |
| Cihan | *We are not. I mean, we are doing journalism.* | 15 |
| Solmaz | He said, we're journalists. We're not people just here to advertise for the *Hizmet* Movement. | 16 |

Cihan cut Solmaz off before she completed her question at Turn 2, but then the *statement → translation → statement → translation* order of speaking went smoothly until Turn 12. At that point, Solmaz became confused, and until Turn 15 the two engaged in a side conversation to clarify Cihan's statement of Turn 11. That statement was clear as a linguistic signal: "*we're not a committee doing the Hizmet Movement's publications.*" It is no more complicated, when viewed without context, than other statements that Solmaz translated without difficulty. Yet the decodability of a signal is not just a property of the signal itself, but also depends on the receiver: Solmaz, in this moment. Solmaz was unable to make sense of his statement because it clashed with her understanding of the Gülen-affiliated media and with the way she had coached me pre-interaction. Before the interview, Solmaz had *defended* the movement media precisely by saying they should be thought of and judged as a community newsletter. Now Cihan was saying the opposite: they were *not* a community publication. The two went back and forth as she made sure that was what he *really* meant. It is unclear whether the second part of her utterance at Turn 14, "*you are that way*," is a question or a rebuttal; it lacks the "*mi*" suffix that indicates a question in Turkish.

When Solmaz did pivot to translate back to me, she departed from the precedent she had established in Turns 4, 6, 8, and 10 of taking on Cihan's subject position (e.g. "we are"). Instead, she translated that last statement with the preface "He said." Changing subject position distanced her from the utterance and signaled the information's unreliability to me.[1] The signal that reached me was not only Cihan's translated statement, but also a key for how decode it: with a grain of salt. Solmaz disagreed with Cihan. She also had to repair the potential damage to her standing as a local expert when Cihan told me the opposite of what Solmaz had previously explained.

This moment of breakdown aside, I found the interview highly informative for my story. Solmaz could make sense of Cihan's words beyond their dictionary definitions because of her experience with the Gülen Movement. She also did a great deal to enhance my capacity as a receiver. If a fixer tells a reporter something that would fit brilliantly into their story, but the reporter cannot make sense of what they are told or see its relevance to their frame, the fixer's utterance is useless noise. When Solmaz coached me beforehand on Gülen Movement lingo and secrecy and when she added side comments to her translation that helped me understand the nuances of Cihan's speech, she effectively expanded my capacity to decode a wider range of signals.

I was able to borrow Solmaz's expertise, contacts, and built-up trust with Gülen-affiliated media, which took her years to develop (Murrell 2015: 82). Solmaz enabled me to quickly gain entry, get the information I needed, and then depart while maintaining my moral distance for our source. Solmaz's changes of subject position and comments encouraging skepticism of Cihan were subtle signals to help me

---

[1] See also Diriker (2004) on the inconsistent subject positions of conference interpreters.

preserve that distance and avoid unwitting co-optation to our source's side.

Solmaz's little interventions also signaled to me that she was on my side, that she was able to split her fixer self from the *Today's Zaman* self that was closer to our sources. After our visit to *Özgür Düşünce*, she seethed over the way Cihan and others at the office had dodged my questions about affiliation with the Gülen Movement.

"Do they think we're stupid? Do they actually think it works to avoid answering, that they're convincing us they're independent?" She took the "we"/"us" subject position, merging herself with me into a team. As a plural pronoun, we were together on the same moral and epistemic side *against* her erstwhile colleagues.

# *Orhan*

I hired Orhan to help me for the same story about the crackdown on the Turkish press. The newsworthy peg on which I thought I could hang the story was the recent seizure of *Zaman*. When I discussed my idea with Orhan at his usual café, he did not suggest any pro-Gülen media sources. He instead encouraged me to contextualize recent events with the Gülen Movement's history of collusion with the government in targeting critical journalists.

Orhan had himself been something of a victim of the Gülen Movement media. When the two Turkish newspapers where he worked in the 2000s came – following government intervention – under new management, both began hiring then-allied AKP loyalists and Gülenists. They pushed out the old guard that included Orhan. He offered that in addition to fixing for this story, he could serve as a source if I wanted to interview him.

Orhan also pushed hard for us to interview someone at the news website OdaTV who had faced prosecution in the Ergenekon trials. Starting in 2008, a series of military officers and journalists were charged (by prosecutors thought to be Gülen Movement adherents, with Erdoğan's blessing) with conspiring to overthrow the AKP government as members of a secret secularist organization called Ergenekon. The Gülen-affiliated media denounced journalists implicated in the alleged plot and published falsified evidence.

I was initially skeptical of using an OdaTV journalist as a source because I considered the outlet too far outside the mainstream. OdaTV was associated with *ulusalcılık*, a strain of Kemalist nationalism intensely hostile to what its proponents see as the twin threats of AKP Islamism and Western imperialism (Gürpınar 2013; Çınar and Taş 2017). OdaTV founder Söner Yalçın was notorious for anti-Semitism and conspiracy theorizing (Baer 2013). Orhan readily acknowledged that the outlet was controversial but nonetheless, on his second or third attempt, convinced me that it would be worth talking to an erstwhile defendant or two of the OdaTV case.

Once we settled on a list of prospective sources, Orhan picked up one of his two cell phones from our café table, asking me which outlet I was writing for as he dialed. I stumblingly said that I had pitched the story to *The Nation* (which ended up rejecting it) and Orhan translated this over the phone into me *working* for *The Nation* as he requested interviews. Orhan was at work convincing both me and sources of each other's legitimacy. Orhan's tone speaking to Barış Terkoğlu, his source at OdaTV, was familiar and jovial: *"How's it going?" "Good, bro."*

We took a ferry across the Bosphorus to OdaTV's office in Kadıköy district later that week. Barış had been indicted in 2011 as a conspirator in the alleged Ergenekon plot after he reported that evidence against other defendants had been planted. Orhan knew Barış's legal case inside and out. He had attended more than a dozen of Barış's court appearances as a fixer for various foreign news organizations.

As Barış described the events leading to his prosecution, Orhan aligned the information to my interest in the prosecution of journalists. He dropped words unimportant to this line of inquiry as he translated. Orhan also moderated Barış's claims by adding words that made them more amenable to a skeptical outsider like me. For example:

| Speaker | Content |
| --- | --- |
| Barış | *Some soldiers were being prosecuted for bombs found in an excavation. I found and published camera recording* (inaudible) *concrete evidence that they were buried there by police.* |
| Orhan | Also I, I also showed some footages that have been founded in Ergenekon case during the investigations that there's some weapons buried in some places. But I found some footage that police was – it is quite possible that police have planted that weapons to that places. |

Orhan subtracted mention of *"soldiers"* – I was interested in journalists' prosecutions, after all – and not simply because he was in a rush. Orhan did find the time to add that this was part of the Ergenekon investigation as clarification for me. Orhan also rendered Barış's *"concrete evidence that they were buried there by police"* into

English as a much softer formulation: "it is quite possible that police have planted that weapons to that places."

It might seem that I am finding patterns in random mistakes. Maybe Orhan just is not a great translator. He does, after all, confusingly conflate the footage Barış obtained with evidence used in the Ergenekon trials in a way that does not serve any interactional purpose. Some of his transformations were simple error. But there was a persistent pattern of Orhan dropping and adding data to align Barış's words with my scripts, especially when his sentences were complex.

Orhan managed the overload of complex sentences through lossy compression (i.e. by losing some information). He was careful to preserve the information that fit my prescriptions but dropped unprescribed data, like the word "*soldiers.*" Take the passage below, in which Barış overloads Orhan's capacity as a transcoder with a long sentence swollen with subclauses:

| Speaker | Content |
| --- | --- |
| Barış | *In brief, the thing I want to say is that* Zaman *newspaper supported this arresting of journalists in Turkey and behaved as a part of the political power's conspiracy against everyone opposed to it and, like an organization mouthpiece or the publication of a structure organized for [the agenda of] the state, just about played a leading role in this matter.* |
| Orhan | Actually *Zaman* newspaper supported, when we look at that period, *Zaman* newspaper has supported the journalism – journalist arrests to be taken, taken the journalism into the lock [i.e. locking up journalists], and they were spokespeople of this mentality in Turkey. |

As he struggled to translate, Orhan left out the more conspiracy theorist–sounding stuff about "*the political power's conspiracy against everyone opposed to it*" and "*a structure organized for the state.*" In Orhan's rendition, *Zaman*'s journalists served merely as "spokespeople" of a "mentality," acting hypocritically but not conspiratorially.

It is worth noting that Barış's sentence above, which took him about 25 seconds to express, was of exceptional length in the original Turkish. From the start, Orhan would interrupt him when he continued too long, tacitly coaching Barış to conform to a conversational rhythm that both minimized translator overload and served my expectation to be included at frequent intervals. After the first few minutes of the interview, Barış's utterances mostly lasted 5 to 15 seconds, and he began to adapt to the enforced conversational rhythm by speaking in shorter, punchy sentences and pausing on his own for dramatic effect as he gave Orhan openings to translate, as in the next passage.

This passage also shows how Orhan used his knowledge of the OdaTV case to fill in Barış's narrative, to read between the lines and add information to Barış's originals:

| Speaker | Content | Turn |
| --- | --- | --- |
| Barış | *First the target would be shown by the Gülen media.* | 1 |
| Orhan | First you started to be appointed by the Gülen Movement and media. | 2 |
| Barış | *It would be explained that you were a putschist [darbeci], that you were a terrorist, that actually you were a person with secret goals working to topple the government.* | 3 |
| Orhan | They started to write and talk about that you're a coup, pro-coup person, that you have some hidden agenda to take the government, to make coup or something. They were always publishing these kind of stories first. | 4 |
| Barış | *What an interesting coincidence: in exactly that same period, pro-Gülen police listened to your phones. They began to follow you with vehicles.* | 5 |
| Orhan | It was such an interesting coincidence that the same time a pro-Gülen police officers and Gülenist other officers was following you, taps your phone. They tapped your phone in the same time, follows you where you go or, you know, take a close look at your personal and private life. | 6 |

The only straightforward mistranslation, obscuring meaning without doing any interactional work that I can discern, was Orhan's use of "appointed" in Turn 2. Other signal distortions were embellishments or reductions of the original that served to bring Barış's utterances into alignment with my coding norms and informational interests. Adding "They were always publishing these kind of stories first" at Turn 4 added emphasis to Barış's statement and clarified the subject doing the defaming to be the Gülen media, whereas Barış's use of the passive voice ("*It would be explained*" in Turn 3) was normative in Turkish but evasive in English. At Turn 4 Orhan also left out "*terrorist*," perhaps predicting that the word would have thrown me off, as there had been no discussion of terrorism in the sense of indiscriminate violence.[1]

Orhan's addition at Turn 6 of "take a close look at your personal and private life," when Barış only says police surveilled him, might be better described as **predictive translation** than as **mistranslation**. Orhan knew from his past reporting that details of defendants' sex lives had been leaked in the press and addressed in court. Barış did get around to mentioning "*your sexual life, your family life, your private relations were published by those newspapers*" but not until 4 minutes later in the interview. Prediction allows a fixer to manage information overload, producing a transcoded signal for the end receiver that combines bits of the transmitter's signal with compatible information already stored in the fixer's memory.

Orhan often folded his own explanations of what Barış was saying seamlessly into his renditions of Barış's words. In this example, Barış was talking about Gülen's pragmatism in instructing his followers to conform to secular norms in order to access and infiltrate state institutions:

| Speaker | Content |
| --- | --- |
| Barış | *When the headscarf [türban] debate was going on at universities, Gülen, instead of fighting, advised his loyalists to take off their headscarves and enter university.* |
| Orhan | For example, when there was this fight come up in universities because of the closed – closed girls – I mean covered girls was forbidden to enter universities. Gülen said – was okay, and said his supporters that "You can go to university uncovered." He suggested that to his supporters. |

Barış formulated his message assuming a receiver who could decode his reference to "*the headscarf debate … at universities*" because they

---

[1] On the expansive meaning of "*terrorist*" in Turkish political discourse, see for example Weise (2016) on Erdoğan's usage of the term.

knew that there had been a secularist ban on headscarved women entering public buildings, which the AKP lifted after years of resistance. Orhan, however, lacked confidence that I possessed the background knowledge to decode Barış's statement and so expanded on the original with the explication "covered girls was forbidden to enter universities."

From the perspective of an information transmission purist, Orhan mixing his own message with Barış's was problematic signal bleed. But for a pragmatist like Orhan, merging explanation with translation efficiently aligned us into coding harmony. The alternative – explaining context and meaning to me in separate side comments – would have been more socially laborious, requiring changes in tone and other signals that he was transitioning back and forth between channel/translator/non-person and transmitter/interlocutor/person roles.

Listening back to the transcripts to note where Orhan diverged from direct translation and where Barış added explanatory notes himself, I could approximately reconstruct Orhan's and Barış's respective predictions of what I did and did not know and where the two diverged. When Barış revealed his prediction that I was unfamiliar with the PKK in explaining, as he discussed the prosecution of a Gülen critic, "*He was accused with making propaganda for the PKK organization – I mean a separatist organization,*" Orhan by contrast revealed his own prediction that I *was* familiar with the PKK by compressing his translation to "charged with being a member of PKK."

Some of Orhan's changes to the signals he transcoded from Barış would have been unnecessary if he had tuned the end receiver (me) beforehand. Solmaz, having coached me on what it signaled when a speaker used *Hizmet* versus *Cemaat* versus *FETÖ* for the Gülen Movement, was sure to preserve the original Turkish appellations when she translated Cihan's words. Orhan provided no such coaching and, predicting that I was an impaired receiver unable to decode the meaning of Turkish labels for the movement, consistently translated Barış's negatively charged "*Cemaat*" into the neutral "Gülen Movement." The effect was a loss of useful information from Orhan's English renditions.

Orhan's signal enhancements (or distortions, depending on perspective) worked in both directions: he also helped Barış make sense of me and to refine his own messaging. When I asked vague, unclear, wordy questions, Orhan would improve them in ways he predicted would elicit a more useful response than direct translations of my originals. Sometimes his interventions were more explicit to me, as when Orhan asked clarifying side questions of me (e.g. Turn 2 below) before translating.

| Speaker | Content | Turn |
|---|---|---|
| Noah | Since, in the last two years since Gülen and Erdoğan have been fighting, have *Zaman* and other newspapers continued to write about – for example about OdaTV? About secular opposition papers? Have they changed the way that they talk about, for example, what you do? | 1 |
| Orhan | (overlapping with my last words) You mean the fight – the fight started – after the fight started? | 2 |
| Noah | Yeah just since after the fight started. | 3 |
| Orhan | *So after the brouhaha [telaş] broke out between Erdoğan and Cemaat, after the fight grew, did* Zaman *continue to target you, journalists like you, for instance OdaTV and such? Or did a change take place in* [Zaman's] *policy?* | 4 |
| Barış | *After the war erupted, both sides actually held back from directly opposing journalists like us.* (Orhan: mm-hmm) *I can even say this: the general trend was that they tried to pull (inaudible), not just me, to their [respective] sides.* (Orhan: mm) *Because they wanted to make alliance.* | 5 |
| Orhan | After the fight come up, both sides, Erdoğan's side and Gülen's side, they hesitate to hit against the journalists like them. Actually I can also say as an addition that they want to pull us near to them in order to make a kind of a coalition against the other side. | 6 |

Orhan narrows my question to focus on what he predicts I really want to know. He asks Barış at Turn 4 not the general question of whether *Zaman* "continued to write about" OdaTV, but specifically *"did Zaman continue to target you?"* He then further helps Barış provide an answer to satisfy me by back-channeling approving "mm-hmm" sounds during Turn 5 as Barış begins to say useful things. This feedback nudged Barış to tune his transmissions for optimal reception.

In other cases, I asked specific questions and Orhan generalized them to align with the response that he predicted Barış was ready to offer.

Below, I try to pin down the details of the pro-Gülen media's role in the attack on Barış as an Ergenekon conspirator. Orhan changes the object of the news under inquiry mid-sentence from the singular *you* [*sen*] to the plural *you all* [*siz*]. Orhan's revision reduces the burden on Barış to recall details of news coverage about him individually and allows him instead the easier task of describing a general pattern:

| Speaker | Content |
| --- | --- |
| Noah | And was the [defamatory] news published first in *Zaman*, in *Taraf*,[2] in – the news about you specifically? |
| Orhan | *Was news coming out about you* (singular) *– about you* (plural) *generally coming out in* Taraf *and* Zaman *first?* |

Orhan's prediction that losing specifics would cost less to me than demanding specifics would cost of Barış may have been incorrect. I have been using the word **predict** rather than **understand** because it suggests the possibility of inaccuracy. Barış may well have remembered which newspaper specifically targeted him first, and if it had been *Zaman*, that would have contributed a good detail to my story about *Zaman*'s seizure.

Late in the interview, I asked Barış what he thought of the counterargument that I had been hearing from pro-Gülen journalists like Cihan: Even if *Zaman* had done wrong in the past, wasn't it better to fight the government's monopolization of the media now by defending *Zaman* and other outlets? And shouldn't freedom of expression be defended even for those who had made mistakes? Orhan suddenly sounded exhausted, almost slurring his words as he translated into Turkish. He uncharacteristically switched back to English midway through translating to ask that I repeat the second half of my question, though I had asked it in clear terms. The function of this paraverbal resistance was to distance Orhan from the question and signal his skepticism of the Gülenist counterargument to Barış.

Taken alone, each of these modulations in the signals Orhan was relaying between Barış and me was small, relatively unimportant. But they added up to help Barış give me useful information while convincing

[2] *Taraf* was another newspaper that published extensively on the Ergenekon and OdaTV cases, though its connections to the Gülen Movement were less clear than *Zaman*'s.

him that Orhan was on his side. Orhan's renditions of Barış's words gave me the impression that our source was both moderate and comprehensible, more so than if Orhan had translated more literally.

Solmaz had signaled to me through her translation choices that Cihan's information was suspect, which served to distinguish her from our interviewee and signal that she was free from Gülenist bias. Orhan translated in ways that reduced the visibility of Barış's bias, which served to sway me to his arguments. It also helped that Barış, under Orhan's rhythmic pressure, switched from lengthy rambles to speaking in short, pithy sentences that fit my frame as neat quotations, like "politics is the art of presenting your problem as if it is everyone's."

Barış ended up with central billing in my article, with a hundred more words about his case than about the pro-Gülen journalist Cihan's. The moderated information Orhan delivered to me from Barış led me to revise my framing and criticize the Gülen Movement media more than I had originally planned.

When I showed the full article to Solmaz after publication, she commented, with a tone and expression that signaled to me that she thought Barış an extremist, that it was very "interesting" the way I had included him in the article as the main voice of the opposition. But by then, even if I had wanted to, even if Solmaz had convinced me I had made an unconscionable mistake, it was too late for me to change the article.

Including an *ulusalcı* journalist like Barış as a prominent voice of the opposition and victim of injustice did not change the general narrative that I presented to an American audience, that the Turkish government was systematically capturing the national press. But spotlighting Barış did matter to Solmaz and potentially to Barış himself, enmeshed as they were in local politics. My article lent him legitimacy on an international stage.

* * *

A fixer enjoys a certain freedom to make choices that matter from an insider perspective so long as they do not challenge the outsider's frame control. They can get creative as long as they work within the Mad Libs template. We can call this constrained freedom the fixer's **frame space** (Goffman 1981: 230–231; Baker 2006: 105–110). The amount of space available to the fixer depends both on the narrowness of their client's demands and on their capacity to choose among different fill-ins to satisfy the reporter's script in good time.

When it came to choosing sources, Orhan (a longtime newsmaker) had more contacts who fit my prescription for a persecuted opposition journalist than Zeynep (a grad student) had contacts who fit my prescription for an official source of PKK conflict statistics. Orhan enjoyed a wider frame space than Zeynep. Orhan could choose the best source from among multiple options: a source who was not too valuable, who would not mind talking to me, and who would predictably make arguments toward which Orhan was well-disposed.

If we zoom in from the selection of sources to the selection of words, fixers similarly operate within limited but significant frame space during a translated interview. The words a source speaks – the signals they send – do not 100 percent determine the message that reaches the end receiver; uncertainty remains in what the final message will be after the fixer transcodes and then the reporter decodes it. Barış's originals were only loosely linked to Orhan's translations; Orhan had some freedom in his word choice (Palmer 2019: 128–130).

Freedom of choice is relational, though: we may have some freedom to act within one frame, but how we use that space is constrained by the other frames around us. When choosing the words for his renditions of Barış's speech, Orhan also had to worry about every other moral expectation I have discussed: filling in my story template, Barış making sense to an outsider, microlevel scripts for the rhythm of conversation, his own situation-transcending disposition on the topic, and so on. Orhan may have enjoyed some freedom of choice in relation to each of these constraints taken individually, but together, the different frame spaces overlapped like a crowded Venn diagram that chained him to its center with little wiggle room.

Orhan's commitment to fit his actions into each of these frame spaces depended on the risk and cost of detection if he did not. For example, the space Orhan had to change Barış's statements to meet my needs was limited by the prescription for high-fidelity translation. Barış's words did not 100 percent determine Orhan's, but they did determine them more than 0 percent because Orhan lacked complete information control. He knew that Barış and I understood enough of each other's language to tell if Orhan was getting too creative. Even if reporter and source do not share a spoken interlanguage, there are always alternative communication channels that disrupt a fixer's control and freedom: body language, emotive inflection, and even the duration of non-understood speech carry information that reporters and sources can use to enforce the coding prescription of accurate translation (Palmer 2019: 118–120).

Orhan mediated the Barış interview in ways that constrained my write-up of the media crackdown story and the information that

I would bring to building story frames in the future. Orhan translated predictively and compressed signals from Barış in order to manage information overload. He enhanced, cleaned up, and smoothed Barış's noisy signals to satisfy my prescriptions, as Orhan understood them.

Useful as prediction and compression may be as transcoding tools, they also homogenize the news. They limit sources' freedom to transmit information to reporters that the fixer does not expect or deem relevant, that might not fit the story template at hand but could expand a reporter's knowledge in other ways. In the interview with Barış, I did not receive information that might have led me in new directions.

At several moments in the interview (one is transcribed above), Barış talked about "*soldiers*" and "*military officers*" tried in the Ergenekon trials, but those words were dropped in Orhan's lossily compressed translations. Orhan thought his job was to transmit information to me about journalists on trial, not soldiers. A few months later, though, the officers once on trial beside Barış would suddenly become newsworthy again.

Some of the very same soldiers purged in the Ergenekon era would return to their posts to replace those who staged a coup – a real, violent attempt to capture the state by force, not just a dubiously evidenced conspiracy theory (Tol and Taşpınar 2016). A noisier translation of Barış's words, full of information less immediately useful to me, might have planted a seed in my mind for a future story. I might have recalled those officers as a topic to revisit. I might have considered Barış as a potential broker to contact them.

# Solmaz

The focus of my story, under Orhan's sway, was shifting to how journalists within Turkey viewed the crackdown on Gülen Movement media differently than their international counterparts. Barış's indictment of *Zaman* contrasted dramatically with the empathetic coverage of the newspaper's plight in the United States and Europe, where *Zaman*'s seizure had yielded headlines like "The Death Blow to Turkish Media" and "This Is the End of Journalism in Turkey" (Arjomand 2016b).

I wondered what Kurdish journalists thought about the demise of the pro-Gülen media. They were far longer-standing victims of state press policy than either the *Hizmet* or the *ulusalcı* press.

Solmaz and I went to the offices of *Özgür Gündem* (Free Agenda) newspaper to interview reporter Çağdaş Kaplan. *Özgür Gündem* was associated with the Kurdish Movement, despite the similarity of its name to pro-Gülen *Özgür Düşünce* (Free Thought). Solmaz had met Çağdaş in the course of her work at *Today's Zaman*. Once the Gülen Movement–affiliated media joined the opposition in late 2013, its journalists, including Solmaz, began to sympathetically cover human rights and press freedom issues related to the Kurds. Nonetheless, compared to my previous fixer Zeynep, who was socially and morally closer to the Kurdish Left and had a refined sense of how to code-switch between a rights activist and a foreign reporter, Solmaz was new to figuring out how to transcode Kurdish Movement speech.

During our conversation with Çağdaş, Solmaz was oddly disinclined to frame issues as specific to the Kurds. As Çağdaş recounted his personal narrative of prosecution, Solmaz compressed her translations such that he seemed to be speaking about the press in general, rather than the Kurdish press specifically. Even the word "Kurdish" kept dropping from her English renditions.

| Speaker | Content | Turn |
|---|---|---|
| Çağdaş | *News that was published on Diçle News Agency with my own signature,* | 1 |
| Solmaz | … The news article that had my own byline for Diçle Haber Ajans | 2 |
| Çağdaş | *live telephone connections that I made with Kurdish channels in Europe,* | 3 |
| Solmaz | the live feeds that I gave to European news outlets, | 4 |
| Çağdaş | *and telephone meetings that I made with news sources,* | 5 |
| Solmaz | and the telephone conversations that I had with my sources, | 6 |
| Çağdaş | *interviews,* | 7 |
| Solmaz | the interviews, | 8 |
| Noah | Mm-hmm | 9 |
| Çağdaş | *these were introduced as evidence and [prosecutors claimed that] these served as propaganda for the PKK Kongra-Gel[1] terror organization, therefore also that I was an organization member.* | 10 |
| Solmaz | They were – these were used as evidence against me saying that I was producing propaganda for the PKK and that I was a member of a terrorist organization. … (32 seconds later) | 11 |
| Çağdaş | *This case – at that time, the AKP government preferred a policy of security on the Kurdish problem and [this case] was opened as a political case. The silencing of the press was wanted, the Kurdish press.* | 12 |
| Solmaz | The – in this period the AKP – the AKP opened this case as a political case for national security and tried us for this reason. | 13 |
| Çağdaş | *I mean the Kurdish press's most important news organizations were raided [basıldı]; silencing them was wanted.* | 14 |
| Noah | Mm-hmm | 15 |
| Solmaz | And the – this was an attack on the Kurdish media, and the Kurdish media is, and these outlets are the most important outlets. And this was a – this was an attempt to silence these Kurdish outlets. | 16 |

[1] The PKK adopted Kongra-Gel, short for the People's Congress of Kurdistan, as its official name in 2003 to mirror a shift in official ideology. Solmaz did not translate "Kongra-Gel," perhaps because she thought it more likely to confuse than to inform me, or perhaps because she was not comfortable using an insider term to refer to the organization.

Following both Çağdaş's Turkish and Solmaz's English, it became apparent that she kept leaving out the word "Kurdish" in her translations to me. This happened three times, in Turns 4 and 13. I cannot know for sure why Solmaz repeatedly lost the word "Kurdish" in translation until my intervention. She may have judged that removing these references would better align his utterances to my script for a story on press freedom in general, not Kurdish press freedom in particular.

It was only after I back-channeled directly to Çağdaş at Turn 15 with an "mm-hmm" *before* Solmaz had a chance to translate his Turkish that she began including the word "Kurdish," perhaps reminded that I was following along his original and had noticed her pattern of omission. Solmaz did not have complete information control over transmissions between Çağdaş and me.[2]

Solmaz also lacked the depth of background knowledge of the recent history of the Kurdish press that she possessed of the pro-Gülen press, which impaired her capacity as a transceiver. She found some of Çağdaş's words and references incomprehensible, whereas she had been able to decode terminology specific to the Gülen Movement and its legal issues to me with ease born out of greater familiarity.

As the interview continued, Çağdaş explained his thirteen months in jail as he was tried with dozens of other journalists for association with the KCK (Union of Kurdistan Communities, an umbrella organization connected to the PKK). Solmaz struggled to translate the legalese name of the special court that tried the KCK cases: *Özel Yetkili Ağır Mahkemesi* (Specially Authorized Heavy Penal Court). In contrast to Orhan, she had never worked as a court reporter or covered journalists' trials.

Then, Çağdaş made an oblique reference to the Gülen–Erdoğan schism that Solmaz missed in her translation, setting the stage for further confusion of the English transcript. The subtlety of Çağdaş's reference to Gülenist misdeeds was likely a courtesy to Solmaz, who he knew had worked for *Today's Zaman*. That interactional gesture of

---

[2] I do not remember why I said "mm-hmm." My policy while reporting was to try to ignore Turkish-language utterances until I later listened to audio recordings, but I may not have been able to help but notice the discrepancy between original and transcoded messages and reflexively signal to Solmaz that I was on to her. My utterance may have also been an unconscious signal to Çağdaş that his message was getting through despite the distortion.

politeness toward what he presumed to be Solmaz's disposition ended up transforming the information that reached me.

| Speaker | Content | Turn |
|---------|---------|------|
| Çağdaş | *Of course the AKP government – I mean changes took place. Changes took place in the political atmosphere in Turkey. When it was proved that this court had done illegal thing[s], these courts were closed down.* | 1 |
| Solmaz | Of course there were lawlessness involved in these cases on, by the part of the AKP and since then this specific type of court has been closed. | 2 |
| Çağdaş | *President Erdoğan personally – at that time he was prime minister – also said these courts were not going to be trustworthy [güven olmayacağını söyledi]* | 3 |
| Solmaz | The prime – the then prime minister himself Erdoğan then said that these cases were, were not secure? (questioning intonation) | 4 |
| Çağdaş | *But he had himself opened [the courts] before that* (inaudible). | 5 |
| Solmaz | But he's also the one that filed them. | 6 |
| Çağdaş | *He closed [the courts] himself.* | 7 |
| Solmaz | And he's also the one who shut them. | 8 |

The events Çağdaş obliquely and succinctly referenced at Turn 1 are as follows: The Specially Authorized Heavy Penal Courts in which the KCK cases were tried had been created in 2004 along with positions of public prosecutors "specially authorized" to investigate civil servants. Such special courts, essentially an anti-terrorism judiciary parallel to the ordinary civilian court system with fewer civil rights protections, were nothing new in Turkey; however, the 2004 reorganization of the system allowed then-allied Erdoğan and Gülen loyalists to take control of the special courts and use them against political opponents (Kaynar 2017).

Prosecutors and judges allegedly affiliated with the Gülen Movement spearheaded, with AKP government support, the KCK trials (as well as the Ergenekon coup plot trials). But, as the rift between Gülen and Erdoğan grew, the special prosecutors started going after government loyalists, particularly those involved in the Kurdish peace negotiations

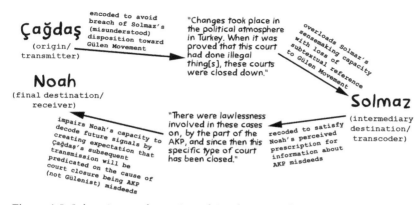

**Figure 4.5** Solmaz's transformation of Çağdaş's speech

of which Gülen apparently disapproved. These investigations culminated in the 2013 corruption scandal that implicated members of Erdoğan's inner circle. The government responded by purging the judiciary of suspected Gülenist prosecutors, judges, and police and passing a law that put an end to the special courts and special prosecutorial powers.

These were the "changes in the political atmosphere" that Çağdaş references at Turn 1. The "illegal things" were wiretaps of senior government officials that pro-Gülen police and prosecutors allegedly leaked via social media (Jenkins 2012; Sinclair-Webb 2014: 15–22; George 2018).

Solmaz may have been critical of the Gülen Movement, but she had spent years working in its media bubble and may not have known the intricacies of this sordid series of events. When she failed to make sense of Çağdaş's narrative, she may have defaulted to portraying Erdoğan and the AKP as the villains of his story. Whatever the reason, she turned Gülenist illegality into AKP illegality at Turn 2 by adding "the lawlessness ... of the AKP" to Çağdaş's original, as shown in Figure 4.5. From Solmaz's words, it seems that Erdoğan reversed his position and turned against the court because of his own party's illegality. That did not fit with what either of us knew of the president, and that first distortion made the rest of Çağdaş's account nonsensical.

The translated narrative's internal consistency continued to crumble in the minutes that followed. The closure of courts in Çağdaş's original

(Turns 3, 5, 7) had become the closure of Çağdaş's individual case in Solmaz's English rendition (Turns 4, 6, 8), but then the case that Solmaz told me had been closed was brought to the constitutional court. In Çağdaş's original, the constitutional court then "dropped" the case (i.e. declined to hear it, pushing it back down to the local court level), which Solmaz, unfamiliar with either Turkish or English legalese, translated as "overturned."

The narrative transmitted to me in English about Çağdaş's case made no sense: the case was tried at a special court, which was closed down because of AKP lawlessness, prompting (AKP leader) Erdoğan to close Çağdaş's case, which then went to the constitutional court, which overturned the case, which was going to have a hearing in a few days at a local court.

* * *

One way to make up for limited capacity is through **interpolation**. In everyday speech, we automatically fill in, or interpolate, words that we do not hear or that are not comprehensibly articulated. These interpolations are based on a missing word's position in a sequence and our knowledge as listeners. If you hear me say, "My name (inaudible) Noah," you can reasonably interpolate the inaudible word to be "is." Fixers make up for impairment of their signal reception by interpolating words they presume a speaker said or implied between words they actually understood. A form of predictive translation, interpolation allows a fixer to manage information overload and to devote less effort to listening and more to figuring out how best to align the message's original with its destination (Bateson 1972: 408–409).

But speech can be unpredictable, and interpolation impairs a listener's ability to pick up on unexpected signals. It reduces the capacity to receive and make sense of surprising new information.

If a fixer interpolates incorrectly, it can cause a domino effect of trouble when the speaker's subsequent utterances fail to fit with the previous translation. When Solmaz did not understand Çağdaş's oblique reference to a special court's closure for Gülenist illegality, she interpolatively reconstructed his statement based on her misunderstanding that we were talking about government misdeeds, to say the court was closed for AKP illegality. That first line of Solmaz's translation reduced Çağdaş's ability to transmit further information that made sense to me, because I expected the rest of his narrative to follow consistently from the (distorted) starting point to which Solmaz had delivered me.

Whereas Orhan had distorted signals from Barış to make his narrative *more* coherent to an outsider, Solmaz's inexpert modulations rendered Çağdaş's narrative incoherent. The signal-to-noise ratio was too low to be useful, like a photo so grainy you can't be confident of any details. In my article, I reduced all the information about Çağdaş's legal travails to a single line that he "has been on trial since 2011."

# *Noah*

Late in the evening of Friday, July 15, 2016, I was at home in Etiler neighborhood idly browsing social media while my then-girlfriend-now-wife Brett rehearsed music when strange reports started to appear in my Twitter feed. Military vehicles had blocked off bridges connecting Istanbul's European and Anatolian sides; soldiers were on the street telling people to go home, that it was not a drill. Turkish Twitter was collectively realizing that a coup d'état was underway. Soldiers appeared in Taksim Square and at Istanbul airport. Our apartment's TV was not working, so I dug a little radio set out of a back closet. At midnight, we listened as the "Peace at Home Council" announced that they were now in charge.

Resistance emerged swiftly, though. The putschists had, as in simpler days of military takeover, only seized the public broadcaster and not bothered to control the more popular private TV or radio stations. Erdoğan appeared on CNN Türk via Facetime video chat on an anchor's cell phone and invited the nation into city squares to resist. Huge crowds of civilians faced off against tanks and armored personnel carriers. Loyalist police and soldiers exchanged fire with the putschists. Brett and I heard the pop of automatic gunfire coming from the nearby bridge across the Bosphorus, then cowered as fighter jets screamed overhead with sonic booms. A contact of mine in Ankara wrote that it looked like Star Wars as jets and helicopters met in combat in the skies over the capital. Mosques around us in Etiler began repeatedly sounding the *ezan*, the Islamic call to prayer, and the *sela*, an eerily beautiful recitation imploring God to forgive the Muslim dead that is usually reserved for funerals and natural disasters (Gill 2016). By 4 a.m. it seemed the coup attempt had been beaten back, though fighting continued in Ankara, and we tried to get some sleep.

The next morning, I cautiously ventured out to our neighborhood's main street, wondering if it would be deserted except for police. But the heavy machines we could hear from our apartment were garbage trucks and not armored vehicles. Our local grocer was doing a brisk business and told me nonchalantly that if there were not at least one coup attempt every couple of decades, it would feel abnormal.

The government immediately accused Fethullah Gülen of orchestrating the plot. In the days and weeks that followed, they set about not only arresting military officers with plausible connections to the coup attempt, but also purging the judiciary, education system, and media of alleged *FETÖ* members. Although the pro-Gülen news media had not communicated support for the coup attempt while it was under way, they were treated as enemies of the state. Dozens of news outlets were shut down by presidential decree, including *Özgür Düşünce* where Solmaz and I had visited. Our source Cihan Acar was arrested and eventually convicted for an interview he had conducted months before the coup attempt (P24 2016).

Some journalists targeted in the post–July 15 purges had nothing to do with the Gülen Movement. Police raided and shut down the pro–Kurdish Movement newspaper *Özgür Gündem*, detaining many of our interviewee Çağdaş Kaplan's colleagues. Çağdaş himself eventually fled the country to avoid a six-year prison sentence as the pro-government press labeled him "a well-known FETÖ terrorist" (*Daily Sabah* 2019; Kaplan 2020).

As a fixer, I interviewed one terrified schoolteacher at a Gülen Movement–affiliated high school that was shut down. The school was not a Gülenist brainwashing machine. It had a solid track record of education in subjects like math and science and no conceivable connection to the coup attempt beyond training students who went on to state-sector careers. But the government was not going to let the crisis go to waste and used the failed coup as a pretext to eliminate competition to the *İmam Hatip* religious schools with which Erdoğan sought to create a loyal "pious generation" (Butler 2018). My schoolteacher source was doubtful he would ever be allowed to teach again.

I had fixed for a handful of clients as part of my research before these events, but after July 15 my fixing career really kicked off. Had I wanted to continue the line of work, the coup attempt might have been for me what the Gezi Park protests were for Elif or the siege of Kobani was for Jimmy: a transformative event generating a demand for fixers that outstrips existing supply, from which arises a new generation of fixers, in the right place at the right time with the right skills.

When I thanked Elif the next month for referring one client to me, she did not even remember doing so. She had been so busy and gotten so many requests that she forwarded to anyone who might fit the call for fixers that she had lost track.

The coup attempt lasted from Friday night through Saturday morning. By Sunday, I had lined up a week of fixing full-time for Michael, a staff writer for a European newspaper. He flew into Istanbul that night.

# Michael and Noah (Day 1)

I met Michael at his hotel in Beyoğlu on Monday morning. He asked me over coffee about Turkish politics and my research. He was filling in for the newspaper's regular Turkey correspondent, who had mistimed her vacation. Michael had reported in Turkey on a couple previous occasions (his usual fixer was already booked) but did not have detailed knowledge of the country. He asked very general questions about contemporary politics and Fethullah Gülen, whom the government had already named as the coup attempt's mastermind. I characterized the Gülen Movement as a wide network with a conspiratorial side but with many affiliates engaged in nothing more sinister than teaching math to children. Orhan would likely have given a less generous briefing, Solmaz a more sympathetic one.

The scope of what Michael was considering for a news story and the questions he asked me about recent events clued me into the frame within which he operated. Michael's editor had drafted the skeleton of a narrative, delegating the blank spaces for Michael to fill (Figure 4.6).

Michael's editor's prescriptions were not very specific, so Michael had a good deal of freedom to choose how to satisfy them. Even so, Michael's frame space was constrained. Michael would have found it difficult to sell his editor on an article about the PKK within that template. But an article about the vast purge of the judiciary underway would fit the bill nicely.

On Saturday, government buildings in Ankara still smoldering, some 3,000 judges and prosecutors were dismissed from their posts and many of them taken into custody. Michael read news about this crackdown in English-language wire agency and newspaper reports, enough to fill in some more blanks on his own. By the time the story reached me, it was already mostly written, with just a few blank spaces left for me to help fill with local color (Figure 4.7).

```
In Turkey, since Friday night's coup attempt,_____.
                                      (account of recent repressive action)
_____claimed that these actions were justified because
(government representative)
_____. But critics such as
               (justification of repressive action)
_____contend that_____.
(opposition source)              (criticism of repressive action)
The_____ is part of a larger trend toward_____.
  (repressive action)                    (broader criticism of government)
```

**Figure 4.6** Frame after editor's fill-ins

```
In Turkey, since Friday night's coup attempt,many judges were detained.

_____claimed that these actions were justified because
(government representative)
conspirators in the judiciary threatened national security : "_____."
                                           (quotation to this effect)
                                          the purge is an opportunistic means of
But critics such as_____ contend that_undermining judicial independence and
                          (opposition source)
_____. The purge of the judiciary is part of a larger
(further criticism of the purges)
trend toward authoritarianism and _____.
               (other political trends, according to expert and/or opposition sources)
```

**Figure 4.7** Frame after Michael's fill-ins

To fill remaining blanks, Michael wanted to find judges, lawyers, or others able to comment on what was happening, who all these detainees were, and how so many pre-identified Gülenists could still work in the judiciary if the state had already been purging them for the previous three years. Michael had read a Reuters article that included one lawyer's full name, and Michael suggested the man as a source. The lawyer was on Facebook. I sent him a message but never received a response. Our ability to fill in the remainder of Michael's frame would depend on my social capital and enterprise.

I remembered another lawyer I had met years ago who remained a Facebook friend, and I messaged her as well. She responded that she was dealing with too much and was too exhausted to talk to the media. I never told Michael about her, lest he prod me to sway her.

I also had a Diyarbakır Bar Association representative's phone number, which Zeynep had given me for my PKK story, though we never called him. Michael and I went down together to the hotel's basement conference room for privacy. My cell phone had no signal down there, so I used Skype to call, which it later occurred to me probably made the call's origin read suspiciously as "unavailable" or as a US number.

The prospective source answered. I introduced myself in my American-accented Turkish as seeking comment on the prosecutors and judges who had been fired and/or detained. He responded, sounding somewhere between terrified and angry, that he was driving and could not talk. I asked if there was a better time for us to talk and, almost yelling, he replied no, and the only thing he had to say was that those detained were Gülenist traitors. We thanked each other and hung up.

I could understand how amid a judicial purge, a lawyer would be afraid to contribute anything except the official government narrative over an unsecure connection to a strange caller. As a reminder, many in Turkey suspect the hand of America behind everything bad in politics. Turkish officials and pro-government media were already heavily insinuating that the United States, where Gülen had lived in exile for decades, had supported the coup attempt.

I relayed the man's scared and hostile tone to Michael. I had failed to recruit a source, but the episode gave Michael a sense of the tension and fear in the air that was ultimately reflected in his article.

At the time, though, I just felt I was failing from the get-go. I did have one more contact to try: Özge, a lawyer and a former flame of mine with whom I had not spoken in years. I set aside my personal hesitance and sent her a private Facebook message. She responded promptly, agreeing to meet us when she returned home from work after 5 p.m. Michael told me that he hoped to be done speaking with sources by 4:30 because he wanted to file his story with his editor by 6 p.m., but Özge could not meet earlier. Timing would be tight.

In the meantime, I walked Michael over to the nearby Human Rights Organization office where I had interviewed Ümit Efe, thinking that İHD might have something to offer about the latest arrests. Ümit was out of the office but those present were friendly. They sat us down on a couch and gave us bottles of water.

The senior representative there had no inside information and so pivoted her answers toward what she wanted to talk about: Kurdish and Alevi issues and the oppression of the Kurdish-leftist Peoples' Democratic Party (HDP) with whom İHD is closely aligned. Each time it was Michael's turn to speak, he reoriented the conversation back toward the judges and prosecutors he wanted to write about that day. I will paraphrase for the sake of brevity into numbered original questions and answers (we can pretend for now that I translated with perfect fidelity):

MICHAEL 1:    Are these latest arrests worrisome to civil society organizations like yours?

İHD 1:        For a long time, the government has been pressuring and arresting all opponents. Since June 7 especially,[1] things have gotten worse.

MICHAEL 2:    What about the judges and prosecutors in particular? Do their arrests raise particular concerns?

İHD 2:        The Gülen Movement and the AKP were allies and co-oppressors for a long time. Two years ago their alliance broke, and in that time other serious problems arose: ISIS, Kobani, Kurdish issues. Before that [at the height of the Kurdish–Turkish peace process], things had been more relaxed. Since and even before June 7, the government has been on a lynching campaign against the HDP and opposition.

MICHAEL 3:    Who are these judges? Are they all Gülenists?

İHD 3:        The government says those detained are all Gülenists, but then there is also the issue of the thousands of conscripted soldiers. These conscripts say they were forced to participate in the coup, and now they are being mistreated and tortured.[2] We are looking into petitioning on behalf of conscripts in detention.

MICHAEL 4:    Since my article has to focus on judges and prosecutors, I wonder: Are you concerned that with 3,000 judges and prosecutors replaced, the system will become more packed with AKP sympathizers and that will be bad for your cause?

İHD 4:        For a long time there has been no judicial independence. The security services decide, the prosecutors give the case to

---

[1] Mentioning this date was a pivot to Kurdish issues. The June 7, 2015, general election marked the AKP's decisive turn against the HDP and contributed to the collapse of the PKK peace process. I quickly explained this in an aside to Michael as I translated.

[2] Mistreatment and suspicious deaths of conscripts was another topic on which İHD had reported extensively. You may remember that Ümit pivoted to discussing soldiers' psychological problems when Zeynep and I interviewed her about PKK conflict death counts.

the court, and the judges pass down sentences. Before the coup attempt, the prosecutors and judges now detained were part of this unjust system. [Kurdish] activists and people in Sur [Diyarbakır's Old City devastated in recent fighting] were arrested without committing any crime. We think this situation will get even worse after the coup attempt. It is good the coup was stopped, but its defeat does not mean that democracy in Turkey is growing.

MICHAEL 5:    And what is your full name?

İHD 5:    (Gives name) Also, in Alevi neighborhoods in Istanbul and Ankara now they are sounding the *sela* [Sunni funeral recitation] day and night on loudspeakers, creating tension.

İHD's representative sought to align Michael and me with the information she was able and wanted to transmit. Each answer would begin with a response that addressed at least the theme of Michael's question (İ1: arrests, İ2: AKP action against Gülen Movement; İ3: claim that Gülenists detained; İ4: judicial independence, İ5: source's name), but then steer toward topics of İHD interest (İ1: Kurds, İ2: Kurds, İ3: conscripts, İ4: Kurds, İ5: Alevis). Our source recognized the prescription that questions should be met with responses that answer them (Goffman 1981: 5–6). She did not have the freedom of choice to say whatever she wanted. To manage this moral conflict, she anchored her utterances to the preceding question by touching on the question's theme but then quickly pivoted to issues outside the scope of Michael's questions or his story.[3]

To be fair, I had done a poor job of matchmaking. I had brought Michael to a source unable to contribute novel information about the latest purges. She was doing her best to contribute *something* of interest to her guests from within her own stock of knowledge. And from her perspective, questions about the judiciary and mass detentions had to be framed within a broader context than Michael was addressing with his narrow focus on the post-coup-attempt crackdown.

---

[3] The folks at İHD were not particularly wily or obstructionist in this regard. They were merely following a tried-and-true formula for press management. A central component of media training that elite sources receive is learning to "pivot" or "bridge" from the question asked to the source's desired messaging. As former US Secretary of Defense Robert McNamara advised, "Never answer the question that is asked of you. Answer the question that you wish had been asked of you" (Morris 2003).

Our source failed to convince Michael to reframe his story. In Michael's article published the next day, there was no mention of Kurdish or Alevi issues. He quoted the İHD representative only as saying that for a long time, there had been no judicial independence in Turkey.

She did, however, spark Michael's interest in the Alevi religious minority. He had not heard of the sect before and asked me about it after the interview. Michael's capacity to decode signals from our source was impaired by his lack of background knowledge, but he was working to upgrade and tune his receiver to the frequency of Turkish society.

I also managed to arrange a source from the government side for Michael: a government representative whom I knew to be a Columbia University alumnus. I had introduced myself to him that morning in a Twitter direct message as a Columbia grad student helping a journalist friend. He responded that we could speak that afternoon and provided his phone number.

After we left İHD, I sat us down at a table in front of a café just down the street to call the government representative. My choice of location was another rookie mistake. As soon as I dialed the number, a succession of motorcyclists drove up and idled roaringly beside us. Noise in the informatic sense can also be noise in the colloquial sense.

I spoke to the government official for just a few seconds, confirming that this was a good time before handing the phone to Michael. They spoke in English. Michael plugged his free ear against engine noise as he asked questions mostly oriented toward pinning down the facts of who was detained, on what charges, and with what planned next steps, without getting confrontational or questioning the official's claims. The two struggled to hear each other over the motorcycles, but otherwise I was pleased that the interview proceeded amicably. Whatever my own politics and skepticism about the official's statements, I was short on AKP sources and hoped to reuse this one. I was sure to send him a friendly follow-up thank you message.

We then headed back to Michael's hotel, where he scanned the international newswires and I scanned the local media. He wrote down notes on the previous two interviews, reducing his workload for the rush to file his story that would follow our final interview.

\* \* \*

We walked over to Özge's apartment building before 5 p.m. and waited outside, Michael noticeably on edge about the time. Özge finally appeared, hustling home from her law firm, and welcomed us. She insisted on serving drinks and slicing melon for us as we sat on her sofa – following her script for hospitality while unwittingly breaching our prescription for a rapid information exchange.

As it happened, Özge was also Alevi and made mention that some of the judges were Alevis and leftists (categories that overlap significantly), and not (Sunni) Gülenists. This time Michael asked me how to spell "Alevi," his interest in the sect growing.

Below, I include transcripts of our interview with Özge. I transcribed the interview after returning from Turkey to New York, and listening back to it was, frankly, tortuous. Sweating and blushing as I transcribed, I shook my head despairingly and almost shouted at my past self whenever I failed to take advantage of a momentary pause or end of a phrase to jump in with a translation: Go! Here's your chance! Translate, damn it! I could almost feel Michael breathing down my neck as I listened, impatient to know what Özge was saying and frustrated that I kept yielding the floor to Özge before I could fully translate or Michael could ask a new question.

I had remembered myself as doing a bad job of translating, in the sense of relaying accurate information, because of Özge's use of technical legal terms. As I listened, though, it became apparent that where information did get lost in translation, my failure related as much to coordinating the conversation as to limited language ability.

A fixer not only translates but also signals to brokered parties when it is their turn to speak. The fixer prescribes whether to respond to a question or address a new topic. Compared to Orhan's more practiced coordination of the interview with Barış for my media crackdown story, I did little to exercise such control over the flow of speech. Whereas Orhan had made the most of limited English abilities by forcing Barış to speak in short, easily translated turns, I made my job more difficult by allowing long speaking turns (Schegloff et al. 1974; Wadensjö 1998: 105–110).

The transcript below begins around 4 minutes into my recording of the interview, after Özge said that some non-Gülenist Alevis were detained. It is a lot to break down, I know. That was precisely the problem for (and co-produced by) me as the fixer, too. Instead of turn numbers, I include the start and end times of each utterance in the righthand column to show duration.

| Speaker | Content | Time |
|---------|---------|------|
| Michael | And does she worry about – you know, this obviously opens a lot of judicial vacancies for the regime. (inaudible) how the regime puts its own people into all those jobs, what effects does it have on Turkish life? | 4:07–4:23 |
| Noah | *And so if the vacancies being created now are filled with AKP – I mean Erdoğan-ist judges and prosecutors, what kind of an effect will there be? I mean for you, for the whole justice system?* | 4:23–4:45 |
| Özge | (sighs) *I mean for us of course the regime is changing; it is slowly changing. Actually, today we were debating this: in the Constitution, the law [of] the Republic of Turkey, is the rule of law [hukuk devleti]. If the rule of law concept is removed, then it will be possible for the death penalty to be introduced in this country today.*[4] *For that reason, of course it is their goal to change the regime. But as you know, we are legalists [hukukçu]. I mean Recep Tayyip Erdoğan's guys can't all of a sudden – I mean judges and prosecutors – they can't instantly take their posts and change everything. Because of that [rule of law], for instance, there is still a court [i.e. due process] for the soldiers who attempted the coup. Of course, they can go step by step until '23.*[5] *Because really they are working step by step. They are working very systematically. But the effect of this on people like me will be like this: with judges and prosecutors we are experiencing very big problems with one-on-one communication. Because we are trying to protect human rights, and on this point they don't want to work, or they* | 4:45–7:09 |

[4] Here Özge is referring to Erdoğan's call, immediately following the coup attempt, for the death penalty to be reinstated. The AKP government abolished capital punishment in 2004 as part of Turkey's European Union accession process, which had faltered by this time.

[5] The Year 2023, the 100th anniversary of the founding of the Republic of Turkey, was a favorite referent of Erdoğan and his supporters. They promised that an ambitious list of economic, infrastructural, and foreign policy goals would come to fruition by that year. Erdoğan would also be up for re-election as president in 2023.

(*cont.*)

| Speaker | Content | Time |
|---------|---------|------|
| | *raise other problems and for that reason one-on-one arguments can increase. Besides that, it is very interesting that – like in the past, public offices could not be entered wearing a headscarf because of secularism. But now we have one judge, a judge in Çağlayan Courthouse in Istanbul. And she comes out to hearings headscarved. And in her official chamber, on the walls are prayers, Arabic writing. And there are [i.e. she makes] interesting admonitions [uyarılar]. For instance, I witnessed one admonition [by this judge]. We go to her chamber a lot and of course we ask questions to be able to do our jobs. If she doesn't understand what you say, she recites in your face, "God is perfect [Suphanallah] God is perfect God is perfect," [then says] "Get out of my face!"*[6] | |
| Noah | (tries to interject in Turkish) | 7:09–7:10 |
| Özge | *[It is] like that. I mean when recounting this to you* (using second person singular), *I can't believe it* (laughs) *but I think these kinds of things will probably increase.* | 7:10–7:21 |
| Noah | It been, they do definitely want to change the regime. And step by step over time – | 7:21–7.27 |
| Michael | Change the – ? | 7:27–7:28 |
| Noah | The regime | 7:28–7:29 |
| Michael | The legal regime? | 7:29–7:30 |
| Noah | The legal regime, step by step over time this has been happening. Right now in the constitution Turkey's defined by a uh legal state, I guess. (to Özge, or maybe to myself in Turkish) *How shall I translate hukuk devleti?* Legal state a – | 7:30–7:48 |
| Michael | The Rule of Law? | 7:48–7:49 |
| Özge | *hukuk devleti* – | 7:49–7:50 |

[6] This passage provides a good illustration of the difference that literary translator Maureen Freely discussed between Turkish and English usages of subjects and objects. To make Özge's passive-voice-heavy statement intelligible in written English, I had to insert six bracketed comments to clarify the subjects or objects of her speech.

*(cont.)*

| Speaker | Content | Time |
| --- | --- | --- |
| Noah | Rule of law, rule of law. If they take out this word, then they can go forward with what they want to do with putting in the death penalty and with these things. However, you do see in Turkey, although they are going step by step in a very systematic way, they still haven't taken over the entire justice system. That's why there is still a justice system in place to deal with the soldiers who were arrested, for instance, that isn't entirely under the control of the – of the government. However, they are moving step by step and she's seen in the last few years, for example, it used to be that in – people, women wearing headscarves were not allowed to enter state, public buildings. However now there's for example at Çağlayan, the big, largest court in Istanbul, there's one court where there's a judge who goes to hearings covered and on her walls there are religious verses. (to Özge) *Stuff like calligraphy, prayers?* (Özge confirms nonverbally) Like calligraphy, Muslim and – | 7:50–9:13 |
| Michael | So she wears her headscarf in court? | 9:13–9:15 |
| Noah | Yeah who wears her headscarf. And – | 9:15–9:17 |
| Michael | What is it on her wall? | 9:17–9:18 |
| Noah | Religious – like – writings. *For instance stuff from the Koran?* (Özge confirms nonverbally) Yeah like things from the Koran, calligraphy. She's, for her this is, it's tough to imagine that this is the case now. And she and other people are pushing for things like human rights and judges who have been installed, the more recent judges aren't really interested in this. And this is going to – she expects this to become even more difficult to get across. And she said for example that the judge who wears the headscarf and has the, you know, religious verses on her wall, when you say something she doesn't understand – (to Özge) *So what does that judge do when you say something she doesn't understand? What did you say? That judge, I mean when you say something she doesn't understand, what does she do?* | 9:18–10:24 |

My translation started off shrewd, if not accurate. I did not render Michael's question (4:07–4:23) about the effect of anticipated judicial appointments on society into Turkish with utmost fidelity but added (4:23–4:45) a specific reference to AKP and Erdoğan, as well as a request for Özge to speak about her personal experience not found in Michael's original. I read between the lines that Michael was interested in Erdoğan and his loyalists in the judiciary, rather than the "regime," a word which in Turkish parlance could have referred instead to the "deep state" that Erdoğan was claiming to combat.[7] Asking about Özge personally, rather than Turkish life generally, likewise enhanced Michael's original question by adding specificity.

I made my own job more difficult, though, by allowing Özge to speak for nearly 3 minutes uninterrupted in her initial response. I failed to enforce a rhythm of short responses. Instead, I had to store many minutes' worth of speech in my memory before taking my turn. Her long response followed by my long translation also prevented Michael from steering the conversation. Over the 8.5 minutes of conversation transcribed above and below, Özge spoke for 217 seconds; I spoke for 265 seconds, mostly in English; Michael held the floor for only 25 seconds.

My noninterruption may have stemmed from a bias toward Özge or from my own disposition toward conducting interviews: as an ethnographic researcher, I had been taught to allow interviewees to say their piece with minimal intervention. Or maybe I just lacked fixing experience. Whatever its reason, my inaction allowed Özge to overload my memory and capacity as a transcoder.

My failure to gracefully coordinate the conversation and the limits of my informational capacity amplified each other in a vicious circle. I rendered Turkish speech into English unclearly with the terms "regime," "covered," and the ambiguous subject "they,"[8] so when Michael *did* have a chance to speak, at 7:27–7:30 (also at 9:13 and

---

[7] "Regime" in Turkish tends to refer to the system of government rather than the government in power, while "state" (*devlet*) tends to refer not to the elected government or president but to the bureaucracy and so-called deep state that persist as governments come and go. Hence, one can be pro-government but anti-regime or anti-state.

[8] "Covered" (*kapalı*) would have been immediately decodable as meaning "headscarved" had I been speaking Turkish; in a state of coding ambivalence, I was letting Turkish codes bleed into my English speech. In the case of "they," I likewise adopted the Turkish coding norm of an ambiguous subject, even though I was not rendering anything Özge said into English but adding my own conclusion to her speech.

12:29, below), he used it to direct side questions to me. He had no opportunity to pursue new lines of inquiry because he was busy providing feedback to check the signal that I relayed to him.

Had I been confident with my translation of *hukuk devleti*, the side conversation from 7:30–7:50 could have been avoided, and I could have continued my turn translating about the headscarved judge sooner. Had I been more familiar with the folksy speech patterns of Turkish Islamists, Özge's account (around 7:00) of the judge's admonition might have better stuck in my mind. With greater informational capacity, I might not have had to pose my side question (10:16–10:24) asking Özge to remind me what the judge would say to her in court.

The informatic function of my question was feedback meant to repair overload. The interactional effect of my question, though, was that it signaled to Özge that it was again her turn to speak.[9] She used the invitation not to resend her original message about the headscarved judge (uttered from around 6:30–7:09) but instead to make a new, long, original statement:

| Speaker | Content | Time |
|---------|---------|------|
| Noah | (interrupting an English-language translation of Özge's previous statement) *So what does that judge do when you say something she doesn't understand? What did you say? That judge, I mean when you say something she doesn't understand, what does she do?* | 10:16–10:24 |
| Özge | *Noah my dear, they* (plural, unstated subject) *try to discredit lawyers because judges and prosecutors, they're bureaucrats. They are directly under the state's control. And we are independent types. Nobody can fire us from our jobs and so forth. Because of that we came to constitute the law's warriors of freedom. I mean we didn't want to, but this kind of situation arose. On this matter the judges – we experienced everything there [at the courthouse]. I got beaten a lot, I don't even know, and nowadays those guys can do* | 10:24–11:09 |

---

[9] Goffman (1981) discusses actions that invite speech in terms of the **ratification** of participation status as a speaker.

*(cont.)*

| Speaker | Content | Time |
| --- | --- | --- |
| | *anything. We, we need to get a signature. We knock on his door. We say "Mr. Prosecutor, can we get a signature?" He goes "Get out!" I mean, like, do you understand?* | |

By trying to preserve signal fidelity, back-channeling to make sure I got it right before I translated, I simultaneously failed to coordinate the interaction in my own best interest. By the time Özge finished speaking, my backlog of information to transcode had grown by another 40 seconds of content.

Then, I dug myself even deeper into the overload hole at 11:09. Instead of seizing on Özge's pause after her question above, *"Do you understand?"* to translate to Michael, I answered it myself.

| Speaker | Content | Timespan |
| --- | --- | --- |
| Noah | *I understand.* | 11:09–11:10 |
| Özge | *Humane relations – and in that way they undermine the lawyers. They throw paper in your face or, I don't know, they don't take a file. A file waits there for months, waits for years. Like, you don't move that file forward.* | 11:10–11:26 |
| Noah | (to Michael) So people like her, lawyers are still, they're, they're independent. They can't just be fired by the government, whereas prosecutors and judges are bureaucrats. It sounds that they're state officials and so they're directly under the control of the state. And so they're able to, to put pressure on independent lawyers not directly, because they're more free, but through the way that they interact with these other officials. So for example, she'll go to the court and she'll have to get just the signature, something very standard, from a prosecutor. So she'll go in and ask for the signature and very rudely they'll just say, "Get out of here," not sign it. Or for example they'll just refuse to take a case file, or you'll give a case | 11:26–12:29 |

*(cont.)*

| Speaker | Content | Timespan |
|---------|---------|----------|
| | file and it will just sit there for months or for years even and they won't address it. And so in these small ways they can make the work of lawyers like her more difficult. | |

By taking Özge's question *"Do you understand?"* to be directed at me (rather than Michael) and responding, I signaled that I was a person in the conversation, not just a channel transmitting her message to Michael. When I back-channeled *"I understand,"* I signaled to Özge that her message had reached its destination and it was yet again her turn. She accordingly added another 15 seconds of speech for Michael to wait on and for me to memorize before I returned to translating.

By the time I got back to speaking English (11:26), more than 4 minutes had elapsed since Özge's original account of the judge's admonition that I had been midway through translating. I made no further attempt to transmit that information to Michael. I do not recall whether I had forgotten about the female judge or just decided to drop the information about her to allow the conversation to move forward. I instead rendered just Özge's latest (10:46–11:26) utterances about rude prosecutors into English.

Having scrutinized transcripts of conversations each of us translated, I do not think that Orhan was a better translator than me at a purely technical level. If you gave us each a standardized test of English–Turkish and Turkish–English translation, I would likely beat him on fidelity. But the real world is not a standardized test. In the real world, Orhan knew better than I did how to play the interactional game of coordinating a turn order that kept his reporter happy and avoided information overload. He knew better than I did how to play the game of feeding both sides what they wanted, including by predicting and interpolating to fill gaps in what he understood. I, on the other hand, made a mess of the interview by trying to translate accurately and politely.

As a result of my failure to coordinate turn-taking, Özge largely determined the direction of talk, and so Michael could not steer the interview back toward information most useful to his story. And the clock was ticking. By the end of the transcript above, we were more than a third of the way through the time Michael had allotted before he had to rush back to his hotel to write.

After half an hour, Michael cut the conversation short, declining Özge's offer of Turkish coffee and thanking her for her time. Özge was surprised at this quick turnaround and offered apologies of her own for not being able to meet us earlier. We all wanted to continue the conversation, but Michael's and Özge's time maps for the day were out of sync to a degree that I was unable to repair.[10]

I walked Michael downstairs and as far as an avenue to hail a taxi back to his hotel, where he managed to file his story just in time for the next morning's edition. Michael, as a broker between his local contacts (Özge and me) on the one hand and his newspaper on the other, was also caught in rhythmic ambivalence. He did his bit to synchronize our social time with his editor's work time through expertise and stress by hammering out an article of over 500 words in the space of a half hour. Michael's own freedom of choice to reflect on and revise his initial frame, to appreciate the nuances of information from Özge, was limited by this time squeeze.

Even if Michael had to go, Özge insisted that she and I catch up and have dinner together. I felt it would be enormously rude, and possibly squander my social capital with a valuable source, to decline the invitation. I swayed to Özge's script, which had the cascade effect of desynchronizing my work time from my private social time and violating a rival moral obligation: my current girlfriend Brett was back at our apartment waiting for me after cooking dinner for two, and I was out with my ex.

\*\*\*

I took the subway home after dinner. Taksim Metro Station was already plastered with posters of the July 15 Martyrs: civilians, police, and soldiers who had died resisting the coup attempt.

As I rode back to Etiler, a 3-minute-long video appeared on the screens of my train car. In it, the denizens of a Turkish city are going about their days when a shadowy figure cuts the cable holding up a massive national flag in the city's central square. The people, seeing the flag fall, fight back against this act of sabotage. They flood into the city

---

[10] Snyder (2016: 13–17) refers to such daily rhythms as **timescapes**, reserving the term **time maps** for longer-term trajectories. I collapse the two terms together simply to avoid having to introduce another set of distinctions.

square, forming a massive human pyramid around the flagpole. A young man climbs to the very top and, holding the severed end of the cable, leaps down, martyring himself in order to raise the flag back to its rightful place. Throughout this sequence, subtitles of the muted voiceover pronounce Turkey's national anthem. The video ends with a portrait of Erdoğan and the slogan, *THE NATION WILL NOT BOW DOWN / TURKEY WILL NOT BE DEFEATED.* There was no way, I thought to myself, it could have been produced in the space of two days, and it seemed to specifically reference the coup attempt: the city square, the people's resistance, the celebration of citizen martyrdom all fit perfectly.

In the days after the coup attempt, conspiracies abounded about the government staging the coup attempt as a ploy to further consolidate power. There were details about Friday and Saturday that did not seem to make sense, for instance, that Erdoğan had flown with his family to Istanbul while putschist F-16 fighter jets were still in the air nearby, pursuing but not attacking his plane (Popp 2017). The European Union commissioner in charge of Turkish accession to the EU accused the government of preparing a list of political enemies in advance to be purged when the opportunity arose, which fit with what Michael and I were learning about the judiciary (Bartunek 2016). The hashtag #darbedegiltiyatro (*"not coup but theater"*) was trending on Twitter, and people I had interviewed in the street the previous day with another reporter had similarly claimed that it had been a ridiculous ploy: real coups were staged before dawn when everyone was asleep, they said, not in the evening when everyone was watching the news.[11]

I had taken those conspiracy theories as outlandish, but this video in the metro unsettled me. Had it been produced in anticipation of the events of Friday and Saturday? And could they be sloppy or arrogant enough to broadcast it just two days later?

---

[11] Government officials had a different explanation for the unusual timing of the coup attempt: the plot had been discovered and so the conspirators were forced to move earlier than planned (Popp 2017).

# Michael and Noah (Day 2)

First thing the next morning, I met Michael at his hotel to debrief about the previous day's interviews and decide on our next topic. Özge had made a strong impression on Michael. She really gave it to the AK Party with both barrels, he commented, and I told him that she did not used to be so political, or for that matter to foreground her Alevi identity.

Alevis in the Republic of Turkey have always to some degree been a community apart from the mainstream. Religious nationalists who equate Sunni Islam with true Turkishness have long targeted Alevis with sectarian attacks and accusations of disloyalty(Lord 2017). When I had dated Özge, though, I had not even realized she was Alevi. It never came up. Yet over the ensuing years, the Turkish government's increasingly open discourse of Sunni majoritarianism and the Syrian civil war, which pitted Sunnis against Alawites and other religious minorities and had the ripple effect of raising sectarian tensions in neighboring Turkey,[1] seemed to have sharpened Özge's Alevi identity.

The previous evening, she and I had dined at a restaurant near Taksim Square, the site of a violent clash during the coup attempt. We could hear pro-government demonstrators at a "democracy vigil" in the square chanting the *tekbir*: "God is greatest" in Arabic. The chant upset Özge; to her, it was an act of aggression in a sectarian culture war.[2]

---

[1] Turkish Alevis and Syrian Alawites are both heterodox sects that revere Ali, but they have very different national histories. Despite these differences, as the Turkish state supported Sunni rebels in Syria against its Alawite-led government and accommodated Sunni Syrian refugees in ways that Alevis in some instances found threatening, Alevi–Sunni tensions in Turkey grew (Çağaptay 2012; ICG 2016b).

[2] The *tekbir* is not a specifically Sunni chant across the Muslim world – it is heard from Iranian Shiites, for example – but in Turkey the chant has come to be associated with Sunni Islam in particular, and secularists see it as a political

She told me about riots since the previous Friday night targeting Alevis in Okmeydanı neighborhood of Istanbul (a long-restive Alevi- and Kurdish-populated area), and that for the first time, she feared sectarian mob violence. She feared for her life. Sunni chauvinists were taking the opportunity provided by the victory of July 15th to assert dominance over political and religious rivals of all stripes, whether or not they had anything to do with the coup attempt (Arjomand 2017: 426–429).

I recounted Özge's worries to Michael as he ate his breakfast. Between Özge and the unprompted mentions of religious persecution in our Human Rights Organization interview, an Alevi seed was planted in Michael's mind. We discussed doing a piece on sectarian tensions. Ultimately, though, Michael was not convinced that the issue was big and urgent enough to take priority for Day Two of reporting.

He decided instead to write an article on Erdoğan supporters who had rushed into the streets to confront soldiers on the night of the coup attempt. The citizen mobilization story's greater novelty than (continued) sectarianism, along with the fact that other international media were covering it heavily, made that story more newsworthy.[3]

Apropos of the popular resistance narrative, I mentioned the video I had seen on the metro and why it raised my suspicions. The production value, with dozens of actors in multiple locations and slick special effects, was just too high for the film to have been created overnight. Michael was intrigued and thought a description of this video could fit in with his story. I told him I would investigate further.

Michael's frame was wide, his script vague. Beyond wanting to talk with government supporters, he had no strong prescription for whom and what I should deliver to him. Michael left me with a generous frame space, though my anticipation of sources' and sub-fixers' moral pressure squeezed me before I even made a phone call. I knew a group of young men in the working-class suburb of Bahçelievler who were Erdoğan fans. I suspected they would know people who had joined the fight at the district police headquarters, if they had not themselves. However, those young men were my sources for a longer-term story I was putting together as a photojournalist. I was wary of introducing

---

Islamist rallying cry. Among Turkish Alevis, not the *tekbir* but *Oh God! Oh Muhammad! Oh Ali!* is the sectarian chant recited at political rallies.

[3] See also Gans ([1979] 2004: 78–82), Shoemaker and Vos (2009: 24–27), and Boyer (2013: 35–42) on considerations of newsworthiness.

them to Michael, who might ask controversial political questions and burn bridges that had taken me (and a couple fixers I hired) much time to build.

Additionally, the experience of cutting short our interview with Özge had made me acutely aware that time constraints shackled Michael, and I wanted to avoid rhythmic ambivalence between his deadlines and sources' schedules. Bahçelievler was on the far side of town, and even taxiing there would risk getting stuck in a traffic jam.

I also had artist friends in Balat, a nearer-by, not-yet-gentrified neighborhood of Fatih district that gave Erdoğan and his AK Party solid majorities in every election. Those friends knew plenty of Erdoğan supporters, but I predicted that it would be a bother and social capital expenditure for me to recruit them as sub-fixers for this story. They were already self-conscious of their neighbors viewing them as socially dangerous outsiders, bohemian weirdos, if not worse. On one occasion, my friend shushed me for chatting about ISIS in English while outdoors, concerned about giving neighbors fodder for suspicious gossip about CIA–Islamic State collusion in Balat. To ask those neighbors to talk to Michael and me (foreign spies) would potentially be socially costly to them, a cost that would be passed on to me through their resentment. Also, they were valuable as sub-fixers for more specialized sources in the arts and media. Why blow my social capital with them to find a pro-Erdoğan source for a one-day story when half the country fit that description?

I opted instead to bring Michael to Kasımpaşa, a neighborhood close to his Beyoğlu-district hotel with a pro-government reputation. The neighborhood is overrepresented in reporting on Erdoğan's popular support both because it is where he grew up and because of its proximity to foreign reporters' lodgings and offices. Visiting in the middle of the day meant that our source recruitment skewed toward older men: shopkeepers and retirees hanging around teashops.

My choice of Kasımpaşa was another kind of translation. I translated Michael's request for pro-government voices into a walk around a particular neighborhood at a particular time. These choices would affect the information he received analogously to the way my word choices did when I translated between Turkish and English.

I did manage to arrange one interview in advance, albeit with another grayhair: a local journalist named Onur running a news site about and for Kasımpaşa residents. Onur told us about the neighborhood's character (always ready for a fight!) and about locals gathering at a loyalist police station before marching on Taksim Square. He opined that the assets of coup plotters should be seized and given to the families of July 15th martyrs. Michael seemed happy with the interview and quoted from it extensively in his article.

I tried but failed to recruit Onur as a sub-fixer by asking him to introduce us to other locals. People here do not like outsider journalists, he told me. Too many have come, and when the locals said Black, the journalist wrote White. I tried to convince Onur that we were different, stressing my Iranian-ness and Michael's anti-imperialist disposition, but to no avail. Sure enough, most people we approached in Kasımpaşa did not want to talk to us, including at the local administrative offices (*muhtarlık*), but we did manage conversations at a café and a mosque.

One effect of my matchmaking with older sources was that they talked about current events with reference to the history they remembered. Their praise for the president was full of references to Erdoğan's time as mayor of Istanbul, from 1994 to 1998. They described how he had literally and metaphorically cleaned up the city.

Their discussion of July 15th too was backward looking. Our sources compared the coup attempt to the 1960 overthrow of Prime Minister Adnan Menderes, to whom Erdoğan has been likened by both supporters and detractors. They referenced the 1997 nonviolent military intervention that toppled the AKP's Islamist predecessor Welfare Party. They talked about their memories of shame over civilian complacency when the military intervened in 1980 and 1997 when explaining their pride at the People's triumph over soldiers days earlier.[4]

Though their ages and positions in Turkish society doubtless shaped their interpretations of events, our sources did not come up with these comparisons on their own. Sources, like every other news contributor, conform to narratives created by others. The day after the coup attempt, a video circulated on social media of police pulling putschist soldiers from a tank while a civilian man shouted that soldiers had staged coups before and *"at that time our father[s] and grandfather[s] were silent, but we will not be silent!"* (Gill 2016). Onur repeated this rallying cry almost verbatim in a quotation that Michael included in

---

[4] These sources referenced these events by day and month, as momentous dates are coded in Turkey: the 1960 coup is 27 May; the 1980 coup is 12 September; the 1997 military memorandum is 27 February. Yet one man ended up directly quoted in Michael's article as referring to "the 1980 coup," words that did not come out of his mouth. Michael and I transcoded the date into compatibility with receivers (newspaper readers in Europe).

his article as original speech. Nonetheless, of all the viral videos and slogans circulating in those days, the one that Onur was most inclined to parrot resonated with his experience living through the 1980 and 1997 military interventions.

I later chatted with my younger pro-government contacts in Bahçelievler about the coup attempt. They offered a different set of cultural references, a different framing of the event and their motivation to resist. The 1960, 1980, and 1997 coups never came up. When they talked about their support for Erdoğan, it related to his actions as prime minister and then president, not his actions as Istanbul mayor when they were toddlers.

Michael's choice of fixer (me) may also have made it easier to arrive at the backward-looking contextualization of July 15th that appeared in his newspaper the next morning. Between interviews, Michael asked me about the references our sources had made, and I gave an enthusiastic account of the history of military intervention in Turkey and of the Menderes era. I was happy to show off my book-learning, one area where I felt competent as a fixer.

Michael was not naïve to the fact that we were collecting a biased sample of old man data. After a few interviews, he advised we talk with some women as well. Choosing me as a fixer made information about Turkish political history more easily accessible to him, but it limited his ability to collect information from women, particularly in a conservative neighborhood like Kasımpaşa. I tried but was repeatedly rebuffed by women on the street and in shops. One young female woman working at a pharmacy did talk with us, but gave short stock answers: Yes, the president grew up in this neighborhood; Yes, people love him here; Yes, he visits here but I have never seen him; Yes, I was happy that Turkey was strong and people supported each other against the coup attempt; No, I did not see anything that night because I stayed home. This source did not make it into the article. The fill-ins she contributed lacked the titillating timbre, the *je ne sais quoi*, of a juicy quotation.

We wrapped up our Kasımpaşa tour mid-afternoon. Michael was not entirely satisfied with the interviews but wanted to avoid the last-minute scramble of the previous evening. While Michael wrote, I was to further research the mysterious high-production-value video that I had seen on the metro. Once home, I searched online for the video and for anyone else discussing its sudden appearance as suspicious. I learned, just before Michael's filing deadline, that I had gotten it completely wrong.

The video had in fact been made for the AKP's 2014 municipal elections campaign but was banned after a short TV run because it illegally used the national flag to advertise for a political party (Reuters 2014). Had I been a Turkish TV watcher two years earlier, I would have known and remembered this controversy – another downside to Michael's choice of fixer.

I quickly called Michael to admit my mistake, and he removed the suggestion in the article that the video was newly created, though he still cited its appearance on metro cars as an illustration of the fervor that the state was drumming up to rally the nation behind Erdoğan. Had I not fessed up in time, though, a major European newspaper would have published that bit of conspiratorial fake news about the government having a premade coup resistance video. I was ashamed of my mistake, but Michael seemed to take it in stride.

We went on to discuss stories for the next day, and the prospect of covering Sunni–Alevi tensions came up again. With my own disposition toward the adventure of a novel subject and against pack journalism, I liked the idea. The issue was receiving little attention outside Turkey despite the explosion of international media coverage following the coup attempt. I also liked the idea because Özge and our Human Rights Organization interviewee had swayed me, and because I thought that I could rely on both as pro bono sub-fixers to report the story. Michael seemed increasingly amenable to the idea of a story on the sectarianism evident in both the latest violence in Alevi neighborhoods and purges of Alevi bureaucrats.

I wrote in my field notes that evening,

[Michael] asks me for story suggestions. I had suggested in morning Alevi angle and I suggest it again now, offering to start looking into it, saying [Özge] could help, also İHD, and we could go to neighborhoods where there have been attacks. ... Now he seems receptive. I think this would be a nice thing to do for [Özge]; for me this is closest thing to activism.

But then Erdoğan announced a state of emergency.[5]

---

[5] Detail-oriented students of Turkey may notice that we are only up to Tuesday, and Erdoğan's state of emergency announcement was on Wednesday night. To reiterate, this book is a work of sociological fiction. I have changed the chronology of events and reporting both for streamlined reading and so that it is more difficult to identify the news articles whose production I describe.

# Michael and Noah (Day 3)

Michael wanted to do the Alevi story. I wrote to Özge, asking if she could help us with contacts for a visit to Okmeydanı, the Alevi neighborhood in central Istanbul where fighting had occurred in recent days.

*"State of emergency was declared don't go,"* she responded.

Michael wanted to go anyway, but now, after steering Michael toward a story about Alevis and sectarianism for the previous two days, I hesitated. I did not know what a state of emergency meant in practice. From what I read on Turkish news websites that morning, everyone was required to have identification ready to show police, who I imagined had a heavy presence in Okmeydanı.

As it turned out, the state of emergency would have little effect on day-to-day reporting. At checkpoints, mostly the entrances to mass transit stations, police ignored me and pulled aside darker-complexioned young men of working-class appearance for ID checks. But I did not know that at the time, and Özge's message had unnerved me. I had also hoped that she would prearrange indoor meetings with people she knew. It would be uncomfortably conspicuous for Michael and me to walk around a neighborhood I had never before visited and talk to strangers, as we had in Kasımpaşa the previous day.

Michael planned to leave Turkey after a week of reporting; being deported a few days early would have been no great inconvenience. I, on the other hand, wanted to stick around to complete my research and, for that matter, to return to Turkey in the future. My time map made me more risk averse than Michael.

Michael and I argued. I refused to visit the neighborhood. I lined up an interview with a representative of an Alevi community association and reached out to an academic who had written a book on Turkish Alevism, but they were not what Michael was looking for. He never wrote the article. After days of work convincing him that the topic was newsworthy and helping him build a sturdy frame around it, I effectively killed the story.

We settled on a safe and ho-hum story about the effect of the coup attempt on tourism instead. We visited Sultanahmet neighborhood and spoke to tourists and shopkeepers. A friend of mine ran a city tour company, and I catalyzed an English-language phone conversation between him and Michael. I promoted my friend shamelessly, citing their top ratings online. This was low-stakes propagandizing, not like openly asking Michael to put in a good word for a political faction, and he agreed with a laugh to give them publicity with prospective tourists back in his country.

The only hitch in the tourism story came when we happened upon some Iranians waiting to take a ferry to the Princes' Islands. I put my Persian language capacity to use for the first time in my brief fixing career, and it turned out that one was not a tourist but a tour guide, organizing trips for Iranian visitors to Istanbul and Antalya. She had interesting things to say about changes in the industry in recent years, about the exodus of Iranians from Turkey after the coup attempt, and about her own fear living in Istanbul in such dangerous days.

When at the end of the interview Michael asked for her name, though, our source hesitated and deliberated with her friends. I suspected from her haircut, piercings, and comportment that she might be one of many LGBT Iranians who fled the Islamic Republic, which criminalized homosexuality, for still relatively liberal Turkey and then worked illegally in Istanbul while applying for asylum or overstaying a tourist visa. Hence our interviewee's concern about her name being published. "*It doesn't need to be real*," I told her in Persian, and after further deliberation with her group she gave us the name "Vaghar," spelling it in English for Michael.

Later, as Michael went over his notes from the interview with me, I mentioned offhandedly that I did not think Vaghar was her real name, without acknowledging my side comment inviting her to invent one. I was surprised, given that it was just a first name and she was not a public figure, that Michael was very disappointed by this. He ended up leaving her interview out of his story as a result.

I was especially surprised that Michael would not use a fake name because it was, by that time, clear to me that details of stories were interchangeable for Michael. This was evident in the mistakes that Michael made. Each day I worked with Michael, I would closely read the story he had written the previous day in his newspaper. There were usually a few little mistakes, which I would point out and Michael would pass on to his editor for correction in the newspaper's online edition.

Without fail, these mistakes were in details that Michael included as local color despite their irrelevance to the story's overall framing from the vantage point of a foreign news editor or reader curious about what was happening, in broad strokes, in Turkey. Michael was sure to mention details like street names, the names of vox pop sources, and the proximity of neighborhoods to famous landmarks, but often got them wrong. Checking the details – he could have consulted me or even Google Maps – was clearly a low priority. What mattered was just that he *had* details; their unique specifics were interchangeable.[1]

Saying that details are interchangeable is not the same as saying that they are unnecessary. If including unique specifics was unnecessary, Michael could have left more space for analysis by excluding them. For that matter, Michael's editor could have saved the cost of flying Michael to Turkey and written an article themselves that filled the same frame.

Specifics create what semiotician Roland Barthes ([1968] 1989) called a **reality effect**: seemingly insignificant details function as a powerful rhetorical tool for convincing an audience of an author's legitimacy as a witness and chronicler. Details also demonstrate reporters' adventurous exposure to local chaos and color.[2]

Getting details wrong only matters when someone notices. Michael was quick to apologize and forward corrections to his editor when I pointed out mistakes. It was important that he believed that the details he included were real. The reality effect operated on him, not just on his editor and readers. Michael would not knowingly use a fake name for "Vaghar" or even include the other information she contributed once he flagged her data as corrupted. A lie violates the journalistic code; a mistake does not.

For my part, when I told Michael that the Iranian's name was likely fake, I inexpertly exposed him to moral contamination instead of insulating him from it. I sabotaged my own reconciliation of the conflict between my client's prescription for a name and my source's prescription for anonymity.

---

[1] See also Blacksin's (2021: 4–6) discussion of war reportage's trope of the generic "victim" story that makes quick, decontextualized sense of a conflict for foreign audiences. Individual victims become interchangeable commodities traded in the global media economy.

[2] See also Tuchman (1978: 82–103) and Zelizer (1993, 2007) on **eyewitnessing** and how the citation of factual detail lends authority to journalism.

# The Chains of Narrative

Story frames are always tacit, and who is handed the tacit authority to fill which tacit blanks is a matter of status within journalism. At each descending level of journalism's hierarchy and each successive link along the chain of information brokerage, from editor to reporter to fixer, the remaining blank frame spaces become narrower, less abstract, and more firmly prescribed by the scripts that surround them.[1] In Figure 4.8, each contributor has the upper hand in exercising frame control over the neighbor to their left and information control over the neighbor to their right.[2]

Within those constraints, though, each contributor has some degree of freedom in filling the blanks allotted to them. Whether frame space is experienced as wide or narrow depends on the capacity of the contributor. Social capital, transcoding capacity, predictive and interpolative abilities, and coordinating expertise each gives an information

---

[1] Everyone's contribution is also constrained by factors preceding the editor's input: preexisting cultural frames (e.g. Orientalist discourse) for making sense of issues and places, journalism's cultural norms for what makes information newsworthy and how a news story should be structured, and story-specific considerations such as coverage of an issue by other news outlets. For fixers, client reporters are the messengers delivering these scripts. Reporters tacitly trace the scripts' outlines through the positive and negative feedback with which they respond to fixers' offerings of story ideas, sources, and translations. Editors play an analogous role vis-à-vis reporters.

[2] The fragile chain of relationships depends on both frame and information control remaining tacit and ambiguous. When it becomes clearly delineated that a fixer is exercising control over the reporter's access and information, or that a reporter is exercising frame control and keeping the fixer segregated from their news organization, the relationship breaks down or at least embittered disillusionment ensues. As Malcolm (1990: 143) writes of the interactions on which newsmaking depends, "If everybody put his cards on the table, the game would be over."

# The Chain of News Production
## –Abbreviated–

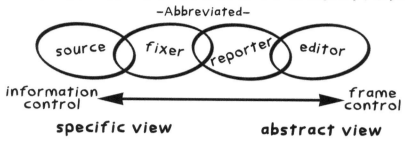

Figure 4.8 The chain of news production (abbreviated)

broker more options to satisfy their interlocutor at the next link in the chain of news production.

As we move leftward along the assembly, from outsider journalist to insider local, details seem to contributors less interchangeable and more determinative of a story's moral standing. Michael needed a name for the local journalist we interviewed in Kasımpaşa to create a reality effect, but it did not much matter for Michael's career whether he got the spelling right. He would leave Turkey soon and never talk to Onur again.

It was more significant for me that Michael spelled Onur's name correctly. I wanted to send Onur the published article, to show him not only that we got his name right, but that, unlike those other foreign journalists he had derided, when he said Black, we had not written White. I cared that Onur approved the story's details, because I wanted to groom him as a source and sub-fixer for future stories. He held more moral sway over me than over Michael.

At each rightward linkage along the chain of news contributors, the perspective becomes more abstract. The fixer subtly pressures a source to contribute a pithy soundbite, carefully chooses which of their words to highlight in translation, and expertly transcodes that utterance to illuminate its subtext for an outsider client, only for their reporter to treat it as interchangeable filler for their frame as they scramble to make their deadline. The reporter subtly pressures their fixer to connect them with the right source, carefully chooses words of that source to highlight as a quotation, and expertly contextualizes that quotation to make sense to an outsider editor, only for their editor to treat it as interchangeable filler for their frame as they juggle content coming in from around the world.[3]

I am being unfair to reporters, more so to editors. It is useful as a thought experiment, though, to imagine a reporter who cares only about filling their frame with maximum expedience. This singularly focused reporter is analogous to a syntactician playing Mad Libs.

For a linguistic **formalist** studying grammar or the structure of sentences or narratives, the particular words a player inserts in the game do not matter. They are interchangeable operators plugged into a pre-scripted formula. But this abstract, disenchanted viewpoint misses the joke, the whole point of the game from the connoisseur player's perspective. The words the player inserts determine whether sentences are funny or boring. The formalist is blind to the difference between the stories in Figures 4.9 and 4.10, because both equally satisfy the abstract parenthetical prescriptions beneath blank spaces:

---

[3] Each stage of template-filling is **relatively autonomous** from the next. I adapt the idea of relative autonomy from Hall ([1973] 2006), who proposed we study the media as composed of four relatively autonomous stages: production, distribution, consumption/reception, and reproduction. Production is only relatively – not fully – autonomous because concerns about the other stages shape how it is done. My argument is that if we zoom in to the production stage, we find a chain of miniature production → distribution→ consumption → reproduction processes linked end to end. A source produces a message, which a fixer distributes through translation to a reporter, who consumes the message and then reproduces it in a new form within the stories they then distribute to their editor, and so on. These miniature chains are likewise relatively autonomous from one another: editors' demands and priorities trickle down to fixers through reporters, but it is the prescriptions of those immediate interlocutors – reporters as well as sources – that directly shape fixers' moral worlds in ways that can have little to do with far-off concerns at news organization headquarters. A news story is the product not of the individual mind of any one contributor, but of the **cybernetic mind** constituted by the chain, the Matryoshka nesting dolls of sub-minds that discern and care about differences on different scales, that successively draw maps of each other's maps at a scale legible to the eye of next mapmaker (Bateson 1972: 453–459).

The**best** way to write an academic monograph is to begin with
(adjective)
a(n)**illustrative** vignette. Then, review the work of prominent
(adjective)
**scholars** who have written on the **subject** you are addressing
(plural job title)                                                    (noun)
and describe the **contributions** of those authors, while also pointing
(plural noun)
out the gaps in their **arguments** that your monograph will **fill** .
(plural noun)                                                   (verb)

Figure 4.9 Story with boring fill-ins

The **flatulent** way to write an academic monograph is to begin with
(adjective)
a(n)**fabricated** vignette. Then, review the work of prominent
(adjective)
**charlatans** who have written on the **wall** you are addressing
(plural job title)                                              (noun)
and describe the **navels** of those authors, while also pointing
(plural noun)
out the gaps in their **teeth** that your monograph will **floss** .
(plural noun)                                                 (verb)

Figure 4.10 Story with funny fill-ins

If a fixer realizes that they get paid the same so long as their fill-ins fit the frame, if they do not think their client is even equipped to appreciate the differences among template-compatible fill-ins, they may take shortcuts. They may turn to the easiest and safest, most predictable and boring sources for story after story.[4]

Yet fixers have their own moral dispositions. They have ideas of what makes a good story beyond their clients' prescriptions and take pride in distinguishing a hackneyed fill-in from an inspired one. In an interview I catalyzed for Michael with an English-speaking academic and activist, I cringed as she stuck to well-worn international progressive slogans and terminology of "the 99%" familiar from New York City's Occupy Wall Street Movement. Predicting the types of political discourse that would make sense to Michael, our source spoke in generic, universalist terms that papered over everything I found interesting and unique about Turkey's politics.

---

[4] Gans ([1979] 2004: 140) similarly notes that it can be safest and most efficient to recycle sources because unfamiliar sources pose a greater risk of breaking frame: "unfamiliar sources may provide new or contradictory information that complicates the general reporter's ability to generalize and summarize."

In the real world, no news contributor is a pure formalist, indifferent to detail so long as detail exists. A reporter might appreciate the way a fixer helps them artfully fill in one of those blanks: a famous source, a clever quotation, a novel explanation. They can act like a teammate playing alongside their fixer, filling in the blanks together in inspired and original ways. I was pleased to see that in his article, Michael ignored the generic filler of progressive verbiage our academic source had contributed, instead focusing for story detail on her personal experience and uncharacteristic confession that she once attacked police officers at a rally in a crazed panic.

A bit of information is, in cyberneticist Gregory Bateson's (1972: 453) words, "a difference that makes a difference." The **connoisseur** reporter learns to distinguish among differences that do not register as information from the formalist perspective.[5] For the formalist, it makes no difference how a player uses their frame space to fill in a template. The distinctions that the connoisseur appreciates but the formalist ignores we might call the **timbre** of a news story.

In music, the timbre of an instrument or voice consists of a combination of audio frequencies above and below the note being played or sung. Timbre is not information formalized in sheet music. On the page, a single tone is written, but the real-life performer includes unwritten semitones, adding their own signals. Timbre is a form of noise from a purist perspective. Yet timbre is what turns sound into music (Clarke 2010: 163–170). A MIDI file produced by composition software can provide nearly noise-free audio, and its high signal-to-noise ratio is precisely what makes the sound soulless and uninspired, lacking musicality and magic compared to a noisy chanteuse or imperfect viola. Timbre is not so much a disruption of signal as an enhancement.[6]

---

[5] The connoisseur journalist is analogous to the practitioner of what Kuhn ([1962] 1970: 36–38) calls **normal science**, who displays "enthusiasm and devotion" as they act as an "expert puzzle-solver" within the boundaries of the prevailing **paradigm**, busying themselves with the "mop-up work" of paradigm articulation, that is, filling in remaining blanks left by the ambiguities of accepted theories (Kuhn [1962] 1970: 23–27).

[6] In the spirit of further jumbling signal transmissions of disparate media: **timbre** is the auditory equivalent of Barthes's (1981: 43–45) visual **punctum**. Whereas the **studium** is what a photograph is *about* as broadly understood by members of a culture, the punctum is the detail that uniquely "pricks" the individual viewer. The punctum confers on the larger image its **advenience**, or adventure (Barthes

What I was most proud of in the stories that I wrote as a reporter were distinctive details that enlivened my articles while conforming to their overall framework. One detail that sticks in my mind was a framed 1994 headline on pro-Kurdish *Özgür Gündem*'s wall that declared, "*IT WILL BURN YOU TOO*" above a photograph of the newspaper's firebombed offices.[7] In my story on the crackdown on opposition media, I put the headline into a context that transformed it into a prophetic address to then-pro-government journalists who turned a blind eye to the plight of the long-suffering Kurdish press, only to face government oppression themselves a decade or two later.

I am not alone in valuing creative details. I attended a few parties with foreign reporters in Istanbul and noticed that when journalists complimented one other's work, they tended to focus on a detail that caught their eye rather than a story's general framing.[8] The connoisseur writes for an insider clique, while the formalist addresses the outsider masses.[9]

Connoisseurship among reporters is not a static quality or reflection of the strength of their character. As with other kinds of connoisseurship, it is easier for resource-rich people to develop and exercise

---

1981: 19); it is a charismatic artifact, the informatic embodiment of the social distinction that the connoisseur chases and the tool with which they distinguish themselves.

[7] On December 3, 1994, three coordinated bombings struck the offices and printing house of *Özgür Ülke* in Istanbul and Ankara. *Özgür Ülke* was the 1994–1995 incarnation of *Özgür Gündem*. Kurdish Movement newspapers, like Kurdish Movement political parties, have been repeatedly shut down by the courts for separatism and association with the PKK and then reopened under different names. The perpetrators of the bombings were never caught, and the Kurdish Movement accused the Turkish state of directing the attack (Simon 2015: 36–37; Kepenek 2019).

[8] Where general framing did come up in casual conversation, it was usually to disparage a colleague who, according to the speaker, had framed an article in a way that diverged ludicrously from what the speaker thought was the reality on the ground. The explanation was usually that the colleague had either been duped by a local political faction – i.e. was too close to the story – or ignorantly clung to received assumptions – i.e. was too far from the story – and served to portray the speaker as a critical outsider or a savvy insider, depending on whether the speaker was chasing status or charisma.

[9] Connoisseurship is also cultivated at journalism schools. Teachers encourage close readings of literary journalism classics, circle and laud the details of student projects that they find compelling, grant grudging B's to students who turn in coursework that satisfies the assignment's formal prescriptions but with uninspired fill-ins.

(Bourdieu 1984). Reporters can act more like connoisseurs when they have time, money, and expertise at their disposal. The same reporters act more like formalists when desperate to meet a deadline, when they cannot afford to pursue numerous leads until they find the perfect character and quotation, when they find themselves in unfamiliar territory where they cannot differentiate a novel fill-in from a hackneyed one.

Michael acted as a connoisseur when he turned up his nose at the platitudes offered by our progressive intellectual source. He kept asking questions until she recounted a juicy personal story of fighting with cops. On another day of our reporting, though, Michael had no time to interview a source before filing his story and so asked me to do the interview myself, then send him a summary. This was a good way to ensure a high signal-to-noise ratio of the transmission he received, to efficiently filter out any noise so that he could snatch any useful information with minimal time expended. But this method also stripped the signal of potentially enchanting timbre (Wiener 1954: 50–51).

When fixers align information *too* well to reporters' frames, news stories can come out sounding like MIDI tracks. When they clean up the noise of sources' statements and translate local realities to fit neatly within reporters' frames, fixers contribute to the production of conformist, formulaic, uninspired stories.

Timbre is not the only form of noise with which journalists contend. Timbre is a kind of domesticated noise that lives inside the acceptable bounds of frame space and does not threaten disorder.[10] The more radical form of noise breaks frame and disrupts the signal needed to fill in a story template (Goffman 1974: 345–377; Serres 2007). This heretical noise challenges orthodox editorial scriptures (Bourdieu 1991: 127–129).[11]

Fixers inevitably contribute information that goes entirely off script. Fixers make introductions to sources who try to steer interviews toward topics they would rather discuss, and fixers only have so much capacity to convert wayward information into useful signals or to tune

---

[10] See also in Clifford's (1983: 139–142) discussion of Bakhtin's concept of **domesticated heteroglossia**: an apparent proliferation of different voices, but which have all been fit into the same perceptual/theoretical framework of a single author and so do not challenge the hegemonic order.

[11] See also Said's (1981: 149–153) discussion of **antithetical knowledge** that challenges institutionalized Orientalist discourse.

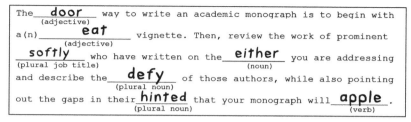

The **door** way to write an academic monograph is to begin with
(adjective)
a(n) **eat** vignette. Then, review the work of prominent
(adjective)
**softly** who have written on the **either** you are addressing
(plural job title)                                    (noun)
and describe the **defy** of those authors, while also pointing
(plural noun)
out the gaps in their **hinted** that your monograph will **apple** .
(plural noun)                                              (verb)

Figure 4.11 Story with frame-breaking fill-ins

their clients to receive them. Fixers also lead reporters to new places, whole worlds of sights, sounds, and smells far in excess of what would fit into any story.

In relation to the immediate story frame that a reporter must fill, such information is useless noise interfering with the useful signal of compatible fill-ins. If a reporter had nothing but noise to fill editors' templates, it would be chaos. Mad Libs turns from fun into gibberish if you break frame by ignoring parenthetical prescriptions (Figure 4.11).

The result is Dadaist poetry at best, and a communication breakdown in a field like journalism that does not tolerate nonsense. When a fixer fails to contribute fill-ins that fit a reporter's frame or a reporter fails to thus satisfy an editor, the story is killed. The contributor loses face and the trust of their superordinate. News is not made. That is what happened to my story about death counts in the PKK conflict: I supplied what no editor demanded, framing my report on the insurgency in a way that did not fit existing templates for how to cover the issue.[12]

But what happens more often is that a contributor transmits a mix of useful signal and useless noise to their nearest neighbor along the news production chain. That neighbor filters out the noise as they transcode the message for the next transceiver in the chain. A story is made, but the noise is not part of it. That very same noise might become useful

---

[12] The reality is a bit more complex because, in the case of my PKK article, news *was* made, not through a professional outlet but through the online publishing platform to which I posted the story when I tired of rejection. My story was still subject to a brokerage process *after* publication, though, and became news only to the niche audience who found it through social media or search engines – less picky gatekeepers than professional editors.

signal if the template were revised, but that first contributor lacks the status to exercise such frame control.

On my first day reporting with Michael, my choice of sources exposed Michael to the noise of repeated references to Alevi issues that had little to do with the story he was writing on purges of the judiciary. At the Human Rights Organization, our source's transmissions contained a low signal-to-noise ratio. She talked about Alevis, Kurds, and conscripts with scant attention to Michael's line of inquiry, and little of her information made the cut for the article he wrote that evening. The same day, we spoke with my lawyer friend Özge, who provided a higher signal-to-noise ratio of information about judicial purges, but nonetheless mentioned Alevi persecution in the context of crumbling secularism. Michael was not initially attuned to our sources' signals; he had never heard of the Alevis, and I had to give him a quick primer on the community. It required the accumulation of redundant signals from İHD, Özge, and me to sensitize Michael to the topic.

Even once Michael could make sense of sources' statements, details about Alevis broke frame. His story about the judiciary would have needed significant revision to fit that information, and neither the sources nor I had the status to force it through.

Exposure to that initially useless noise, however, put Michael on the trail of a whole new story about Sunni–Alevi tensions and led him to consider filling his editor's framework in ways that he did not realize possible when his plane first landed in Istanbul. What was noise in Story Frame 1 became signal in Story Frame 2 (Serres 2007). Setting aside that Story Frame 2 never became news because I refused to bring Michael to Okmeydanı during the state of emergency, the point is: in noise that subverts the order of hierarchically imposed frames lies the potential for change, for new beginnings (Clarke 2010: 164; Collins et al. 2010: 10–11).[13]

---

[13] This is not a new idea, and it is worth quoting a few scholars from various disciplines who have expressed it with a more beautiful timbre. Cyberneticist Gregory Bateson (1972: 410) writes, "All that is not information, not redundancy, not form, and not restraints – is noise, the only possible source of *new* patterns." Philosopher Michel Serres (2007: 21) writes, "The bit of noise, the small random element, transforms one system or one order into another." Translation theorist Mona Baker (2006: 98), citing psychologist Jerome Bruner, writes that "breaches of canonical scripts are what makes a narrative worth telling." Historian of science Thomas Kuhn ([1962] 1970: 52–65) argues along

Sometimes noise is simply nonsense that degrades useful signal. But other times, information that is useless in the short term is essential in the long term. Without the disruption of noise, the reporter learns nothing new enough to change their framing, nothing to goad them into breaking frame themselves and challenging their editor to revise their respective, perhaps Orientalist, image of the world.[14]

The templates with which contributors at each link in the chain of news production contend are, after all, not immaculately conceived by editors or anyone else, but rather accrue through repeated iterations of storytelling. I have been drawing the chain as a line, but it is a loop that feeds back into itself: producers are also consumers.

Templates are constantly, if glacially, shifting as contributors along the chain break the frames of their neighbors. Those neighbors repair and reuse their frames, but with slightly altered dimensions.[15]

Contributors do not necessarily experience their subordinates' frame breaks as mere distracting noise or as unwelcome defiance of the chain of command. If we take a further step away from the **formalist**, past the **connoisseur**, we arrive at the **adventurer**, the seeker of chaos, of frame-breaking noise. For the xenophile adventurer, surprising information that does not fit their story frame, or even their cognitive framework for making sense of the world, provides the excitement that makes journalism worth pursuing (Simmel [1911] 1971: 190–194).

If the formalist listens to whatever is playing on the Top 50 Pop Chart that week, if the connoisseur appreciates the timbre of pre-Romantic classical music and its variations within the safe confines of familiar patterns, the adventurer is an avant-garde jazz cat.

the same lines that the seed of scientific revolution is sown when scientists become aware of anomalies that violate their "paradigm-induced expectations."

[14] Similarly, in a study of fixers in Iraq, some interviewed journalists "referred to the danger of fixers understanding too well what their journalist wanted," filtering out noise that the fixers anticipated would not fit their client's expectations. For instance, sources' talk about "resistance" early in the US occupation got filtered out when the dominant frame for news from Iraq was still democratization and gratitude toward American liberators, only for that "noise" to become important information later on as story frames changed in the face of accumulating, unignorable signals of a growing insurgency (Palmer and Fontan 2007: 14–18).

[15] See also Baker (2006: 101) on "narrative accrual," Burt (2007: 58–92) on the connection of brokerage to creativity and learning, and Mignolo (2000) on the productive challenge that "border thinking" can pose to dominant regimes of knowledge.

Miles Davis said, "There are no wrong notes in jazz: only notes in the wrong places" (Klotz 2017). What is dissonant noise in one measure is melodic signal in another. To recognize that potentiality of a disruption, though, requires a receptive capacity to process new signals, an expertise developed through extensive coaching and recurrent exposure to noise.[16]

Pianist Herbie Hancock recounted a case of Davis's adventurous trumpet playing:

Right in the middle of his solo, I played the wrong chord … and Miles paused for a second. Then he played some notes that made my notes right … which astounded me. I couldn't believe what I heard. Miles was able to make something that was wrong into something that was right. … Miles didn't hear it as a mistake. He heard it as something that happened, just an event. And so that was part of the reality of what was happening at that moment. … Since he didn't hear it as a mistake, he felt that it was his responsibility to find something that fit. … We can look for the world to be as we would like it to be … but I think the important thing is that we grow. And the only way we can grow is to have a mind that's open enough to be able to accept situations, to be able to experience situations as they are and turn them into medicine. Turn poison into medicine. (Hancock 2014)

Like Davis, the journalist-adventurer searches for new ideas in the noise that disrupts expectations. As compared to the connoisseur, they value not just the clever adoption of domesticated timbre but the thrill of taming of wild noise. They pursue the charismatic mystique gained from the mastery of disorder and transubstantiation of noise into signal (Simmel [1911] 1971: 190–194), conferred by publication of that scoop of journalistic lore that shatters the dominant frame using a frequency of reality to which no other peer was attuned.[17] Signal is a

---

[16]  Again, it is important not to uncritically attribute expertise to individual heroism. As Bourdieu (1984) argued, the capacity for aesthetic distinction may appear to be an individual's magic but is actually socially patterned and instilled through long-term participation in a social field.

[17]  Another paradox: The adventurer is more vulnerable to doubts about their objectivity and professionalism because they challenge the field's doxa (Bourdieu 1991) and so jarringly remind colleagues of the adventurer's subjectivity. Yet in so doing, the adventurer practices the substantive objectivity advocated by media critics since Walter Lippmann (1922): "a radical enlargement of the range of attention" that overcomes received stereotypes. The formalist, by contrast, maintains the appearance of objectivity among peers by unquestioningly adhering to the stereotypes of the doxa (Pedelty 1995: 7–8). See also Galison's (2015: 61) discussion of journalistic objectivity as "a kind of cultivation of self, a

supply to satisfy editorial demand, but noise is what makes it exciting, even magical, to report.

It is possible to be an adventurer because our cognitive frames are not as limited as the frames of news stories. A reporter can learn a great deal in the process of reporting that does not make it into their current project but is stored in memory for future use. Whether they have the bandwidth to decode frame-breaking information and to store it in their memory, though, depends on the dispositions that particular reporter has cultivated and on the situation in which they receive that information. When a deadline looms or burnout sets in, everyone reverts to formalism, just with varying degrees of resistance.

Formalist, connoisseur, adventurer.[18] Every editor, reporter, and fixer is a mixture of all three, though in different and changing measures. The direction a news contributor leans at any moment is a negotiation between the competing moral pulls of the current story's short-term prescriptions and the long-term value of cultivating expertise and mystique, both in oneself and in one's teammates. The higher the signal-to-noise ratio a fixer provides their client, the less room there is for surprise or change. But the lower the signal-to-noise ratio, the less a reporter is able to satisfy their immediate need to write a story. A very low signal-to-noise ratio makes it difficult to put together a story on deadline and can even make sources' messages incomprehensible. Between the efficient formalist and charismatic adventurer, between the order of the dominant frame and the allure of the scoop, the connoisseur adopts a compromise posture. They search for a timbre inspiringly different enough to win distinction but not so different as to bring disorder.[19]

A savvy reporter recruits and manages fixers with the goal of obtaining an optimal signal-to-noise ratio for their situation. I did well to hire Solmaz for the interview at the pro-Gülen newspaper *Özgür*

---

re-making of who we are that alters our perception and therefore our assessment of our world."

[18] The ideal types of the **formalist, connoisseur,** and **adventurer** correspond, albeit at the production rather than consumption end of the circulation of media, to Hall's ([1973] 2006: 170–173) categories of **dominant-hegemonic, negotiated,** and **oppositional** positions of reception.

[19] The optimal signal-to-noise ratio can vary depending on channel-specific prescriptions for how quickly stories make sense to audiences. A daily TV news show has fewer seconds of attention per story, and so less capacity to coach their audience into making sense of information than does a long-form magazine.

*Düşünce.* As a former employee of the movement's media wing, she coached and translated in ways that allowed our source's timbre to resonate meaningfully in my ears and to open me up to new ideas. Had I been savvier, though, I might not have hired Solmaz for the interview at pro-Kurdish *Özgür Gündem*, during which she added noise of a quantity and quality that a connoisseur would disdain.

A savvy fixer, for her part, learns to cater to her reporter's sense-making capacity and desired signal-to-noise ratio. This personalization of service can take the form of a calculus: How much social capital do they want to risk for a client who cannot tell the difference between a *mot juste* and a cliché? Or it can take the form of a spur-of-the-moment addition of a few explanatory words into a translation that would not, in the fixer's reflexive judgment, make sense to their client if translated literally.

In summary: Within the constraints of their moral world and informatic capacity, a fixer sizes up the client, decides what information they are prepared to receive and how much coaching effort is worth expending to increase their receptive capacity, introduces them to a source selected to provide enough signal to satisfy the client's immediate needs with the right measure of noise sprinkled in, and then cleans up any excessive noise through strategic distortion of the information transmitted from source to reporter.

# From Local to Global

# Strategic Ambiguity

Part V will be about change: change in the lives and strategies of our protagonists, change in Turkey and Syria and of international perceptions of those countries, change within the field of journalism, change in the way we should understand who controls the media and how.

But first, remember Victor Louis, fixer extraordinaire between the Soviet Union and the West? Louis and his British wife might have lived in Communist Russia, but they were famous for entertaining foreign guests at a dacha festooned with high-tech Western gadgets and precious antiques. A carpet that had once belonged to Catherine the Great decorated their living room (Vronskaya 1992; Whitney 1992; Schechter 2012).

From his lowly origins as a political prisoner whom the KGB likely paroled in exchange for spying on foreign diplomats and journalists, Louis made the most of his marginal but opportune place on the fault lines between the First and Second Worlds as he fixed for the *New York Times*, *London Evening News*, *France-Soir*, and others.

Louis turned the very ambiguity of his position into a strategic asset, alternately playing the part of worried citizen, objective reporter, and political insider. In one case of à la carte fixing, Louis traveled to Denmark to meet with a young Strobe Talbott (later US deputy secretary of state), who was translating Soviet leader Nikita Khrushchev's memoirs for *Time* magazine. Louis brought a suitcase full of tape recordings by Khrushchev and haggled expertly over the terms of their exchange – Time Inc.'s use of the tapes and his own cut of the profits – under the guise of a righteous outsider to journalism and its callous transactionalism (Ufberg 2016). Talbott remembered,

He would cast himself in the role of the naïve but proud amateur entrepreneur who is only just learning how unfair and exploitative the big time can be. His petulance was fine tuned to transmit just a hint of threat that he might walk out at any moment, shocked and disgusted at the bullying greed he had encountered. He bluffed not from a position of faked strength, but from one of faked weakness. ... (Schechter 2012: loc. 2493)

In other interactions with reporter colleagues, Louis would strenuously deny their jokes and insinuations that he was KGB affiliated and claim to be nothing but a professional journalist (Whitney 1992). Still other times, Louis played up those very affiliations when it served to signal his status beyond journalism. Louis reminisced in his memoir,

> I gave up trying to persuade people that I was not working for any agency beside my newspaper. But I also learned that it was much more beneficial to belong to a mysterious department than to be just a journalist. I was treated with respect and sometimes even with servility in most countries. I was received by ministers, heads of state, assistants to presidents and vice-presidents. The aura of a man belonging to a mysterious government body, even if it is the secret police, would open many doors for me which would be slammed in front of an ordinary journalist. I have learned to puff my cheeks, spread a tail like a peacock and prophesy as if I really were "the hand of Moscow." (Schechter 2012: loc. 2526)

Louis was polyvocal in his self-presentation: he would play the part of the activist, the journalist, or the spy depending on the situation and audience, defying clear-cut singular classification of his role. He was not a central player in the established fields of diplomacy, intelligence work, or journalism, but parlayed his marginal position in each field into a central position at their murky intersection.

Part of the key to Louis's success was that he remained largely behind the scenes. When Louis delivered a scoop to a European or American journalist about Kremlin power struggles and Cold War military interventions, their name – not his – appeared in the byline.[1]

Fixers are rarely credited as co-authors, even today. A chain of brokers creates the news, but often, especially in print journalism, a story is credited to just a single person (Bossone 2014; Murrell 2015; Plaut and Klein 2019a). Usually this is the reporter who wrote the story, though sometimes a byline will go to whoever is in the location that best signals charismatically *being there* to the public audience, even if that person contributed little (Zelizer 2007). News readers

---

[1] Less generously, Victor Louis's uncredited provision of information to Western Bloc journalists could be considered information laundering: layering "dirty" information through legitimate-seeming front organizations to obscure its sourcing (Arjomand 2019).

might use bylines to evaluate articles as information sources, but bylines obscure as much as they reveal about the newsmaking process.

When, for instance, the Syrian fixer Leyla worked on one newspaper article about the siege of a suburb in southern Syria, she corresponded with a staff reporter in New York, finding sources and interviewing several on her own, remotely, from her apartment in Gaziantep before sending along summaries. The reporter in New York wrote the article based on his and Leyla's interviews and research, but then the newspaper decided to give the byline to a different staff reporter based in Beirut. The latter had been otherwise occupied and contributed to the story only by reading it over and making a couple of edits, but Beirut was closest to where the events had taken place. At the bottom of the article, Leyla and the New York reporter were at least ambiguously acknowledged as having "contributed."

News stories, like scientific discoveries, political change, and other cultural products, are generated through complex processes of brokerage and conflict among networks of actors (Latour 1988b: 13–16, 2005b). The fiction that fits more comfortably with our limited sensemaking capacities, though, is that a cultural product exists because a Great Man has willed it into being (a low-status woman or self-effacing machine rarely gets the credit).[2]

For the reporters, scientists, and politicians who get to be Great Men, the virtues of this simplified representation of social process are obvious. For those who do not get credit, anonymity in newsmaking has both downsides and upsides.

When news organizations do not publicly acknowledge the contributions of fixers, their status in the field of journalism is left ambiguous. This ambiguity justifies fixers' subordination to foreign reporters (Blacksin 2021: 14–15). Fixers sometimes fight for credit because accumulating shared bylines with high-status reporters sends a signal to other clients that those fixers are trustworthy and professional. Many of those I interviewed recalled their bylines at prominent publications with pride and complained about cases when reporters contributed little to a story but received all the credit for the fixer's knowledge and labor.

---

[2] See Murrell (2015: 23–29) on the power of the myth of the swashbuckling Great Man among foreign news correspondents specifically.

Yet some of those same fixers embrace strategic ambiguity:[3] they want authorial credit sometimes but anonymity other times (Palmer 2019: 169–190; Plaut and Klein 2019a, 2019b: 1705). Those same interviewees of mine sometimes turned down bylines or complained to me of their name appearing on a story despite their wishes. Credit can be dangerous. Credited authors and the news outlets publishing their work are the ones targeted when stories generate blowback. Remaining behind the scenes can be a defensive strategy, a means of circumventing conflict when a fixer's time map indicates that they will stay in place longer than their clients.

When reporting on the Turkish domestic media, I scheduled interviews around journalist sources' court appearances. They were hit by a steady flow of criminal and civil suits in retaliation for their reporting, most of which were dropped only after wasting many hours of their time. Enough charges have stuck, though, that Turkey has been the world's leading jailer of journalists off and on since 2012. The Committee to Protect Journalists even started a special weekly "Turkey Crackdown Chronicle" blog series in 2016 to keep up with legal and other attacks on the domestic opposition media. After the coup attempt, the crackdown intensified further (Beiser 2016; Över 2017: 330–335).

Fixers have avoided this legal onslaught. The only case of a fixer facing prosecution for his work in recent years occurred was Mohammed Rasool, an Iraqi-Kurdish fixer detained alongside his clients in Diyarbakır while covering the PKK conflict (*Vice News* 2015; *Evrensel* 2017). The near absence of legal action against fixers was especially striking after the coup attempt given that the State of Emergency Law contained provisions that could have been weaponized against fixers:[4]

Anyone who spreads or conveys false or exaggerated news or information with intent to create panic among the public shall … be liable to additional

---

[3] In an influential argument about communication within organizations, Eisenberg (1984) uses **strategic ambiguity** to mean signals that can be decoded in multiple ways, a subject addressed in Part IV. Here in Part V, I use the term to refer rather to the instability of fixers' alignment to the scripts of the parties they broker and of their participation status in the fields they bridge.

[4] The State of Emergency Law was in effect from July 2016, after the coup attempt, until July 2018, after Erdoğan's reelection as president with greatly expanded constitutional powers (Hürtaş 2018).

punishment of imprisonment for between three months and one year and a minimum fine of five thousand Turkish liras. If such crime is committed by a person in association with a foreigner, the additional term of imprisonment shall not be for less than one year together with a fine of thirty thousand liras. If the crime involves publication and/or the use of broadcasting media, the penalty shall be double and imposed on both the person primarily responsible for the crime and anyone else connected with its commission. (Republic of Turkey Official Gazette 1983: Part 5, Article 25, Clause 2)

No Turkish translators, fixers, or producers were prosecuted for spreading "false or exaggerated news or information with intent to create panic among the public … in association with a foreigner," despite state officials' frequent public accusations that the international media were doing just that.

Fixers have escaped the crackdown on the Turkish media because of their ambiguous status in journalism. Fixers and their teammates have some freedom of choice to present them alternately as 1) professionals closely affiliated to eminent news organizations or 2) mere translators carrying out a mechanical function, not really journalists and so no more liable than an assistant who prepared the reporter's tea or took care of his kids. Claim 1 and Claim 2 together constitute a useful arsenal for fighting state oppression.

Playing the close-affiliation-to-powerful-foreigners card made the Turkish state hesitant to target fixers for fear of international outcry. When Rasool was jailed in 2015, his lengthy pre-trial detention prompted unusually vocal condemnation from the international press and civil society organizations, as compared to most cases of jailed Turkish journalists (*Vice News* 2015). Despite souring relations with the United States and European Union, Turkey's standing in the world is tied to diplomacy and international public opinion and vulnerable to Claim 1. Erdoğan and other AKP leaders routinely disparage foreign reporters and publications (e.g. Hughes et al. 2014), and a few foreign journalists have been deported or denied residency or re-entry into the country (Lepeska 2016), but the Turkish government has stopped short of weaponizing the courts against the international press as it has against domestic journalists.

Affiliation with international news organizations is not enough, though. Turkish dual citizens in the less ambiguous role of reporters for foreign outlets have been targeted less than domestic colleagues but more than fixers. Around the time of my final research trip to Turkey, a Dutch-Turkish columnist was detained for insulting the president and a German-Turkish correspondent was indicted for spreading terrorist propaganda (BBC 2016; Shalal 2017).[5]

Playing the mere-non-person-translator card (Claim 2) in combination with the it's-not-worth-the-international-outcry card (Claim 1), however, allows fixers to fly under the radar of government surveillance or at least avoid retaliation. Since fixers are not usually credited as co-authors, Claim 2 is an option: they can distance themselves from reporters and present themselves as technicians with no control over stories. As long as they did not talk politics or pick fights with government supporters on social media, several fixers told me, they could avoid attracting unwanted attention.

The trade-off for anonymity is status within journalism. Each of our protagonists experienced the competing pulls of safe invisibility and professional visibility. Some of them came to feel trapped on the murky margins of the professional field, denied trust and frame control. Some became disenchanted altogether with journalism and looked for other possibilities. Others adopted a detached, commodified view of newsmaking and their relationships with clients, acting more like salespeople than teammates. Some sought to abandon ambiguity in order to claim professional status and rise through the ranks of journalism. Others embraced the possibilities afforded by their ambiguous position and, like Victor Louis before them, became central players of emergent fields in the trading zones between journalism and other worlds. As some fixers advanced within or departed from journalism altogether, spaces opened up for a new generation of brokers.

[5] In another recent case, prosecutors indicted two Turkish *Bloomberg News* reporters for attempting to "destabilize the economy" through reporting on the fall of the Turkish lira and panic in the country's banking sector (RSF 2019).

# Leyla and Aziz

Aziz's abduction in Aleppo made the couple more guarded and suspicious about working with the foreign press. The international community's response was a harsh reminder of their marginal status in journalism. Foreign reporters who reached out to Leyla while Aziz sat in a Jabhat al-Nusra prison cell probed whether Aziz had conspired in his clients' kidnapping. Those clients' governments did nothing, as far as the couple could tell, to secure Aziz's release when they negotiated ransoms for their own citizens.

After Aziz's release and return to Turkey, he and Leyla continued to assist journalists like Geert and Orhan whom they already knew and trusted, but they were leery of new clients. Leyla told me that her husband's abduction had cemented an unease she had already felt over fixing work. Leyla and Aziz were disenchanted in both the Weberian and colloquial senses: the inner order of journalism made sense to them, and they did not like what they saw. The two were aware that they held very limited control over the framing of stories, that reporters arrived with preformulated scripts seeking brief adventure and local color and then abruptly left once they got what they came for.

For Leyla, journalism was a disruption of her career as a literary translator and language teacher, and she sought not adventure but a return to the normalcy of life before civil war and displacement. For Aziz, journalism was not just a disruption but, increasingly, a threat to his political activism and local ties. In their early days as fixers in Turkey, his clients framed the conflict in Syria as an Arab Spring revolutionary struggle against a dictator, in alignment with the Syrian opposition in exile that Aziz supported. But by 2015, according to Aziz, American and European media became disproportionately focused on ISIS and equivocal about Assad regime atrocities.

Aziz complained that an interviewee could tell a reporter ten things, but the reporter would just cherry-pick the one that suited the story they already had planned. Clients, feigning strategic alignment with

Aziz and sources, would claim they had humanitarian motivations but then fixate on uncomfortable details about rebel factions and rebel misdeeds or salacious details about ISIS. They might learn that the government had killed a hundred people, but for the reporter it would not be newsworthy. If ISIS killed three people, though, it would be a story.

It was not just the way clients framed stories that bothered Aziz, but their disrespect for sources' prescriptions more generally. On one occasion, a rebel source gave a reporter a photograph of himself on the promise, which Aziz convinced him to trust, that the reporter would use the source's photo only privately as a writing aid. A week later, the reporter published that photo in an article without informing Aziz or the source.

Aziz felt alienated from the stories he helped produce.[1] He grew pickier about accepting new clients and came to prefer Japanese reporters over Europeans or Americans. Only the Japanese, he told me, were consistently respectful to sources and sent him their stories to review in advance.[2]

After a couple of years in Turkey, Leyla and Aziz got visas to Sweden. Aziz planned to go to graduate school to study politics. Leyla planned to return to literary translation and look for employment as a teacher of Arabic.

Orhan, Leyla and Aziz's original recruiter and meta-fixer, meanwhile complained that the constant turnover of his Syrian friends as

---

[1] If we substitute the word "fixer" for "worker" and "story" for "product," Marx ([1844] 1978: 72) provides a fitting description of Aziz's dismay with news stories into which he contributed his effort and social capital, only for his client to adopt framings and transmit information that he thought damaged the Syrian rebel cause or threatened a valued source's security:

The worker [fixer] puts his life into the object; but now his life no longer belongs to him but to the object. ... The alienation of the worker in his product [news story] means not only that his labor becomes an object, an external existence, but that it exists outside him, independently, as something alien to him, and that it becomes a power on its own confronting him. It means that the life which he has conferred on the object confronts him as something hostile and alien.

[2] Other fixers, more closely aligned with Euro-American journalism, negatively profiled Japanese reporters for the same reason that Aziz liked them. Japanese journalists, I was told, were too complacent about accepting sources' claims uncritically and too willing to grant sources discretion to guide stories.

they migrated to Europe made his job more difficult. Many were on a raft to a Greek island or in a car to the Bulgarian border as soon as they had earned enough money to pay a smuggler. Orhan had to keep finding new Syrian sub-fixers to keep up with demand from client reporters.

# Orhan

When Orhan first started fixing, he coached clients that Turkish opposition journalism was under siege, that Ergenekon and Sledgehammer coup plot trials were a sham, that Erdoğan was an authoritarian amassing power. They mostly dismissed Orhan as an embittered Kemalist. In their view, the big picture was that AK Party was democratizing Turkey, integrating the country into Europe, and performing an economic miracle. Information he contributed that did not fit into the prevailing Euro-American narrative did not immediately change these clients' minds. Orhan's reporters might mention contradictions to that narrative in their stories, but framed them as minor glitches, mere noise interfering with the stronger signal of the triumph of democracy and establishment of a "Turkish Model" for the whole region.

Orhan lacked frame control, and his control over information to clients was undermined by another class of brokers who circumvented him to speak directly to the international press. Media-friendly, English-speaking liberal and Gülenist intellectuals presented the AKP as democrats reforming civil–military relations for the first time in the Republic of Turkey (Akyol 2015; Yeşil 2016: loc. 74–106).

Although Orhan had logged years of experience as a journalist in the Turkish press before he began fixing, his worldview and political disposition set him apart from his clients. He did not share the same interpretation of events or assumptions about the big picture as foreign media insiders. His clients limited his frame control because they did not see him as objective (Bourdieu 1991; Zelizer 1993; Schultz 2007). Orhan's subjectivity stuck out to foreign reporters more than that of the liberal intellectual pundits because Orhan's views were dissonant with the reporters' own subjective sense of Turkish politics.

Orhan's heretical and frustrated contributions gradually accumulated with other signals reaching European and American reporters that Erdoğan was not a liberal democratic model for the Muslim

World.[1] Turkey's European Union accession process stalled; the AKP gradually purged liberal and moderate party members; the Gülen Movement broke with Erdoğan and went from burnishing to tarnishing his government's global reputation (Kınıklıoğlu 2015). If there was a decisive paradigm shift in Orhan's clients' coverage of Turkey, it was the Gezi Park protests of 2013. The government responded violently to protesters who reframed Erdoğan's reform and development agenda as an illiberal power grab, who articulated an alternative political vision that made sense to foreign reporters. Orhan's clients flipped their script. The prevailing frame for reporting Turkey went from democratization to authoritarianism.

In Aziz's case, the distance between his clients and his own political disposition widened over the course of his fixing career. For Orhan, the dominant frame shifted over time in his favor. By the time clients came around to his view of the Turkish government, though, Orhan had already begun to view his job more like manufacturing and sales than artisanal teamwork.

Disenchanted by his clients' intransigent frame control but enjoying rising day rates, Orhan began to take a certain distance from the stories he worked on. He came to care less about stories' inspired originality, more about efficiency: minimizing the amount of work it took to fulfill clients' prescriptions. Re-using sources was efficient. The more times he interviewed the same person, the more easily he could transcode their statements to fit clients' expectations and the less carefully he needed to listen. When he had a good set of sources to fill an in-demand frame, he would sell them over and over to different clients.

Once I began to work as a reporter, Orhan would send me text messages occasionally to advertise his network of sources and pitch story ideas. When the Kremlin called on Russian citizens to boycott Turkey after Turkey shot down a Russian jet over the Syrian border (*Daily Sabah* 2016), Orhan texted me that he had great contacts in the Russian tourism industry of southern Turkey. Orhan's salesmanship homogenized news coming out of Turkey: the same blanks were filled with the same local details in many different stories on the same topic as Orhan kept busy with a steady stream of clients from around the world.

[1] See also Kuhn's ([1962] 1970) discussion of how the accumulation of anomalous signals eventually leads to epistemic shift and Bourdieu (1991: 127–136) on the effects of heretical discourse that breaks the doxic frame.

Other freelance news contributors likewise sell multiple versions of the same story. As a struggling freelance reporter, José had to cover the same topic in articles for several news outlets just to break even financially. Fixers' anonymity, though, makes recycling coverage both easier and more morally dubious from the news audience's perspective. If José double-dipped, a careful reader could tell that the same news contributor was pushing an issue in multiple publications. When Orhan double-dipped, that reader would see the names of different reporters bylining the various stories. Orhan's role as a common element among stories would be untraceable. When Orhan succeeded at pitching similar stories to numerous clients, the perception for a devoted news reader would be that the topic was important enough and the interviewees representative enough that multiple news organizations had independently chosen them and were independently corroborating one another's claims.

The oversight of editors who prescribed original content also constrained José's recycling. If he wanted to publish multiple articles on the same issue, he made a point of quoting different sources in each one. Orhan's anonymity afforded him greater freedom to recycle sources up and down his client list.

Orhan's double-dipping may have been invisible to news audiences and even to faroff editors worrying about the big picture, but Orhan had limited control over reporters' information about his recycling game. The word-of-mouth networks among foreign reporters on which Orhan relied for client referrals were also information channels that those reporters used to keep tabs on which colleagues were reporting what, where, and with whose help. And if a client did not learn from colleagues that Orhan was double-dipping, they might figure it out as they searched online for previous coverage of the issue Orhan had pitched.

Connoisseur and adventurous reporters disapproved of Orhan double-dipping. Orhan would promise them thrilling, exclusive access, but then they would learn with disappointment that the contact whom Orhan had promised was not a virgin source but had already been with other reporters.[2] Those clients came to view Orhan less as a teammate than as a calculating salesman. They distrusted Orhan, and

---

[2] See also Murrell's (2015: 110–111) discussion of reporters' disapproval of fixers "selling pups."

his over-rationalized approach to fixing threatened their pursuit of adventure and the elusive scoop.

Orhan developed a working routine that objectified sources into generic products and clients into generic buyers. As a fixer, he went from connoisseur to formalist to insulate himself from the disappointment and alienation that he felt when he poured himself into a story, only to see it framed in alignment with a client's preconceptions and against Orhan's sense. In a vicious circle, Orhan had adopted a commodifying, detached disposition toward his stories out of frustration over his lack of frame control. This cynical approach to fixing in turn made clients further distrust Orhan and reject his input at the level of story framing.

Orhan's connoisseur-journalist self did not disappear altogether. He rather split off his connoisseurly disposition from fixing work and reserved it for articles he wrote himself. After several years' hiatus, he began to contribute to the Turkish press again as a reporter and opinion writer, to author articles for highbrow news websites too niche for the government to bother shutting down. They paid little, but Orhan was subsidized by his fixing day job.

# Burcu, Elif, and Solmaz

When a news contributor's social and moral link to the field of international journalism tightens, they gain greater frame control, more moral sway to change their foreign colleagues' minds. Yet at the same time, the moral drive to challenge those foreign colleagues with frame-breaking information and the capacity to access fresh perspectives weaken as that contributor's dispositions, social network, and field of vision align with their foreign teammates'. We might call this the **Producer's Paradox**, the flip side of the **Fixer's Paradox**.

It took years for Burcu to establish herself as XYZ's lead producer in Turkey. She became the highest-ranked Turkish employee at the channel's Istanbul bureau, and it was not long before she felt bored and limited. Back when she had freelanced as a fixer, Burcu had developed relationships with an exotic array of sources. Even years later, she might bump into an old source from Kasımpaşa or Fatih, and they would remember her name and chide her for never coming around the neighborhood anymore. The reason Burcu no longer visited was that, once she rose to the top, she was largely chained to the office desk. When she did go into the field with a reporter and act as a translator, it was usually for interviews with government officials or celebrities, VIPs who had the media training to treat Burcu as a non-person and speak directly to the reporter. They rarely remembered her name. She felt she had lost the excitement of new connections and deep relationships with sources that she now delegated to her stable of sub-fixers including Elif.

Some of the few new connections Burcu did make were with a fresh cohort of public relations bureaucrats, and these relationships were adversarial. President Erdoğan's capture and politicization of the bureaucracy accelerated from a creep to a sprint following the 2016 coup attempt. He oversaw the purge of his former Gülen Movement allies, along with insufficiently loyal bureaucrats of all stripes who were falsely labeled Gülenist. A constitutional referendum the next year abolished the prime ministry effective 2018 and further consolidated the bureaucracy under the president's personal control (Koru 2017).

When Burcu had first started fixing in the early 2000s, the place to register for press card accreditation, apply for filming permits, or request interviews with top officials was the Prime Ministry Directorate General of Press and Information. It was a small office staffed by career civil servants who were sticklers about paperwork but relatively apolitical and autonomous. If applying for a permit to bring a large television crew to a hot spot like Diyarbakır, Burcu would be careful to present the reporting agenda as ethnological more than political and to avoid taboo worlds like "guerilla" or "protest." But by and large, if she crossed her t's and dotted her i's, she could expect interactions with the directorate to go smoothly.

Things changed when, with the dissolution of the prime ministry, the press and information directorate was replaced with the Presidency of the Republic of Turkey Directorate of Communications. Erdoğan loyalists staffed this new office and used their administrative powers to leverage political control over both the national and international media. News outlets that reported critically on Erdoğan and the AKP had little hope, for instance, of receiving permission to cross the Syrian border into territory within Turkey's sphere of influence. When Burcu submitted routine film permit requests, the new directorate would selectively deny permission to individual Turkish and foreign XYZ employees without explanation. She suspected that a growing number of her colleagues were blacklisted for their journalism or for signing petitions that called for Turkish–Kurdish peace or condemned the purge of pro-peace academics from universities.

Disheartened by the loss of adventure, growing acrimony, and shrinking space for her to negotiate unity between her channel and the state, Burcu considered leaving Turkey. Per her XYZ producer contract, Burcu had the right to request posting anywhere in the world. If she wanted to work at XYZ's Brazil bureau, she could ask. But she did not ask, felt that it would be weird to ask, she told me. There was still a marked difference between her and her American and European colleagues who would come and go from Turkey. Whatever the status she attained in the organization, there was an unspoken understanding that her position and value in the organization were geographically rooted. She was not a global news producer or correspondent like them; she was their Turkey producer. This difference was, I think, based in good part on the way Burcu had come up through the organization's ranks: as a fixer whose value was linked to her connection to local society, rather than to academic credentials or ties with upper management at XYZ's US headquarters. Burcu thus felt she had hit a ceiling and was unsure where she would go from her current position: "What will I be? A senior producer? A *more* senior producer?"

Burcu was in her 40s with no kids to weigh down her moral scales in favor of stability. She wanted adventure before so much time had passed at the XYZ office that she found herself old and settled (Simmel 1911 [1971]: 197–198). Rather than go back to freelance fixing, she decided to foray into a strange new world, that of entrepreneurship. Burcu created a production company that catered to international media, not just news and documentary but also serial television and film industries.[1] Her hard-earned expertise and connections were still useful, but the challenges of running a startup and diversifying into new forms of media felt fresh and exciting.

Burcu's departure from XYZ created a job opening for a producer, which Elif filled. Being a fixer, Elif told me after accepting XYZ's offer, isn't really a career. It's a job, and if you are good at it then you become a producer or reporter.

Elif had contemplated becoming a reporter herself, pitching stories of her own directly to editors. She was well positioned to make the transition from fixer to reporter, as her bicultural upbringing between Turkey and the United States endowed her with a well-developed capacity to broker between worlds and, more than Orhan, with the cultural disposition to convince other news contributors that she was not *too* local.

Ultimately, Elif preferred to stay behind the scenes. She was not jealous of foreign reporters for getting public credit for stories and having their faces appear on screen. As a blonde in Turkey, she told me, she had always gotten more than enough attention and did not covet visibility. She also did not want tax auditors showing up at her father's company because her name bylined a report critical of the government. For Elif, the role of producer offered the right balance of status and anonymity.

Just as Burcu's re-positioning had opened space for Elif to move from fixer to producer, Elif's promotion created an opening in XYZ's

---

[1] See also Plaut and Klein (2019b: 1703) on the significant portion of fixers who found or work for production companies.

stable of freelance fixers. Solmaz, after assisting me for her first fixing gig, had decided that she had no future in Turkish national media. Government capture and repression of opposition outlets continued apace, so Solmaz turned full-time to the international press. She became one of Elif's go-to sub-fixers, starting in 2016 even before Elif's promotion. Hiring Solmaz was a boon to XYZ, because she gave them access to sources affiliated with the Gülen Movement.

After the coup attempt, Gülenists were top public enemies, living in fear to talk with anyone they did not know. Freshly departed from the pro-Gülen newspaper *Today's Zaman*, Solmaz was up to date on the movement and retained trust among affiliated journalists as *one of us*, though this trust gradually diminished over time as her old contacts came to recognize the shift of her allegiance and perspective away from them.

\*\*\*

News contributors' moral worlds and social networks are chained to the roles they perform, but only loosely. There was a lag period when Burcu had developed the capacity to convince foreign colleagues that she was an objective professional producer who should be trusted with frame control over stories, but she still had good contacts in Kasımpaşa from her fixer days. In this period, Burcu also considered her producing job an exciting learning experience and found adventure in rubbing elbows more closely with the powerful.

The residual connections, expertise, and dispositions of a past field position, which we can call **role memory**, permit a news contributor to bridge worlds. There is a career-progress sweet spot for each link along the chain of news contributors when role memory of a previously occupied link has not yet faded but understanding of the next link along the chain has developed. In this sweet spot, a contributor can optimally broker both access and sensemaking.

Gradually, though, contributors settle into new worlds and old ties weaken. After several years as a producer at XYZ, Burcu was no longer in touch with a diverse list of friends that cut across neighborhoods, classes, and ideologies. She was less attuned to her old sources' evolving worlds and could no longer comfortably ask for help on short notice. Her contact list of government officials and sub-fixers, however, grew much longer. Burcu became reliable for routine stories but lacked exposure to worlds outside of journalism's normal ambit to generate new, frame-breaking ideas.

Burcu had to depend more and more on sub-fixers as she became more internationally oriented, both because she lost the social capital needed at the local end of the chain of news contributors and because she needed a buffer to protect her objective, detached producer self from the contaminating bias of local-ness. She found herself subcontracting the most interesting work she used to do herself. She was better equipped to unify biased sub-fixers' and adventurous reporters' worlds with the world of the faraway news organization headquarters than she was to unify sources' increasingly distant worlds with those of reporters.

One indicator that a contributor might be passing the social and moral sweet spot for their position is boredom. As producing TV news became a predictable routine, Burcu began to feel the tug of adventure toward the greener grass of a fresh new field. She departed XYZ in pursuit of a position – founder of a media startup – that was familiar enough for her expertise and connections to be useful but unfamiliar enough to be exciting. Burcu's replacement at XYZ, Elif, rose to producer rank with a set of social ties and dispositions less aligned to the organization, leading to a new round of productive conflict over what stories to cover and how.

# Nur

Nur worked nonstop with reporters in the southeast throughout 2015 and 2016 on the refugee crisis, the collapsing Kurdish peace process, and legal attacks on the Peoples' Democratic Party (HDP) that the government opportunistically redoubled after July 15th. The party had nothing to do with the coup attempt, but the government ramped up plans already under way to prosecute HDP lawmakers under anti-terrorism laws. Erdoğan used state of emergency powers to replace democratically elected HDP mayors with state-appointed "trustees," much as his prosecutors had forced opposition media outlets into trusteeship.

Like Orhan, Nur grew frustrated with her lack of frame control over stories, even if most clients were sympathetic to the Kurdish Movement and critical of the government. There were some reporters like Alison who worked closely with Nur for years and would come to Diyarbakır looking to develop ideas for stories that she was excited to investigate. But most reporters, she told me, arrived "as a baby," wide eyed and ignorant. She had to explain everything to them and fill in the same derivative templates again and again as existing clients flew off to other countries and new clients parachuted in.

Unlike Orhan, Nur did not settle into the role of the salesperson and formalist frame-filler. She had entered into journalism to help her community and the peace process and was unwilling to let her idealism devolve into cynical routine.

After three years as a fixer, the endless stream of bad news – both disheartening politics and lackluster journalism – had left Nur exhausted, but also with savings in the bank. She felt that she needed a break and also that if she continued to work in Diyarbakır, her status in journalism would be permanently stuck at the fixer level. She had worked hard to split her activist self from her journalist self, but when the stakes were deadly high, Nur's local moral world weighed on her, and her clients noticed. Her mentor İsmet had coached her on presenting herself as an objective professional to rise in her clients' estimation, but İsmet himself had only risen in status to a producer once he began to work abroad, away from the issues most important to him.

Continuing to work in your country of origin can be a professional stigma, signaling to other journalists that you are a Local and not a Global, limiting your prospects of upward mobility. The Turkish citizens who do become high-status reporters and producers in the international press are those with foreign educational credentials and transnational cultural fluency gleaned from years living abroad.

Nur decided that she needed to leave Turkey for her career to move forward. She would have to go to where she was an outsider and establish herself not as a Kurdish fixer, but as a global journalist. Nur was accepted into Columbia Journalism School in New York, and we met on campus during her first J-school semester and my last one as a sociology teaching assistant. She was skeptical that they were teaching anything practical that she had not already learned on the job, but the program was helpful for connections to American editors and newsrooms. Nur would report around the world for a few years and then, she hoped, return to Turkey, where she could use her global credentials to assert greater frame control, to tell local stories as she saw fit.

For her master's thesis project, Nur traveled to Colombia, a country that had long attracted her curiosity because of parallels to her own society. Colombia seemed like Kurdistan in the jungle with its smuggling-heavy economy and long-running leftist insurgency. A Colombian former client reporter offered for Nur to stay with her family, the script flipped so she was now the insider and Nur the outsider. The next I heard from Nur, she was complaining on social media about an unscrupulous Colombian fixer.

# Karim and Habib

Karim and Habib each carved out influential positions for themselves in emergent fields, trading zones between various international actors and the Syrians and Afghans of concern to them (Collins et al. 2010; Galison 2010).[1]

Karim arrived in Turkey in 2013 a desperate refugee. He transformed over the next years from a marginal player to a central node in a network of information about Syria that incorporated reporters, fixers, sources, government agencies, and NGOs.

I first got in touch with Karim in 2015 after Leyla, shocked that I had not talked to him yet, told me, only half-joking, "He's the king of fixers." The first time we met, Karim and I sat in a Lavazza coffee shop in the shadow of Istanbul's Galata Tower, and he told me war stories and showed me shrapnel scars. Two dark-suited British men stopping for takeaway coffee greeted Karim cordially, even deferentially. They're from the embassy, he told me nonchalantly.

While I continued my fieldwork, Karim continued consolidating his network centrality. He began to coach newcomers to the field of fixing. A young Syrian-American woman named Rima, who came to Istanbul for an internship at a foreign news bureau and effectively worked as their Syria fixer, met Karim at a journalist party. Rima was going to leave the party alone late at night after a few drinks, but he offered to make sure that, unfamiliar as she was with the city, she got back to her apartment safely. Rima did not trust a stranger to walk her home, so as a compromise the two ended up in a café talking shop over tea and baklava until dawn.

He was like ... "[Reporters are] going to ask for stories that are sexy. They're going to ask for things that their editors want but might not always

---

[1] For a comparable case of subaltern intermediaries developing a power base in an emergent trading zone, see Raman's (2012) study of South Indian clerks employed by the British colonial government.

be what is right. And you have to make a decision that you can go to sleep at night with ... because being the middle person can be a good thing and can be a bad thing. And you can be a vehicle like for reinforcing stereotypes and for reinforcing bad narratives and untrue narratives. And you can be the trust that they use to do things that are not ethical [i.e. they can use you to earn the trust of sources only to breach sources' or journalism's norms]. And then they can say they didn't do it; their fixer did." And so these are like a lot of things that it really helped to have in the back of my head, because it was easier for me to recognize them later on and it wasn't as much of a shock. And [Karim] also explained rates to me [for] print, radio, broadcast, documentary, freelance, staff. ... He was like, "Besides screwing yourself over [if you accept less than the going rate], you're screwing everyone else over in the city. And you're screwing the people further south who get paid a little bit higher because they're closer to the border. And you're screwing over the people in Syria who get paid extra." He was like, "So when one person knocks their rate down it hurts everyone."

In coaching new fixers to balance foreign and Syrian scripts and act in solidarity with other fixers, Karim was working to turn Syrian affairs brokerage (he coached Syrians working in the NGO sector too) into a shared, recognized, and regulated moral world of its own. He was encouraging his fellow brokers to treat their perspectives and their labor not as secondary to that of their clients or as lonely and ambiguous, but as belonging to an orderly field with its own internal organization and morality.[2]

In a self-reinforcing process, Karim's growing centrality and reputation lent weight to his coaching and other moral pressures. Everyone knew and could vouch for him, and if you violated his prescriptions, he could badmouth you to everyone.

---

[2] Galison (2010) describes the same process in the academic world: new subfields like biochemistry emerge with moral worlds (standards, methodologies, vocabularies, and so forth) that are generated out of exchange between existing fields like biology and chemistry. These emergent subfields contain thinned-out versions of either parent subfield, yet this stripped-down combination, Galison (2010: 48) argues, "is not a lesser version of something else; rather, it is a register of scientific interaction that is supple and effective in its domain." Likewise, the moral orders that Karim and Habib respectively stitched together were supple and effective at attaining the goal of facilitating transcultural information exchange while minimizing normative breaches that would threaten future iterations of brokerage.

Karim's role memory of working on the ground in Syria, and Syrian sources' memory of Karim as a revolutionary comrade, faded as his stay in Turkey extended. But he found, or made, a new world around him.

If Karim was King of (Syrian) Fixers, then he reigned together with Sally, the Canadian reporter with whom he often worked. Between this king and queen was a combination of contacts and credibility with both sources and news organizations that placed them at the center of the Turkish hub of Syrian reporting.

Every collaboration on a news story was an opportunity for mutual apprenticeship. Sally learned from Karim about Syria; Karim learned from Sally about journalism.

As the two grew closer, they began to share bylines and then to share a bed, and after a year of blurry lines between working and dating, they decided to marry. Sally was less comfortable than Karim with ambiguity in their relationship because she had to worry more about the foreign press corps gossip mill, being shamed and likened to rookie freelancers who bedded their fixers in tacit reciprocity for unpaid labor or for an exotic touch of adventure. Some women reporters criticized colleagues for crossing professional lines by flirting their way to discounts or strategically finding boyfriends who could help them on stories. These critics – generally high-status reporters who, unlike hustling freelancers, had the financial means to keep their professional and sexual selves neatly split – argued that normalizing the mixture of business with pleasure encouraged fixers to sexually harass respectable women clients.

Both Sally and Karim also recognized that their marriage would make it much easier – as compared to applying for asylum – for Karim to move to North America if and when necessary. By the end of 2016, the tide of the Syrian Civil War had turned in the Assad regime's favor. The Syrian government finally won the siege of Aleppo and mopped up resistance across most of the country. Although Turkey began a direct military intervention into Syria that year to prop up a Sunni Arab rebel enclave in northern Syria as a counterweight to both Assad and the Syrian Kurds, the resultant stalemate gave Karim little hope for his homeland's future. Karim came to draw a time map for himself that did not involve returning to the Syria he once knew or the Syria he had hoped to help create in the heady early days of revolution.

\*\*\*

Habib arrived in Turkey less desperate than Karim, but also less connected. When Habib first tried his hand at fixing as a university student, his older brother Abdullah was his bridge to the worlds of both journalism and refugee affairs. With each successive tie Habib established with a reporter, NGO worker, Turkish government official, asylum seeker, call-shop owner, or smuggler, though, his centrality grew in the network of people participating in the spike of Afghan migrations to Europe and the spike of media interest in that migration. The more links Habib secured, the more valuable he became for his capacity to connect those different participants with one another. The more relationships Habib catalyzed among his acquaintances, the more densely interconnected the network around him became.

Habib remained a marginal figure in each of the recognized fields he bridged – journalism, humanitarianism, organized crime, and the state – but he was central in a hybrid, emergent field that we might label The Istanbul–International Afghan Refugee Industry (Figure 5.1). Habib achieved what network sociologists call **closure**, when a social network encloses around the nucleus of a node that was previously a bridge spanning gaps among disconnected groups (Burt 2007).

That Habib was at the moral center of the trading zone among these groups became apparent to me in the course of reporting my story about Afghans in Istanbul. Habib got word through his smuggler contact Wahid that an Afghan woman had arrived in Zeytinburnu neighborhood seeking to travel to Europe. A woman traveling alone through the smuggling network was extremely unusual.

Habib and I met the woman, actually a shy headscarved teenager whom I will call Mariam, at a restaurant. She was accompanied by an associate of Wahid named Soltan. Mariam told us that she had escaped an abusive home and was hoping to begin a new life in Europe, where her younger sisters could eventually join her. Soltan told us that he was generously helping Mariam because they were from the same *qom*, an ambiguous term of group identification that can mean anything from family to tribe to ethnicity to nation. Soltan and his wife were hosting Mariam in their apartment for free to keep her safe, he said. Mariam stayed quiet, mostly.

I expressed my outsider skepticism about Soltan's claims of altruism as soon as Habib and I parted company with them. Habib, the insider, was more credulous of Soltan's story. He had known Soltan for years

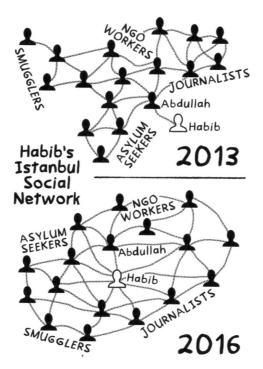

**Figure 5.1** Simplified and stylized sketch of Habib's social network, 2013 and 2016

and trusted that he was telling the truth. Habib culture-talked me toward alignment with Soltan's narrative, explaining that group solidarity was very important to Afghans.

A few days later, though, we were back in Zeytinburnu for another interview when Habib received a phone call from Mariam. She arranged to meet us in the neighborhood's central square without explanation. Mariam arrived crying, carrying a plastic shopping bag that contained all her possessions. She told us a very different version of events than we had heard at the restaurant. Soltan had been raping her – notwithstanding his wife and kid in the next room – in what he said was a fair exchange for shelter and the promise of assistance reaching Europe. When the wife protested, Soltan resolved his marital conflict by kicking Mariam out.

"I'm going to kill him," Habib kept repeating as he paced back and forth, figuring out a plan to help Mariam. The rules by which Habib played were not the rules of any one of the fields he brokered. Against humanitarian code, he used his NGO credentials and access to establish reciprocal relationships with smugglers; against journalistic code, he obtained consent for interviews by leveraging those smugglers' control over migrants; against the smuggler code, he exposed the exploitation of those migrants. But there were nonetheless rules to the emergent field in which Habib was a central arbiter. There was a moral code negotiated from among those intersecting fields. Soltan had breached that code.

Habib arranged for Mariam to stay with a female friend whom Habib knew through the expat social scene until he could find her a place at a women's shelter where he had contacts through his NGO work. He found Mariam a lawyer through an organization that provided legal advocacy to migrants who helped her apply for refugee status and press charges against Soltan. He fixed for other reporters who brought media attention to her case.

Soltan was convicted of rape and went to prison. After a long wait, Mariam's refugee status was approved, and she moved to the United States.

# *José*

In 2003, Istanbul Pride became the first LGBT parade in a Muslim-majority country. Every subsequent year turnout swelled. Around 100,000 people marched from Taksim Square down İstiklal Boulevard in 2014. In 2015, though, police attacked and dispersed revelers with water cannons and rubber bullets (Knight 2015). In June 2016, a month before the coup attempt, Grey Wolves joined Islamists in threatening to attack marchers, and Istanbul's governor banned the event on grounds of security concerns, establishing a precedent that the governorate would follow in subsequent years (AP 2016). Some defied the ban, and riot police responded with more rubber bullets.

José was there. After police detained a few activists and chased the rest from İstiklal Boulevard, small groups formed on side streets to chant and wave rainbow flags until scattered by a charge of teargas and truncheons. Usually, José had by now learned, the cops would stay on the main boulevard rather than pursue protesters down Beyoğlu's maze of side streets. Riot police were themselves outsiders, bused in from out of town in a deployment strategy that helped keep officers unsympathetic to protesters but also meant they were unfamiliar with the field of battle.

José, by contrast, had spent many an evening bar-hopping those side streets and knew them intimately. Camera in hand, he played the same game of cat and mouse as the demonstrators, running from a police advance only to double back through a different back alley or shopping arcade. On one side street, José happened on a pair of confused policemen who had separated from the phalanx and gotten lost chasing protesters. He laughed, took the cops' photo, and told them in Turkish (which he had been working hard to improve through private study and by dating Turkish guys) that they were headed the wrong way and should go back to their bus.

The policemen were not amused. They demanded his passport, press card, and the memory card from his camera. José handed over his passport and, in a slight of hand he had picked up from a photojournalist friend, fiddled with his camera before handing them a blank card instead of the one he had been using.

José worried for a moment that he was in too deep when they told him he was detained and should sit on the curb while they radioed their commander. But then a clanging started above them. Residents of the street's apartments banged together pots and pans, more and more joining the cacophony by the moment. The police suddenly looked scared. Then water splashed down, hurled from buckets by old ladies. Then glass bottles shattered around the two policemen. They threw José's passport back in his face, turned tail, and ran to cheers and jeers. José knew he had been stupid to provoke them, but he was also elated: the neighborhood had taken his side against the police. He was the insider.

* * *

While others of our protagonists struggled to convince colleagues that they possessed the professionalism and objectivity of an outsider, José struggled with the change of dispositions that came with becoming an insider.

By his fourth year in Turkey, José felt that he was finally developing an appreciation for the nuances of Turkish culture and politics. He could conduct interviews on his own in Turkish unless the topic was technical or new to him. Increasingly, other foreign reporters turned to José for contacts, relying on him as an unlabeled, pro bono fixer.

The better José got to know the country, though, the less his ideas about what was interesting aligned with editors'. José grew increasingly frustrated with their constrictive templates. His pitches would be met with responses that the proposed story was "in the weeds" or "inside baseball," meaning that the editors could not make sense of the information as fitting a frame familiar to foreign audiences. His editor at the syndicated news website where José had a string, which sold stories to small newspapers without foreign correspondents of their own, encouraged him instead to focus on 500-word articles on big, breaking events. José complained that he had to expend a majority of those words on background information bringing a reader assumed to know nothing about Turkey up to speed, background information that he had written many times before. Editors would also enrage José by slapping headlines on his articles that had little to do with their nuanced content, instead trumpeting the standard clichés that José took pride in avoiding.

If José wanted to escape his frustration and do work that he found interesting again, he decided, he could not go on as a freelance writer in Istanbul. He could choose to embrace the "Turkey expert" path and go to graduate school or apply for think tank jobs, where his superordinates and his audience would not mind him diving into the weeds.

Or he might find a job as a columnist at a Turkey-based English-language publication, with all the compromises and insecurity that entailed. Writing opinion pieces in the Turkish press would make him even more visible to the government than reporting for a foreign website did, so he worried about being able to stay in Turkey in the future. José had seen foreign colleagues deported or denied re-entry into the country after authoring reports critical of the government, and he thought his own days of publicly criticizing the government while renewing his residency might be numbered.

He even considered going from reporting to full-time fixing. As a fixer, José mused, he could still do the part of the job that he found most interesting – finding and talking with sources, tracking all the latest developments – but without the stress of dealing with editors, the compromise of authoring formulaic articles that undermined his expertise claim to fellow Turkey insiders, or the danger of public visibility.

Or José could relocate and start over as a reporter someplace new, somewhere he did not know too well, where he could enjoy the adventure of discovery anew. As a fresh outsider to a new place, his sense of the optimal signal-to-noise ratio between the familiar and unfamiliar would better align with that of editors. He chose this last option and moved to North Africa.

\*\*\*

I took a journalism class as an undergraduate and remember my teacher, a veteran foreign reporter, saying that she wrote her best stories within the first year or two of arriving in a new place. After that, she didn't see what an outsider would, and what she found interesting was often uninteresting or incomprehensible to an outside audience.

Something is lost in the learning and linking process that transforms a person into an insider. Even as a news contributor gains an appreciation for local nuance, they can also lose the ability to see things that are unremarkable from an insider perspective. As media theorist Marshall McLuhan ([1967] 2003: 106) put it, "we don't know who discovered water, but we're pretty sure it wasn't a fish."

During the course of my work as a fixer with Michael on a story about government supporters in Kasımpaşa neighborhood, we talked politics with some men in a tea shop. They sang Erdoğan's praises, yet a portrait of Mustafa Kemal Atatürk hung on the wall. I write "yet," but this was not a noteworthy contradiction to someone who lives in Turkey and comes every day into contact with people who idolize both leaders. I did not even notice the portrait.

But Michael, with eyes that were outsider enough to see Atatürk and insider enough to recognize him, did notice it. "Who's that?" Michael asked, knowing full well but using the question to elicit a conversation about Atatürk's and Erdoğan's comparative virtues. "We worship God first and Atatürk second," they told us. But what about Atatürk's secularism? Michael asked, and they responded that such details were beside the point. Atatürk led our first war of independence; now Erdoğan is leading our second.

Their response, though unoriginal, got to the heart of the ideological flexibility and importance of personal magnetism in Turkish popular politics too often missing from reductionist international discussions of the struggle between Kemalism and Islamism (Demiralp 2012).[1] It perhaps challenged readers of Michael's article to adjust their frame for making sense of Turkey. That moment in our reporting was possible because Michael, as a relative outsider, could see an opportunity to draw out our sources that did not occur to me. To my relative-insider eyes, the Atatürk portrait had blended into the background and did not register as information.

The sweet spot for a reporter is insider enough to provide connoisseurly fill-ins, but not so much as to rebel against the frames imposed by outsider editors. José passed that spot. When editors' templates went from useful guidelines to chains constricting him, José needed a new country and editors needed a fresh pair of outsider eyes.

The chains of editorial oversight do not chafe the minds of all foreign reporters equally. Alison and Geert were both old hands in Turkey compared to José, but for their own reasons adopted the disposition of the connoisseur more than the adventurer. They came to delight in the

---

[1]  See also Çınar and Taş (2017: 684–685) on Erdoğan's turn toward an *ulusalcı*-inspired discourse highlighting Turkey's War of Independence as a key moment of national history, one being relived in contemporary resistance to the imperialist West and its collaborators within Turkey.

puzzle solving of news production, in cleverly conveying their own distinctive timbre within the confines of their editors' prescriptions.

Enough foreign reporters do cycle through Turkey like José, though, to provide stable revenue for non–upwardly mobile fixers. Sales-oriented fixers like Orhan can routinize their work by recycling the same contacts, coaching, and story ideas in ways impossible without turnover in the Turkish foreign press corps. Orhan could not have repeatedly sold José, Alison, or Geert the same sources and information that he sold to José's replacement, the next stringer the syndicated news website hired as their man in Istanbul. Turnover in reporters, as in fixers, helps keep the system running.

# Temel and Noah

Several of our protagonists' careers underwent great change over the 2010s. Yet I have argued that when we zoom out, we see that continuous individual-level changes are a part of a larger stability, a dynamic equilibrium in the field of international journalism.

It is a tidy model for making sense of continuities in newsmaking, but doesn't any tale of stability run up against the zeitgeisty narrative of radical change in the way information circulates around the globe? Aren't social media and automated translation transforming international journalism and making fixers obsolete? How long will this book's model of morally motivated, status- or adventure-seeking brokers struggling for control over professional production chains remain relevant? Furthermore, aren't distinctions and hierarchies among local and global news contributors outdated colonial holdovers that have no place in an industry that should focus on reforming itself toward equity and social justice?

I will try to answer those questions in reverse order. First, a parable: I asked my trusty, wholly invented fixer Temel to bridge the gap between a source and me. Literally. The source and I were on opposite sides of a canyon, so I could not reach her on my own. Temel stretched, fingers clinging to one side and toes on the other, to span the gap, and I walked across him to the source's side and conducted my interview. After I crossed back, though, I felt bad about stepping all over Temel and pulled him up so that he could respectably stand beside me in journalism territory. The problem was that once Temel was on my side, there was again a chasm to cross. We needed a new broker to walk over for story access.

Media ethics advocates have argued that for the sake of equity, news organizations should bring fixers more closely into the fold of journalism, whether by providing them more public credit or by hiring them on official contracts and granting them the same benefits and protections as reporters. Some argue that news outlets need not rely so

298

heavily on foreigners, who parasitize the credit and money due their subordinates, when outlets could simply deputize fixers and other local news contributors as their reporters (Bossone 2014; Plaut and Klein 2019b; Borpujari 2019; Khan 2019). Within journalism, reformists are increasingly granting fixers bylines and recognizing their contributions with awards. Existing, labeled fixers in pursuit of status within the field of journalism welcome such measures.

Imagine the reformers are successful. Those fixers become more closely and publicly tied to news organizations' moral worlds. For a time, those newly formalized fixers are in a sweet spot, enjoying new-found status to assert frame control while still providing insider access. But gradually, like Burcu, their ties with other worlds weaken as those with journalism strengthen. The reform also reduces the ambiguity and anonymity of their positions, which further constrains fixers' capacity to productively breach journalistic norms to create unities with sources. Formalizing the status of existing fixers pulls them over to journalism's side of the canyon, opening up new gaps that require new linkages.

For journalism to continue, a new, informal stable of sub-fixers is assembled to restore the chain of production, to fill the blanks that staff fixers no longer can, sub-fixers to whom immorality can be safely outsourced. Those new brokers, ambiguous in the affiliation to journalism, have more freedom to act in breach of journalism's moral scripts without contaminating the news organizations they serve. The newcomers have different labels than the formalized fixers, their recruitment accompanied by a new round of boundary-work. Editors, producers, reporters, and fixers convince themselves and others that those informal sub-fixers are not really journalists deserving recognition or protection. Journalism finds its pro-fixer revolution devolving into a reproduction of the same pattern of continual turnover that already existed. Where there is a gap, either there will be a broker or there will be a silence.

Some scholars of "network journalism" have argued to the contrary that we are witnessing a process of **disintermediation** in the production and consumption of news (Bardoel and Deuze 2001; Hermida 2010; Heinrich 2012). Some have claimed that technology is making brokers obsolete, freeing the media from undemocratic gatekeeping and allowing direct-to-source access (Shirky 2008: 81–108). This technological argument is tied to a macroeconomic argument: old media business models are failing, advertising revenues can no longer support the costs of news bureaus around the world, and so a revolution of egalitarian newsmaking is inevitable.

Disintermediation claims are contradicted first by evidence that, as news outlets cut back on staff reporters in country after country, they do not stop covering the world or cover it entirely remotely. They just rely on a slightly different assemblage of professional brokers: NGOs, wire agencies, freelancers, stringers, and especially parachutists covering expansive regions (Boyer 2013; Powers 2018; Wright 2018). Parachutists cannot function without fixers, and so fixing is a growth industry (Murrell 2015; Palmer 2019; Plaut and Klein 2019a). "Citizen," "participatory," and "ambient" journalisms likewise rely on intermediaries ranging from social media influencers to "open-source intelligence" investigators to those same old professional journalists if they are to reach global audiences.

Just as importantly, disintermediation claims too often carry a pro-human bias, considering all the world merely a passive stage and men and women the active players. If we look at the Internet and see a system without brokers, it is because we discriminate against non-humans, assuming them to lack agency and morality (Wiener 1954: 15–27; Latour 1988a; Czarniawska 2011: 176).

Before considering artificially intelligent brokers, it is worth pointing out how even simple machines can act comparably to human fixers. Let us return to my parable.

To avoid asking Temel to plank the canyon again, with the combination of danger and exploitation that bridging method entailed, I tossed a walkie-talkie over to our source across the canyon. Now, I thought, we could communicate directly without mediation. But it turned out that walkie-talkie also acted as a broker and had its own moral world and capacities that shaped my reporting. It would force us into a one-at-a-time rhythm of speech, distort our signals, and introduce noise according to dispositions embodied in its engineering. It could only make sense of certain registers of communication and only span a gap of a certain distance. The access it provided me would be limited to whoever held it on the other side of the canyon.

Today's machine brokers are no mere walkie-talkies. Reporters can now use social media platforms instead of day-rate fixers to find and contact sources, auto-translate instead of day-rate translators to make sense of sources' linguistic signals, ride-share applications instead of day-rate drivers to bring themselves into the same physical spaces as sources.[1]

Non-humans are the ultimate non-persons, casually overlooked and exempted from the scrutiny required of an active player.[2] We might label humans as brokers and non-humans as media or tools, but whether I use Temel or Twitter to find and communicate with a source, I will be relying on an intermediary who regulates my access to and sense of the world.

Imagine that instead of a walkie talkie, Twitter replaces Temel as my bridge across the canyon. It is easy to walk over an algorithm and not notice it, to think that I am on solid ground. But Twitter's algorithms for determining which tweets to show and in what order, how to rank results when I enter a search term or click a hashtag, and whom to suggest I follow have their own biases (e.g. in favor of sponsored content), sensemaking capacities (e.g. reading Unicode text but not images of handwriting), moral dispositions (e.g. hiding or removing content flagged as violating community standards), and access limitations (e.g. only displaying Twitter content). Within those constraints, the algorithms would balance my prescriptions (as they understand them based on usage data) with potential sources' prescriptions (e.g. for privacy when they protect their tweets) and signal to me (with blue checkmarks and follower counts) that some were more trustworthy and newsworthy than others (Halavais 2014; Brake 2017; Tüfekçi 2017; Gillespie 2018).[3]

Twitter would behave differently than Temel, if not qualitatively then quantitatively. It would have different biases of different magnitudes, which would require more complicated methods to decipher than did figuring out Temel's political allegiance and cultural disposition. (An army of scholars and investigative journalists auditing

---

[1] Technology also provides alternative pathways to information that can be used to check human fixers' work and break their information control. Reporters use Internet search engines and social media to learn about sources and events instead of or in addition to relying on their fixers' guidance (Hermida 2014; Carlson 2016: 239–241; Bruns 2018: 195–202).

[2] All of the aforementioned technologies are of course human run. Just as every apparently autonomous human broker is aided by non-human assistants like phones and cars, every apparently autonomous non-human broker has humans behind the scenes designing and maintaining it in ways often invisible to users.

[3] The same brokerage pattern would hold true if I used Facebook or Google as my fixer instead of Twitter (Pariser 2011; Avila et al. 2018; Fung 2018).

algorithms, analyzing ad personalization, and parsing content moderation policies has struggled to map the shifting sands of platform bias.) Twitter would transmit a different timbre of information and different signal-to-noise ratio than would my human sidekick or other non-human brokers.

In pre-Internet days, if a foreign reporter wanted an alternative source of information for a story that circumvented their fixer, they would look to domestic newspapers and televisions as their brokers. Those media demanded the reporter align to their encoding of information in local languages, and in so doing dramatically change the reporter's receiving capacity and worldview. A person always learns more than just words when they study a foreign language.

Even if the reporter stuck to the English-language media of the nearest metropolis, they would find feature stories mostly unrelated to the reporter's existing interests and framework for making sense of the country. Those analog non-human fixers provided a low signal-to-noise ratio, exposing the reporter to much information that broke frame, information that was useless to the reporter for their immediate script but that could perhaps sow the seeds of new ideas.

The signal-to-noise ratio that the latest non-human fixers can provide is much enhanced from the one-size-fits-all mass media. Online platforms closely surveil users to build fine-grained profiles of their dispositions. The platforms then personalize the information that they feed those users in newsfeeds and search results, favoring content similar to that with which a user has previously interacted. These algorithmic brokers retain their clients' attention by leading them to the information they are predisposed to seek while filtering out the noise of contradictory or irrelevant information. At every moment of interaction with brokered parties, they are learning how to reinforce existing frames.

Online platforms' delivery of a high signal-to-noise ratio has drawn a great deal of criticism for fracturing society into a patchwork of "filter bubbles," "social silos," or "echo chambers" of insulated worlds of like-minded insiders who are hostile to and understand little of outside worlds (Pariser 2011). Journalists are vulnerable to this bubble effect as online platforms become increasingly important brokers of their access and sensemaking. Whereas collaboration with human fixers can expose reporters to a healthy dose of outside noise, reliance on social media might keep them more insulated against frame-breaking information. Reliance on non-human fixers may thus increasingly contribute to the homogenization of the news as machine learning becomes more sophisticated.

The pattern of human fixers, at least in the cases of Turkey and Syria, is that they tend to be recruited from the ranks of opponents to the dominant political faction, which in each of these countries not only controls the state but has also captured the domestic media (Finkel 2015). Turkey and Syria fixers tend to be disposed toward contributing to international narratives in ways that counterbalance the dominant power structures of those countries.[4]

Contrary to optimism about social media's liberating potential to diversify political discourse, states are increasingly working to control the Internet through censorship and cooptation. A transcendent disposition of corporate algorithmic brokers, subsidiary to their interest in profit, is to avoid compromising the position of their parent companies in countries of operation.

Governments threaten to block social media platforms' access to their countries' markets, and platforms sometimes toe the line and filter, remove, or reduce the visibility of information sources that displease those states (Morozov 2011: 211–218; Tüfekçi 2017: 132–163). In the Turkish case, the degree and method of compliance with state prescriptions for online content has varied from one company to the next. One recent study found Google News to be particularly biased, directing Turkish users to pro-government news outlets over their independent competitors (Kızılkaya and Ütücü 2021: 38–47).

Since the Gezi Park protests and corruption scandal of 2013, Turkey has issued tens of thousands of requests to Twitter to remove content and shut down user accounts, in many cases for criticism of the government, and intermittently blocked access to the site itself, among thousands of other websites (Sözeri 2016). Twitter has refused the vast majority of those requests, but the platform's resistance may soon be broken (Büyük 2021).

The Turkish state ramped up efforts to control online platforms' content moderation policies again in 2020 with a law requiring social

---

[4] The pattern of fixers being opposition disposed is not universal. Iranian, Chinese, and North Korean states have each made efforts to control and turn fixers into tools for surveilling and influencing reporters on the states' behalf. There is evidence, however, that even in these cases, fixers balance reporters' and states' respective prescriptions, along with moral dispositions of their own that do not align with either (Niknejad 2014; French 2016; Seo 2019).

**Figure 5.2** Public service announcement displayed on a metro train screen in Istanbul in July 2016: "PROFILES SUPPORTING TERROR WILL BE MADE KNOWN TO SECURITY. Citizens can notify [the following Directorate General of Security] email addresses of profiles and pages supporting terror activities." Photograph by author

media companies with over a million daily users in the country to establish offices in Turkey. Those companies, ranging from Twitter and Facebook to LinkedIn and Pinterest, would be forced to promptly comply with government requests to block or remove content from their sites and to store user data inside Turkey, within reach of law enforcement agencies. Platforms, including Twitter, that refused to establish Turkish offices were punished with fines, advertising bans, and bandwidth throttling until they complied (bianet 2021; Twitter 2021).

Tweets are especially vulnerable to state information control because of their public visibility. The Turkish government now encourages its citizens to report subversive social media posts under the guise of counterterrorism efforts (Figure 5.2). Turkish Twitter has become a dangerous place to express opposition viewpoints. The country leads the world in jailing its citizens for social media posts (HRW 2018).[5]

---

[5] See also Tüfekçi (2017: 148–154) on the Turkish government's efforts to censor and punish political activism on Facebook and Instagram.

The state has also worked to scrub the Internet of inconvenient information through its control of mass media: after seizing *Zaman*, for instance, state "trustees" deleted the newspaper's entire online archive (Sözeri 2016). The Turkish state has had limited success with these and other tactics to control the Internet. Nonetheless, the information about Turkey to which online algorithmic fixers can connect a reporter, particularly if that reporter is inside the country without a means to bypass website censorship, has been systematically modified by state intervention.

Of course, human fixers must also worry about state surveillance and coercion. My point is not that one kind of brokerage is always better or worse or that absolute, incommensurable differences exist between human fixers and non-human information brokers. To the contrary, we should be comparing all instances of information brokerage along the same axes of variation.

The division of labor among various human and non-human news brokers is shifting, as are the techniques of mediation to access information and manage its overload. They always have been shifting, hand in hand with technological and economic change (Czarniawska 2011; Bozdağ 2013; Örnebring and Conill 2016: 214–215). Rather than claiming a break from the past in the form of disintermediation, we need to consider today's and tomorrow's cyborg journalism in comparison and continuity with longer-standing variants.

# Coda: Filling in the Blanks

Fixers bridge the gap between reporters and sources with a range of matchmaking, coaching, and transcoding tools. Their capacity and freedom to unify reporters and sources and control information and story frames are constrained, however, by those brokered parties' perceptions of them, the presence of alternative pathways of communication that circumvent them, the limits of their expertise and social capital, and the magnitude of conflict between parties. The unstable positions of all news contributors in macrolevel struggles for political, cultural, and economic power underlie their prescriptions for what should be done and how. Not only brokered parties' competing demands, but also fixers' own pasts and expected futures weigh on them as they navigate the moral dangers of brokerage. Fixers' management of moral threats transforms the objects of exchange between reporters and sources: the information that becomes news. Reporter–fixer–source interactions also transform all sides of the triad, leading them to adopt new dispositions and aspirations as their respective careers progress.

My way of explaining the news demands that we pay attention to the microlevel of each news contributor's perspective and behavior. The danger is that with this fine-grained approach, I miss the forest for the trees, the signal for the noise.

Grander theorists of media have argued that, however news production looks on the microlevel of individual journalists and however much they think their contributions matter, the larger and more important pattern is that news reflects and serves the geopolitical and economic interests of the powerful (Marx and Engels [1845] 2006; Said 1978, 1981; Herman and Chomsky 1988). According to this line of thinking, the powerful impose hegemonic Orientalist, nationalist, and/or neoliberal narratives on Turkey and Syria and delegate the filling in of details to news contributors who are punished or silenced if they break frame. Variety among those delegated details does not register as differences that make a difference from the wide-angle perspective of global inequality and domination.

This book is not intended to refute big picture templates for making sense of journalism. My aim is rather to fill in the lower-order blanks left in grand theorists' frames, blanks that they themselves cannot fill from their outsider vantage point.[1] For example, journalism about the Syrian conflict might indeed follow an Orientalist template, but does Orientalism express itself in condemnation of the barbarism of the Assad regime, or the barbarism of the rebels fighting the regime? Which specific rebel group, among many involved in similar activities, does a news story single out as hero or villain? How moving is the anecdote about the hero and how decisively damning the evidence against the villain? The grand theorist is silent on these details and lacks the tools to explain the variation in informational content and framing even among media from the same countries with similar ownership and market orientations. Those details may be unimportant from an abstract, generalizing perspective, but they can be enormously consequential for the people and groups cast as heroes or villains. For a Syrian rebel group, media coverage could be decisive in their competition with other groups to attract foreign patronage or avoid foreign airstrikes.

I also break the grand theorist's frame, gently, by showing how revisions of narrative can travel not only *down*, but also *up* journalism's hierarchical chain. Fixers convince reporters to change their minds, reporters convince editors, and so on until the news changes the minds of its audience. I encourage the grand theorist to see that outlier stories that do not align to dominant narratives are more than mere noise. They have an order of their own, an order that exists at the

---

[1] Mills ([1959] 2000: 48) similarly argued that Talcott Parsons's grand structural-functionalist theory of the social system was not useful for elucidating any particular real-world issue of concern to real people:

What is "systematic" about [Parsons's] grand theory is the way it outruns any specific and empirical problem. It is not used to state more precisely or more adequately any new problem of recognizable significance. It had not been developed out of any need to fly high for a little while in order to see something in the social world more clearly, to solve some problem that can be stated in terms of the historical reality in which men and institutions have their concrete being. Its problem, its course, and its solutions are grandly theoretical.

level of the moral worlds of news contributors. The local details – who becomes a fixer (or a source or reporter or editor), to what end, with what capacities, and under what conditions – change the news.

To provide the analytical tools to fill in these lower-order blanks, I have linked together ideas from multiple scholarly fields into a framework that does full justice to none of them (Galison 2010). Much as a fixer creates a fragile unity among disparate worlds, I did my best to align theories from fields including cultural anthropology, journalism studies, organizational sociology, science studies, and information theory through additions, subtractions, and substitutions to each school of thought that would horrify a purist of any one of those fields.[2]

I have shifted my vocabulary from chapter to chapter because contributors of each field have produced sets of vocabulary and dichotomies useful for answering different relevant sub-questions of my study. Cultural anthropologists contrast purity with danger; journalism critics, objectivity with bias; moral philosophers, order with disorder; organizational sociologists, status with status threat; telecommunication engineers, signal with noise.

The interlanguage that I use to talk about news fixers borrows from all of these scholarly traditions, clustering together terms from across fields that seem to me to get at the same general notions. **Disorder**, **adventure**, and **noise** are not quite synonyms but are conceptually linked. We could map the linkages among clustered concepts into a network, as in Figure 5.3.

I found it useful to mix and match jargon because the interests of these various academic fields intersect in the figure of the news fixer. How a fixer transcodes depends on their status in brokered fields, which can be compromised by the perception of bias, which is signaled

---

[2] I also tried to satisfy multiple, conflicting coding scripts among my academic and nonacademic target readers for what constitutes an interesting and valuable book. At various points, a sociologist reader might have wondered why I was rambling through yet another tale of newsmaking without the preface of a clear topic sentence that stated the distinctive theoretical contribution of that chapter. A journalist reader might have wondered why I was rambling through yet another set of esoteric theoretical distinctions instead of focusing on the juiciest newsmaking tales. If you found yourself frustrated by too much or too little detail or abstraction or historical, political, or cultural context, I hope that you can forgive me with the understanding that it is not easy to unify the moral worlds of multiple audiences, whether news contributors or book readers.

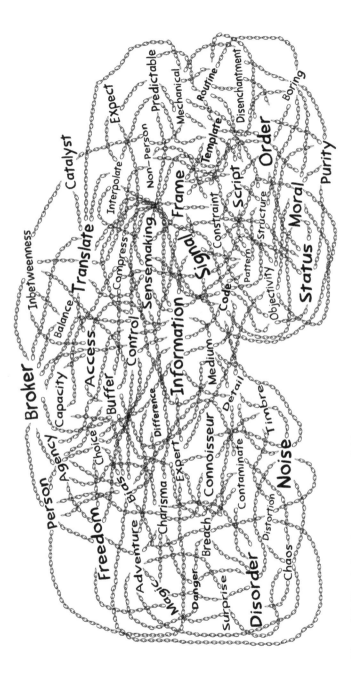

Figure 5.3 Vocabulary for an emergent field

through embodied dispositions. The distinction between whether information is signal or noise depends on whether its transmitter is prescribed the role of person or non-person, which is signaled by their label, which has been negotiated based on an evaluation of their expertise and professional purity.

My hope is that the interlanguage assembled on these pages is useful for other contributors to the hybrid, emergent field of broker studies.

# *Appendix: Sociological Fiction*

A map *is not* the territory it represents, but, if correct, it has a *similar structure* to the territory, which accounts for its usefulness.

Alfred Korzybski, *Science and Sanity*, 58

## Truth and Fiction

If you have skipped ahead to this appendix before reading the rest of the book, be warned that I will reference ideas and characters introduced in previous chapters.

The characters of this book are fictional composites, each constructed through the selective remixing of data I collected about multiple real people. I created composite characters first and foremost to protect the anonymity of research participants. Simply changing names is oftentimes not enough to protect anonymity, especially when describing people who are well known to each other or the public (Vidich and Bensman [1958] 2000: 398–399; Scheper-Hughes 2000; Jerolmack and Murphy 2019). I have described the production of news stories that could be found and matched to individual reporters and, with a bit more digging or insider access, to individual fixers, if I did not take further anonymizing measures.

To deal with the problem of unmasking, many ethnographic researchers scramble details and chronology, usually with the unelaborated claim that their changes are not significant (Jerolmack and Murphy 2019: 804–809). A composite narrative takes such scrambling to its logical conclusion in detaching the character on the page from the real person in the world.

In this appendix, I will explain how I created this book's characters and how my use of fiction aligns with a long line of thought about social scientific methods and ethics. In demonstrating that the use of fiction is actually commonplace in the social sciences, I am not attacking social science as fake. I am saying that the responsible and systematic creation of fiction is an essential tool of social science. Fiction done right is more truthful than nonfiction done wrong. Embracing the fiction label is also an ethical choice: social scientists and journalists alike too often use the claim that they are sticking to observed facts as a rhetorical device to gain unquestionable authority and dodge difficult questions about their biases, worldviews, limited access, and creative shaping of the stories they tell (Clifford 1983: 127–130).

Fiction, broadly defined, is a representation of people and events that is produced from the author's imagination and not limited to correspondence with phenomena that can be individually observed in the real world.[1] That guiding authorial imagination can be socio-logical: connecting personal experience to larger social patterns and trends (Mills [1959] 2000). The method for producing fictional people and events sequences can be scientific: following a systematic logic based on differences that are observed in the real world and theorized to be distinct in their causes and effects.

Sociologists often use fiction as a thinking tool and a means to compress and organize data, although they rarely label their work as such. Every sociological argument of causation employs – implicitly or explicitly – counterfactual "what if" fictions. We imagine a parallel world identical to the real one except for one small difference and then consider how things would have turned out differently, using data from a control group or comparative case as an approximate stand-in for the fictional alternative reality (Weber 1949; Griffin 1993: 1101). Mathematical models of society are alternative realities con-taining limited sets of elements that change and affect each other according to rigidly predictable rules. Such a model is not an accurate representation of reality but is nonetheless useful because it "tells us what would be true *if* that were the way [the world] changed ... as a way of understanding the dynamics of how something might be working, even though it doesn't work just the way the model specifies" (Becker 2007: 161–162). Statistics create fictional average members of invented categories to compare with one another. Statisticians

---

[1] A conception of truth that limits itself to correspondence with individually observed phenomena is useful for propositions about "moderate-sized specimens of goods," but less so for propositions about moral truths, social facts, or interactional patterns (Austin 1962: 6–14).

calculate differences between average outcomes that do not necessarily correspond to any real person's experience and use those calculations to infer how the lives of members of one category would be different in a fictional world in which they were members of the other category.

I do not point out the fictive nature of social scientific methods to discredit them. My point is to reject the idea that fiction and science are incompatible. Fictions can be more effective than – or essential complements to – descriptions of actual events and individuals for explaining social patterns and trends and devising theoretical tools that can be applied to other cases (Fassin 2014).[2]

Social scientists mediate between their data sources and their readers (Fassin 2017). Their representations of society necessarily compress complex social realities in order to make sense to readers (Becker 2007: 2–18). Without lossily compressing data – the hours of recordings, page upon page of field notes, thousands of survey responses, or millions of bits of internet metadata that the researcher has collected – it is impossible to form intelligible arguments, to make comparisons across cases, or to create a formal theory that explains more than the case at hand (Danto 1962; Becker 2007: 17–25; Emerson et al. 2011; Vaughan 2012).

The statistical fiction of the average member of a group allows the compression of data into neatly expressible tables and graphs by combining individual experiences. Narrative fictions can elucidate causal relationships by combining the most revelatory highlights of their data into a single story.

There are nonetheless key differences between literature and social science, not in the act of fictionalization, but in the how and the why of it. Anthropologist Clifford Geertz (1973: 15–16) writes, "Anthropological writings are ... fictions, in the sense that they are 'something made,' 'something fashioned' – the original meaning of *fictiô* – not that they are false, unfactual, or merely 'as if' thought

---

[2] Narratologists like White (1980: 27) have even argued that the world can *only* be made coherent through fiction: "value attached to narrativity [and causal theorizing, he might have added] in the representation of real events arises out of a desire to have real events display the coherence, integrity, fullness, and closure of an image of life that is and can only be imaginary." Without imposing meaning, order, and closure on events to draw them into a fictional unity, the historian or sociologist could only write a chronicle or transcript (Danto 1962; White 1980: 10–27).

experiments."[3] Geertz writes that the important difference between Gustave Flaubert's novel *Madame Bovary* and an ethnographic account of a Moroccan named Cohen "does not lie in the fact that [Bovary's] story was created while Cohen's was only noted. The conditions of their creation, and the point of it ... differ. But one is as much a *fictiô* – 'a making' – as the other."

The point of fashioning social science is to explain patterns and trends and offer tools for interpreting the world. As for the conditions of their respective creations, literature and social science have different criteria for inclusion of content into a story, for separating signal from noise. Literature selects or invents information based on dramatic rather than analytic license. "Drama," Alfred Hitchcock told fellow filmmaker François Truffaut, is "life with the dull bits cut out" (Truffaut and Scott 1985: 103). Social science might be said to be life with the causally irrelevant bits cut out.[4]

If Hitchcock had made a film about NASA's 1986 *Challenger* space shuttle disaster, he would almost certainly have devoted more time to the sensory experience of the astronauts inside the space shuttle than does sociologist Diane Vaughan (1997), whose landmark book on the subject ignores that dimension of reality. After all, the astronauts' feelings did not cause the erosion of O-rings in *Challenger*'s solid

---

[3] The purer fiction of the "'as if' thought experiment" also has its place in social science. Goffman (e.g. 1969: 93) frequently invented characters and situations as exemplars of theoretical arguments, a function that my parabolic character Temel served. Parables are rarely useful as sources of surprising data with which to refine theory; rather, they allow authors to illustrate ideas with greater freedom than that afforded by real data.

[4] The selections made according to the logics of dramatic vs. analytic license often coincide. In a naturalistic/realist fictional story, relatability is part of what makes readers care about characters and continue to turn pages. Readers put themselves in fictional characters' shoes and believe that given the circumstances (however foreign or fantastical), those characters' actions make sense (Keen 2006: 214–216). This evaluation of relatability is grounded in tacit comparison to data that readers have unwittingly been gathering their whole lives about how society works (Becker 2007: 247–251). Selecting data based on aesthetic appeal can meanwhile have analytic utility. Katz (2001, 2002) argues that the "neglected practical wisdom" embedded in gut feelings about what makes for a "luminous description" or poignant moments often reflects good causal reasoning: "Ethnographic data *should* systematically over-dramatize the colorful character of people, their settings and their conduct, for reasons rooted in the logic of empirically grounding and testing causal explanation" (Katz 2001: 467). Drama may clue us in to causal relevance.

rocket booster. Vaughan devotes more attention to the faxing of data charts than Hitchcock would have, because the mode of information transmission from Thiokol engineers to NASA headquarters, however boring, *did* have a causal effect on the launch decision that led to the disaster (Vaughan 1997: 287–326).

The social scientist's analytic license allows them to ignore some data and highlight others in order to create a world for the reader in which research subjects' lives are objectified into evidence, fill-ins for the scientist's causal argument. When social scientists discuss methodology, much of the debate concerns the boundaries of analytic license and the assumptions that underlie authors' simplifications.

The problem, with social science as with journalism, is that the easiest, most convenient way to select and order information is to fall back on a premade template. Researchers necessarily rely on existing theoretical frameworks to make sense of their findings and manage information overload. Those frames should, however, be subject to constant revision in response to new data (Tavory and Timmermans 2014). If they overrely on received wisdom, they risk missing inconvenient trees that might disrupt their expectation for how the forest looks.

Researchers should not have too much freedom to write whatever they like, and factuality in and of itself is too weak a constraint. A bullshit argument can be factually accurate (Frankfurt 2005). It is easy to cherry-pick real data in an untruthful way to confirm a preexisting worldview with no surprises. Not just reality, but the methods by which it is selected, interpreted, and ordered are important for the reliability of a sociological claim (Katz [1983] 2015).

Quantitative researchers follow standardized procedures for constraining their selection and rejection of data. They have developed statistical measures of significance that distinguish signal from noise and techniques to control for the influence of factors outside of the scope of their studies. Such procedures are, however, impossible to imitate in ethnographic research. My data consisted not of numerically coded counts of phenomena, controlled experimental results, or responses to standardized survey questions, but of my qualitative observations of study participants' and my own socially situated actions (Katz [1983] 2015; Small 2009).

When it comes to ethnographic writing that uses composite characters, the cherry-picking problem expands. When data collected on multiple real people get pooled together to form a single composite character, it is even easier to cobble together just-so narratives that conveniently conform to the claims toward which the ethnographer is predisposed.

The challenge for me, then, was to develop a systematic method for clustering multiple participants and selecting which data from which participant to include in what order that held me as accountable as possible to reality. This was not just an ethical but an analytical imperative: for researchers to change their minds and come up with new ideas, they must expose themselves to the surprises of inconvenient information, to noise that disrupts the clean signal of a bias confirmed (Duneier 2011).

## Step One: Compression

There are two steps to creating composite character narratives: 1) deciding how to compress or cluster individual participants into characters and 2) deciding what data to attribute to those characters and in what chronological order. At Step One, my aim was to compress multiple participants into composite characters based on their similarity in a way that enriched rather than impoverished analysis.[5]

I created what I call a **sequence table**: a series of entries arranged chronologically that summarize research participants' careers in the news media and the backgrounds that brought them into those careers. The entries in the sequence table were drawn directly from the coding that I applied to my data. To **code**, in social scientific jargon, means to apply brief metadata descriptions to your original notes, recordings, and so forth. I applied codes based on their hypothesized causal relevance to the variation I hoped to explain: similarities and differences in the ways fixers manage expectations, shape the news, and use fixing to accomplish other goals.

Table A.1 is an invented sequence table, which is shorter and so more readable than the actual sequence tables I created for the characters who have appeared in this book. Each "case" column consists of data about a single real-world research participant.

[5] My method for measuring similarity among participants' life sequences draws on and remixes ideas from Ragin's (2008) Qualitative Comparative Analysis, Propp's (1970) methodology for typologizing folktale sequences, and Abbott's (1995) sequence analysis.

**Table A.1** *Participant sequence (open coding)*

| Participant A | Participant B | Participant C |
| --- | --- | --- |
| Raised in Istanbul | Raised in Istanbul | Raised in Diyarbakır |
| Attended English-language school in Turkey | Moved to United States for elementary school | Learned English |
| Attended English-language university in Turkey | Attended English-language school in Turkey | Attended Turkish university |
| Moved to United States | Attended US university | Reported for wire agency in Turkey |
| Attended US university | Reported for US media in United States | Started fixing full-time |
| Moved to Turkey | Married American spouse | Did military service |
| Got day job in business | Reported for Turkish English-language media | Became staff producer for foreign TV |
| Started fixing part-time | Started fixing full-time | Moved to Russia |
| Quit day job | Became staff producer for US TV news | Reported for foreign TV in Russia |
| Started fixing full-time | | |

Depending on how specific the inputted codes are, it may be that initially no **participant sequence** matches another, as in Table A.1. I must then refine the codes through a process of abstracting specifics into generalities to identify similarities. There must be some basic forms of similarity, unless I have made a mistake in bringing together these cases into a single study. The sequence table is not only a tool for determining similarity, but also a visual aid for transitioning from "open" coding that merely describes data to "selective" coding that sorts data into categories of core causal relevance that serve as the building blocks of theory (Strauss and Corbin 1998). I use the codes and tables to mutually refine each other.

Eventually, I am left with several stripped-down **character sequences** into which multiple participants more or less fit. In some cases, I add variables as I notice their importance across multiple participants'

**Table A.2** *Basic character sequence (selective coding)*

| Character: Ayşe (includes Participants A & B) | Character: Cemal (includes Participant C) |
|---|---|
| Raised in western Turkey | Raised in western Turkey |
| Attended university abroad | Attended university in western Turkey |
| Worked non-media job | Worked as reporter for domestic media |
| Socialized with foreigners in Istanbul | Became fixer |
| Became fixer | Worked as reporter outside Turkey |
| Promoted to producer | |

careers. I think through what variables might be added to differentiate participants who appear similar on the table but whom I know to be very different in real life.[6] For instance, I add "socialized with foreigners in Istanbul" as social ties to foreigners figured into both Participant A's and B's initial recruitment as fixers in contrast to other participants.

If a young participant's sequence looks much like the beginning of an older participant's sequence, I infer that the younger participant is earlier on a similar trajectory to their elder and cluster them together, even though the shorter sequence would need numerous additions at the end to match the longer one. Participants do not always fit squarely into characters. Participant C in Table A.1 has much but not all in common with Character Cemal in Table A.2 (e.g. Diyarbakır is in Eastern Turkey) – and so I end up with participants who bridge multiple characters.

The number of characters I create represents a balance between imperatives to show patterns and to show variations. Were I to treat everyone who participated in my study as unique – and indeed, no two life stories are ever quite the same – then it would be impossible to generalize about patterns that were common to multiple people. Were

---

[6] This interrogation of sequence acts as a stage of the "ethnographic trial" recommended by Duneier (2011), who suggests that once they have constructed a tentative argument, ethnographers should conduct a thought experiment. They should seek out an "inconvenient sample" of data by asking themselves if there are any "witnesses" who could be brought forth to provide testimony containing contradictory facts that would make the ethnographers revise their arguments.

I, by contrast, to lump everyone into a single archetypal character, The Fixer, in order to discover one overarching pattern, then I would leave none of the person-to-person variation that is essential to refining arguments and explaining causes and effects through comparison.

Sequence tables are meant as an aid to comparative analysis, not as a substitute for it. When attributing data from Participant C to Character Cemal, I must acknowledge the incomplete match between the two. Being raised in the Kurdish-majority city of Diyarbakır, for instance, might be causally connected to differences in Participant C's real career – not just whether he works as a fixer but how he does the job – that are not captured by my simplified table. Where those differences are significant enough, and the variation of Participant C from other participants composing Cemal noteworthy enough, I create a minor side character. This minor character retains Participant C's relevant background (e.g. raised in Diyarbakır) and carries out an action of Participant C that is incompatible with Cemal. Tim, Pınar, and Rima were among characters conceived in this manner.

The process of comparing rows challenged me to come up with novel theories obscured by my initial assumptions. For example, I initially conceptually divided my research subjects into the categories "local fixer" and "foreign reporter," assuming the two labels corresponded to separate roles requiring different skills and so resulting from different trajectories. But when I plotted everyone onto the same huge sequence table, I found that the table failed to neatly divide reporters from fixers or foreigners from locals. Turks, Kurds, Syrians, Afghans, Europeans, and Americans never conveniently sorted themselves into national clusters or into separate foreign reporter and local fixer clusters. Some participants went from trajectories similar to others labeled "fixer" to trajectories similar to others labeled "reporter"; others, vice versa (that cluster became José). Sequences did sort themselves into clusters such as transnational elites who quickly rose in status (Elif) and Turkish domestic press journalists who grew disillusioned with the international media and got stuck at *fixer* level (Orhan).

The process of building the sequence table encouraged me to think beyond the hidebound divisions received from my participants' and my own initial categories and labels. I had to consider the fuzziness of those categories and how and why individuals move between labels or are prevented from doing so.

The logical end of considering myself as a participant in the world of international journalism and questioning the neat correspondence of roles and experiences to clear-cut labels – fixer, reporter, researcher – was to plot myself on the sequence table along with my subjects. Noah the recurring character is a composite. His narrative includes the experiences of others, and some things I did are attributed to others according to the same ethical and analytic constraints that guided all my compressing and remixing: protecting participants and attributing data based on similarity of individuals' trajectories and on the causal logic discussed in the next section.

Stripping down lived experiences into such table entries inevitably means that certain entries look the same but have very different meaning in actual participants' lives. The compressed representation of the table fails to capture much of the richness of the ethnographic data collected. Yet there is an important difference between quantitative methodologies, which convert participants into data series and then analyze only those data series, and this compositing method. The sequence table is used only to systematically think through degrees of similarity and difference among participants, and not as a way of thinning down the data I ultimately include in character narratives. When it comes to writing narratives, I remix my data with the sequence table as a guide and flexible template, but I include the same richness of description that I would in conventional ethnographic writing.

## Step Two: Remixing

Now that I had my cast of characters, how could I mix and match data from multiple participants into each character's narrative? How could I force myself to rethink my assumptions, rather than craft a tale around them? I needed a system for limiting my freedom of choice, for holding my assemblage of information into fiction accountable to the real world.

The solution lay in relying on the cause-and-effect logic inherent to narrative. This logic guided my judgment of which information to include in each character narrative and in what order. A narrative consists of bits of information linked together in a sequential chain to form a coherent story – whether or not that story is told in chronological order (Stone 1979: 3). Narrative explains what it includes late in a sequence by what happens earlier in that sequence; it justifies the inclusion of what happens early by its relevance to what happens later. Every event that an author includes in a narrative limits their freedom to choose what happens next or what happened before (Mitchell 1983: 199–200; Griffin 1993: 1098–1099).

Any social scientist telling a narrative story that explains an event, pattern, or trend must be careful in selecting from raw material for inclusion in a narrative and interrogate themselves about what is causally relevant (Griffin 1993). For authors of a composite narrative, this problem expands beyond selecting from data of what actually did occur in a sequence of events in the real world to the more creative exercise of creating sequences that never *really* occurred but are objectively possible: they *could* have occurred (Weber 1949).

This method allowed me to determine what data I should *not* include, but sometimes left me with multiple data (that conflicted with one another but not with what else happened in the narrative) that I *could* include within bounds of objective possibility, analytic license, and causal reasoning. Since I was interested in showing the variety of behaviors that fell within my general theme of news fixing rather than in proving what sequence of a fixing career was most likely, I "sampled for range." I included data in each narrative that were as different as possible from other character's narratives, illuminating variations in behaviors and career paths in the sharpest possible relief. Making my characters different from one another provided fodder for comparison and theory-building (Katz [1983] 2015: 133–136, 2001: 467; Weiss 1994: 22–24; Small 2009: 13; Vaughan 2014).

My approach and challenges will not shock anyone who has written a realist novel or short story or play. *Of course* an author should question whether their story's characters make sense. *Of course* those characters make sense when their thoughts and behaviors are explained by the combination of the situation in which they find themselves and precedent events of their lives.[7] *Of course* there should be variety among characters.

---

[7] Besides realism/naturalism, there are other kinds of literature with norms of dramatic license less constrained by narrative logic and objective possibility. Absurdism and surrealism can powerfully jar us into reflecting on the careful arrangement of our world precisely by breaking with familiar causal paths. Allegorical characters can provide food for philosophical thought without behaving like real people in the real world.

But in a field like sociology, "statistical" logic too often takes precedence over causal logic because it seems like the more scientific option. Statistical logic dictates that the pattern to be identified and included in a social scientist's story is the one most common among study participants. Statistical logic makes sense when a researcher is analyzing quantitative data collected according to statistical standards of randomization and sample size, but it does not make sense for narrative ethnography (Mitchell 1983; Small 2009).

Nonetheless, that was the approach adopted in the only sociology book I have found in which the author explains how they moved from raw data to a composite character narrative: Marion Goldman's (1999) *Passionate Journeys*. Goldman (2002: 160) writes, to defend her composite character method as falling within the legitimate bounds of analytic license, "No major event such as marriage, divorce, or childbirth was recorded unless it was shared by the majority of [participants] in a group." The problem with Goldman's *majority-rules* approach is that it follows a logic of "statistical" fiction without actually having a statistically significant or random sample and without attention to whether the selected characteristics and experiences brought together into a single character are logically compatible with one another. Goldman, at least according to her own methodological appendix, ignores the logics of sequence and causality.

Imagine I used the same method of data selection as Goldman. Imagine that of seven participants whom I cluster into the composite character Ayşe, four (including Participant A above) went to elite private high schools in Istanbul and three (including Participant B) spent their teenage years in the United States. Four of the seven (including the three research participants who grew up partially abroad along with one who lived almost all of her life in Turkey but whose mother is American) speak English with native fluency. The "statistical," *majority-rules* approach dictates that I select the data that are roughly similar across the greatest number of informants for inclusion in Ayşe's narrative. Thus, I write that Ayşe has two Turkish parents, spent her teenage years at private school in Istanbul, and speaks English like an American native speaker. This sequence is a problem for my narrative because, logically, someone who grew up entirely in Turkey without a foreign parent would be unlikely to possess such bilingual fluency. The character would not meet the standard of objective possibility.

If, however, I use causal logic instead of statistical logic to constrain my selection of data, Ayşe turns out differently. I infer that Participant A's and B's time abroad influenced their language abilities by comparing them with participants who did not spend time abroad. In the interest of variation among characters, I create an Ayşe character who speaks English fluently because none of my other characters does, and compose her teenage years accordingly: She grows up in the United States, even though that was only true of a minority of the participants who constitute her. I also determine that an observation I made of a fixer–reporter relationship breaking down because of language problems ought not be attributed to Ayşe, because I logically infer that a fixer who spent years living and studying abroad would be immune to such linguistic difficulties. Perhaps I create a side character to function as carrier of that observation, if it is interesting enough.

## Checking the Truth of Fiction

I claim to hold myself accountable to empirical reality, but how can *you* know whether I am telling the truth? An outside reader cannot fact-check fiction. My access to the data is different from yours; it must be in order to protect my sources. You know only what I tell you about my study participants. You can find internal inconsistencies within my writing but cannot independently audit information excluded from my narratives. A few readers may also be insiders to the world of news production in Turkey and Syria and able to fact-check parts of this book, but most will have to find other ways to evaluate my arguments.

Rather than fact-checking my work, you should **utility-check** it through external comparison and application. Social scientific claims are tools to help make sense of the social world (Jackson 1995: 163). Tools are checked by their usefulness in solving a user's problems. The user, in this case reader, is also a contributor in the chain of knowledge production, whether they conduct a formal comparative analysis or just consider whether my book offers them a useful new frame for making sense of issues they care about.

Precise replication of my study is not possible the way it is of statistical and experimental studies with standardized procedures or publicly available datasets. Nobody could re-run my study by somehow duplicating my fieldwork and compositing process and checking whether they ended up with the same fictional characters.

We can and constantly do, however, "replicate" qualitative studies in our minds whenever we think through whether the author's arguments hold up in other cases we know (Katz [1983] 2015: 142–143). My arguments can be retested in the same way they are developed: through the search for inconvenient, disconfirming data in analogous cases. The difference is that the analogies you draw will have to be external to my study, because you do not have access to my fieldnotes or memories.

Any reader for whom my research is of potential use will be able to find external analogies against which to test my claims. (If they cannot, it means that my research is irrelevant to their lives, and it matters little whether my claims are true or not.) It is not difficult to find comparable cases of the processes that my research addresses: indirect communication through a broker, hierarchies of status that license or restrain social action, moral ambivalence when faced with divergent expectations, the transformation of information as it is relayed from one person to the next.

Comparative cases need not be similar overall to that of fixers in Turkey or Syria in substantive historical context, individuals involved, or level of analysis; they need only be comparable to my case on a particular axis of interest (Vaughan 1992, 2014). I offer leads to external analogies that I found useful in this book's footnotes, wherein I compare our protagonists to doormen, AIDS activists, colonial clerks, biochemists, and more. I control your access to the information I collected and to my research participants, but I cannot control your access to those studies I cite or to other comparative cases that you find on your own.

Labeling my work as fiction will, I hope, helpfully guide users to utility-check my work in this way. The label makes other forms of verification more transparently impractical, even absurd.[8]

## The Composite Compromise

Generations of debates over how to write ethnography and social science more generally have pitted **chroniclers** against **theorists**. The

---

[8] See Katz's ([1983] 2015: 124) discussion of how Goffman "enfranchised his readers to make up their minds about the empirical validity of his analyses in the private voting booths of their own intimate experiences" through the very weakness of his writing's factual authority.

ideal chronicler records everything without prejudice to causal relevance or theoretical frame (Danto 1962: 152–155). The ideal theorist includes only what information supports their argument.

From the theorist's camp, anthropologist E. E. Evans-Pritchard attacked his predecessor Bronislaw Malinowski's "haphazard" documentation of a jumble of data, asserting that "facts can only be selected and arranged in light of theory." (quoted in Clifford 1983: 126) From the chronicler's camp, historians charged that G. W. F. Hegel and his intellectual descendants like Karl Marx cherry-picked convenient evidence that fit their premade ideological frame, chaining readers to their worldview. Hegelian "philosophy of history," the chroniclers charged,

consists of nothing but plot; its story elements exist only as manifestations, epiphenomena, of the plot structure, in the service of which its discourse is disposed. Here reality wears a face of such regularity, order and coherence ... presenting an aspect of such wholeness and completeness that it intimidates rather than invites to imaginative identification. (White 1980: 24)

In other words, the grand theorists' transmissions carried an oppressively high signal-to-noise ratio.

Revisiting the Evans-Pritchard versus Malinowski conflict decades later, anthropologist James Clifford pointed out the potential value of the latter's chronicle:

[Malinowski] published much data that frankly he did not understand. The result was an open text subject to multiple reinterpretations. ... In the modern, authoritative monograph there are, in effect, no strong voices present except that of the writer. But, in *Argonauts* and *Coral Gardens* we read page after page of magical spells, none in any essential sense the ethnographer's words. (Clifford 1983: 136)

The uncontrolled noisiness of Malinowski's writing makes it a dataset for future re-interpreters. His chronicle is democratic in allowing readers the freedom to make sense of that which Malinowski could not. The clean signal of the modern monograph, Clifford warned, can be not just authoritative but authoritarian.[9] Noise can outlive signal, but not if the author silences it so that their own voice can dominate.

---

[9] In Hall's ([1973] 2006) terminology, possibilities for "negotiated" and "oppositional" decoding increase when messages are transmitted with a lower signal-to-noise ratio.

I have been framing research as an exercise in theory building. But people do not read ethnography only for the theory. The concerns of the chronicler should be taken seriously. Ethnographic writing also functions as a primary source on which others build their own theories and as a rough draft for other thinkers to refine (Clifford 1983:141; Tavory and Timmermans 2014: 111–120; Vaughan 2014: 68–83; Jerolmack and Murphy 2019). The chain of knowledge production is not linear but circular.[10]

The chronicler counsels the author against purifying their signals to smoothly slide into their theoretical frames. The chronicler recommends instead that the author transmit richly textured information that readers can use to their own ends.

The disposition of the chronicler runs up against problems of overload and incomprehensibility. Few reader-users have the time to sift through thousands of pages of unedited fieldnotes and hours of recordings to draw their own conclusion. The pragmatic balance lies somewhere between the chronicler and the theorist, between the access offered by a noisy transmission and the sense made by a clean one (Becker 2007: 92–108).

Some forms of writing are noisier than others. Directly quoted speech is more likely to contain data in excess of a theoretical argument than is indirect paraphrasing or description (Clifford 1983: 136–141).[11] Prose description is noisier than a chart. Descriptions of real situations are noisier than parables and thought experiments.

---

[10] See also Sanjek's (2014: 59) discussion of the "anthropological triangle of ethnography, comparison, and contextualization" in which comparative theory and historical context shape the conduct and interpretation of ethnographic fieldwork, and ethnography in turn generates new theoretical thinking and new demands for contextual data.

[11] Even when it comes to quotations, though, speech is not transcoded into written quotations in neutral fashion but actively transformed by the author, in their capacity as broker between source and reader. Decisions with analytic and rhetorical implications about not just *what* to quote but *how* to quote, for instance, whether to standardize colloquial and vernacular speech or to use nonstandard orthography to represent it, are inherent to the transcription process (Bucholtz 2000). Malcolm (1990: 157–158) argues in *The Journalist and the Murderer* that the writer is more theorist than chronicler (she uses the term "stenographer") in their crafting of quotations:

Texts containing dialogue and monologue derived from a tape [recording] – however well edited the transcript may be – tend to retain some trace of their origin (almost a kind of metallic flavor) and lack the atmosphere of truthfulness

Compositing does not prevent the inclusion of rich detail. Remixing real situations and quotations rather than fictionalizing them outright offers a compromise: elements of a chronicle can appear at the level of descriptions of *situations*, but not at the *biographical* level. Compositing intentionally makes it impossible for reader-users to track individual participants through courses of their careers. (I created composites precisely to keep that information out of the hands of the wrong readers.) The subtraction of biographical data constrains reader-users from developing their own interpretations about how and why participants changed over time.

A further hindrance to using my book as a chronicle is that I do not simply remove biographical information but replace it with fill-ins from other sources. These biographical changes could contaminate a reader-user's re-interpretation of situational detail. A theorist of gender might, for instance, take my account in Part III of Geert mocking Nur for her emotional connection to a source as evidence of misogyny and that male reporters read stereotypically female responses among fixers as signals of pro-source bias. In reality, however, that account is based on a female reporter mocking a male fixer. The reader's hypothesis about the gendering of "objectivity" is not necessarily wrong, but there

present in work where it is the writer's own ear that has caught the drift of the subject's thought. . . . The quotations in this book . . . are not . . . identical to their speech counterparts. . . . Fidelity to the subject's thought and to his characteristic way of expressing himself is the sine qua non of journalistic quotation – one under which all stylistic considerations are subsumed. Fortunately for reader and subject alike, the relatively minor task of translating tape-recorderese into English and the major responsibility of trustworthy quotation are in no way inimical; in fact . . . they are fundamentally and decisively complementary.

In the book, Malcolm herself provides paragraphs-long quotations of interviewees who all speak uncannily similarly to the prose Malcolm writes in non-quotation passages, which suggests a heavy theoretical hand in distilling subjects' "characteristic way of expressing" into a written signal that generates an "atmosphere of truth," i.e. reality effect. In contrast to Malcolm, I stick to tape-recorderese whenever possible in this book, although in my use of ellipses (. . .) and explanatory additions (e.g. inserting [recording] above to help you make sense of what Malcolm means by "a tape") I cannot help but act as a writer-theorist, not just a stenographer-chronicler. I also transcribe utterances as dictionary words rather than as strings of phoneme, breathing sounds, volume changes, and pauses. Had I instead used the Jefferson Transcription System of the Conversation Analysis school of sociology, I would have given readers greater access to the raw, noisy speech of my interlocutors, yet anyone but Conversation Analysis insiders would struggle to make sense of what characters were saying (Jefferson 2004).

is too much unknown to the reader about that particular datum and its context for it to serve as solid evidence.

The **Composite Compromise** is that fictionalization constrains your ability to mine my study for empirical data in support of other arguments. This is the authoritarian streak in my writing. It is not wrong to read against the grain of my interpretations, and indeed I hope that my stories and arguments can inspire thinking beyond and in different directions than my own. But you should treat this book as no more reliable a data source than a well-researched novel. You will need to go collect your own evidence elsewhere to test hypotheses derived from this text.

## Conclusion

Any means of representing society incorporates trade-offs between empiricism and strength of theory. Journalism sacrifices aesthetics for facts and literature does the opposite; quantitative methods of social science sacrifice data richness for statistical generalizability and qualitative methods do the opposite. The trade-offs of fictionalization must be acknowledged: creating a composite character narrative as outlined above sacrifices biographical data for robust anonymization. The method also loses fact-check-ability but encourages comparative utility-checking. I have tried to make these trade-offs as transparent as possible by labeling my book as sociological fiction and explaining precisely what I mean by that term: an unreal account systematically constrained by real data that illustrates patterns and variations of social life.

Ethnographic research generally and composite narratives specifically face little external constraint when it comes to selection and arrangement of data. The methodological constraints I imposed at compression and remixing stages are tools for internal accountability. I used them to help transcend my own initial assumptions, make sense of my participants' worlds, and create maps with structural similarities to the territories they represent. I would like to think that the function of this appendix has been not just to salvage a claim to scientific authority for myself as my *just-the-facts* authority crumbles, but to provide tools that other reader-authors find useful or can at least fashion into more useful forms for their own adventures.

# Bibliography

Abbott, Andrew. 1981. "Status and Status Strain in the Professions." *American Journal of Sociology* 86(4):819–835.

———. 1995."Sequence Analysis: New Methods for Old Ideas." *Annual Review of Sociology* 21:93–113.

———. 2017. "The Infinite Nature of the Social Process." Lecture. Networks and Time Workshop, Department of Sociology, Columbia University, April 4.

Abu-Lughod, Lila. [1986] 2016. *Veiled Sentiments: Honor and Poetry in a Bedouin Society*. University of California Press.

Ackerman, Elliot. 2019. *Places and Names: On War, Revolution, and Returning*. Penguin.

Akçam, Taner. [1999] 2006. *A Shameful Act: The Armenian Genocide and the Question of Turkish Responsibility*. Translated by Paul Bessemer. Macmillan.

Akyol, Mustafa. 2015. "How Erdogan Lost the Liberals." *Al Jazeera*, November 19.

Alsaafin, Linah. 2015. "Syria's Eastern Ghouta: The Latest Casualty of War." *Middle East Eye*, February 6.

Amnesty International. 2015. "'We Had Nowhere to Go': Forced Displacement and Demolitions in Northern Syria." October 13.

Andén-Papadopoulos, Kari, and Mervi Pantti. 2013. "The Media Work of Syrian Diaspora Activists: Brokering between the Protest and Mainstream Media." *International Journal of Communication* 7:2185–2206.

Anderson, Chris W. 2011. "Between Creative and Quantified Audiences: Web Metrics and Changing Patterns of Newswork in Local US Newsrooms." *Journalism* 12(5):550–566.

Anderson, Elijah. 1994. "The Code of the Streets." *Atlantic Monthly*, May.

AP (Associated Press). 2016. "Turkey Uses Tear Gas to Break Up Gay Pride Gathering." June 26.

Arjomand, Noah. 2015. "The Folly of Double Government: Lessons from the First Anglo-Afghan War for the 21st Century." Afghanistan Analysts Network, June 7.

———. 2016a. "Afghan Exodus: Smuggling Networks, Migration and Settlement Patterns in Turkey." Afghanistan Analysts Network, September 10.

2016b. "Inside Turkey's Media Crackdown." *Dissent*, April 28.

2016c. "Nobody Knows How Many Have Died in the Turkey-PKK Conflict." Bullshit.ist, September 15. bullshit.ist/nobody-knows-how-many-have-died-in-the-turkey-pkk-conflict-c09c49b131ee

2017. "Every Turk Is Born a Soldier." *Public Culture* 29(3):418–432.

2019. "Information Laundering and Globalized Media – Part 1: The Problem." Center for International Media Assistance, August 20. cima .ned.org/blog/information-laundering-and-globalized-media-part-i-the-problem/

Ashkok, Ahbishekh H., John Baugh, and Vikram K. Yeragani. 2012. "Paul Eugen Bleuler and the origin of the term schizophrenia (Schizopreniegruppe)." *Indian Journal of Psychiatry* 54(1):95–96.

Austin, J. L. 1962. *Sense and Sensibilia*. Oxford University Press.

Avila, Renata, Juan Ortiz Freuler, and Craig Fagan. 2018. "The Invisible Curation of Content: Facebook's New Feed and Our Information Diets." World Wide Web Foundation.

Aydın, Hasan, and Burhan Özfidan. 2014. "Perceptions of Mother Tongue (Kurdish) Based Multicultural and Bilingual Education in Turkey." *Multicultural Education Review* 6(1):21–48.

Baban, Feyzi, Suzan Ilcan, and Kim Rygiel. 2016. "Syrian Refugees in Turkey: Pathways to Precarity, Differential Inclusion, and Negotiated Citizenship Rights." *Journal of Ethnic and Migration Studies* 43(1):41–57.

Baer, Marc David. 2013. "An Enemy Old and New: The Dönme, Anti-Semitism, and Conspiracy Theories in the Ottoman Empire and Turkish Republic." *The Jewish Quarterly Review* 103(4):523–555.

Baker, Mona. 2006. *Translation and Conflict: A Narrative Account*. Routledge.

Bardoel, Jo, and Mark Deuze. 2001. "Network Journalism: Converging Competences of Media Professionals and Professionalism." *Australian Journalism Review* 23(2):91–103.

Barthes, Roland. [1968] 1989. "The Reality Effect." Pp. 14–148 in *The Rustle of Language*. Translated by Richard Howard. University of California Press.

   1981. *Camera Lucida: Reflections on Photography*. Translated by Richard Howard. Hill and Wang.

Bartunek, Robert-Jan. 2016. "Turkey Government Seemed to Have List of Arrests Prepared: EU's Hahn." Reuters, July 18.

Bass, Abraham Z. 1969. "Refining the 'Gatekeeper' Concept: A UN Radio Case Study." *Journalism Quarterly* 46:69–72.

Bateson, Gregory. 1972. *Steps to an Ecology of the Mind*. Ballantine Books.

Bauman, Zygmunt. 1991. *Ambivalence and Modernity*. Polity Press.

BBC (British Broadcasting Corporation). 2016. "Dutch Journalist Detained in Turkey for Erdogan Tweet." April 24.

Bearman, Peter. 2005. *Doormen*. University of Chicago Press.

Becker, Howard S. [1963] 1997. *Outsiders: Studies in the Sociology of Deviance*. The Free Press.

    2007. *Telling about Society*. University of Chicago Press.

Beebee, Thomas O. 2010. "Shoot the Transtraitor!: The Translator as *Homo Sacer* in Fiction and Reality." *The Translator* 16(2):295–313.

Beiser, Elana. 2015. "Syria, France Most Deadly Countries for the Press." Committee to Protect Journalists, December 29.

    2016. "Turkey's Crackdown Propels Number of Journalists in Jail Worldwide to Record High." Committee to Protect Journalists, December 13.

Bellamy, Catherine, Simone Haysom, Caitlin Wake, and Veronique Barbelet. 2017. "The Lives and Livelihoods of Syrian Refugees: A Study of Refugee Perspectives and Their Institutional Environment in Turkey and Jordan." Humanitarian Policy Group.

Benjamin, Walter. [1923] 1996. "The Task of the Translator." Pp. 253–263 in *Walter Benjamin: Selected Writings. Volume 1: 1913–1926*. Edited by Marcus Bullock and Michael W. Jennings. The Belknap Press of Harvard University Press.

Benson, Rodney, and Erik Neveu, eds. 2005. *Bourdieu and the Journalistic Field*. Polity Press.

Berkowitz, Dan, Craig Allen, and Diana Beeson. 1996. "Exploring Newsroom Views about Consultants in Local TV: The Effect of Work Roles and Socialization." *Journal of Broadcasting & Electronic Media* 40(4):447–459.

Bernet, Brigitta. 2006. "Assoziationsstörung. Zum Wechselverhältnis von Krankheitsund Gesellschaftdeutung im Wek Eugen Bleulers (1857–1939)." Pp. 169–193 in *"Moderne" Anstaltpsychiatrie im 19. Und 20. Jahrhundert – Legitimation und Kritik*. Edited by Heiner Fangerau and Karen Nolte. Franz Steiner Verlag.

bianet (Bağımsız İletişim Ağı). 2021. "Twitter ve Pinterest'e reklam yasağı." January 19. bianet.org/bianet/ifade-ozgurlugu/237804-twitter-ve-pinterest-e-reklam-yasagi

*BirGün*. 2018. "Muharrem İnce: Erdoğan Beyaz Türk, Ben Zenci." June 10.

Bishara, Amahl. 2013. *Back Stories: U.S. News Production & Palestinian Politics*. Stanford University Press.

Blacksin, Isaac. 2021. "Situated and Subjugated: Fixer Knowledge in the Global Newsroom." *Journal of Applied Journalism & Media Studies* 1–22.

Bonacich, Edna. 1973. "A Theory of Middleman Minorities." *American Sociological Review* 38:583–594.

Borpujari, Priyanka. 2019. "The Problem with 'Fixers.'" *Columbia Journalism Review*, Summer.

Bossone, Andrew. 2014. "The Thankless Work of a 'Fixer.'" *Columbia Journalism Review*, April 30.

Boteach, Shmuley. 2015. "Mad about Miri." *Observer*. May 11.

Bourdieu, Pierre. 1977. *Outline of a Theory of Practice*. Translated by Richard Nice. Cambridge University Press.

  1984. *Distinction: A Social Critique of the Judgement of Taste*. Translated by Richard Nice. Harvard University Press.

  [1986] 2011. "The Forms of Capital." Pp. 81–93 in *Cultural Theory: An Anthology*. Edited by Imre Szeman and Timothy Kaposy. Wiley-Blackwell.

  1991. *Language and Symbolic Power*. Edited by John B. Thompson. Translated by Gino Raymond and Matthew Adamson. Polity Press.

  1993. *The Field of Cultural Production: Essays on Art and Literature*. Edited by Randal Johnson. Columbia University Press.

  1999. "The Social Conditions of the International Circulation of Ideas." Pp. 220–228 in *Bourdieu: A Critical Reader*. Edited by Richard Shusterman. Blackwell.

  2002. "Habitus." Pp. 27–35 in *Habitus: A Sense of Place*. Edited by Jean Hillier and Emma Rooksby. Ashgate Publishing.

Boyer, Dominic. 2013. *The Life Informatic: Newsmaking in the Digital Era*. Cornell University Press.

Bozdağ, Engin. 2013. "Bias in Algorithmic Filtering and Personalization." *Ethics and Information Technology* 15(3):209–227.

Brake, David R. 2017. "The Invisible Hand of the Unaccountable Algorithm: How Google, Facebook and Other Tech Companies Are Changing Journalism." Pp. 25–46 in *Digital Technology and Journalism*. Edited by Jingrong Tong and Shih-Hung Lo. Palgrave Macmillan.

Breindl, Yana. 2016 "Activists as News Producers." Pp. 250–265 in *The SAGE Handbook of Digital Journalism*. Edited by Tamara Witschge, C. W. Anderson, David Domingo, and Alfred Hermida. SAGE Publications.

Brown, Eileen. 2015. "Twitter Brings Tweet Translation to iOS, Android and Windows 8 Phones." *ZD Net*, January 23. zdnet.com/article/twitter-brings-tweet-translation-to-ios-android-and-windows-8-phones/

Bruns, Axel. 2018. *Gatewatching and News Curation: Journalism, Social Media, and the Public Sphere*. Peter Lang.

Bucholtz, Mary. 2000. "The Politics of Transcription." *Journal of Pragmatics* 32:1439–1465.

Bunce, Mel. 2010. "'This Place Used to be a White British Boys' Club': Reporting Dynamics and Cultural Clash at an International News Bureau in Nairobi." *The Round Table* 99(410):515–528.

Burt, Ronald S. 2007. *Brokerage & Closure: An Introduction to Social Capital.* Oxford University Press.

Butler, Daren. 2018. "With More Islamic Schooling, Erdogan Aims to Reshape Turkey." Reuters, January 25.

Büyük, Hamdi Fırat. 2021. "Report: Turkey Remains World Beater in Twitter Censorship." *Balkan Insight*, January 13. balkaninsight.com/2021/01/13/report-turkey-remains-world-beater-in-twitter-censorship/

Çağaptay, Soner. 2012. "Are Syrian Alawites and Turkish Alevis the Same?" The Washington Institute Policy Analysis, April 17.

Campbell, Deborah. 2017. *A Disappearance in Damascus: Friendship and Survival in the Shadow of War.* Picador.

Carey, James. [1989] 2009. "A Cultural Approach to Communication." Pp. 11–28 in *Communication as Culture: Essays on Media and Society.* Routledge.

Carlson, Matt. 2016. "Sources as News Producers." Pp. 236–249 in *The SAGE Handbook of Digital Journalism.* Edited by Tamara Witschge, C. W. Anderson, David Domingo, and Alfred Hermida.

Catar, Sabina. 2015. "Kurdish Political Parties in Syria." Pp. 112–138 in *The Kurds: History – Religion – Language – Politics.* Edited by Alexander Schahbasi and Thomas Scrott. Published by Wolfgang Taucher, Mathias Vogl, and Peter Wedinger. Austrian Federal Ministry of the Interior.

Cattani, Gino, Simone Ferriani, and Paul D. Allison. 2014. "Insiders, Outsiders, and the Struggle for Consecration in Cultural Fields: A Core-Periphery Perspective." *American Sociological Review* 79(2):258–281.

Çetin, Fethiye. 2012. *My Grandmother: An Armenian-Turkish Memoir.* Translated by Maureen Freely. Verso Books.

Chibnall, Steve. 1977. *Law-and-Order News: An Analysis of Crime Reporting in the British Press.* Tavistock.

Çınar, Alev, and Hakkı Taş. 2017. "Politics of Nationhood and the Displacement of the Founding Moment: Contending Histories of the Turkish Nation." *Comparative Studies in Society and History* 59(3):657–689.

Clarke, Bruce. 2010. "Communication." Pp. 131–144 in *Critical Terms for Media Studies.* Edited by W. J. T. Mitchell and Mark B. N. Hansen. University of Chicago Press.

Clifford, James. 1983. "On Ethnographic Authority." *Representations* 2:118–146.

1997. *Routes: Travel and Translation in the Late Twentieth Century.* Harvard University Press.

Collett, Elizabeth. 2016. "The Paradox of the EU-Turkey Refugee Deal."
    Migration Policy Institute, March.
Collins, Harry, Robert Evans, and Michael E. Gorman. 2010. "Trading
    Zones and Interactional Expertise." Pp. 7–24 in *Trading Zones and
    Interactional Expertise: Creating New Kinds of Collaboration*. Edited
    by Michael E. Gorman. MIT Press.
Corke, Susan, Andrew Finkel, David J. Kramer, Carla Anne Robbins, and
    Nate Schenkkan. 2014. "Democracy in Crisis: Corruption, Media and
    Power in Turkey." Freedom House Special Report.
CPJ (Committee to Protect Journalists). n.d.-a. "Journalists Killed." Online
    Database. cpj.org/data/killed/
    n.d.-b. "Journalists Imprisoned." Online Database. cpj.org/data/
    imprisoned/
    2015. "Turkey Deports Dutch Reporter Frederike Geerdink." September
    9. cpj.org/x/6590
*Cumhuriyet*. 2015. "'New York Times diye bir paçavra var.'" May 30.
Czarniawska, Barbara. 2011. *Cyberfactories: How News Agencies Produce
    News*. Edward Elgar.
Dabashi, Hamid. 2011. *Brown Skin, White Masks*. Pluto Press.
*Daily Sabah*. 2016. "Erdoğan Expressed Regret for Downing of Russian Jet
    in Letter to Putin: Kremlin." June 27.
    2019. "Al-Jazeera Continues to Spread Anti-Turkey Propaganda by
    Adopting a Biased Narrative." November 7.
Danto, Arthur C. 1962. "Narrative Sentences." *History and Theory* 2
    (2):146–179.
Davies, Nick. 2009. *Flat Earth News: An Award-Winning Reporter Exposes
    Falsehood, Distortion and Propaganda in the Global Media*. Vintage.
Demiralp, Seda. 2012. "White Turks, Black Turks? Faultlines Beyond
    Islamism and Secularism." *Third World Quarterly* 33(3):511–524.
Deuze, Mark. 2005. "Toward Professional Participatory Storytelling in
    Journalism and Advertising." *First Monday* 10(7).
Dick, Murray. 2011. "Search Engine Optimisation in UK News
    Production." *Journalism Practice* 5(4):462–477.
Diriker, Ebru. 2004. *De-/Re-Contextualizing Conference Interpreting:
    Interpreters in the Ivory Tower?* John Benjamins.
Douglas, Mary. [1966] 2001. *Purity and Danger: An Analysis of the
    Concepts of Pollution and Taboo*. Routledge.
Duneier, Mitchell. 2011. "How Not to Lie with Ethnography." *Sociological
    Methodology* 41(1):1–11.
Ehraim, Zaina. 2019. "Hurma." Pp. 206–217 in *Our Women on the
    Ground: Essays by Arab Women Reporting from the Arab World*.
    Edited by Zahra Hankir. Penguin Books.

Ehrenreich, Barbara, and Arlie Russell Hochschild. 2003. "Introduction." Pp. 1–13 in *Global Woman: Nannies, Maids, and Sex Workers in the New Economy*. Edited by Barbara Ehrenreich and Arlie Russell Hochschild Metropolitan Books.

Eisenberg, Eric M. 1984. "Ambiguity as Strategy in Organizational Communication." *Communication Monographs* 51(3): 227–242.

Emerson, Robert M., Rachel I. Fretz, and Linda L. Shaw. 2011. *Writing Ethnographic Fieldnotes*, 2nd ed. University of Chicago Press.

Emirbayer, Mustafa. 1997. "Manifesto for a Relational Sociology." *American Journal of Sociology* 103(2):281–317.

*Evrensel*. 2017. "Vice News Muhabirlerinin Yargılanmasına Başlandı." February 27.

Fanon, Frantz. 1967. *Black Skin, White Masks*. Translated by Charles Lam Markmann. Grove Press.

Fassin, Didier. 2014. "True Life, Real Lives: Revisiting the Boundaries Between Ethnography and Fiction." *American Ethnologist* 41(1):40–55.

2017. "Epilogue: The Public Afterlive of Ethnography." Pp. 311–343 in *If Truth Be Told: The Politics of Public Ethnography*. Edited by Didier Fassin. Duke University Press.

Ferguson, Michael. 2013. "White Turks, Black Turks, and Negroes: The Politics of Polarization." *Jadaliyya*, June 29. jadaliyya.com/Details/28868

Filkins, Dexter. 2014. "When Bombs Aren't Enough." *The New Yorker*, October 10.

Finkel, Andrew. 2000. "Who Guards the Turkish Press? A Perspective on Press Corruption in Turkey." *Journal of International Affairs* 54(1):147–166.

2015. "Captured News Media: The Case of Turkey." *Center for International Media Assistance*.

Fishman, Mark. 1980. *Manufacturing the News*. University of Texas Press.

Fleming, E.J. 2004. *The Fixers: Eddie Mannix, Howard Strickling and the MGM Publicity Machine*. McFarland & Company.

Foster, Johanna E., and Sherizaan Minwalla. 2018. "Voices of Yazidi Women: Perceptions of Journalistic Practices in the Reporting on ISIS Sexual Violence." *Women's Studies International Forum* 67:53–64.

Frankfurt, Harry G. 2005. *On Bullshit*. Princeton University Press.

Freely, Maureen. 2006. "Cultural Translation." Pp. 145–151 in *Writing Turkey: Explorations of Turkish History, Politics, and Cultural Identity*. Edited by Gerald MacLean. Middlesex University Press.

French, Piper. 2016 "Unbylined: A Q&A with a Chinese Fixer." *Roads & Kingdoms*, September 13. roadsandkingdoms.com/2016/unbylined-a-qa-with-a-chinese-fixer/

Fung, Brian. 2018. "Here's What We Know about Google's Mysterious Search Engine." *Washington Post*, August 28.

Galison, Peter. 2010. "Trading with the Enemy." Pp. 25–52 in *Trading Zones and Interactional Expertise: Creating New Kinds of Collaboration*. Edited by Michael E. Gorman. MIT Press.

    2015. "Chapter 4: The Journalist, the Scientist, and Objectivity." Pp. 57–75 in *Objectivity in Science: New Perspectives from Science and Technology Studies*. Edited by Flavia Padovani, Alan Richardson, and Jonathan Y. Tsou. Springer.

Gambetta, Diego, and Heather Hamill. 2005. *Streetwise: How Taxi Drivers Establish Their Customers' Trustworthiness*. Russell Sage Foundation.

Gans, Herbert J. [1979] 2004. *Deciding What's News: A Study of CBS Evening News, NBC Nightly News, Newsweek, and Time*. Northwestern University Press.

Geertz, Clifford. 1973. "Thick Description: Toward an Interpretive Theory of Culture." Pp. 3–30 in *The Interpretation of Cultures*. Basic Books.

George, Alan. 2003. *Syria: Neither Bread nor Freedom*. Zed Books.

George, Ella. 2018. "Purges and Paranoia." *London Review of Books* 40 (10):22–32.

Giddens, Anthony. 1991. *The Consequences of Modernity*. Polity Press.

Gieryn, Thomas F. 1983. "Boundary-Work and the Demarcation of Science from Non-Science: Strains and Interests in Professional Ideologies of Scientists." *American Sociological Review* 48:781–795.

Gill, Denise. 2016. "Turkey's Coup and the Call to Prayer: Sounds of Violence Meet Islamic Devotionals." *The Conversation*, August 10. theconversation.com/turkeys-coup-and-the-call-to-prayer-sounds-of-vio lence-meet-islamic-devotionals-63746

Gillespie, Tartleton. 2018. *Custodians of the Internet: Platforms, Content Moderation, and the Hidden Decisions That Shape Social Media*. Yale University Press.

Gleick, James. 2011. *The Information: A History, A Theory, A Flood*. Pantheon Books.

Goffman, Erving. 1959. *The Presentation of Self in Everyday Life*. Anchor Books.

    1963. *Stigma: Notes on the Management of Spoiled Identity*. Prentice-Hall.

    1967. "On Face-Work." Pp. 5–46 in *Interaction Ritual: Essays on Face-to-Face Behavior*. Pantheon Books.

    1968. *Asylums: Essays on the Social Situation of Mental Patients and Other Inmates*. AldineTransaction.

    1969. *Strategic Interaction*. Ballantine Books.

    1974. *Frame Analysis: An Essay on the Organization of Experience*. Harper & Row.

1981. *Forms of Talk*. University of Pennsylvania Press.

1983. "The Interaction Order: American Sociological Association, 1982 Presidential Address." *American Sociological Review* 48(1):1–17.

Goldman, Marion. 1999. *Passionate Journeys: Why Successful Women Joined a Cult*. University of Michigan Press.

2002. "Voicing Spiritualities: Anchored Composites as an Approach to Understanding Religious Commitment." Pp. 146–161 in *Personal Knowledge and Beyond: Reshaping the Ethnography of Religion*. Edited by James V. Spickard, Shawn Landres, and Meredith B. McGuire. New York University Press.

Göle, Nilüfer. 2013. "*Gezi* – Anatomy of a Public Square Movement." *Insight Turkey* 15(3):7–14.

Goode, William J. 1960. "A Theory of Role Strain." *American Sociological Review* 25(4):483–496.

Griffin, Larry J. 1993. "Narrative, Event-Structure Analysis, and Causal Interpretation in Historical Sociology." *American Journal of Sociology* 98(5):1094–1133.

Gürakar, Esra Çeviker. 2016. *Politics of Favoritism in Public Procurement in Turkey: Reconfigurations of Dependency Networks in the AKP Era*. Palgrave Macmillan.

Gürpınar, Doğan. 2013. "The Reinvention of Kemalism: Between Elitism, Anti-Elitism and Anti-Intellectualism." *Middle Eastern Studies* 49 (3):454–476.

Gürsel, Zeynep Devrim. 2016. *Image Brokers: Visualizing World News in the Age of Digital Circulation*. University of California Press.

Gutman, Roy. 2017a. "Have the Syrian Kurds Committed War Crimes?" *The Nation*, February 7.

2017b. "America's Favorite Syrian Militia Rules with an Iron Fist." *The Nation*, February 13.

Hakyemez, Serra. 2017. "Turkey's Failed Peace Process with the Kurds: A Different Explanation." Brandeis University Crown Center for Middle East Studies, Middle East Brief No. 111.

Halavais, Alexander. 2014. "Structure of Twitter: Social and Technical." Pp. 29–42 in *Twitter and Society*. Edited by Katrin Weller, Axel Bruns, Jean Burgess, Merja Mahrt, and Cornelius Puschmann. Peter Lang.

Hall, Stuart. 1981. "The Whites of Their Eyes: Racist Ideologies and the Media." Pp. 28–52 in *Silver Linings: Some Strategies for the Eighties*. Edited by George Bridges and Ros Brunt. Lawrence & Wishart.

[1973] 2006. "Encoding/Decoding." Pp. 163–173 in *Media and Cultural Studies: Keyworks*. Edited by Meenakshi Gigi Durham and Douglas M. Kellner. Blackwell.

1997. "The Work of Representation." Pp. 13–74 in *Representation: Cultural Representations and Signifying Practices*. Edited by Stuart Hall. Sage.

Hallin, Daniel C., and Paolo Mancini. 2004. *Comparing Media Systems: Three Models of Media and Politics*. Cambridge University Press.

Hancock, Herbie. [SafaJah]. 2014. *Miles Davis According to Herbie Hancock* (video). YouTube. youtube.com/watch?v=FL4LxrN-iyw.

Hannerz, Ulf. 2012. *Foreign News: Exploring the World of Foreign Correspondents*. University of Chicago Press.

Hansen, Suzy. 2017. *Notes on a Foreign Country: An American Abroad in a Post-American World*. Farrar, Straus and Giroux.

HDN (Hürriyet Daily News). 2014. "CHP's Motion on Mine Accidents in Soma Rejected by AKP Two Weeks Ago." May 14.

Hecker, Pierre. 2016. *Turkish Metal: Music, Meaning, and Morality in a Muslim Society*. Routledge.

Heinrich, Ansgard. 2012. "Foreign Reporting in the Sphere of Network Journalism." *Journalism Practice* 6(5–6):766–775.

Hendrick, Joshua D. 2013. *Gülen: The Ambiguous Politics of Market Islam in Turkey and the World*. New York University Press.

Herman, Edward, and Noam Chomsky. 1988. *Manufacturing Consent: The Political Economy of the Mass Media*. Pantheon Books.

Hermida, Alfred. 2010. "Twittering the News: The Emergence of Ambient Journalism." *Journalism Practice* 4(3):297–308.

2014. "Twitter as an Ambient News Network." Pp. 259–372 in *Twitter and Society*. Edited by Katrin Weller, Axel Bruns, Jean Burgess, Merja Mahrt, and Cornelius Puschmann. Peter Lang.

Hoffman, Max. 2019. "The State of the Turkish-Kurdish Conflict." Center for American Progress, August 12.

Hochschild, Arlie Russell. 1983. *The Managed Heart: Commercialization of Human Feeling*. University of California Press.

HRW (Human Rights Watch). 2011. "Turkey: Arrests Expose Flawed Justice System." November 1

2018. "Turkey: Crackdown on Social Media Posts." March 27.

Hughes, Everett. 1962. "Good People and Dirty Work." *Social Problems* 10 (1):3–11.

Hughes, Thomas, Jo Glanville, and Christophe Deloire. 2014. Open letter to President Erdogan. Article 19, English PEN, and Reporters Without Borders, September 23.

Hunter, Duncan. 2018. "Book Breaking and Book Mending." *Slate*, July 25. slate.com/human-interest/2018/07/academic-publishing-and-book-breaking-why-scholars-write-books-that-arent-meant-to-be-read.html

Hürtaş, Sibel. 2018. "Is Turkey's State of Emergency Really Over?" *Al Monitor*, July 19. al-monitor.com/pulse/originals/2018/07/turkey-state-of-emergency-really-over.html

ICG (International Crisis Group). 2016a. "The Human Cost of the PKK Conflict in Turkey: The Case of Sur." March 17.

2016b. "Turkey's Refugee Crisis: The Politics of Permanence." November 30.

İnce, Adem. 2018. *Turkey's Kurdish Question from an Educational Perspective*. Lexington Books.

İneli-Ciğer, Meltem. 2015. "Implications of the New Turkish Law on Foreigners and International Protection and Regulation No. 29153 on Temporary Protection for Syrians Seeking Protection in Turkey." *Oxford Monitor of Forced Migration* 4(2):28–36.

İnsan Hakları Derneği. 2016. "2015 İnsan Hakları İhlalleri Raporu." March 9.

Irwin, Will. 1909. *The Confessions of a Con Man*. B. W. Huebsch.

Jackall, Robert. 1988. *Moral Mazes: The World of Corporate Managers*. Oxford University Press.

Jackson, Louis E., and C. R. Hellyer. 1914. *A Vocabulary of Criminal Slang: With Some Examples of Common Usages*. Modern Printing Company.

Jackson, Michael D. 1995. *At Home in the World*. Duke University Press.

Jefferson, Gail. 2004. "Glossary of Transcript Symbols with an Introduction." Pp. 13–31 in *Conversation Analysis: Studies from the First Generation*. Edited by Gene H. Lerner. John Benjamins Publishing Company.

Jenkins, Gareth. 2012. "The Snake That Doesn't Touch Me: Turkey's Special Authority Courts." *Turkey Analyst* 5(5), March 5.

Jerolmack, Colin, and Alexandra K. Murphy. 2019. "The Ethical Dilemmas of Social Scientific Trade-Offs of Masking in Ethnography." *Sociological Methods & Research* 48(4):801–827.

Jerolmack, Colin, and Shamus Khan. 2014. "Talk Is Cheap: Ethnography and the Attitudinal Fallacy." *Sociological Methods & Research* 43(2):178–209.

Johnson, Glen. 2015. "For Syrian Armenians, Exodus Evokes Flight from Genocide a Century Ago." *Los Angeles Times*, March 1.

2016. "Former Beauty Queen Convicted of Insulting Turkey's President by Sharing Poem on Social Media." *Los Angeles Times*, May 31.

Judt, Tony. 2010. "Edge People." *New York Review of Books*, February 23.

Kaplan, Çağdaş. 2020. "I Will Come Back One Day." *Friedrich Naumann Foundation*, June 16.

Karakaş, Burcu. 2019. "KCK Basın Davası: 'Basın özgürlüğünü baskılamaya yönelik bir dava.'" *Deutsche Welle Türkçe*, January 1.

Karaveli, Halil M. 2012. "The Coalition Crumbles: Erdogan, the Gülenists, and Turkish Democracy." *The Turkey Analyst* 5(4), February 20.

Katz, Jack. [1983] 2015. "A Theory of Qualitative Methodology: The Social System of Analytic Fieldwork." *Méthod(e)s* 1(1):131–146.

1999. *How Emotions Work*. University of Chicago Press.

2001. "From How to Why: On Luminous Description and Causal Inference in Ethnography (Part I)." *Ethnography* 2(4):443–473.

2002. "From How to Why: On Luminous Description and Causal Inference in Ethnography (Part II)." *Ethnography* 3(1):63–90.

Kaynar, Ayşegül Kars. 2017. "Political Trials and the Second Jurisdiction of the State: Normalcy of the Exception." Pp. 25–37 in *Contemporary Turkey at a Glance II: Turkey Transformed? Power, History Culture*. Edited by Meltem Ersoy and Esra Özyürek. Springer.

Keen, Suzanne. 2006. "A Narrative Theory of Empathy." *Narrative* 14(3):207–236.

Kepenek, Evrim. 2019. "'Özgür Ülke'den Geriye Cesaret Kaldı.'" bianet, December 3. bianet.org/1/19/216617-ozgur-ulkeden-geriye-cesaret-kaldi

Keshishian, Vahakn. 2015. "Between Anticipation and Misery: The Syrian-Armenian Refugees of Lebanon." *The Armenite*, January 13. thearmenite.com/2015/01/anticipation-misery-syrian-armenian-refugees-lebanon/

Khan, Altaf. 2019. "Fixers in Corporate Media: Pashtun Journalists under Threat in North Western Pakistan." *Conflict & Communication Online* 18(1):1–9.

Kınıklıoğlu, Suat. 2015. "Turkey's Self-Inflicted Disaster." *The New York Times*, October 19.

Kızılkaya, Emre, and Burak Ütücü. 2021. "'The New Mainstream Media' Is Rising (and It Seeks Support)." International Press Institute, March.

Klockars, Carl B. 1974. *The Professional Fence*. The Free Press.

Klotz, Kelsey. 2017. "The Art of the Mistake." *The Common Reader*, May 15.

Knight, Kyle. 2015. "Dispatches: Violent Crackdown at Istanbul's Pride Parade." Human Rights Watch, June 30.

Knightley, Phillip. 2004. *The First Casualty: The War Correspondent as Hero and Myth-Maker from the Crimea to Iraq*. Updated edition. Johns Hopkins University Press.

Koru, Selim. 2017. "Erdogan Goes for the Death Blow against Turkey's Bureaucracy." *Foreign Policy*, April 14.

Korzybski, Alfred. [1933] 1994. *Science and Sanity: An Introduction to Non-Aristotelian Systems and General Semantics*. 5th ed. Institute of General Semantics.

Kuhn, Thomas S. [1962] 1970. *The Structure of Scientific Revolutions*. University of Chicago Press.

Kurt, Mehmet. 2017. *Kurdish Hizbullah in Turkey: Islamism, Violence and the State*. Pluto Press.

Larkin, Brian. 2013. "The Politics and Poetics of Infrastructure." *Annual Review of Anthropology* 42:327–343.

Latour, Bruno (under pseudonym Jim Johnson). 1988a. "Mixing Humans and Nonhumans Together: The Sociology of a Door-Closer." *Social Problems* 35(3):298–310.

1988b. *The Pasteurization of France*. Translated by Alan Sheridan and John Law. Harvard University Press.

2005a. "From Realpolitick to Dingpolitick." Pp. 14–44 in *Making Things Public: Atmospheres of Democracy*. Edited by Bruno Latour and Peter Weibel. MIT Press.

2005b. *Reassembling the Social: An Introduction to Actor-Network-Theory*. Oxford University Press.

Lepeska, David. 2016. "How I Became Another Victim of Erdogan's Press Crackdown." *Foreign Policy*, May 2.

Letsch, Constanze. 2014. "'Their Fight Is Our Fight': Kurds Rush from across Turkey to Defend Kobani." *The Guardian*, September 26.

Levine, Donald. 1985. *The Flight from Ambiguity: Essays in Social and Cultural Theory*. University of Chicago Press.

Levinger, Matthew. 2018. "Master Narratives of Disinformation Campaigns." *Journal of International Affairs* 71(1.5):125–134.

Lewis, Bernard. 2004. "From Babel to Dragomans." Pp. 18–32 in *From Babel to Dragomans: Interpreting the Middle East*. Oxford University Press.

Lippmann, Walter. 1922. *Public Opinion*. Harcourt, Brace and Company.

Lohr, Steve. 2006. "This Boring Headline is Written for Google." *New York Times*, April 6.

Lord, Ceren. 2017. "Rethinking the Justice and Development Party's 'Alevi Opening.'" *Turkish Studies* 18(2):278–296.

Lutz, Catherine A. 1988. *Unnatural Emotions: Everyday Sentiments on a Micronesian Atoll and Their Challenge to Western Theory*. University of Chicago Press.

MacFarquhar, Neil, and Anne Barnard. 2016. "How a Reporter's Quest for Online Bargains Led to a Network of Syrian Contacts." *New York Times*, February 16.

Mahmood, Saba. 2004. *Politics of Piety: The Islamic Revival and the Feminist Subject*. Princeton University Press.

Mahoney, Robert. 2015. "A Year After James Foley and Steven Sotloff Murders, More Awareness of Risks." *Syria Deeply*, August 19. newsdeeply.com/syria/community/2015/08/19/a-year-after-james-foley-and-steven-sotloff-murders-more-awareness-of-risks

Malas, Nour. 2019. "Binet el-Balad. Pp. 80–96 in *Our Women on the Ground: Essays by Arab Women Reporting from the Arab World.* Edited by Zahra Hankir. Penguin Books.

Malcolm, Janet. 1990. *The Journalist and the Murderer.* Vintage Books.

Mamdani, Mahmood. 2004. *Good Muslim, Bad Muslim: America, the Cold War, and the Roots of Terror.* Pantheon Books.

Marcus, Aliza. 2007. *Blood and Belief: the PKK and the Kurdish Fight for Independence.* New York University Press.

Marx, Karl. [1844] 1978. "Economic and Philosophic Manuscripts of 1844." Pp. 66–125 in *The Marx-Engels Reader.* Edited by Robert C. Tucker. 2nd ed. W. W. Norton & Company.

Marx, Karl, and Freidrich Engels. [1845] 2006. "The Ruling Class and the Ruling Ideas." Pp. 9–12 in *Media and Cultural Studies: Keyworks.* Edited by Meenakshi Gigi Durham and Douglas M. Kellner. Blackwell Publishing.

McClelland, Mac. 2014. "How to Build a Perfect Refugee Camp." *The New York Times,* February 13.

McCombs, Maxwell E., and Donald L. Shaw. 1972. "The Agenda-Setting Function of Mass Media." *Public Opinion Quarterly* 36(2):176–187.

McLuhan, Marshall. [1967] 2003. *Understanding Me: Lectures and Interviews.* Edited by Stephanie McLuhan and David Staines. McClelland & Stewart.

McNelly, John T. 1959. "Intermediary Communicators in the International Flow of News." *Journalism Quarterly* 36(1):23–26.

Mears, Ashley. 2015. "Working for Free in the VIP: Relational Work and the Production of Consent." *American Sociological Review* 80 (6):1099–1122.

Merton, Robert K. 1972. "Insiders and Outsiders: A Chapter in the Sociology of Knowledge." *American Journal of Sociology* 78(1):9–47.

    1976. *Sociological Ambivalence and Other Essays.* The Free Press.

Mignolo, Walter. 2000. *Local Histories/Global Designs: Coloniality, Subaltern Knowledges, and Border Thinking.* Princeton University Press.

Mills, C. Wright. [1959] 2000. *The Sociological Imagination.* Oxford University Press.

Mitchell, J. Clyde. 1983. "Case and Situation Analysis." *Sociological Review* 31(2):187–211.

Moon, Ruth. 2019. "Beyond Puppet Journalism: The Bridging Work of Transnational Journalists in a Local Field." *Journalism Studies* 20 (12):1714–1731.

Morozov, Evgeny. 2011. *Net Delusion: The Dark Side of Internet Freedom.* PublicAffairs.

Morris, Errol (director). 2003. *The Fog of War: Eleven Lessons from the Life of Robert S. McNamara.* Sony Pictures Classics.

Murrell, Colleen. 2015. *Foreign Correspondents and International Newsgathering: The Role of Fixers.* Routledge.

NPR (National Public Radio). 2012. "NPR Ethics Handbook." May 2.

*New York Times.* 2004. "Ethical Journalism: A Handbook of Value and Practices for the News and Editorial Departments." September.

Nicey, Jérémie. 2016. "Semi-Professional Amateurs." Pp. 222–s235 in *The SAGE Handbook of Digital Journalism.* Edited by Tamara Witschge, C. W. Anderson, David Domingo, and Alfred Hermida. SAGE Publications.

Niknejad, Kelly Golnoush. 2014. "This Is How Tehran Bureau Covers Iran." *Columbia Journalism Review,* September 30.

Nordland, Rod. 2014a. "2 Star-Crossed Afghans Cling to Love, Even at Risk of Death." *The New York Times,* March 9.

2014b. "Afghan Newlyweds, Facing Threats, Find Brief Respite in Mountains." *The New York Times,* April 21.

2014c. "Newlyweds on the Run: A Challenge in Reporting." *The New York Times,* April 24.

Ombudsman Institution of the Republic of Turkey. Grand National Assembly of Turkey. 2018. *Syrians in Turkey: Special Report.* Elma Technical Printing.

Ong, Aihwa. 1999. *Flexible Citizenship: The Cultural Logics of Transnationality.* Duke University Press.

Örnebring, Henrik, and Raul Ferrer Conill. 2016. "Outsourcing Newswork." Pp. 207–221 in *The SAGE Handbook of Digital Journalism.* Edited by Tamara Witschge, C. W. Anderson, David Domingo, and Alfred Hermida. SAGE Publications.

Över, Defne. 2017. "Political Destabilization in Turkey: The Case of Journalism, 1980–2013." PhD dissertation, Department of Sociology, Cornell University.

*P24.* 2016. "Olağanüstü Hal'de Gazeteciler – 3." July 28. platform24.org/guncel/1653/olaganustu-hal-de-gazeteciler—3

Packer, George. 2009. "It's Always the Fixer Who Dies." *The New Yorker,* September 10.

Palazzolo, Joe, and Michael Rothfeld. 2020. *The Fixers: The Bottom-Feeders, Crooked Lawyers, Gossipmongers, and Porn Stars Who Created the 45th President.* Penguin Random House.

Palmer, Lindsay. 2019. *The Fixers: Local News Workers and the Underground Labor of International Reporting.* Oxford University Press.

Palmer, Jerry, and Victoria Fontan. 2007. "'Our Ears and Our Eyes': Journalists and Fixers in Iraq." *Journalism* 8(1):5–24.

Pariser, Eli. 2011. *The Filter Bubble: How the New Personalized Web Is Changing What We Read and How We Think.* Penguin.

Park, Robert. 1928. "Human Migration and the Marginal Man." *American Journal of Sociology* 31(6):881–893.

Paterson, Chris, Kenneth Andresen, and Abit Hoxha. 2012. "The Manufacture of an International News Event: The Day Kosovo was Born." *Journalism* 13(1):103–120.

Pattillo, Mary. 2007. *Black on the Block: The Politics of Race and Class in the City.* University of Chicago Press.

Payaslian, Simon. 2007. "Diasporan Subalternities: The Armenian Community in Syria." *Diaspora* 16(1–2):92–132.

Pedelty, Mark. 1995. *War Stories: The Culture of Foreign Correspondents.* Routledge.

Pendry, Richard. 2011. "Sub-Contracting Newsgathering in Iraq." *Ethical Space* 8(3-4):14–20.

Phillips, Robert A. 2010. "Ethics and Network Organizations." *Business Ethics Quarterly* 20(3):533–543.

Plaut, Shayna, and Peter W. Klein. 2019a. "The Practice of Fixing and the Role of Fixers in Global Journalism." Pp. 1354–1367 in *The Oxford Encyclopedia of Journalism Studies.* Edited by Henrik Örnebring. Oxford University Press.

2019b. "'Fixing' the Journalist-Fixer Relationship: A Critical Look towards Developing Best Practices in International Reporting." *Journalism Studies* 20(12):1696–1713.

Popp, Maximillian. 2017. "Revisiting Turkey's Failed Coup Attempt." *Spiegel Online*, July 6. spiegel.de/international/world/turkey-coup-a-chronology-of-events-a-1155762.html

Powers, Matthew. 2018. *NGOs as Newsmakers.* Columbia University Press.

Propp, Vladimir. 1970. *Morphology of the Folktale.* University of Texas Press.

Rabinow, Paul. 1977. *Reflections on Fieldwork in Morocco.* University of California Press.

Ragin, Charles C. 2008. "What Is Qualitative Comparative Analysis (QCA)?" eprints.ncrm.ac.uk/250/1/What_is_QCA.pdf

Raman, Bhavani. 2012. *Document Raj: Writing and Scribes in Early Colonial South India.* Chicago: University of Chicago Press.

RSF (Reporters Without Borders) and bianet (Bağımsız İletişim Ağı). 2016. "Kalyon Group." Media Ownership Monitor: Turkey. turkey.mom-rsf.org/en/owners/companies/detail/company//kalyon-group/

2017. "Fixers – Field Reporting's Unseen Facilitators." October 4.

2019. "Business Reporters Now Being Harassed in Turkey." June 20.

Republic of Turkey Official Gazette. 1983. *Act No. 2935: State of Emergency Law.* October 25.

Reuters. 2014. "Turkey's Erdogan Threatens to 'Ban the Ban' on His Electoral Film." March 20.

2020. *Handbook of Journalism.*

Rhimes, Shonda (creator). 2012–2018. *Scandal* (television series). ABC.

Said, Edward. 1978. *Orientalism.* Pantheon Books.

1981. *Covering Islam: How the Media and the Experts Determine How We See the Rest of the World.* Pantheon Books.

Sanjek, Roger. 1993. "Anthropology's Hidden Colonialism: Assistants and Their Ethnographers." *Anthropology Today* 9(2):13–18.

2014. *Ethnography in Today's World: Color Full before Color Blind.* University of Pennsylvania Press.

Scalbert-Yücel, Clémence. 2009. "The Invention of a Tradition: Dikarbakır's Dengbêj Project." *European Journal of Turkish Studies* 10:1–25.

Schanberg, Sydney. [1980] 2013. *The Death and Life of Dith Pran.* RosettaBooks. Kindle edition.

Schechter, Jerrold. 2012. "The Jones Project." Locations 2482–2591 in *Albest: Untold Stories from the Correspondents for the Legendary Time-Life New Service.* Edited by John Stacks. Xlibris. Kindle edition.

Schegloff, Emanuel, Gail Jefferson, and Harvey Sacks. 1974. "A Simplest Systematics for the Organization of Turn-Taking for Conversation." *Language* 50(4):696–735.

Scheper-Hughes, Nancy. 2000. "Ire in Ireland." *Ethnography* 1(1):117–140.

Scheufele, Dietram A., and David Tewksbury. 2007. "Framing, Agenda-Setting, and Priming: The Evolution of Three Media Effects Models." *Journal of Communication* 57(1):9–20.

Schudson, Michael. 2003. *The Sociology of News.* W. W. Norton & Company.

Schudson, Michael, and Chris Anderson. 2009. "Objectivity, Professionalism, and Truth Seeking in Journalism." Pp. 108–121 in *The Handbook of Journalism Studies.* Edited by Karin Wahl-Jorgensen and Thomas Hanitzsch. Routledge.

Schultz, Ida. 2007. "The Journalistic Gut Feeling: Journalistic Doxa, News Habitus and Orthodox News Values." *Journalism Practice* 1(2):190–207.

Seo, Soomin. 2016. "Marginal Majority at The Postcolonial News Agency: Foreign Journalistic Hires at the Associated Press." *Journalism Studies* 17(1):39–56.

2019. "One Foot in Prison and One Foot Out: State Appointed Local Journalistic Labor in North Korea." *Journalism Studies* 20 (12):1747–1763.

Serres, Michel. 2007. *The Parasite.* Translated by Lawrence R. Schehr. University of Minnesota Press.

Shafak, Elif. 2006. "Women Writers, Islam, and the Ghost of Zulaikha." Pp. 153–156 in *Writing Turkey: Explorations of Turkish History, Politics, and Cultural Identity*. Edited by Gerald MacLean. Middlesex University Press.

Shalal, Andrea. 2017. "Jailed German-Turkish Reporter Sees Turkey Drifting Toward Fascism." Reuters, November 10.

Shannon, Claude E. [1949] 1964. "The Mathematical Theory of Communication." Pp. 31–125 in *The Mathematical Theory of Communication*. University of Illinois Press.

Shankland, David. 2003. *The Alevis in Turkey: The Emergence of a Secular Islamic Tradition*. Routledge.

Shin, Jae-Hwa, and Glen T. Cameron. 2005. "Different Sides of the Same Coin: Mixed Views of Public Relations Practitioners and Journalists for Strategic Conflict Management." *Journalism and Mass Communication Quarterly* 82(2):318–338.

Shirky, Clay. 2008. *Here Comes Everybody: The Power of Organizing without Organizations*. Penguin.

Shoemaker, Pamela J., and Tim P. Vos. 2009. *Gatekeeping Theory*. Routledge.

Simmel, Georg. [1903] 1971. "The Metropolis and Mental Life." Pp. 324–339 in *On Individuality and Social Forms*. Edited by Donald N. Levine. University of Chicago Press.

[1908] 1971. "The Stranger." Pp.143–149 in *On Individuality and Social Forms*. Edited by Donald N. Levine. University of Chicago Press.

[1911] 1971. "The Adventurer." Pp. 187–198 in *On Individuality and Social Forms*. Edited by Donald N. Levine. University of Chicago Press.

1950. "The Triad." Pp. 145–169 in *The Sociology of Georg Simmel*. Edited and translated by Kurt H. Wolff. The Free Press.

Simon, Joel. 2014. "Is It Time to End Media Blackouts?" *Columbia Journalism Review*, September 3.

2015. *The New Censorship: Inside the Global Battle for Media Freedom*. Columbia University Press

Sinclair-Webb, Emma. 2014. "Turkey's Human Rights Rollback: Recommendations for Reform." Human Rights Watch, September.

Skjerdal, Terje. 2020. "Checkbook Journalism/Payment for Coverage." Pp. 256–259 of volume 1, *The International Encyclopedia of Journalism Studies*. Edited by Tim P. Vos, Folker Hanusch, Dimitra Dimitrakopoulou, Margaretha Geertsema-Sligh and Annika Sehl. Wiley.

Small, Mario. 2009. "'How Many Cases Do I Need?': On Science and the Logic of Case Selection in Field-Based Research." *Ethnography* 10 (1):5–38.

Smith, Hannah L. 2019. *Erdoğan Rising: The Battle for the Soul of Turkey*. William Collins.

Smith, Ron F. 2008. *Ethics in Journalism*. 6th ed. Blackwell.

Snyder, Benjamin H. 2016. *The Disrupted Workplace: Time and the Moral Order of Flexible Capitalism*. Oxford University Press. Kindle edition.

Soley, Lawrence C. 1992. *The News Shapers: The Sources Who Shape the News*. Praeger.

Sönmez, Mustafa. 2014. "Conflict between Gülen Movement and Turkey's Ruling AKP Reflected in Business World." *Hürriyet Daily News*, January 11.

Sontag, Susan. [1977] 1989. *On Photography*. Farrar, Strauss & Giroux.

Sözeri, Efe Kerem. 2016. "The Reality of Life under Turkey's Internet Censorship Machine." *The Daily Dot*, July 5. dailydot.com/layer8/turkey-censorship-real-life/

Stein, Aaron. 2014. "ISIS in Turkey: Using Open Source to Find Out." *Bellingcat*, October 1. bellingcat.com/resources/case-studies/2014/10/01/isis-in-turkey-using-open-source-to-find-out/

Stone, Lawrence. 1979. "The Revival of Narrative: Reflections on a New Old History." *Past and Present*, 85:3–24.

Stovel, Katherine. 2013. "The Broker's Dilemma." Lecture. Networks and Time Workshop, Department of Sociology, Columbia University, April 3.

Stovel, Katherine, and Lynette Shaw. 2012. "Brokerage." *Annual Review of Sociology* 38:139–158.

Strauss, Anselm, and Juliet Corbin. 1998. *Basics of Qualitative Research: Techniques and Procedures for Developing Grounded Theory*. SAGE Publications.

Swidler, Ann. 1986. "Culture in Action: Symbols and Strategies." *American Sociological Review* 51:273–286.

Swidler, Ann, and Susan Cotts Watkins. 2017. *A Fraught Embrace: The Romance & Reality of AIDS Altruism in Africa*. Princeton University Press.

Tavory, Iddo, and Stefan Timmermans. 2014. *Abductive Analysis: Theorizing Qualitative Research*. University of Chicago Press.

Terry, Don. 2011. "The Fixer." *Columbia Journalism Review*, April 11.

Tezcür, Murat Güneş, and Clayton Besaw. 2016. "Violence in Turkey Is Increasingly Resembling Violence in Syria – Here's Data to Show Why." *Political Violence @ a Glance*, September 23. politicalviolenceataglance.org/2016/09/23/violence-in-turkey-is-increasingly-resembling-violence-in-syria-heres-data-to-show-why/

Tol, Gönül, and Ömer Taşpınar. 2016. "Erdogan's Turn to the Kemalists." *Foreign Affairs*, October 27.

*Toronto Star*. 2011. "Toronto Star Newsroom Policy and Journalistic Standards Guide." December 7.

Truffaut, François, and Helen G. Scott. 1985. *Hitchcock*. Simon and Schuster.

Tuchman, Gaye. 1978. *Making News: A Study in the Construction of Reality*. The Free Press.

Tüfekçi, Zeynep. 2017. *Twitter and Tear Gas: The Power and Fragility of Networked Protest*. Yale University Press.

Tumber, Howard, and Jerry Palmer. 2004. *Media at War: The Iraq Crisis*. Sage.

Turner, Victor. 1967. *The Forest of Symbols: Aspects of Ndembu Ritual*. Cornell University Press.

Twitter Public Policy. 2021. "An Update on Twitter in Turkey." March 19. blog.twitter.com/en_us/topics/company/2021/update-twitter-turkey.

Ufberg, Ross. 2016. "The Jones Project: Smuggling Nikita Khrushchev's Memoirs Out of the USSR." *Lapham's Quarterly*, September 27.

UNHCR (United Nations High Commissioner for Refugees). 2018. *Global Trends: Forced Displacement in 2018*.

Vaughan, Diane. 1992. "Theory Elaboration: The Heuristics of Case Analysis." Pp. 173–202 in *What Is a Case? Exploring the Foundations of Social Inquiry*. Edited by Charles Ragin and Howard S. Becker. Cambridge University Press.

    1997. *The Challenger Launch Decision: Risky Technology, Culture, and Deviance at NASA*. University of Chicago Press.

    2012. "Ethnographic Analytics." Paper presented, AJS Conference, "Causal Thinking and Ethnographic Research" University of Chicago, March 8–9.

    2014. "Theorizing: Analogy, Cases, and Comparative Social Organization." Pp. 61–84 in *Theorizing in Social Science: The Context of Discovery*. Edited by Richard Swedberg. Stanford University Press.

*Vice News*. 2015. "Free Rasool: VICE News Staff on the Journalist Now Imprisoned for a Month in Turkey." September 27. vice.com/en_us/article/a39378/free-rasool-vice-news-staff-on-the-journalist-now-imprisoned-for-a-month-in-turkey

Vidich, Arthur J., and Joseph Bensman. [1958] 2000. *Small Town in Mass Society: Class, Power, and Religion in a Rural Community*. University of Illinois Press.

Vronskaya, Jeanne. 1992. "Obituary: Viktor Louis." *The Independent*, July 20.

Wadensjö, Cecilia. 1998. *Interpreting as Interaction*. Longman.

Weaver, Warren. [1949] 1964. "Recent Contributions to the Mathematical Theory of Communication." Pp. 3–28 in *The Mathematical Theory of Communication*. University of Illinois Press.

Weber, Max. [1918] 1946a. "Science as a Vocation." Pp. 129–156 in *From Max Weber: Essays in Sociology*. Edited and translated by Hans H. Gerth and C. Wright Mills. Oxford University Press.

[1921] 2010. "The Distribution of Power within the Community: Classes, Stände, Parties." Translated by Dagmar Waters, Tony Waters, Elisabeth Hahnke, Maren Lippke, Eva Ludwig-Glück, Daniel Mai, Nina Ritzi-Messner, Christina Veldhoen, and Lucas Fassnacht. *Journal of Classical Sociology* 10(2):137–152.

[1922] 1946b. "The Sociology of Charismatic Authority." Pp. 245–252 in *From Max Weber: Essays in Sociology*. Edited and translated by Hans H. Gerth and C. Wright Mills. Oxford University Press.

1949. "Objective Possibility and Adequate Causation in Historical Explanation." Pp. 164–188 in *The Methodology of the Social Sciences*. Translated by Edward Shils and H. Finch. The Free Press.

Weir, Peter (director). 1982. *The Year of Living Dangerously*. McElroy & McElroy and Metro-Goldwyn-Mayer.

Weise, Zia. 2016. "In Erdogan's Turkey, Everyone Is a Terrorist." *Foreign Policy*, March 24.

Weiss, Robert. 1994. *Learning From Strangers: The Art and Method of Qualitative Interview Studies*. The Free Press.

White, Hayden. 1975. *Metahistory: The Historical Imagination in Nineteenth-Century Europe*. Johns Hopkins University Press.

1980. "The Value of Narrativity in the Representation of Reality." *Critical Inquiry* 7(1):5–27.

White, Jenny. 2013. *Muslim Nationalism and the New Turks*. Princeton University Press. Kindle edition.

Whitney, Craig R. 1992. "Victor Louis, 64, Journalist, Dies; Conduit for Kremlin to West." *The New York Times*, July 21.

Wiener, Norbert. 1954. *The Human Use of Human Beings: Cybernetics and Society*. Da Capo Press.

Wright, Kate. 2018. *Who's Reporting Africa Now? Non-governmental Organizations, Journalists, and Multimedia*. Peter Lang.

Yannakakis, Yanna. 2008. *The Art of Being In-Between: Native Intermediaries, Indian Identity, and Local Rule in Colonial Oaxaca*. Duke University Press.

Yanik, Lerna K. 2006. "'Nevruz' or 'Newroz'? Deconstructing the 'Invention' of a Contested Tradition in Contemporary Turkey." *Middle Eastern Studies* 42(2):285–302.

Yassin-Kassab, Robin, and Leila Al-Shami. 2016. *Burning Country: Syrians in Revolution and War*. Pluto Press.

Yeşil, Bilge. 2016. *Media in New Turkey: The Origins of an Authoritarian Neoliberal State*. University of Illinois Press. Kindle edition.

Zaloom, Caitlin. 2006. *Out of the Pits: Traders and Technology from Chicago to London*. University of Chicago Press.

Zelizer, Barbie. 1993. "Journalist as Interpretive Communities." *Critical Studies in Mass Communication* 10:219–237.

———. 2007. "On 'Having Been There': 'Eyewitnessing' as a Journalistic Key Word." *Critical Studies in Media Communication* 24(5):408–428.

Zeydanlıoğlu, Welat. 2012. "Turkey's Kurdish Language Policy." *International Journal of the Sociology of Language* 217:99–125.

Zorza, Victor. 1971. "The Khrushchev Memoirs: Who Forged What." *The Guardian*, January 21.

# Index

Abdullah (character), 35, 171, 290
accreditation, 49, 63, 83–84, 281
activists as news contributors, 26–27,
    39, 81–85, 88, 94–100, 145, 191,
    229, 285, *See also* non-
    governmental organizations
    (NGOs)
Actor-Network Theory, 108, 269
adventure, 15, 42–43, 54, 70, 164, 180,
    251, 261–263, 279, 281–282, 289,
    308
Afghanistan/Afghans, 14–15, 34–36,
    91–93, 171–174, 290–292
Aleppo, 158–160, 289
Alevis, 72, 150, 231–233, 243–244,
    248–250, 260
Alison (character), 26–28, 54, 75–76,
    152, 285, 296
ambivalence, 105–108, 118–119, 129,
    150, 178
  coding, 111–113, 117, 131, 135,
    251, 308
  rhythmic, 111–113, 131, 148–149,
    233, 241
  sociological, 106, 135
  strategic, 116–118, 125–126, 154–155
analytic license, 314, 322
anonymity, 282
  of fixers, 2, 33, 61–62, 141, 167,
    268–272, 278
  of research participants, 6, 311
  of sources, 120, 250–251, 274
Antakya, 31
Armenia/Armenians, 114, 132,
    150–153
Assad, Bashar al-, 25, 29–30
audience segregation, 108, 126, 151,
    155, 167, 178
Aziz (character), 73–75, 157–161,
    273–275, 277

bias, 2, 54, 66, 69, 76, 116, 119, 146,
    178, 180, 308
  of non-humans, 301–302
boundary-work, 49, 67, 77, 79, 93, 98,
    168–170, 299
Brigitte (character), 133–135
brokerage
  as object of study, 305, 310
  by non-humans, 54, 87, 299–305
  chains in news production, 94–97,
    299, 306
  definition, 50
Burcu (character), 60, 64–71, 83, 112,
    115, 119–126, 161, 280–284

Chad (character), 130–132
codes/coding, 106, 112, 145–146,
    183–189, 292, 306
  in social research, 316–320
composite characters, 5–8, 10,
    311–328
compression (of information), 100,
    185, 208, 215–216, 313, 316–320
connoisseurship, 256–258, 278–279,
    296
coups d'état, 246
  1997 intervention, 16
  2016 attempt, 224–225, 227,
    241–242
credit (in journalism), 2, 63, 167,
    268–270, 289
culture talk, 174, 291

Damascus, 29–30
DDT (news organization), 32, 80,
    83–84, 162, 166
Democratic Unity Party (PYD), 139,
    146
disenchantment, 41, 272–273, 276–279
disintermediation, 299–300, 305

For EU product safety concerns, contact us at Calle de José Abascal, 56–1°,
28003 Madrid, Spain or eugpsr@cambridge.org.